EXPLAINING SOCIAL BEHAVIOR
MORE NUTS AND BOLTS FOR THE SOCIAL SCIENCES

This book is an expanded and revised edition of the author's critically acclaimed volume *Nuts and Bolts for the Social Sciences*. In twenty-six succinct chapters, Jon Elster provides an account of the nature of explanation in the social sciences; an analysis of the mental states – beliefs, desires, and emotions – that are precursors to action; a systematic comparison of rational-choice models of behavior with alternative accounts; a discussion of what the social sciences may learn from neuroscience and evolutionary biology; and a review of mechanisms of social interaction ranging from strategic behavior to collective decision making. He offers an overview of key explanatory mechanisms in the social sciences, relying on hundreds of examples and drawing on a large variety of sources – psychology, behavioral economics, biology, political science, historical writings, philosophy, and fiction. In accessible and jargon-free language, Elster aims at accuracy and clarity while eschewing formal models. In a provocative conclusion, he defends the centrality of qualitative social science in a two-front war against soft (literary) and hard (mathematical) forms of obscurantism.

Jon Elster is Professor (Chaire de Rationalité et Sciences Sociales) at the Collège de France. A Fellow of the American Academy of Arts and Sciences and Corresponding Fellow of the British Academy, he is a recipient of fellowships from the John Simon Guggenheim Foundation and the Russell Sage Foundation, among many others. Dr. Elster has taught at the University of Chicago and Columbia University and has held visiting professorships at many universities in the United States and Europe. He is the author or editor of thirty-four books, most recently *Closing the Books: Transitional Justice in Historical Perspective* and *Retribution and Restitution in the Transition to Democracy*.

EXPLAINING SOCIAL BEHAVIOR

《《《

More Nuts and Bolts
for the Social Sciences

Jon Elster

COLLÈGE DE FRANCE

CAMBRIDGE
UNIVERSITY PRESS

CAMBRIDGE UNIVERSITY PRESS
Cambridge, New York, Melbourne, Madrid, Cape Town, Singapore, São Paulo

Cambridge University Press
32 Avenue of the Americas, New York, NY 10013-2473, USA
www.cambridge.org
Information on this title: www.cambridge.org/9780521771795

First published 2007

Printed in the United States of America

A catalog record for this publication is available from the British Library.

Library of Congress Cataloging in Publication Data
Elster, Jon, 1940–
    Explaining social behavior : more nuts and bolts
for the social sciences
/ Jon Elster
    p.   cm.
Expanded and rev. ed. of: Nuts and bolts for the social sciences, 1989.
    Includes bibliographical references and index.
    ISBN-13: 978-0-521-77179-5 (hardback)
    ISBN-13: 978-0-521-77744-5 (pbk.)
1.   Social sciences – Methodology. 2.   Social interaction. I.   Elster, Jon,
1940 – Nuts and bolts for the social sciences. II.   Title.
    H61.E434 2007
    302 – dc22   2006022194

ISBN 978-0-521-77179-5 hardback
ISBN 978-0-521-77744-5 paperback

For Jonathan and Joanna

CONTENTS

PREFACE

This book began as a revision of a book I published in 1989, *Nuts and Bolts for the Social Sciences*. It ended up as a quite different and more ambitious kind of book. It covers a much greater variety of topics, in considerably more detail, and in a different spirit. Although nine chapters have the same headings as chapters in the earlier book, only Chapter 9 and Chapter 24 remain substantially the same.

Although comprehensive in scope, the book is not a treatise. It is both less and more than that. It is an elementary, informal, and personal presentation of ideas that have, I believe, considerable potential for illuminating social behavior. I use plenty of examples, many of them anecdotal or literary, others drawn from more systematic studies. The very occasional use of algebra does not go beyond high school level. At the same time, the book has a methodological and philosophical slant not usual in introductory-level presentations. There is an effort to place the social sciences within the sciences more generally – the natural sciences as well as the humanities. There is also an effort to make the reader keep constantly in mind how general principles of scientific explanation constrain the construction of theories with explanatory pretensions.

The style of the bibliographical notes to each chapter reflects the rise of the Internet, in particular of Wikipedia, Google.com, and Scholar .Google.com. Since readers can find most relevant references in a matter of minutes, I have omitted sources for many of the statements and findings in the text. Instead I try to point readers to important source-books, to some modern classics, to books and articles that are the sources of claims that might be harder to track down on the Internet, and to authors from whom I have taken so much that not mentioning them would justify a pun on my name (*Elster* in German means magpie).

Although the main text contains few references to contemporary scholars, I refer extensively to Aristotle, Seneca, Montaigne, La Rochefoucauld, Samuel Johnson, H. C. Andersen, Stendhal, Tocqueville, Proust, and other classical writers who remain literally inexhaustible sources of causal hypotheses. We would be cutting ourselves off from many insights if we ignored the mechanisms suggested by philosophy, fiction, plays, and poetry. If we neglect twenty-five centuries of reflection about mind, action, and interaction in favor of the last one hundred years or the last ten, we do so at our peril and our loss. I cite these authors not so much to appeal to their authority as to make the case that it is worth one's while to read widely rather than narrowly. In direct opposition to what I perceive as the relentless professionalization of (especially American) social science, which discourages students from learning foreign languages and reading old books, the present volume is an extended plea for a more comprehensive approach to the study of society.

❮❮❮

In preparing the manuscript I received assistance and comments from many people. I should first thank my students at Columbia University for their incisive questioning and comments in the course where I first presented the material that turned into this book. Suggestions from Pablo Kalmanovitz were particularly useful. In Collioure, Aanund Hylland and Ole-Jørgen Skog spent three days with me discussing a draft of the whole book. In Oslo, Hylland, Karl O. Moene, and John Roemer continued the discussion over a day and a half. Their comments not only saved me from many (many!) errors but also suggested how I could supplement and consolidate the exposition. I am grateful to Roemer in particular for urging me to write a conclusion. I received written comments on the whole manuscript from Diego Gambetta, Raj Saah, and an anonymous reviewer. Gambetta's comments were particularly detailed and helpful. I had useful conversations with Walter Mischel about the ideas – largely originating with him – presented in Chapter 10. I also received valuable written comments from George Ainslie on the ideas – many of them raised by him – presented in Part I of the book. Bernard Manin commented constructively on Chapter 25. Robyn Dawes offered incisive comments on Chapter 7 and Chapter 12. Finally, over the several last years I have presented drafts of chapters for this book to the members of the "Monday group" that has met weekly in New York City each fall and more occasionally in the spring since 1995: John Ferejohn, Raquel Fernandez, Russell Hardin, Stephen Holmes, Steven Lukes, Bernard Manin, Pasquale Pasquino, Adam Przeworski, and John Roemer. I thank them all for their friendly and constructive objections.

I dedicate the book to Jonathan and Joanna Cole – they will know why.

❬❬❬

I cite Montaigne's *Essays* from the translation by M. Screech (London: Penguin, 1971); Proust from the new translation edited by C. Prendergast (London: Penguin, 2003); Pascal's *Pensées* from the translation by A. J. Krailsheimer (London: Penguin, 1995); La Rochefoucauld's *Maxims* from the translation by L. Tancock (London: Penguin, 1981); La Bruyère's *Characters* from the translation by H. van Laun (New York: Scribner, 1885); Stendhal's *On Love* from the translation by G. Sale, S. Sale, and J. Stewart (London: Penguin, 1975); and Tocqueville's *Democracy in America* from the new translation by A. Goldhammer (New York: Library of America, 2004). Other translations from French are mine.

❬❬❬

INTRODUCTION

❀ ❀ ❀

This book is about explaining social behavior. In the first part, I spell out my conception of explanation, and in the remaining four parts, I construct a toolbox of concepts and mechanisms that apply to particular cases. Needless to say, it does not aspire to completeness. Rather than trying to spell out the gaps, which will be obvious, let me begin by enumerating a sample of the puzzles that, I submit, can be illuminated by the approach I am taking. In the Conclusion, I return to the same puzzles with brief references to the explanations I have cited in earlier chapters.

The examples and the explanations must be taken with two caveats. First, I do not claim that all the explananda are well-established facts. In an actual explanation, this is of course a crucial first step – it makes no sense to try to explain what does not exist. For the purpose of building a toolbox, however, one can be less rigorous. Second, even for the explananda whose existence is well documented I do not claim that the explanations I cite are the correct ones. I only claim that they satisfy a minimal condition for an explanation – that they logically imply the explananda. The puzzles and explanations are intended to show "if this kind of thing happens, here is the kind of mechanism that might explain it" as well as "if this mechanism operates, here is the kind of thing it can produce." Given these caveats, here are the puzzles, arranged somewhat arbitrarily (since many puzzles could fit in several categories) according to the four substantive parts of the book.[1]

I ⬿ The Mind

- Why do some gamblers believe than when red has come up five times in a row, red is more likely than black to come up next?

---

[1] Although the list overlaps somewhat with a list of puzzles presented in Chapter 12 as challenges to rational-choice theory, it has no polemical purpose, only that of inciting the reader's curiosity.

- Why do other gamblers believe than when red has come up five times in a row, black is more likely than red to come up next?

- Why do preferences sometimes change through the sheer passage of time?

- Why do many people who seem to believe in the afterlife want it to arrive as late as possible?

- Why are people reluctant to acknowledge, to themselves and others, that they are envious?

- Why are people reluctant to acknowledge, to themselves and others, that they are ignorant?

- Why, among sixteenth-century converts to Calvinism, did the belief that people were predestined either to heaven or to hell induce greater peace of mind than the belief that one could achieve salvation through good works?

- Why is it (sometimes) true that "Who has offended, cannot forgive"?

- Why is shame more important than guilt in some cultures?

- Why did the French victory in the 1998 soccer World Cup generate so much joy in the country, and why did the fact that the French team did not qualify beyond the opening rounds in 2002 cause so much despondency?

- Why do women often feel shame after being raped?

- Why do humiliating rituals of initiation produce greater rather than lesser loyalty to the group into which one is initiated?

II ⌢ Action

- Why do more Broadway shows receive standing ovations today than twenty years ago?

- Why may punishments increase rather than decrease the frequency of the behavior they target?

- Why are people unwilling to break self-imposed rules even when it makes little sense to follow them?

- Why is the pattern of revenge "Two eyes for an eye" instead of "An eye for an eye"?

- Why is the long-term yield on stocks much larger than that on bonds (i.e., why does not the value of stocks rise to equalize the yields)?

- Why do suicide rates go down when dangerous medications are sold in blister packs rather than bottles?

- Why did none of thirty-eight bystanders call the police when Kitty Genovese was beaten to death?

- Why did some individuals hide or rescue Jews under the Nazi regimes?

- Why did President Chirac call early elections in 1997, only to lose his majority in parliament?

- Why are some divorcing parents willing to share child custody even when their preferred solution is sole custody, which they are likely to get were they to litigate?

- Why are poor people less likely to emigrate?

- Why do some people save in Christmas accounts that pay no interest and do not allow for withdrawal before Christmas?

- Why do people pursue projects, such as building the Concorde airplane, that have negative expected value?

- Why, in "transitional justice" (when agents of an autocratic regime are put on trial after the transition to democracy), are those tried immediately after the transition sentenced more severely than those who are tried later?

- Why, in Shakespeare's play, does Hamlet delay taking revenge until the last act?

III ⟿ Lessons from the Natural Sciences

- Why are parents much more likely to kill adopted children and stepchildren than to kill their biological children?

- Why is sibling incest so rare, given the temptations and opportunities?

- Why do people invest their money in projects undertaken by other agents even when the latter are free to keep all the profits for themselves?

- Why do people take revenge at some material cost to them and with no material benefits?

- Why do people jump to conclusions beyond what is warranted by the evidence?

IV ⟿ Interaction

- Why do supporters of a Socialist party sometimes vote Communist and thereby prevent their party from winning?

- Why do some newly independent countries adopt as their official language that of their former imperialist oppressor?

- Why are ice cream stalls often located beside each other in the middle of the beach, when customers would be better off and the sellers no worse off with a more spread-out location?

- Why does an individual vote in elections when his or her vote is virtually certain to have no effect on the outcome?

- Why are economically successful individuals in modern Western societies usually slimmer than the average person?

- Why do people refrain from transactions that could make everybody better off, as when they abstain from asking a person in the front of a bus queue whether he is willing to sell his place?

- Why did President Nixon try to present himself to the Soviets as being prone to irrational behavior?

- Why do military commanders sometimes burn their bridges (or their ships)?

- Why do people often attach great importance to intrinsically insignificant matters of etiquette?

- Why do passengers tip taxi drivers and customers tip waiters even when visiting a foreign city to which they do not expect to return?

- Why do firms invest in large inventories even when they do not anticipate any interruption of production?

- Why, in a group of students, would each think that others have understood an obscure text better than he has?

- Why are votes in many political assemblies taken by roll call?

- Why is logrolling more frequent in ordinary legislatures than in constituent assemblies?

Suggested explanations for these phenomena will be provided at various places in the book and briefly summarized in the Conclusion. Here I only want to make a general remark about two types of explanation that are *not* likely to be useful. As readers will see in the very first chapter, with several reminders along the road, one of the aims of the book is to inculcate skepticism toward two common lines of reasoning. First, with very few exceptions the social sciences cannot rely on functional explanation, which accounts for actions or behavioral patterns by citing their consequences rather than their causes. Do norms of tipping exist because it is more efficient to have customers monitor waiters than to have the owner do it? I do not think so. Second, I now believe that rational-choice theory has less explanatory power than I used to think. Do real people act on the calculations that make up many pages of mathematical appendixes in leading journals? I do not think so.

On three counts at least, rational-choice theory is nevertheless a valuable part of the toolbox. If understood in a qualitative commonsense way, it is capable of explaining much everyday behavior. Even when it does not explain much, it can have immense conceptual value. Game theory, in particular, has illuminated the structure of social interaction in ways that go far beyond the insights achieved in earlier centuries. Finally, human beings *want* to be rational. The desire to have sufficient reasons for one's behavior, and not simply be the plaything of psychic forces acting "behind one's back," provides a permanent counterforce to the many irrationality-generating mechanisms that I survey in this book.

Even though I am critical of many rational-choice explanations, I believe the concept of *choice* is fundamental. In the book I consider several alternatives to choice-based explanation and conclude that although they may sometimes usefully supplement that approach, they cannot replace it. The fact that people act under different *constraints*, for instance, can often explain a great deal of variation in behavior. Also, in some cases one may argue that *selection of agents* rather than *choice by agents* is responsible for the behavior we observe. By and large, however, I believe that the subjective factor of choice has greater explanatory power than the objective factors of constraints and selection. This is obviously an intuition that cannot be proved in any rigorous sense, and in any case social scientists ought to have room for all the factors in their toolbox.

《《《

I

EXPLANATION AND MECHANISMS

This book relies on a specific view about explanation in the social sciences. Although not primarily a work of philosophy of social science, it draws upon and advocates certain methodological ideas about how to explain social phenomena. In the first three chapters, these ideas are set out explicitly. In the rest of the book they mostly form part of the implicit background, although from time to time, notably in Chapters 14 through 17 and in the Conclusion, they return to the center of the stage.

I argue that all explanation is causal. To explain a phenomenon (an *explanandum*) is to cite an earlier phenomenon (the *explanans*) that caused it. When advocating causal explanation, I do not intend to exclude the possibility of intentional explanation of behavior. Intentions can serve as causes. A particular variety of intentional explanation is *rational-choice explanation*, which will be extensively discussed in later chapters. Many intentional explanations, however, rest on the assumption that agents are, in one way or another, *irrational*. In itself, irrationality is just a negative or residual idea, everything that is not rational. For the idea to have any explanatory purchase, we need to appeal to specific forms of irrationality with specific implications for behavior. In Chapter 12, for instance, I enumerate and illustrate eleven mechanisms that can generate irrational behavior.

Sometimes, scientists explain phenomena by their *consequences* rather than by their causes. They might say, for instance, that blood feuds are explained by the fact that they keep populations down at sustainable levels. This might seem a metaphysical impossibility: how can the existence or occurrence of something at one point in time be explained by something that has not yet come into existence? As we shall see, the problem can be restated so as to make explanation by consequences a meaningful concept. In the biological sciences, evolutionary explanation offers an example. In the social sciences, however, successful instances of such explanation are few and far between. The blood-feud example is definitely not one of them.

The natural sciences, especially physics and chemistry, offer *explanations by law*; laws are general propositions that allow us to infer the truth of one statement at one time from the truth of another statement at some earlier time. Thus when we know the positions and the velocity of the planets at one time, the laws of planetary motion enable us to deduce and predict their positions at any later time. This kind of explanation is *deterministic*: given the antecedents, only one consequent is possible. The social sciences offer few if any law-like explanations of this kind. The relation between explanans and explanandum is not one-one or many-one, but one-many or many-many. Many social scientists try to model this relation by using *statistical* methods. Statistical explanations are incomplete by themselves, however, since they ultimately have to rely on intuitions about plausible causal *mechanisms*.

《《《

Chapter 1

EXPLANATION

❀ ❀ ❀

Explanation: General

The main task of the social sciences is to explain social phenomena. It is not the only task, but it is the most important one, to which others are subordinated or on which they depend. The basic type of explanandum is an *event*. To explain it is to give an account of why it happened, by citing an *earlier event* as its cause. Thus we may explain Ronald Reagan's victory in the 1980 presidential elections by Jimmy Carter's failed attempt to rescue the Americans held hostage in Iran.[1] Or we might explain the outbreak of World War II by citing any number of earlier events, from the Munich agreement to the signing of the Versailles Treaty. Even though in both cases the fine structure of the causal explanation will obviously be more complex, they do embody the basic *event-event* pattern of explanation. In a tradition originating with David Hume, it is often referred to as the "billiard-ball" model of causal explanation. One event, ball A hitting ball B, is the cause of – and thus explains – another event, namely, ball B's beginning to move.

Those who are familiar with the typical kind of explanation in the social sciences may not recognize this pattern, or not see it as privileged. In one way or another, social scientists tend to put more emphasis on *facts*, or states of affairs, than on events. The sentence "At 9 A.M. the road was slippery" states a fact. The sentence "At 9 A.M. the car went off the road" states an event. As this example suggests, one might offer a *fact-event* explanation to account for a car accident.[2] Conversely, one might propose an *event-fact* explanation to account for a given state of affairs, as when asserting that the attack on the World Trade Center in 2001

---

[1] To anticipate a distinction discussed later, note that, Carter did not *fail to attempt* but *attempted and failed*. A nonaction such as a failure to attempt cannot have causal efficacy, except in the indirect sense that if others perceive or infer that the agent fails to act, they may take actions that they otherwise would not have.

[2] The voter turnout example discussed later provides another illustration.

explains the pervasive state of fear of many Americans. Finally, standard social-science explanations often have a *fact-fact* pattern. To take an example at random, it has been claimed that the level of education of women explains per capita income in the developing world.

Let us consider the explanation of one particular fact, that 65 percent of Americans favor, or say that they favor, the death penalty.[3] In principle, this issue can be restated in terms of events: How did these Americans *come to favor* the death penalty? What were the formative events – interactions with parents, peers, or teachers – that caused this attitude to emerge? In practice, social scientists are usually not interested in this question. Rather than trying to explain a brute statistic of this kind, they want to understand *changes* in attitudes over time or *differences* in attitudes across populations. The reason, perhaps, is that they do not think the brute fact very informative. If one asks whether 65 percent is much or little, the obvious retort is, "Compared to what?" Compared to the attitudes of Americans around 1990, when about 80 percent favored the death penalty, it is a low number. Compared to the attitudes in some European countries, it is a high number.

Longitudinal studies consider variations over time in the dependent variable. *Cross-sectional* studies consider variations across populations. In either case, the explanandum is transformed. Rather than trying to explain the phenomenon "in and of itself," we try to explain how it varies in time or space. The success of an explanation is measured, in part, by how much of the "variance" (a technical measure of variation) it can account for.[4] Complete success would explain all observed variation. In a cross-national study we might find, for instance, that the percentage of individuals favoring the death penalty was strictly proportional to the number of homicides per 100,000 inhabitants. Although this finding would provide *no* explanation of the absolute numbers, it would offer a *perfect* explanation of the difference among them.[5] In practice, of course,

---

[3] Answers fluctuate. Also, the number of people who favor the death penalty for murder goes down drastically when life imprisonment without parole is stated as the alternative.

[4] As economists sometimes say, they are interested only in what happens "at the margin."

[5] Strictly speaking, the causal chain might go in the other direction, from attitudes to behavior, but in this case that hypothesis is implausible.

perfect success is never achieved, but the same point holds. Explanations of variance do not say anything about the explanandum "in and of itself."

An example may be taken from the study of voting behavior. As we shall see later (Chapter 12), it is not clear why voters bother to vote at all in national elections, when it is morally certain that a single vote will make no difference. Yet a substantial fraction of the electorate do turn out on voting day. Why do they bother?

Instead of trying to solve this mystery, empirical social scientists usually address a different question: Why does turnout vary across elections? One hypothesis is that voters are less likely to turn out in inclement weather, because rain or cold makes it more attractive to stay home. If the data match this hypothesis, as indicated by line C in Figure 1.1, one might claim to have explained (at least part of) the variance in turnout. Yet one would not have offered *any* explanation of why the line C intersects the vertical axis at P rather than at Q or R. It is as if one took the first decimal as given and focused on explaining the second. For predictive purposes, this might be all one needs. For explanatory purposes, it is unsatisfactory. The "brute event" that 45

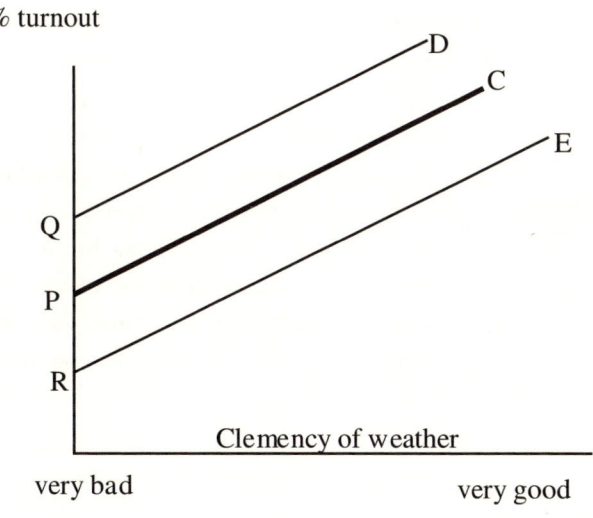

FIGURE 1.1

percent or more of the electorate usually turn out to vote *is* an interesting one, which cries out for an explanation.

The ideal procedure, in an event-event perspective, would be the following. Consider two elections, A and B. For each of them, identify the events that cause a given percentage of voters to turn out. Once we have thus explained the turnout in election A and the turnout in election B, the explanation of the difference (if any) follows automatically, as a by-product. As a bonus, we might also be able to explain whether identical turnouts in A and B are accidental, that is, due to differences that exactly offset each other, or not. In practice, this procedure might be too demanding. The data or the available theories might not allow us to explain the phenomena "in and of themselves." We should be aware, however, that if we do resort to explanations of variance, we are engaging in a second-best explanatory practice.

Sometimes, social scientists try to explain *nonevents*. Why do many people fail to claim social benefits they are entitled to? Why did nobody call the police in the Kitty Genovese case?[6] Considering the first question, the explanation might be that the individuals in question *decide* not to claim their benefits, because of fear of stigma or concerns with self-image. Since making a decision *is* an event, this would provide a fully satisfactory account. If it fails, social scientists would, once again, look at the *differences* between those who are entitled to benefits and claim them and those who are and do not. Suppose the only difference is that the latter are unaware of their entitlement. As an explanation, this is helpful but insufficient. To go beyond it, we would want to explain *why* some entitled individuals are unaware of their entitlement. To discover that because they are illiterate, they are unable to read the letters informing them about their rights would also be helpful but insufficient. At some point in the explanatory regress, we must either come to a positive event, such as a conscious decision not to become literate or a conscious

---

[6] For more than half an hour on March 27, 1964, thirty-eight respectable, law-abiding citizens in Queens, New York, watched a killer stalk and stab a woman in three separate attacks in Kew Gardens. Twice their chatter and the sudden glow of their bedroom lights interrupted him and frightened him off. Each time he returned, sought her out, and stabbed her again. Not one person telephoned the police during the assault; one witness called after the woman was dead.

decision by officials to withhold information, or turn to those who do seek the benefits to which they are entitled. Once we have explained the behavior of the latter, the explanation why others fail to seek their benefit will emerge as a by-product.

Considering the Kitty Genovese case, there is no variation in behavior to explain, since *nobody* called the police. Accounts of the case indicate that several of the observers *decided* not to call the police. In terms of proximate causes this provides a fully satisfactory account, although we might want to know the reasons for their decision. Was it because they feared "getting involved" or because each observer assumed that someone else would call the police ("Too many shepherds make a poor guard")? Some of the observers, however, apparently did not even think about calling the police. One man and his wife watched the episode for its entertainment value, while another man said he was tired and went to bed. To explain why they did not react more strongly one might cite their shallow emotions, but that, too, would be to account for a negative explanandum by citing a negative explanans. Once again, their behavior can only be explained as a by-product or residual. If we have a satisfactory explanation of why some individuals thought about calling the police, even if in the end they decided not to, we shall have the only explanation we are likely to get of why some did not even think about it.

In the rest of this book I shall often relax this purist or rigorist approach of what counts as a relevant explanandum and an appropriate explanation. The insistence on event-focused explanations is a bit like the principle of methodological individualism, which is another premise of the book. In principle, explanations in the social sciences should refer only to individuals and their actions. In practice, social scientists often refer to supraindividual entities such as families, firms, or nations, either as a *harmless shorthand* or as a *second-best approach* forced upon them by lack of data or of fine-grained theories. These two justifications also apply to the use of facts as explananda or as explanantia, to explanations of variance rather than of the phenomena "in and of themselves," and to the analysis of negative explananda (nonevents or nonfacts). The purpose of the preceding discussion is not to hold social scientists to pointless or impossible standards, but to argue that at the level of first principles the event-based approach is intrinsically superior. If scholars keep that fact in mind they may, at least sometimes, come up with better and more fruitful explanations.

Sometimes, we might want to explain an event (or rather a pattern of events) by its consequences rather than by its causes. I do not have in mind explanation by *intended* consequences, since intentions exist prior to the choices or actions they explain. Rather, the idea is that events may be explained by their *actual* consequences, typically, their *beneficial* consequences for someone or something. As a cause must precede its effect, this idea might seem to be incompatible with causal explanation. Yet causal explanation can also take the form of explanation by consequences, if there is a loop from the consequences back to their causes. A child may initially cry simply because it feels pain, but if the crying also gets it attention from the parents, it may start crying more than it would have otherwise. I argue in Chapters 16 and 17 that this kind of explanation is somewhat marginal in the study of human behavior. In most of the book, I shall be concerned with the simple variety of causal explanation in which the explanans – which might include beliefs and intentions oriented toward the future – precedes the occurrence of the explanandum.[7]

In addition to the fully respectable form of functional explanation that rests on specific feedback mechanisms, there are more disreputable forms that simply point to the production of consequences that are beneficial in some respect and then without further argument assume that these suffice to explain the behavior that causes them. When the explanandum is a *token*, such as a single action or event, this kind of explanation fails for purely metaphysical reasons. To take an example from biology, we cannot explain the occurrence of a neutral or harmful mutation by observing that it was a necessary condition for a further, advantageous one. When the explanandum is a *type*, such as a recurrent pattern of behavior, it may or may not be valid. Yet as long as it is not supported by

---

[7] For some purposes, it may be useful to distinguish among causal, intentional, and functional explanation. Physics employs only causal explanation; biology additionally admits functional explanation; and the social sciences further admit intentional explanation. At the most fundamental level, though, all explanation is causal.

a specific feedback mechanism, we should treat it as if it were invalid. Anthropologists have argued, for instance, that revenge behavior has beneficial consequences of various kinds, ranging from population control to decentralized norm enforcement. (Chapter 22 offers many other examples.) Assuming that these benefits are in fact produced, they might still obtain by accident. To show that they arise nonaccidentally, that is, that they sustain the revenge behavior that causes them, the demonstration of a feedback mechanism is indispensable. And even when one is provided, the initial occurrence of the explanandum must be due to something else.

The Structure of Explanations

Let me now turn to a more detailed account of explanation in the social sciences (and, to some extent, more generally). The first step is easily overlooked: before we try to explain a fact or an event we have to establish that the fact *is* a fact or that the event actually did take place. As Montaigne wrote, "I realize that if you ask people to account for 'facts,' they usually spend more time finding reasons for them than finding out whether they are true. . . . They skip over the facts but carefully deduce inferences. They normally begin thus: 'How does this come about?' But does it do so? That is what they ought to be asking."

Thus before trying to explain, say, why there are more suicides in one country than in another, we have to make sure that the latter does not tend, perhaps for religious reasons, to underreport suicides. Before we try to explain why Spain has a higher unemployment rate than France, we have to make sure that the reported differences are not due to different definitions of unemployment or to the presence of a large underground economy in Spain. If we want to explain why youth unemployment is higher in France than in the United Kingdom, we need to decide whether the explanandum is the rate of unemployment among young people who are actively searching for jobs or the rate among young people overall, including students. If we compare unemployment in Europe and the United States, we have to decide whether the explanandum is the unemployed in the literal sense, which includes the incarcerated population, or in the technical sense, which only includes those searching for work.[8] Before we try to explain why revenge takes the form of "tit for tat" (I kill one of yours each time you or yours kill one of mine), we should verify that this is actually what we observe rather than, say, "two tits for a tat" (I kill two of yours each time you or yours kill one of mine). Much of science, including social science, tries to explain things we all know, but science can also make a contribution by establishing that some of the things we all think we know simply are not so. In that case, social science may also try to explain *why* we think we know things that are not so, adding as it were a piece of knowledge to replace the one that has been taken away.[9]

Suppose now that we have a well-established explanandum for which there is no well-established explanation – a *puzzle*. The puzzle may be a surprising or counterintuitive fact, or simply an unexplained correlation. One small-scale example is "Why are more theology books stolen from Oxford libraries than books on other subjects?" Another small-scale example, which I shall explore in more detail shortly, is "Why do more Broadway shows receive standing ovations today than twenty years ago?"

Ideally, explanatory puzzles should be addressed in the five-step sequence spelled out in the following. In practice, however, steps (1), (2), and (3) often occur in a different order. We may play around with different hypotheses until one of them emerges as the most promising, and then look around for a theory that would justify it. If steps (4) and (5) are carried out properly, we may still have a high level of confidence in the preferred hypothesis. Yet for reasons I discuss toward the end of the next chapter, scholars might want to limit their freedom to pick and choose among hypotheses.

---

[8] In either of the last two cases, some individuals may take up a career as criminals or students because they do not think they would get a job if they tried. For some purposes, one might want to count these among the unemployed; for other purposes, not.

[9] Just as science can help explain popular beliefs in nonfacts, it can help explain popular beliefs in false explanations. For instance, most of those who suffer from arthritis believe arthritic pain is triggered by bad weather. Studies suggest, however, that there is no such connection. Perhaps we should drop the search for the causal link between bad weather and arthritic pain and instead try to explain why arthritics believe there is one. Most likely they were once told there was a connection and subsequently paid more attention to instances that confirmed the belief than to those that did not.

1. Choose the theory – a set of interrelated causal propositions – that holds out the greatest promise of a successful explanation.
2. Specify a hypothesis that applies the theory to the puzzle, in the sense that the explanandum follows logically from the hypothesis.
3. Identify or imagine plausible accounts that might provide alternative explanations, also in the sense that the explanandum follows logically from each of them.
4. For each of these rival accounts, refute it by pointing to additional testable implications that are in fact *not* observed.
5. Strengthen the proposed hypothesis by showing that it has additional testable implications, preferably of "novel facts," that are in fact observed.

These procedures define what is often called the *hypothetico-deductive method*. In a given case, they might take the form shown in Figure 1.2. I shall illustrate it by the puzzle of increasing frequency of standing ovations on Broadway. It is not based on systematic observations or controlled experiments, but on my casual impressions confirmed by newspaper reports. For the present purposes, however, the shaky status of the explanandum does not matter. If there are in fact more standing ovations on Broadway than there were twenty years ago, how could we go about explaining it?

I shall consider an explanation in terms of the rising prices of Broadway tickets. One newspaper reports the playwright Arthur Miller as saying, "I guess the audience just feels having paid $75 to sit down, it's their time to stand up. I don't mean to be a cynic but it probably all changed when the price went up." When people have to pay seventy-five dollars or more for a seat, many cannot admit to themselves that the show was poor or mediocre, and that they have wasted their money. To confirm to themselves that they had a good time, they applaud wildly.

More formally, the explanation is sought in the hypothesis "When people have paid a great deal of money or effort to obtain a good, they tend (other things being equal) to value it more highly than when they paid less for it."[10] Given the factual premise of rising prices, this

---

[10] A similar idea is sometimes used to defend the high fees of psychotherapists: patients wouldn't believe in the therapy unless they paid a lot for it. But no therapists to my knowledge state that they donate 50 percent of their fee to Red Cross.

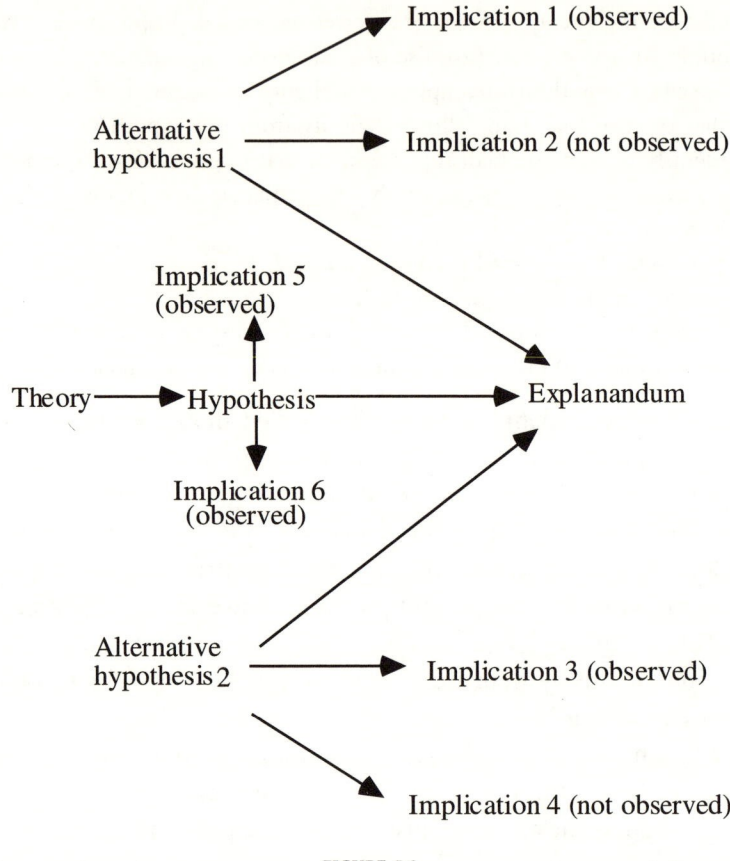

FIGURE I.2

proposition passes the minimal test that any explanatory hypothesis must satisfy: If it is true, we can infer the explanandum. But this is a truly minimal test, which many propositions could pass.[11] To strengthen our belief in this particular explanation, we must show that it is supported from below, from above, and laterally.

---

[11] The human mind seems to have a tendency to turn this minimal requirement into a sufficient one. Once we have hit upon an account that *may* be true, we often do not pause to test it further or to consider alternative accounts. The choice of an account may be due to the idea of *post hoc ergo propter hoc* (after it, therefore because of it), or to an inference from the fact that a given account is *more plausible than others* to the conclusion that it is *more likely than not* to be correct.

An explanation is supported *from below* if we can deduce and verify observable facts from the hypothesis over and above the fact that the hypothesis is intended to explain. It must have "excess explanatory power." In the case of the Broadway shows, we would expect fewer standing ovations in shows whose prices for some reason have not gone up.[12] Also, we would expect fewer standing ovations if large numbers of tickets to a show are sold to firms and given by them to their employees. (This would count as a "novel fact.") Even if these tickets are expensive, the spectators have not paid for them out of their own pocket and hence do not need to tell themselves that they are getting their money's worth.

An explanation is supported *from above* if the explanatory hypothesis can be deduced from a more general theory.[13] In the present case, the explanatory proposition is a specification of the theory of cognitive dissonance proposed by Leon Festinger. The theory says that when a person experiences an internal inconsistency or dissonance among her beliefs and values, we can expect some kind of mental readjustment that will eliminate or reduce the dissonance. Typically, the adjustment will choose the path of least resistance. A person who has spent seventy-five dollars to see a show that turns out to be bad cannot easily make herself believe that she paid less than that amount. It is easier to persuade herself that the show was in fact quite good.

Although not without problems, the theory of cognitive dissonance is pretty well supported. Some of the support is from cases that are very different from the one we are considering here, as when a person who has just bought a car avidly seeks out ads for that very brand of car, to bolster his conviction that he made a good decision. Some of the support arises from quite similar cases, as when the painful and humiliating initiation

---

[12] We would *not* necessarily expect fewer people to rise to their feet in the cheaper sections. They might feel foolish sitting when others are rising; also, they might have to get up to see the actors who would otherwise be blocked from view by those standing in front of them.

[13] More accurately: if it is a *specification* of a more general theory. The relation between a general theory and a specific explanatory hypothesis is rarely a deductive one. For one thing, there may be some slack in the theory itself (see Chapter 2). For another, a given theory can usually be operationalized in many different ways.

rituals of college fraternities and sororities induce strong feelings of loyalty. I am not saying that people would consciously tell themselves, "Because I suffered so much to join this group, it must be a good group to belong to." The mechanism by which the suffering induces loyalty must be an unconscious one.

An explanation receives *lateral support* if we can think of and then refute alternative explanations that also pass the minimal test. Perhaps there are more standing ovations because today's audiences, arriving in busloads from New Jersey, are less sophisticated than the traditional audience of blasé New York denizens. Or perhaps it is because shows are better than they used to be. For each of these alternatives, we must think of and then disconfirm additional facts that would obtain if they were correct. If standing ovations are more frequent because audiences are more impressionable, we would expect them also to have been frequent in out-of-town performances twenty years ago. If shows are better than they used to be, we would expect this to be reflected in how well they are reviewed and how long they play before folding.

In this procedure, the advocate for the original hypotheses also has to be the devil's advocate. One has consistently to *think against oneself* – to make matters as difficult for oneself as one can. We should select the strongest and most plausible alternative rival explanations, rather than accounts that can easily be refuted. For similar reasons, when seeking to demonstrate the excess explanatory power of the hypothesis, we should try to deduce and confirm implications that are novel, counterintuitive, and as different from the original explanandum as possible. These two criteria – refuting the most plausible alternatives and generating *novel facts* – are decisive for the credibility of an explanation. Support from above helps but can never be decisive. In the long run it is the theory that is supported by the successful explanations it generates, not the other way around. Emilio Segrè, a Nobel Prize winner in physics, said that some winners confer honor on the prize whereas others derive honor from it. The latter are, however, parasitic on the former. Similarly, a theory is parasitic on the number of successful explanations it generates. If it is able to confer support on a given explanation, it is only because it has received support from earlier explanations.

What Explanation Is Not

Statements that purport to explain an event must be distinguished from *seven other types of statement*.

First, causal explanations must be distinguished from *true causal statements*. To cite a cause is not enough: the causal mechanism must also be provided, or at least suggested. In everyday language, in good novels, in good historical writings, and in many social scientific analyses, the mechanism is not explicitly cited. Instead, it is suggested by the way in which the cause is described. Any given event can be described in many ways. In (good) narrative explanations, it is tacitly presupposed that only causally relevant features of the event are used to identify it. If told that a person died as a result of having eaten rotten food, we assume that the mechanism was food poisoning. If told that he died as a result of eating food to which he was allergic, we assume that the mechanism was an allergic reaction. Suppose now that he actually died because of food poisoning, but that he was also allergic to the food in question, lobster. To say that he died because he ate food to which he had an allergy would be true, but misleading. To say that he died because he ate lobster would be true, but uninformative. It would suggest no causal mechanism at all and be consistent with many, such as that he was killed by someone who had taken an oath to kill the next lobster eater he observed.

Second, causal explanations must be distinguished from statements about *correlations*. Sometimes, we are in a position to say that an event of a certain type is invariably or usually followed by an event of another kind. This does not allow us to say that events of the first type cause events of the second, because there is another possibility: the two might be common effects of a third event. In his *Life of Johnson*, Boswell reports that a certain Macaulay, although "with a prejudice against prejudice," affirmed that when a ship arrived at St. Kilda in the Hebrides, "all the inhabitants are seized with a cold." While some offered a causal explanation of this (alleged) fact, a correspondent of Boswell's informed him that "the situation of St. Kilda renders a North-East Wind indispensable before a stranger can land. The wind, not the stranger, occasions an epidemick cold." Or consider the finding that children in contested custody cases are more disturbed than children whose parents have reached a private custody agreement. It could be that the custody dispute itself explains the difference, by causing pain and guilt in the children. It could also be, however, that custody disputes are more likely to occur when the parents are bitterly hostile toward each other and that children of two such parents tend to be disturbed. To distinguish between the two interpretations, we would have to measure suffering before and after the divorce. A third possibility is canvassed later.

Here is a more complex example, my favorite example, in fact, of this kind of ambiguity. In *Democracy in America*, Alexis de Tocqueville discussed the alleged causal connection between marrying for love and having an unhappy marriage. He points out that this connection obtains only in societies in which such marriages are the exception and arranged marriages the rule. Only stubborn people will go against the current, and two stubborn persons are not likely to have a very happy marriage.[14] In addition, people who go against the current are treated badly by their more conformist peers, inducing bitterness and unhappiness. Of these arguments, the first rests on a noncausal correlation, due to a "third factor," between marrying for love and unhappiness. The second points to a true causal connection, but not the one that the critics of love marriages to whom Tocqueville addressed his argument had in mind. Marrying for love causes unhappiness only in a context where this practice is exceptional. Biologists often refer to such effects as "frequency dependent."[15]

---

[14] Here the "third factor" is a character trait, stubbornness, rather than an event.

[15] The first mechanism is a *selection effect*, the second a genuine *aftereffect*. The distinction applies quite widely. If we ask why someone in a certain state (e.g., being in a certain occupation, being unemployed, or being hospitalized for mental illness) is more likely to remain in that state the longer she has already been there, either mechanism (or both) might be at work. The long-term unemployed, for instance, might form a subset of the population with skills for which there is little demand; alternatively, all employed individuals might be equally likely to lose their jobs, but once they lose them, the state of being unemployed changes them (or the perception of them by employers) so that their likelihood of reentering the labor market declines over time. The "labeling theory" of mental illness or crime rests on the (dubious) assumption that aftereffects dominate selection effects.

In addition to the "third-factor" problem, correlation may leave us uncertain about the *direction* of causality. Consider an old joke:

Psychologist: You should be kind to Johnny. He comes from a broken home.
Teacher: I'm not surprised. Johnny could break any home.

Or as the comedian Sam Levinson said, "Insanity is hereditary. You can get it from your children." The implication is that a disturbed child may cause the parents to divorce rather than that a divorce causes the disturbance. Similarly, a negative correlation between how much the parents know about what their adolescent children are doing and the children's tendency to get into trouble need not show that parental monitoring works, but only that teenagers intent on getting into trouble are unlikely to keep their parents informed about what they are doing.

Third, causal explanations must be distinguished from statements about *necessitation*. To explain an event is to give an account of why it happened *as* it happened. That it might also have happened in some other way, and would have happened in some other way had it not happened the way it did, does not provide an answer to the same question. Consider a person who suffers from cancer of the pancreas, which is certain to kill her within a year. When the pain becomes unendurable, she kills herself. To *explain* why she died within a certain period, it is pointless to say that she *had to* die in that period because she had cancer.[16] If all we know about the case are the onset of cancer, the limited life span of persons with that type of cancer, and the death of the person, it is plausible to infer that she died because of the cancer. We have the earlier event and a causal mechanism sufficient to bring about the later event. But the mechanism is not necessary: it could be pre-empted by another. (In the example the preempting cause is itself an effect of the preempted cause, but this need not be the case; she might also die in a car accident.) To find out what actually happened, we need

---

[16] James Fitzjames Stephen writes that "the law is perfectly clear that, if by reason of [an] assault [a man] died in the spring of a disease which must have killed him, say, in the summer, the assault was the cause of his death."

more finely grained knowledge. The quest never ends: right up to the last second, some other cause could preempt the cancer.[17]

Statements about necessitation are sometimes called "structural explanations." Tocqueville's analysis of the French Revolution is an example. In his published book on the topic, he cites a number of events and trends from the fifteenth century to the 1780s and asserts that the revolution, against this background, was "inevitable." By this he probably meant (1) that any number of small or medium-sized events would have been sufficient to trigger it and (2) that it was a virtual certainty that *some* triggering events would occur, although not necessarily the ones that actually did happen or when they did happen. He also seems to argue (3) that after 1750 or perhaps 1770 there was nothing anyone could have done to prevent the revolution. Although Tocqueville left notes for a second volume in which he intended to account for the revolution as it *did* happen, one might argue that if he successfully established (1), (2), and (3), there was no need to take this further step. The problem with this line of reasoning is that in many interesting social-science questions (and in contrast to the cancer example), claims such as (1), (2), and (3) are very hard to establish by methods untainted by hindsight.[18] A stronger argument can be made when similar events happen independently of each other at the same time, suggesting that they were "in the air." The study of simultaneous discoveries in science provides an example.

Fourth, causal explanation must be distinguished from *storytelling*. A genuine explanation accounts for what happened, as it happened. To tell a story is to account for what happened as it *might* have happened (and perhaps did happen). I have just argued that scientific explanations differ from accounts of what *had to* happen. I am now saying that they also

---

[17] Causal preemption should be distinguished from causal overdetermination. The latter is illustrated by a person's being hit simultaneously by two bullets, each of which would have been sufficient to kill her. The former is illustrated by a person's being killed by one bullet, preempting the operation of another fired a few seconds later.

[18] The American Revolution is perhaps a more plausible candidate for a structural explanation. An acute neutral observer such as the French minister Choiseul observed as early as 1765 that the independence of the American colonies was inevitable. For a detached French commentator such as Raymond Aron, the independence of Algeria was also a foregone conclusion well before it came about. The French Revolution is more akin to the collapse of Communism – inevitable mainly in hindsight.

differ from accounts of what *may* have happened. The point may seem trivial, or strange. Why would anyone want to come up with a purely conjectural account of an event? Is there any place in science for speculations of this sort? The answer is yes – but their place must not be confused with that of explanation.

Storytelling can suggest new, parsimonious explanations. Suppose that someone asserts that self-sacrificing or helping behavior is conclusive proof that not all action is self-interested, and that emotional behavior is conclusive proof that not all action is rational. One might conclude that there are three irreducibly different forms of behavior: rational and selfish, rational and nonselfish, and irrational. The drive for parsimony that characterizes good science should lead us to question this view. Might it not be the case that when people help others it is because they expect reciprocation, and that when they become angry it is because that helps them to get their way? By telling a story about how rational self-interest *might* generate altruistic and emotional behavior, one can transform an issue from a philosophical one into one that is amenable to empirical research.[19] A just-so story can be the first step in the construction of a successful explanation. In fact, many of the "answers" I offer in the Conclusion to the puzzles I presented in the Introduction have a strong flavor of just-so stories.

At the same time, storytelling can be misleading and harmful if it is mistaken for genuine explanation. With two exceptions stated in the next paragraph, "as-if" explanations do not actually explain anything. Consider for instance the common claim that we can use the rational-choice model to explain behavior, even though we *know* that people cannot perform the complex mental calculations embodied in the model (or in the mathematical appendixes of the articles in which the model is set out). As long as the model provides predictions with a good fit with the observed behavior, we are entitled (it is claimed) to assume that agents act "as if" they are rational. This is the operationalist or instrumentalist view of explanation, which originated in physics and was later adopted

---

[19] In this particular case, the just-so stories happen to be false, since people also help others in one-shot interactions and getting angry may cause others to refrain from interacting with them.

by Milton Friedman for the social sciences. The reason, it is claimed, we can assume that a good billiards player knows the law of physics and can carry out complex calculations in his head is that this assumption enables us to predict and explain his behavior with great accuracy. To ask whether the assumption is *true* is to miss the point.

This argument may be valid in some situations, in which the agents can learn by trial and error over time. It is valid, however, precisely because we can point to a *mechanism* that brings about nonintentionally the same outcome that a superrational agent could have calculated intentionally.[20] In the absence of such a mechanism, we might still accept the instrumentalist view if the assumption enabled us to predict behavior with very great accuracy. The law of gravitation seemed mysterious for a long time, as it seemed to be based on the unintelligible idea of action at a distance. Yet because it made possible predictions that were accurate to many decimal points, Newton's theory was uncontroversially accepted untill the advent of the theory of general relativity. The mysterious workings of quantum mechanics are also accepted, albeit not always without qualms, because they allow for predictions with even more incredible accuracy.

Rational-choice social science can rely on neither of these two supports. *There is no general nonintentional mechanism that can simulate or mimic rationality.* Reinforcement learning (Chapter 16) may do it in some cases, although in others it produces systematic deviations from rationality. Some kind of social analog to natural selection might do it in other cases, at least roughly, if the rate of change of the environment is less than the speed of adjustment (Chapter 17). In one-shot situations or in rapidly changing environments, I do not know of any mechanism that would simulate rationality. At the same time, the empirical support for rational-choice explanations of complex phenomena tends to be quite weak. This is of course a sweeping statement. Rather than having to explain what I mean by "weak," let me simply point to the high level of

---

[20] At this first occurrence in the book of the word "agent" it may be worthwhile to note that many scholars prefer "actor." Perhaps economists think in terms of agents, sociologists in terms of actors. Although it does not really matter which term we use, I prefer "agent" because it suggests agency; "actor," by contrast, suggests an audience that may or may not be present.

disagreement among competent scholars about the explanatory force of competing hypotheses. Even in economics, in some ways the most developed among the social sciences, there are fundamental, persistent disagreements among "schools." We *never* observe the kind of many-decimal-points precision that would put controversy to rest.

Fifth, causal explanations must be distinguished from *statistical explanations*. Although many explanations in the social sciences have the latter form, they are unsatisfactory in the sense that they cannot account for individual events. To apply statistical generalizations to individual cases is a grave error, not only in science but also in everyday life.[21] Suppose it is true that men tend to be more aggressive than women. To tell an angry man that his anger is caused by his male hormones rather than argue that it is unjustified by the occasion is to commit both an intellectual and a moral fallacy. The intellectual fallacy is to assume that a generalization valid for most cases is valid in each case. The moral fallacy is to treat an interlocutor as governed by biological mechanisms rather than as open to reason and argument.

Although statistical explanations are always second best, in practice we may not be able to do any better. It is important to note, however, that they are inevitably guided by the first-best ideal of causal explanation. It appears to be a statistical fact that citizens in democracies live longer than citizens in nondemocratic regimes. Before we conclude that the political regime explains longevity, we might want to *control for* other variables that might be responsible for the outcome. It might be that more democracies than nondemocracies have property X, and that it is really X that is responsible for life expectancy. But as there are indefinitely many such properties, how do we know which to control for? The obvious answer is that we need to be guided by a causal hypothesis. It seems plausible, for instance, that citizens in industrialized societies might live

---

[21] The converse fallacy – using an individual case to generate or support a generalization – is equally to be avoided. Proust wrote that the housekeeper Françoise in the Narrator's family "was as likely to take the particular for the general as the general for the particular." This combination can be pernicious. Suppose you observe a member of group X telling a lie. Generalizing, you form the belief that members of group X tend to lie. Next, observing another member of the group, you assume he is lying. Finally, the (unverified) assumption is used as further evidence for the generalization.

longer than citizens of less developed societies. If industrial societies also tend to be more democratic than nonindustrial regimes, that could account for the observed facts. To make sure that it is democracy rather than industrialization that is the causal factor, we have to compare democratic and nondemocratic regimes at the same level of industrialization, and see whether a difference persists. Once we feel reasonably confident that we have controlled for other plausible causes, we may also try to find out *how* – by which causal chain or mechanism – the regime type affects life span. I discuss this second step in the next chapter. Here, I only want to note that our confidence is inevitably based on *causal intuitions* about what are (and what are not) plausible "third factors" for which we need to control.[22]

Sixth, explanations must be distinguished from *answers to "why questions."* Suppose we read a scholarly article and see to our surprise that the author does not refer to an important and relevant article, causing us to ask ourselves, "Why does he not cite it?" Our curiosity may be perfectly satisfied if we learn that he was in fact unaware of that earlier work (although we might also want to know why he had not explored the literature more thoroughly). But "He did not cite it because he was not aware of it" is not an explanation. If read as an explanation it would imply, absurdly, citing a nonevent to explain another nonevent. Suppose, however, that we discover that the author was aware of the article but *decided* not to cite it because he himself had not been cited in it. In that case the answer to the why question also provides an explanation. There is an event, the decision to not cite the article, caused by an earlier event, the anger triggered by not being cited.

Finally, causal explanations must be distinguished from *predictions*. Sometimes we can explain without being able to predict, and sometimes predict without being able to explain. True, in many cases one and the same theory will enable us to do both, but I believe that in the social sciences this is the exception rather than the rule.

---

[22] For instance, there is no plausible causal mechanism that should make us control for the population size of democratic and nondemocratic regimes. Although one cannot exclude a causal link between population size and average life span, social science has not established any such connection; nor can I imagine a noncontrived one.

I postpone the main discussion of why we can have explanatory power without strong predictive power to the next chapter. In brief preview, the reason is that in many cases we can identify a causal mechanism after the fact, but not predict before the fact which of several possible mechanisms will be triggered. The special case of biological explanation is somewhat different. As further discussed in Chapter 16, evolution is fueled by the twin mechanisms of random mutations and (more or less) deterministic selection. Given some feature or behavioral pattern of an organism, we can explain its *origin* by appealing to a random change in the genetic material and its *persistence* by its favorable impact on reproductive fitness. Yet prior to the occurrence of the mutation, no one could have predicted it. Moreover, as the occurrence of one mutation constrains the subsequent mutations that can occur, we may not even be able to predict that a given mutation will occur sooner or later. Hence structural explanations are unlikely to be successful in biology. The phenomenon of *convergence* – different species' developing similar adaptations because they are under similar environmental pressures – has a structural flavor but does not allow us to say that the adaptations were inevitable.

Conversely, we may have predictive power without explanatory power. To predict that consumers will buy less of a good when its price goes up, there is no need to form a hypothesis to explain their behavior. Whatever the springs of individual action – rational, traditional, or simply random – we can predict that overall people will buy less of the good simply because they can afford less of it (Chapter 9). Here there are several mechanisms that are constrained to lead to the same outcome, so that for predictive purposes there is no need to choose among them. Yet for explanatory purposes, the mechanism is what matters. It provides understanding, whereas prediction offers at most control.

Also, for predictive purposes the distinction among correlation, necessitation, and explanation becomes pointless. If there is a lawlike regularity between one type of event and another, it does not matter – for predictive purposes – whether it is due to a causal relation between them or to their being common effects of a third cause. In either case we can use the occurrence of the first event to predict the occurrence of the second. Nobody believes that the first symptoms of a deadly disease cause the later death, yet they are regularly used to predict that event. Similarly, if knowing a person's medical condition allows us to predict that he will not be alive one year from now, the prediction is not falsified if he dies of a car accident or if he takes his life because the illness is too painful.

〈〈〈

Bibliographical Note

The general view of explanation and causation on which I rely is set out in more detail in J. Elster, D. Føllesdal, and L. Walløe, *Rationale Argumentation* (Berlin: Gruyter, 1988) (English translation in preparation). For applications to human action I refer the reader to D. Davidson, *Essays on Actions and Events* (Oxford University Press, 1980). My criticism of functional explanation is set out in various places, notably in *Explaining Technical Change* (Cambridge University Press, 1983). Details of the Kitty Genovese case are found in A. M. Rosenthal, *Thirty-Eight Witnesses* (Berkeley: University of California Press, 1999). A convenient access to Festinger's views is in L. Festinger, S. Schachter, and M. Gazzaniga (eds.), *Extending Psychological Frontiers: Selected Works of Leon Festinger* (New York: Russell Sage, 1989). The examples of "child-to-parent" effects are from two stimulating books by J. R. Harris, *The Nurture Assumption: Why Children Turn Out the Way They Do* (New York: Free Press, 1998) and *No Two Alike* (New York: Norton, 2006). I discuss Tocqueville's views on causality in "Patterns of causal analysis in Tocqueville's *Democracy in America*," *Rationality and Society* 3 (1991), 277–97, and his views on the French Revolution in "Tocqueville on 1789," in C. Welch (ed.), *The Cambridge Companion to Tocqueville* (Cambridge University Press, 2006). Milton Friedman's defense of "as-if" rationality in "The methodology of positive economics" (1953) is reprinted in M. Brodbeck (ed.), *Readings in the Philosophy of the Social Sciences* (London: Macmillan, 1969). A recent defense of the "as-if" approach in political science is R. Morton, *Methods and Models: A Guide to the Empirical Analysis of Formal Models in Political*

Science (Cambridge University Press, 1999). As most other defenders of the approach, she does not offer a reason why we should *believe* in the "as-if" fiction. A partial exception is D. Satz and J. Ferejohn, "Rational Choice and Social Theory," *Journal of Philosophy* 91 (1994), 71–87. The discussion of "why questions" draws on B. Hansson, "Why explanations," forthcoming in *Theoria*. The independence of the law of demand from motivational assumptions was noted in G. Becker, "Irrational behavior in economic theory," *Journal of Political Economy* 70 (1962), 1–13.

Chapter 2

MECHANISMS
❀ ❀ ❀

Opening the Black Box

Philosophers of science often argue that an explanation must rest on a *general law*. To explain an event is to cite a set of initial conditions together with a statement to the effect that whenever those conditions obtain an event of that type follows. In this chapter I offer two objections to this idea, one moderate and relatively uncontroversial, the other more radical and open to dispute.

The first objection is that even if we can establish a general law from which we can deduce the explanandum (the second objection denies that we can always do this), this does not always amount to an explanation. Once again, we may refer to the distinction between explanation on the one hand and correlation and necessitation on the other. A general law to the effect that certain symptoms of a disease are always followed by death does not explain why the person died. A general law based on the fundamental nature of the disease does not explain the death if the disease was preempted by a suicide or a car accident.

To get around these problems, it is often argued that we should replace the idea of a general law with that of a *mechanism*. Actually, as I use the term "mechanism" in a special sense later, I shall use the phrase "causal chain" to denote what I have in mind here.[1] Rather than trying to explain an event E by the statement "Whenever events $C_1, C_2, \ldots, C_n$ occur, an event of type E follows," one may try to establish the causal chain that leads from the causes $C_1, C_2, \ldots, C_n$, up to E. This step is often referred to as "opening the black box." Suppose we know that heavy smokers are much more likely than others to get lung cancer. This fact might be due to the fact either that smoking is a cause of lung cancer or that people disposed to smoking also are disposed to the cancer

---

[1] In some of my earlier writings I used "mechanism" to denote what I now call "causal chains." In more recent work I began to use "mechanism" in the sense defined later in this chapter. I should probably have chosen a different terminology, but it is too late now.

(perhaps genes predisposing for lung cancer are linked to genes that make some people more readily addicted to nicotine).[2] To establish the former explanation, we will have to exhibit a chain of physiological cause-effect relations that begins with heavy smoking and ends with lung cancer. The final explanation will be more fine-grained, have more causal links, and be more convincing than the black-box statement "Smoking causes cancer."

Or suppose that somebody asserted that high unemployment causes wars of aggression and adduced evidence for a law-like connection between the two phenomena. Once again, how can we know that this is a causal effect and not a mere correlation? Perhaps high fertility rates, which cause unemployment, also motivate political leaders to initiate aggressive wars? Unsuccessful wars would at least cut down the population size, and successful ones would provide new territories for expansion and migration. To eliminate this possibility, we would first control for fertility rates (and other plausible "third factors") and see whether the connection remains. If it does, we would still not be satisfied until we are provided with a glimpse inside the black box and told *how* high unemployment causes wars. Is it because unemployment induces political leaders to seek new markets through wars? Or because they believe that unemployment creates social unrest that must be channeled toward an external enemy, to prevent revolutionary movements at home? Or because they believe that the armament industry can absorb unemployment? Or could it be that the unemployed tend to vote for populist leaders who are likely to eschew diplomacy and instead use wars to resolve conflicts?

Consider the last proposal in more detail. *Why* would the unemployed vote for irresponsible populist leaders rather than for politicians from one of the established parties? Once again, one can imagine a number of ways of opening this particular black box. Perhaps the natural clientele of populist politicians are more likely to vote when they are unemployed, because their opportunity cost of voting (that is, the value of their time) is less than it is when they have a job. Or perhaps

---

[2] As noted later, the second explanation was at one point seriously proposed.

populist leaders are more likely to propose instant solutions to the unemployment problem. Or perhaps they offer policies that would punish those whom the unemployed believe to be responsible for their plight or to benefit from it, be they capitalists or an economically successful ethnic minority.

Consider the last proposal in more detail. *Why* would the unemployed want to punish capitalists or affluent minorities? Isn't that just another black-box statement? One way of spelling it out would be by asserting that the unemployed are motivated by material self-interest. If the state could confiscate the wealth of these elites, the funds could be used for redistribution to benefit the unemployed. Or perhaps they are motivated by a desire for revenge, which would incite them to punish the elite even if they would not benefit in material terms. If the rich are seen as engaging in ruthless downsizing to increase their profits, those who lose their jobs can use the ballot box to get even. Or the unemployed might simply be envious of the clever minority members who succeed where they failed and use the ballot box to cut them down to size.

As far as I know, high unemployment does not cause wars of aggression. The whole exercise is hypothetical. Yet I believe it supports the idea that the credibility of an explanation increases with the extent to which general laws are spelled out in terms of a causal chain. At the level of general laws we can never be sure that we have controlled for all relevant "third factors." There may always be some cause lurking in the wings that would account for both the explanandum and its alleged cause. If we increase the number of links in the causal chain, we reduce this danger.

The danger cannot, however, be eliminated. Specifying a causal chain does not mean giving up on general laws altogether, only going from general laws at a high level of abstraction to laws at a lower level of abstraction. We might, for instance, replace the universal law "High unemployment causes wars" by the less abstract laws "Populist leaders are war prone" and "The unemployed vote for populist leaders." The latter law, in turn, might be replaced by the conjunction of "The unemployed are envious of rich minorities" and "Those who envy rich minorities vote for populist leaders." As with any other law, these might turn out to be mere correlations. If being envious of minorities and being unemployed are common effects of a joint cause, the electoral success of war-prone leaders would be due not to unemployment but to a factor causally correlated with it. Yet at this more fine-grained level, there are fewer factors to control for. The better we focus the causal story, the easier it is to make sure that we are not dealing with mere correlation.

Explanations in terms of (very) general laws are also unsatisfactory because they are too opaque. Even if presented with an ironclad case for a universal link between unemployment and wars of aggression and a persuasive argument that all remotely plausible "third factors" have been controlled for, we would still want to know *how* unemployment causes wars. We might believe that the explanation is correct, and yet not be satisfied with it. As I noted in the previous chapter, this was the status of explanations relying on the law of gravitation before general relativity. Action at a distance was so mysterious that many refused to believe it could be the last word. As the law allowed for correct predictions to many decimal points, skeptics had to accept that things happened "as if" it were true, although they would not accept the existence of a force that could "act where it was not."

Mechanisms

Readers may well have said to themselves that the instances of alleged universal laws in this exercise are pretty implausible. I agree. In part, their lack of plausibility may be due to the limits of my imagination in concocting the examples, but I believe there are deeper reasons too. There are simply very few well-established general laws in the social sciences. The "law of demand" – when prices to up, consumers buy less – is well supported, but as laws go it is pretty weak.[3] The law of gravitation, for instance, says not only that as the distance between two objects increases the attractive force between them decreases: it tells us by

---

[3] Moreover, for some goods demand goes *up* when prices go up. Consumers may be attracted to a good because it is expensive (the "Veblen effect") or buy less of a good such as bread when its price falls because they can afford to replace some of it by higher-quality goods such as meat (the "Giffen effect").

how much it decreases (inversely with the square of the distance). There is nothing like the law of gravitation in the social sciences.[4]

The law of demand and Engel's law, according to which the fraction of income used on food declines as income increases, are what we might call *weak laws*. For any change (up or down) in the independent variable they allow us to predict the *direction* or the sign of a change (up or down) in the dependent variable. They do not allow us, however, to predict the *magnitude* of the change. Although weak, such laws have some content, since they allow us to rule out a whole range of possible values of the dependent variable. They do not help us, however, to single out the value that will be realized within the nonexcluded range.

The law of demand is not only weak, but also badly suited for explanatory purposes. As we saw in Chapter 1, it is compatible with several assumptions about how consumers behave. To *explain* why consumers buy less of a good when it becomes more expensive we would have to adopt and test a specific assumption about individual consumer reactions to price changes. The key word is "individual." In the social sciences, a satisfactory explanation must ultimately be anchored in hypotheses about individual behavior. This principle – known as "methodological individualism" – is the premise for the present book as a whole. It implies that psychology and perhaps biology must have a fundamental importance in explaining social phenomena. If I am hesitant about biology, it is not because I believe it is incapable in principle of explaining aspects of human behavior, but because I think it is largely too undeveloped to do the job.

To explain individual behavior, we mostly have to rely on what I call *mechanisms*. Roughly speaking, mechanisms are *frequently occurring and easily recognizable causal patterns that are triggered under generally unknown conditions or with indeterminate consequences*. They allow us to explain, but not to predict. It has been argued, for instance, that for every child who becomes alcoholic in response to an alcoholic environment,

---

[4] To be sure, it is often said that the strength of altruistic feelings toward others varies inversely with their social distance from the agent. Yet the idea of "social distance" is more like a metaphor than like a concept, and in any case "varies inversely" is much less precise than "varies inversely with the square of the distance."

another eschews alcohol in response to the same environment. Both reactions embody mechanisms: doing what your parents do and doing the opposite of what they do. We cannot tell ahead of time what will become of the child of an alcoholic, but if he or she turns out either a teetotaler or an alcoholic we may suspect we know why.

I do not claim that there is any kind of objective indeterminacy at work here; indeed that concept has little meaning outside quantum mechanics. I am claiming only that we can often explain behavior by showing it to be an instance of a general causal pattern, even if we cannot explain why that pattern occurred. The mechanisms of conformism (for instance, doing what your parents do) and of anticonformism (doing the opposite of what they do) are both very general. If we can show the behavior of a child with an alcoholic parent to be an instance of one or the other mechanism, we have provided an explanation of the behavior. One might object that as long as we have not shown why the child became (say) an alcoholic rather than a teetotaler we have not explained anything. I would certainly agree that an account showing why one rather than the other outcome occurred would be a better one, and I do not deny that we might sometimes be able to provide one. But to subsume an individual instance under a more general causal pattern is also to provide an explanation. To know that the child became an alcoholic as a result of conformism is to remove some of the opaqueness of the outcome, although some will remain as long as we do not also explain why the child was subject to conformism.

I said that a mechanism is "a frequently occurring and easily recognizable causal pattern." Proverbial folk wisdom has identified many such patterns.[5] In my preferred definition, "A proverb has been passed down through many generations. It sums up, in one short phrase, a general principle, or common situation, and when you say it, everyone knows exactly what you mean." Moreover, proverbs often state mechanisms (in the sense used here) rather than general laws. Consider, in particular, the striking tendency for proverbs to occur in mutually exclusive pairs. On the one hand, we have "Absence makes the heart grow fonder," but on

---

[5] As we shall see in Chapter 10, however, proverbs are not always wise.

the other "Out of sight, out of mind." On the one hand we may think
that forbidden fruit tastes best, but on the other that the grapes beyond
our reach are sour. On the one hand, "Like attracts like," but on the
other "Opposites attract each other." On the one hand, "Like father, like
son," but on the other "Mean father, prodigal son." On the one hand,
"Haste makes waste," but on the other "He who hesitates is lost." On
the one hand, "To remember a misfortune is to renew it," but on the
other "The remembrance of past perils is pleasant." (As noted later, the
last two are in fact not mutually exclusive.) Many other examples could
be cited.

Many pairs of opposite mechanisms do not appear to be captured
by proverbs. Consider for instance what we may call the spillover-
compensation pair. If a person who works very hard at the job goes on
vacation, would we expect her to carry over the same frenetic pace to her
leisure activities (spillover effect) or on the contrary to relax utterly
(compensation effect)? Or would we expect citizens in democracies to be
prone or averse to religion? If they carry over the habit of deciding for
themselves from the political to the religious sphere (spillover), we would
expect weak religious beliefs. If the lack of a superior authority in politics
leads them to seek authority elsewhere (compensation), a democratic
political regime would rather tend to favor religion. A contemporary
question, which still seems to be undecided, is whether violence
on television stimulates real-life violence (spillover) or attenuates it
(compensation).

Similar mechanisms can apply to relations among individuals.
Consider the question of explaining donations to charity. One individual
may be mainly concerned with the efficiency of giving. If others give
little, his donation will make more of an impact and hence he is more
likely to give; if others give much his donation matters less and he may
not make any. Another donor may be more concerned with fairness
(among donors). If others give little, she cannot see why she should give
more; conversely if others give much she may feel compelled to follow
suit. The same pair of mechanisms may apply in collective-action
situations. As a popular movement grows, some individuals may drop
out because they do not believe they make much of a difference

any more, whereas others may join because they do not feel they should stay on the sidelines while others are paying the cost (Chapter 24).

Even proverbs that are not matched with an opposite proverb often express mechanisms rather than laws. The proverb "The best swimmers drown" would be absurd if taken to mean that the propensity to drown invariably increases with swimming skill. Yet for some swimmers it may indeed be the case that their confidence in their swimming skill increases more rapidly than their skill, causing them to take unwarranted risks ("Pride goes before a fall"). Or consider a proverb to which I shall return several times in this book, "We believe easily what we hope and what we fear."[6] Although the proverb is implausible if read literally, as a universal law, it is a useful reminder that in addition to the well-known phenomenon of wishful thinking, there is a less-well-understood propensity to what we might call *countermotivated thinking*.[7] Consider, finally, the proverbial claims "Too many shepherds make a poor guard" and "Too many cooks make the soup too salty." Again, the value of the proverbs is not to state a universal law, but to suggest mechanisms. The first proverb might be true if each shepherd believes that everybody else is keeping watch (remember the Kitty Genovese case), and the second if each cook believes that nobody else is adding salt to the soup.

When defining mechanisms, I also said that they "are triggered under generally unknown conditions or with indeterminate consequences." Most of the proverbial mechanisms that I have cited so far fall in the first category. We do not know which conditions will trigger conformism or anticonformism, wishful thinking or counterwishful (countermotivated) thinking, adaptive preferences (sour grapes) or counteradaptive preferences (the grass is greener). We know that at most one member of each pair will be realized, but we cannot tell which. The qualification

[6] Although this proverb does not state a pair of contrary propositions, we might imagine proverbial statements to the effect that "we believe easily what we hope" and "we disbelieve easily what we hope." We are in fact often biased against what we hope because we overcorrect for wishful thinking.

[7] The idea might be defined more broadly, to include both disbelieving what one hopes and believing what one fears. In the previous note, I cited a possible way in which the first variety might come about. As for the second, perhaps the desire to prepare oneself for the worst tends to strengthen the belief that the worst will occur. The mere process of running through a mental scenario might engrave it on the mind and raise its status from remotely possible to plausible or even probable.

"at most" is important, because some people may not be subject to either member of these mechanism pairs. Genuine autonomy means being neither conformist nor anticonformist. People's beliefs may be independent of their desires, and their desires independent of their opportunities.

In other cases, proverbs suggest the simultaneous triggering of two mechanisms with oppositely directed effects on the outcome. In that case, the indeterminacy lies in determining the *net effect* of the mechanisms rather than in determining which of them (if any) will be triggered. Consider for instance "Necessity is the mother of invention" and "It is expensive to be poor." The first proverb asserts a causal link between poverty and a strong *desire* for innovation, the second a link between poverty and few *opportunities* for innovation. Because behavior is shaped by desires as well as by opportunities (Chapter 9), we cannot in general tell whether the net impact of poverty on innovation is positive or negative. Or consider the pair of proverbs mentioned earlier, "To remember a misfortune is to renew it" versus "The remembrance of past perils is pleasant." The first proverb relies on what has been called an "endowment effect": the memory of a bad experience is a bad experience.[8] The second relies on a "contrast effect": the memory of a bad experience enhances the value of the present.[9] In general we cannot tell whether the net effect of an early bad experience on later welfare will be positive or negative.

Once again, we are not restricted to proverbs. Consider for instance two nonproverbial mechanisms involved in what has been called "the psychology of tyranny." If the tyrant steps up the oppression of the subjects, two effects are likely to occur. On the one hand, harsher punishments will deter them from resistance or rebellion. On the other hand, the more he behaves as a tyrant the more they will hate him. Like any bully, he is likely to inspire hatred as well as fear. If hatred dominates fear, oppression will backfire. In countries occupied by Germans during

---

[8] Conversely, the memory of a good experience is a good experience. Thus Tennyson: "'Tis better to have loved and lost than never to have loved at all."

[9] Conversely, the memory of a good experience devalues the present. Thus Donne: "'Tis better to be foul than to have been fair."

World War II, members of the resistance sometimes exploited this mechanism when they killed German soldiers to provoke a reprisal, on the assumption that the deterrence effect would be dominated by the "tyranny effect."[10] Or consider the somewhat similar case of a person who faces a barrier or impediment to her goal. This threat to her freedom of action may induce what psychologists call "reactance" – a motivation to recover or reestablish the freedom. The effects of the barrier and the consequent reactance oppose each other, and in general we cannot tell which will be the stronger.[11] As an illustration, think of the effect of hiding from a small boy a drum his parents do not want him to play with.[12]

Even when we know the net effect, we may not be able to explain it. Suppose we were somehow able to observe and measure a zero net effect of the endowment and contrast effects with regard to a good experience in the past. This outcome might come about in two ways. Although the three-star French meal I had last year reduced my pleasure from later meals in more ordinary French restaurants, this negative effect on my welfare is exactly offset by the memory of what a great meal it was. Yet the observation of a zero net effect is also perfectly consistent with both endowment and contrast effects of zero – as well as with both effects very and equally strong. As long as we do not know which is the case, we cannot claim to have explained the outcome. To assess the strength of each effect, we might look at the outcome in a situation in which the other is not expected to occur. If, as seems plausible, my pleasure from Greek cooking is unaffected by the three-star French meal, we can identify the strength of the pure endowment effect.

[10] Sometimes the hatred found a different target. In three villages in Central and Northern Italy where the Germans undertook savage reprisals in 1944, some villagers were still hostile to the partisans fifty years later because they were seen as indirectly or even "truly" responsible for the massacre. When A causes B to kill C, relatives and friends of C may direct their anger at A rather than B. In the resistance movements that were fighting German occupational troops, both mechanisms were observed.

[11] A special feature of this example is that one of the two competing effects (the reactance) is induced by the other (the barrier). In the other examples, the two effects are caused simultaneously by a common cause (e.g., the tyrant's oppression).

[12] In another illustration of reactance, children (and adults too) may refuse all proposals about how to spend the day, *even the one they prefer*, because they do not want to feel imposed upon.

A related indeterminacy can arise with regard to the first type of mechanisms, those that are triggered under "generally unknown conditions." Consider again the case of an alcoholic parent. If we look at the whole population of alcoholics (or a large representative sample), suppose that their children on average drink neither more nor less than the children of nonalcoholics. Disregarding for simplicity the influence of genetic factors, this hypothetical finding might be understood in two ways. On the one hand, it could be that children of alcoholics are neither conformist nor anticonformist: that is, their drinking behavior might be shaped by the same causes as that of children of nonalcoholics. On the other hand, it could be that half the children of alcoholics are conformist and the other half anticonformist, leaving a net effect of zero.

Similarly, theories of voting behavior have identified both an underdog mechanism and a bandwagon mechanism. Those subject to the former tend to vote for the candidate who is behind in preelection polls, whereas those subject to the latter vote for the front-runner. If the two types are evenly mixed, there might be no noticeable net effect, so that the polls would be good predictors of the actual vote. A lack of influence of polls on voting in the aggregate would not show, however, that individuals are unaffected by the polls. Weak aggregate effects of TV violence on real-life violence could mask strong opposite effects on subgroups. In all these cases, a neutral aggregate could reflect either a homogeneous population of unaffected individuals or a heterogeneous population of individuals who are all strongly affected but in opposite directions. The need to dispel this ambiguity provides yet another argument for methodological individualism. To explain behavior at the aggregate level, we must look at the behavior of the individual components.

Molecular Mechanisms

I have been considering what we might call "atomic" mechanisms – elementary psychological reactions that cannot be reduced to other mechanisms at the same level. One might well ask how far these psychological mechanisms will take us in explaining social phenomena.

The answer is that we can use atomic mechanisms as building blocks in more complex "molecular" mechanisms. Again, we may begin with proverbs. Two proverbs say, "The fear is often greater than the danger" and "Fear increases the danger." Taken together, they imply that excessive fear may create its own justification. An English proverb says that "there is a black sheep in every flock." A French proverb tells us that "it takes only one bad sheep to spoil a flock." Taking them together, we may infer that every flock will be spoiled.[13]

Consider for instance a self-governing collegial body such as a university department or a workers' cooperative. The following scenario is sufficiently frequent and intelligible to qualify as a molecular mechanism. First, by the laws of probability any group of twenty or more is likely to contain at least one garrulous and contrary person, a "spoiler," defined by the dictionary as "one who mars the chance of victory for an opponent, while not being a potential winner." Second, in a group that contains a person of this kind collective self-government is very difficult. Discussions go on forever; previous decisions are constantly put into question; a spirit of formalism replaces informal collegiality; bad blood is created; and so on. In the end, the group will welcome the move to government by a smaller executive committee or even by a single individual.

Leaving proverbs behind, let us consider another molecular mechanism. For centuries or millennia, elites have been wary of democracy as a regime form because they thought it would allow for all sorts of dangerous and licentious behavior. Yet opportunities for dangerous behavior will not by themselves produce such behavior: the motive must also be there. Might democratic regimes somehow restrain the desires of the citizens to do what democracy allows them to do? This was Tocqueville's claim. He thought that to satisfy a need for authority for which politics did not provide, democratic citizens would turn to religion, which tends to limit and restrain what the citizens desire. The critics of democracy got it wrong, he argued, because they focused only on opportunities

---

[13] I am taking a bit of a liberty with these proverbs. In its literal meaning the French phrase *une brebis galeuse* refers to a sheep with a skin disease caused by an arachnidan parasite.

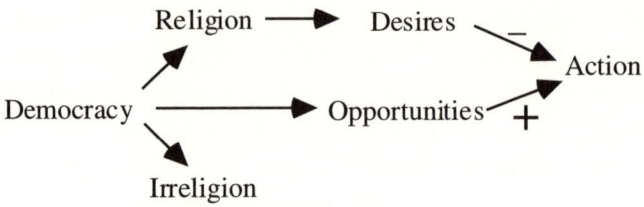

FIGURE 2.1

while neglecting desires. Although he stated this argument as if it yielded a universal law, it is more plausibly understood in terms of mechanisms. For one thing, if the spillover effect rather than the compensation effect is at work, the lack of political authority will weaken religion rather than strengthen it. For another, even if the spillover effect is at work, we cannot conclude anything about the net effect. If the opportunity set is greatly expanded and the desires only weakly restrained, the net effect of democracy may be to increase rather than reduce the incidence of the behavior in question.

The two pairs of mechanisms are summarily represented in Figure 2.1. *If* the influence of democracy on religion is mediated by the compensation effect rather than the spillover effect, democratic societies will be religious. *If* the negative effect of democracy on desires (mediated by religion) is strong enough to offset the positive effect of democracy on opportunities, democratic citizens will behave moderately.[14]

Mechanisms and Laws

Often, explaining by mechanisms is the best we can do, but sometimes we can do better. Once we have identified a mechanism that is "triggered under generally unknown conditions," we may be able to identify the triggering conditions. In that case, the mechanism will be replaced by a law, albeit usually a weak one in the sense defined earlier.

---

[14] In addition, Tocqueville claimed that the tyranny of majority opinion would exercise a moderating influence. "Some governments seek to safeguard mores by condemning the authors of licentious books. In the United States, no one is condemned for such works, but no one is tempted to write them."

Common sense assumes that a gift will make the recipient feel grateful. If he does not, we blame him. The classical moralists – from Montaigne to La Bruyère – argued that gifts tend to make recipients resentful rather than grateful. It seems that both common sense and the moralists are on to something, but they do not tell us when we can expect the one or the other outcome. A moralist from classical antiquity, Publilius Syrus, stated *triggering conditions*: a small gift creates an obligation, a large one an enemy.[15] By appealing to the size of the gift as a triggering condition, we have transformed the pair of mechanisms into a (somewhat) law-like statement.[16] To cite another example, we might be able to state when a tension between a desire and a belief ("cognitive dissonance") is resolved by modifying the belief and when it is resolved by modifying the desire.[17] Purely factual beliefs may be too recalcitrant to be easily modified (Chapter 7). The person who paid seventy-five dollars for a ticket to a Broadway show cannot easily fool himself into thinking he only paid forty dollars. He will normally, however, be able to find some attractive aspects of the show and persuade himself that these are more important than the ones in which it is deficient.

Earlier, I mentioned the contrast between the "forbidden fruit" mechanism and the "sour grapes" mechanism. In some cases, we may be able to predict which will be triggered. In an experiment, subjects in one condition were asked to rank four records according to their attractiveness and told that the next day they would receive one of them, chosen at random. Subjects in another condition ranked the records and were told that the next day they would be able to choose one of them. The next day, all subjects were told that the record they had ranked third was unavailable and asked to rank the four records again, as part of an attempt to discover how listening to a record for the second time might affect one's evaluation of it. As predicted by reactance theory, subjects in the first condition displayed the "sour grapes" effect by downgrading the value of the

---

[15] I am cheating a bit here, to get the example right, since Syrus refers to loans rather than to gifts. Although it seems plausible that both the loan and the gift of a large sum of money can make the recipient feel resentful, they probably do so in different ways.

[16] Only "somewhat," since the exact size at which gratitude turns into resentment will be highly context dependent. The same remark applies to the other cases discussed in the text.

[17] Recall, however, that the tension may be left unresolved.

unavailable option whereas those in the second showed the "forbidden fruit" effect by upgrading it. (A control group who were not told about the elimination showed no change.) The crucial difference is that the second group experienced a threat to their freedom while the first did not.

Let me consider, however, a more complex example. With regard to the pair of proverbs "Absence makes the heart grow fonder" and "Out of sight, out of mind," there is actually a third proverb suggesting a triggering condition: "A short absence can do much good." La Rochefoucauld proposed a different condition: "Absence lessens moderate passions and intensifies great ones, as the wind blows out a candle but fans up a fire." These plausible propositions are not very strong laws. To be able to predict the course of passion, we would have to know what counts as a short absence (three weeks?) and as a strong passion (one that keeps you awake at night?). Also, we would have to specify how duration of absence and strength of passion *interact* to generate increase or decrease of passion during an absence. Let me pursue the last issue.

Interaction Among Causes

In general, the social sciences are not very good at explaining how causes interact to produce a joint effect. Most commonly, one assumes that each cause contributes separately to the effect (an "additive model"). To explain income, for instance, one may assume that it is caused in part by parental income and in part by parental education, and then use statistical methods to determine the relative contributions of these two causes. For the example I have discussed, this approach might not be adequate. The duration of the absence might not make a separate contribution to the strength of the post-absence emotion; rather its effect might depend on the strength of the pre-absence emotion. This interaction effect is shown in Figure 2.2.

Some scholars argue, though, that the world – or at least the part of it they study – simply does not exhibit many interactions of this kind. It is rarely the case, they claim, that for low levels of independent variable X the dependent variable Z increases (decreases) with dependent variable Y, whereas for high levels of X an increase in Y causes a decrease (increase)

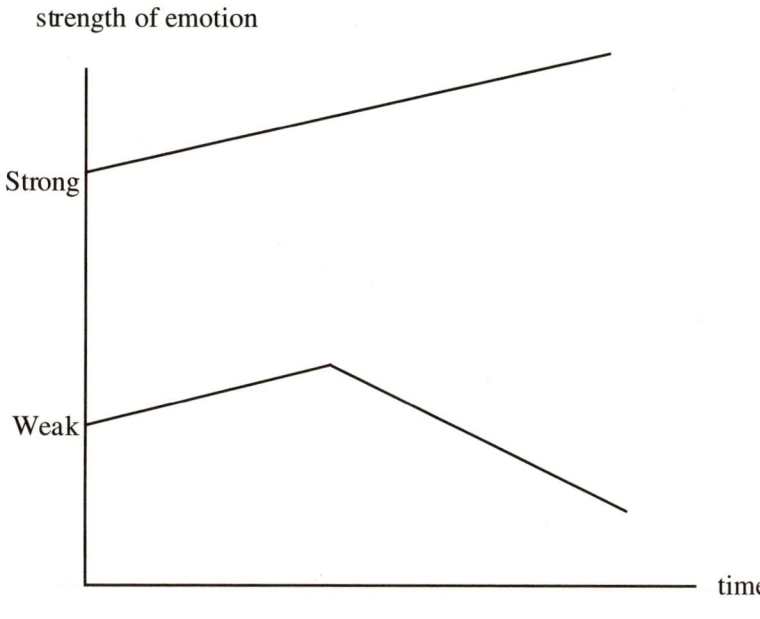

strength of emotion

Strong

Weak

time

FIGURE 2.2

in Z. The hypothesized relation in Figure 2.2 would (if it exists) be an exception. At most, they argue, what we find is that at low levels of X, Y has little effect on Z, whereas it does have an effect at higher levels of X. In explaining income, for instance, one may assume that parental income contributes more or less at different levels of parental education. This kind of interaction can be captured by a multiplicative interaction term so that Z is a function of X, Y, and XY. By contrast, the *reversal* of the causal effect of Y on Z at higher levels of X cannot be captured in this way. If we can believe the claim that such reversals are rare, however, we need not worry much about them.

The existence of an interaction effect may be subject to the same kind of indeterminacy that we find in mechanisms more generally. Consider the interaction between age and basic political attitudes as causes of extremism. One might guess that the youth organizations will be to the left of the parties themselves, giving the Young Conservatives a lighter shade of blue. Alternatively, the youth organizations of the political parties will be more extreme than the parties themselves – Young Conservatives a darker shade of blue and Young Socialists a more vivid shade of pink. Both guesses seem plausible, and both patterns have in fact been observed. Or consider the interaction between preconsumption mood and drug consumption as causes of postconsumption mood. One might guess that drugs such as alcohol or cocaine are *mood lifters*, attenuating depressions and turning contentment into euphoria. But one might also suspect drugs to be *mood multipliers*, making bad moods worse and good moods better. Again, both guesses seem plausible and both patterns are observed. In both cases, the first mechanism is compatible with an additive model, whereas the second implies a reversal effect.

When faced with recalcitrant data adding an interaction term, or "curve fitting," is not the only possible response. There is an alternative strategy, that of "data mining." In a curve-fitting exercise, one keeps the dependent and independent variables fixed and shops around, as it were, for a mathematical function that will give a good statistical fit. In a data-mining exercise, one keeps the mathematical function fixed (usually a simple additive model) and shops around for independent variables that have a good fit with the dependent variable. Suppose that by a "good fit" we mean a correlation that would only have a 5 percent probability of occurring by chance. In any study of a complex social phenomenon such as income, one can easily list a dozen variables that might conceivably affect it.[18] Also, there are probably half a dozen different ways of conceptualizing income. It would be very unlikely if none of the independent variables showed a correlation at the 5 percent level with one of the definitions of income.[19] The laws of probability tell us that the most

---

[18] Thus in one longitudinal study of the relation between maternal practices and child outcomes, only 35 of 552 correlations were statistically significant "at the $p < 0.05$ level" (meaning that there was 1 chance in 20 that they obtained by chance), a fact only evident to those who read the appendixes of the book. In the reprint edition, these were deleted.

[19] Theory may suggest that bad weather depresses stock market traders, causing them to sell. Scholars report, however, the opposite result when bad weather is defined as 100 percent cloud cover. By changing the definition of bad weather to cloud cover above 80 percent, the sign of the correlation magically reverses.

improbable coincidence would be if improbable coincidences never occurred.[20]

Once a scholar has identified a suitable mathematical function or a suitable set of dependent or independent variables, she can begin to look for a causal story to provide an intuition to back the findings. When she writes up the results for publication, the sequence is often reversed. She will state that she started with a causal theory; then looked for the most plausible way of transforming it into a formal hypothesis; and then found it confirmed by the data.[21] This is bogus science. In the natural sciences there is no need for the "logic of justification" to match or reflect "the logic of discovery." Once a hypothesis is stated in its final form, its genesis is irrelevant. What matters are its downstream consequences, not its upstream origins. This is so because the hypothesis can be tested on an indefinite number of observations over and above those that inspired the scholar to think of it in the first place. In the social sciences (and in the humanities), most explanations use a finite data set. Because procedures of data collection often are nonstandardized, scholars may not be able to test their hypotheses against new data.[22] And if procedures *are* standardized, the data may fail to reflect a changing reality. It is impossible to explain consumption patterns, for instance,

[20] I have two personal experiences. The first time I visited New York I bought tickets for two Broadway shows, one built around the music of Fats Waller and the other around that of Duke Ellington. There were few tickets left, so I had to take what I could get – which, in both shows, was row H, seat 130. This was merely uncanny, but another coincidence felt more significant. There are two experiences I've only had once. One is being invited to a dinner party and then forgetting I'd been invited. The other is being invited to a dinner party and then having the host call me up half an hour before I was supposed to be there, to tell me he had to cancel because of illness. The coincidence, which made me think for a second that someone was watching over me, is that this was one and the same party.

[21] Hence there are three problems about using correlation as a guide to causality. First, the correlation may arise purely by chance and have no causal interpretation. Second, the correlation may have an indirect causal interpretation if the two correlated phenomena are common effects of a "third factor." Third, the direction of causality might be ambiguous.

[22] One could get around or at least mitigate this problem by exercising self-restraint. If one has a sufficiently large data set, one can first concentrate on a representative sample and ignore the rest. Once one has done one's best to explain the subset of observations, one can take the explanation to the full data set and see whether it holds up. If it does, it is less likely to be spurious. Another way of keeping scholars honest would be if journals refused to consider articles submitted for publication unless the hypotheses to be tested together with the procedures for testing them had been deposited with the editor (say) two years in advance. The alcohol researcher Ketil Bruun adopted this practice.

without taking account of new products and of changing prices of old ones.

There is no doubt that sharp practices of this kind occur. I do not know how common they are, only that they are sufficiently widespread to cause thoughtful social scientists to worry. The main cause of the problem is perhaps our inadequate understanding of multifactorial causality. If we had strong intuitions about how several causes can interact to produce an effect, there would be no need to rely on the mechanical procedure of "adding an interaction term" when an additive model fails. Yet because our intuitions are weak, we do not really know what to look for, and then tinkering with models seems the only alternative – at least if we retain the ambitious goal of providing law-like explanations. Given the dangers of tinkering, perhaps we should lower our ambitions instead.

❮❮❮

BIBLIOGRAPHICAL NOTE

Many of the ideas in this chapter are adapted from Chapter 1 of my *Alchemies of the Mind* (Cambridge University Press, 1999). There I also cite works by Raymond Boudon, Nancy Cartwright, and Paul Veyne that advocate similar proposals. A recent statement is P. Hedström, *Dissecting the Social* (Cambridge University Press, 2005). Useful ways of thinking about psychological mechanisms also include F. Heider, *The Psychology of Interpersonal Relations* (Hillsdale, NJ: Lawrence Erlbaum, 1958), and R. Abelson, *Statistics as Principled Argument* (Hillsdale, NJ: Lawrence Erlbaum, 1995). The latter also offers wise and witty remarks about the pitfalls of statistical analysis. A standard brief exposition of the idea that science explains by general laws is C. Hempel, *Philosophy of Natural Science* (Englewood Cliffs, NJ: Prentice-Hall, 1966). The principle of methodological individualism is thoroughly covered in Part 4 of M. Brodbeck (ed.), *Readings in the Philosophy of the Social Sciences*

(London: Macmillan, 1969), and in Part 6 of M. Martin and L. McIntyre (eds.), *Readings in the Philosophy of Social Science* (Cambridge, MA: MIT Press, 1994); see also K. Arrow, "Methodological individualism and social knowledge," *American Economic Review: Papers and Proceedings* 84 (1994), 1–9. I have written more systematically on proverbs in "Science et sagesse: Le rôle des proverbes dans la connaissance de l'homme et de la société," in J. Baechler (ed.), *L'acteur et ses raisons: Mélanges Raymond Boudon* (Paris: Presses Universitaires de France, 2000). The idea of the "psychology of tyranny" is taken from J. Roemer, "Rationalizing revolutionary ideology," *Econometrica* 53 (1985), 85–108. The study of subjects who were promised records is J. Brehm et al., "The attractiveness of an eliminated choice alternative," *Journal of Experimental Social Psychology* 2 (1966), 301–13. A general introduction to reactance theory is R. Wicklund, *Freedom and Reactance* (New York: Wiley, 1974). Skepticism about interaction that induces reversal effects is found in R. Hastie and R. Dawes, *Rational Choice in an Uncertain World* (Thousand Oaks, CA: Sage, 2001), Chapter 3. The footnoted story of the 6 percent significant correlations is told in R. R. McCrae and P. T. Costa, "The paradox of parental influence," in C. Perris, W. A. Arrindell, and M. Eisemann (eds.), *Parenting and Psychopathology* (New York: Wiley), pp. 113–14. The footnoted example of the impact of bad weather on stock market traders is taken from P. Kennedy, "Oh no! I got the wrong sign! What should I do?" *Journal of Economic Education* 36 (2005), 77–92, which also contains useful comments on the costs (and benefits!) of data mining more generally.

Chapter 3
INTERPRETATION
❀ ❀ ❀

Interpretation and Explanation

In many writings on the humanities, the focus has been on *interpretation* rather than explanation. In the German tradition, a contrast was often drawn between the "spiritual sciences" (*Geisteswissenschaften*) and the natural sciences (*Naturwissenschaften*). In the former, we are told, the proper procedure is that of interpretation or "understanding" (*Verstehen*). For the latter the appropriate language is that of explanation (*Erklären*). Max Weber wrote, for instance, that natural science does not aim at "understanding" the behavior of cells.

We may then ask whether the social sciences rely on understanding or on explanation. I believe this question is wrongly put. In my view, to interpret *is* to explain. Interpretation is nothing but a special case of the hypothetico-deductive method (Chapter 1). Scholars in the humanities cannot, for instance, use "empathy" as a privileged shortcut to the interpretation of behavior, since one scholar's empathetic understanding may differ from that of another. To decide among conflicting inter-pretations they have to confront these interpretive hunches or hypotheses (for that is what they are) with *experience*. As I argued in Chapter 1, experience includes not only the facts we are trying to understand, but also *novel facts* that we might not otherwise have thought about investigating.[1]

Interpretation is directed to human actions and to the product of human actions, such as works of art. In Chapter 14 I address the issue of interpretation of literary works, more specifically works in which we need to understand the actions of the characters as well as the choices of the

---

[1] In the experimental sciences, "novel facts" can mean facts that are literally new, as when one exposes rats or human beings to conditions that do not occur naturally. In the humanities and nonexperimental social sciences, "novel" must be taken in the epistemic sense of "previously unsuspected" rather than in the ontological sense of "previously nonexisting."

author. In trying to understand other literary works, as well as the "wordless arts" of painting, sculpture, or instrumental music, this two-tier issue does not arise. Yet in these art forms too, the choices of the artist lend themselves, in principle, to much of the same analysis as that which I shall propose for authorial decisions. The artists make choices according to some criterion of "betterness" that neither they nor we may be able to formulate explicitly, but that is revealed in practice when they discard one draft, one sketch, or one recording in favor of another. Yet the relation between the criterion of betterness and human psychology is more complicated and less well understood in the wordless arts than in (classical) fiction. I shall not attempt to deal with them.

Rationality and Intelligibility

The remainder of this chapter, therefore, will be directed to the interpretation of *action*. Interpreting an action requires us to explain it in terms of the antecedent beliefs and desires (motivations) of the agent. Moreover, we should explain these mental states themselves in a way that makes sense of them, by locating them within the full desire-belief complex. An isolated desire or belief that does not have the normal kind of solidarity with other mental states is just a brute fact that may allow us to explain behavior but not to understand it.

A paradigm mode of explaining action is to demonstrate that it was performed because it was *rational* (Chapter 11). To do so, it is not enough to show that it had good consequences for the agent: it must be understood as optimal from the agent's point of view. It is a fact, for instance, that if people attach high value to future consequences of present behavior, that is, have a low rate of time discounting (Chapter 6), their lives go better. It is also plausible that higher education may shape time preferences in that direction. These two premises do not, however, amount to a rational-choice explanation of why people decide to become educated. For an explanation to get off the ground one would have to show that people have the requisite beliefs about the impact of education on the ability to delay gratification, and that they are subjectively motivated to acquire that ability.[2] Trying to explain the choice by its beneficial consequences is a form of "rational-choice functionalism" – combining the two approaches I warned against in the Introduction – that sheds no light on the meaning of the behavior.

If behavior is rational, it is ipso facto also intelligible. Irrational behavior can also, however, be intelligible. I shall distinguish among three varieties of intelligible but irrational behavior and contrast them with some cases of unintelligible behavior.

The first arises when the machinery of decision making (see Figure II.1) is *truncated* in one way or another. By virtue of its peculiar urgency, a strong emotion may prevent the agent from "looking around" (i.e., gathering information) before acting. Rather than adopting a waiting strategy similar to that of the Roman general Fabius the Cunctator (hesitator), the agent rushes into action without taking the time to consider the consequences. Another form of truncation arises in weakness of will, traditionally understood as acting against one's own better judgment (Chapter 6). The person who has decided to quit smoking yet accepts the offer of a cigarette acts on a reason, namely, a desire to smoke. For an action to be rational, however, it has to be optimal in light of the totality of reasons, not just one of them. I shall have occasion, however, to question this understanding of weakness of will.

A second variety arises in the *short-circuiting* of the machinery of decision that occurs when belief formation is biased by the agent's desires. Wishful thinking, for instance, is irrational, but fully intelligible. A subtler form of motivated belief formation arises when the agent stops gathering information when the evidence gathered so far supports the belief he would like to be true.[3] These forms of motivated belief formation are, in their way, optimizing processes: they maximize the pleasure the agent derives from his beliefs about the world rather than the pleasure he can expect from his encounters with the world.

---

[2] In Chapter II I argue that the idea of being motivated to be motivated by long-term consequences is conceptually incoherent, but that is a separate point from the one I am making here.

[3] In an age of greater statistical innocence, Gregor Mendel, the discoverer of the laws of inheritance, apparently practiced this method of "quitting when you're ahead" in his experiments.

A third variety is what we might call a *wire-crossing* in the machinery of decision. We can easily understand why the mind might engage in cognitive dissonance reduction (of which wishful thinking is one variety), but why should it also pursue dissonance *production*? The idea, cited in Chapter 2, that we believe easily what we fear is an example. Why would fear of a bad outcome make us see it as more likely than is warranted by our evidence? If the belief is supported neither by the evidence nor by our desires, why adopt it? Clearly, nothing is being optimized. In one sense such behavior is harder to understand than actions arising from truncation and short-circuiting, since *there is nothing in it* for the agent, no partial or short-term goal that it satisfies. Nevertheless it is intelligible (as I understand that idea) because it arises from the belief-desire system of the agent.

Actions that elude interpretation include those caused by compulsions and obsessions, phobic behavior, self-mutilations, anorexia, and the like. To be sure, such behavior has the effect, which explains why it is performed, of relieving the anxiety the agent feels if she does not perform it. Yet washing one's hands fifty times a day or walking up fifty flights of stairs to avoid taking the elevator is not like using a tranquilizer. Taking Valium may be as rational and intelligible as taking aspirin, but compulsive and phobic behavior is unintelligible because it is not part of an interconnected *system* of beliefs and desires. Or to take an example from John Rawls, we would find it hard to understand the behavior of someone who devoted his time to counting blades of grass unless it was linked to some other goal, such as winning a bet.

Wishful thinking is intelligible, as is counterwishful thinking. The belief of a disturbed individual that the dentist in the building next door is directing X rays at him to destroy his mind is not. By contrast, paranoid beliefs in politics are intelligible because they are rooted in the desires of the agent. A strongly anti-Semitic person is motivated to entertain absurd beliefs about the omnipotent and evil nature of the Jews (see Chapter 7). It is not that she wants Jews to *have* these features, but she is motivated to *believe* they do because the belief can rationalize her urge to destroy them. Even contradictory beliefs may be intelligible. An anti-Semite may on different occasions characterize the Jews as "vermin" *and* assert their omnipotence. The very same people who say that "Jews are always trying to push in where they are not wanted" also believe that "Jews are clannish, always sticking together." One and the same Muslim may assert that the Israeli intelligence service Mossad was behind the attacks on the World Trade Center on September 11, 2001, *and* take pride in the event.

Understanding Civil Wars

Let me give two extended examples to flesh out the ideas of intelligible beliefs and desires, both taken from studies of civil wars past and present. I shall then draw on the same studies and some others to address the basic hermeneutic question of how we can impute or establish motivations and beliefs.

Consider first the belief in predestination, which was a main issue dividing Calvinists and Catholics in the wars of religion. At its origin was the intense religious anxiety experienced by many believers in pre-Reformation times, due to uncertainty about one's salvation. How could one be sure – could one ever be sure – that one had done enough to achieve it? Looking back to his earlier years, Calvin wrote in 1539 that even when he had satisfied the demands of the church to confess his sins and efface God's memory of them by doing good works and penance, "I was far removed from certainty and tranquility of conscience. For each time that I delved into myself or lifted my heart up to You, I was struck by such an extreme horror that neither purgations nor disculpations could cure me."

What relieved him from anxiety was the shift from a conception of God as immanent in the world, an oppressive and threatening presence, to a conception of God as absolutely transcendent. Crucially, this idea was linked to the doctrine of double predestination: since God had chosen from eternity who would be saved and who would be damned, there was *nothing one could do* for one's salvation and hence no reason to worry that one had not done enough. The key interpretive issue concerns the link between this belief in predestination and the relief from anxiety. A priori, this effect of the doctrine seems unintelligible. Calvin taught that the elect was a small minority, ranging (in different statements) from one in a hundred to one in five. What could generate more anxiety than the belief that one was very likely to be among the damned and that there was nothing one could do to escape an eternity of burning in hell? Would not conversion from Catholicism to Calvinism be to go, literally, from the frying pan into the fire?

The answer is probably to be found along the lines first sketched by Max Weber. Given their belief in predestination, the Calvinists could not hold that rational and systematic effort would bring them salvation, but they could and did hold that it would give them the subjective *certainty* of salvation. Calvin himself wrote that "the vocation of the elect is like a demonstration and testimony of their election." And it seems in fact that conversion to Calvinism effectively eliminated uncertainty about salvation. I return to this form of "magical thinking" in Chapter 7. Here I merely want to emphasize how the twin mechanisms of wishful thinking and magical thinking lend intelligibility to the belief in predestination.

Consider next the intelligibility of motivations. Why are young Palestinians willing to give their life in suicide missions? Their main motivation – to obtain or defend a national homeland – is not difficult to understand.[4] It is a cause that may be as compelling as was the defense of democracy in the struggle against Hitler. What may seem puzzling is the *strength* of the motivation. Some additional causal factors are needed to make it intelligible. I shall discuss half a dozen of these and conclude in favor of one of them.

Prior to September 11, there was a widespread belief that the typical suicide bomber in the Middle East was a single young unemployed man, perhaps sexually starved, for whom a religious movement could fill a vacuum that would otherwise be occupied by family and work. Then overnight, after the attack on the World Trade Center, experts on terrorism decided that they had to "rewrite the book." Even before then,

---

[4] By claiming that this is their main motivation, I am not denying that there may be others, such as the desire for posthumous glory or fame, the material benefits that will accrue to the family of the suicide attacker, revenge for the Israeli killing of a friend or relative, or social pressure to volunteer for a mission. As I note in the introduction to Part II, I am skeptical about the motivational power of religious benefits in the form of a privileged access to paradise.

however, the frequent if fluctuating deployment of female suicide bombers should have led scholars to question this stereotype. In the second Intifada, the use of female suicide bombers, some of them mothers or highly educated people, has been even more striking.

The often cited factors of poverty and illiteracy also seem to have limited causal efficacy, at least as features of the individual suicide attackers. Among Palestinian suicide bombers, income and education tend in fact to be higher than in the general population. Explanations in terms of poverty are also unsatisfying because it is not clear how poverty would generate the required motivation. In one common view, the gains from blowing oneself up have to be weighed against the cost of blowing oneself up – one's life. If life is not highly valued, the cost is less. According to this approach, a life in misery and poverty is worth so little to the individual that the costs of suicide become negligible. I am skeptical about this argument, since I think that poor people find their lives as worth living as anyone else. That people adjust their aspirations to their circumstances so that they maintain a more or less constant level of satisfaction ("the hedonic treadmill") is a pretty well-established psychological finding.

A more plausible factor than absolute deprivation is *relative deprivation*, that is, the gap between expectations and reality experienced by the many educated Palestinians who are now without any prospect of decent employment. Downward social mobility could have the same effect. Yet the most relevant features seem to be permanent feelings of *inferiority* and *resentment*. The first of these emotions is based on *comparison* between oneself and others, the second on *interaction* between oneself and others. Generally speaking, interaction-based emotions are more powerful than comparison-based ones. Many writers on the Palestinian suicide bombers emphasize the intense resentment caused by the daily humiliations that occur in the interaction with the Israeli forces. Beyond the degrading checks and controls to which the Palestinians are subject, there is also their awareness that many Israelis think all Arabs "lazy, cowardly, and cruel," as a Jerusalem taxi driver said to me some twenty years ago.

If this account is correct, the strong resentment of those who currently occupy the desired homeland enables us to *understand* the willingness to die of the Palestinian suicide attackers. The desire to fight the Israelis derives its strength from being embedded in a larger motivational complex. There is, however, an alternative view. Palestinian suicide attackers are usually kept on a short leash by their handlers, who are ready to provide additional pressures in case the primary motivation should fail when the time of action approaches. One would-be suicide attacker in Iraq, who was captured and disarmed because he was visibly nervous, said that for three days before his mission he had been locked up in a room with a mullah who had talked about paradise and fed him "a special soup that made him strong." The mental state that actually triggers the act of detonating the bomb may therefore be ephemeral and something of an artifact rather than a stable feature of the person. While terms such as "brainwashed" or "hypnotized" may be too strong, there is evidence that some of the attackers were in a trancelike state in the minutes before they died. When, as in such cases, an intention is isolated from the overall desire-belief system of the person, no interpretation is possible. The behavior of the handlers and more generally the organizers of the mission can, of course, be the object of interpretation.

A Hermeneutic Dilemma

It is well and good to claim that behavior must be explained in terms of the antecedent mental states – desires and beliefs – that cause them, but how do we establish these prior causes? On pains of circularity, we cannot use the behavior itself as evidence. We must look at other evidence, such as statements by the agent about his motivation, the consistency of his nonverbal behavior with these statements, the motives imputed to him by others, and the consistency of *their* nonverbal behavior with these imputations. Yet how can we exclude the possibility that these verbal and nonverbal forms of behavior were purposefully chosen to make an audience believe, falsely, that a particular motivation was at work? Professions and allegations of motivations can themselves be motivated. The question is central in collective decision making. As I argue in Chapter 25, all methods for consolidating individual preferences into a social decision create incentives for the participants in the process to misrepresent their preferences.

Consider, as an example, the motives of leaders and followers in civil wars. The parties have professed, or their opponents have imputed to them, one of three motives: *religion, power,* and *money.* Those who profess religious motives are often accused of using them as a disguise for their real motives, be they political or pecuniary. During the French wars of religion (1562–98), the warring parties constantly accused each other of using religion as a pretext for their political or even pecuniary aims. There were some bases for these charges. Henri de Navarre (later Henri IV) converted six times in his life, and the last conversion, in 1593, was widely suspected of opportunism. His father, Antoine de Bourbon, had already made it clear that his faith was for sale to the highest bidder. He accompanied the queen regent to mass, and his Protestant wife to communion. On his deathbed, he sought consolation from both religions. A leading reformer, Cardinal de Châtillon, married after his conversion but retained both his title as cardinal and the revenue from his bishopric. Another prelate, Antoine Carraciolo, bishop of Troyes, also wanted to combine a Protestant ministry with the income from his bishopric. A leading Catholic, Henri duc de Guise, was perfectly willing to seek an alliance with the Calvinists against King Henri III.

In the contemporary world, too, religion is sometimes used as a pretext for politics, and politics as a pretext for money. The goals of the Chechnyan insurgents and of some Palestinian organizations, notably the Fatah, were originally exclusively political. When they took on a religious mantle, it was largely to attract a larger following. In Palestine, the rivalry with the unquestionably religious Hamas made this a necessity for organizational survival. In the Philippines, the terrorist group Abu Sayyaf has used the demand for an independent Islamic state as a pretext for kidnapping for huge ransoms. In Colombia, it remains uncertain whether the Revolutionary Armed Forces of Colombia (FARC) retains its original motivation to fight social injustice or whether it has by now degenerated into a mafia. In all these cases, as in the French wars of religion, the imputation of motives is often fraught with uncertainty. It may be hard to know, notably, whether motives of leaders and of followers are completely concordant.

There are many reasons why people might want to misrepresent their motivations and those of their opponents. For one thing, each society has a normative hierarchy of motivations (Chapter 4) that induces a desire to present oneself as animated by a noble motivation rather than by a baser one, and to impute a low-ranked motivation to the opponent. In the French wars of religion as in the English civil war, each side presented itself as religiously motivated and the other as merely hungry for power. For another, if one can make others attach credence to profession of a particular motivation, it may be easier to achieve one's aims. Because the image of a terrorist can be more daunting than that of a common criminal, mercenary kidnappers may increase the chances of concessions by waving the banners of a cause. In Colombia, many kidnappings are committed by common criminals who try to provoke fear among the families of victims by claiming to belong to a guerrilla group. Kidnappings are scarier if the terrorists are thought to be willing to take drastic measures if something goes wrong, and less willing to bargain over deadlines or haggle about money. If they cannot obtain what they demand, they can at least "make a statement" by killing their victims.

The problem of self-serving bias in statements about the intentions of social agents is serious, but not insurmountable. A simple way around it might be to consider the *objective interests* of the agent and assume that in the absence of strong evidence to the contrary they coincide with her subjective motivation, regardless of what she says about the latter. Alternatively, one might identify the *actual consequences* of her action and assume that in the absence of strong evidence to the contrary they are what she intended to bring about. (Either idea might apply to the choice of higher education discussed earlier.) The fact that there exist these *two* procedures for shifting the burden of proof suggests, however, that neither is acceptable. Both objective interests and actual consequences can suggest useful hypotheses about subjective motives, but neither has a presumption in its favor.

Historians and social scientists have developed other ways of handling the problem that, especially when combined, can yield reasonably certain conclusions. One technique is to go beyond statements made before an audience and to look for those less likely to be motivated by a desire for misrepresentation. Letters, diaries, reported conversations, drafts, and the like, can be invaluable sources. We know, from letters they wrote to their wives, that some delegates to the French Assemblée Constituante in 1789 voted against bicameralism and royal veto because they thought their lives might be in danger if they voted otherwise. In the assembly, they justified their votes by the public interest. In trying to excavate the motivations behind the massacre on St. Bartholomew's night in 1582 historians have found it useful to go beyond the biased accounts of the participants and rely on reports by foreign diplomats who had an interest in getting it right. In nineteenth-century England, deathbed statements were exempt from the usual rules about hearsay evidence. The first draft of a document may say more about the beliefs and motives of the author than a later published version. It is instructive, for example, to compare the drafts of Marx's *The Civil War in France* or of his letter to Vera Sassoulitch with the official versions.

There may also be a sharp contrast between what actors may say in public and what they say behind closed doors. Although the published debates of the French Assemblée Constituante in 1789–91 are endlessly fascinating, two factors conspire to make them less than reliable as evidence about mental states. On the one hand, the public setting constrained the delegates to use public-interest arguments only; naked group interest was inadmissible. On the other hand, their vanity was stimulated by speaking before a thousand fellow delegates and a thousand auditors in the galleries. In both respects, the American Federal Convention was more conducive to sincerity. Because the number of delegates was small (55, compared to 1,200 in Paris) and the proceedings were shrouded in secrecy, interest-based bargaining could and did occur. At the same time, as Madison wrote many years later, "Had the members committed themselves publicly at first, they would have afterwards supposed consistency required them to maintain their ground, whereas by secret discussion no man felt himself obliged to retain his opinions any longer than he was satisfied of their propriety and truth, and was open to the force of argument." Nor did the fear of future revelations chill the debates, as the secrecy was supposed to extend indefinitely and was in fact broken only by the publication of Madison's notes many decades later. Strategic reasons for misrepresentations are blunted if sincerity carries no cost.

Social scientists may also remove the cost of sincerity by creating an artificial veil of ignorance. Suppose a scholar wants to study the relation between sexual orientation and some other variables of interest. It may be difficult to induce subjects to give true answers to questions whether they have ever had sexual experiences with members of the same sex, even if they are assured that answers will be anonymized. To get around this problem the researcher can instruct them to answer honestly in case they had any such experience and, if they never had, to flip a coin to decide whether to answer yes or no. If they comply – and they have no reason not to comply – and the sample is large enough, the data will be just as good as if everyone had answered truthfully.

Another technique to see whether the nonverbal behavior of the agents is consistent with their professed motivation is to ask: do they put their money where their mouth is? When in 2003 the Bush administration cited its certainty that Sadaam Hussein had weapons of mass destruction as its main reason for invading Iraq, did it also deploy the requisite measures to protect American soldiers from this threat? Some behavioral patterns may reveal the true motivation of kidnappers. In 1996 in Costa Rica, kidnappers (mainly, ex-contras from Nicaragua) demanded a $1 million ransom in addition to job guarantees for workers, a cut in food prices, a rise in the Costa Rican minimum wage, and the release of fellow rebels from prison. When they were offered $200,000, they were satisfied and did not insist on the political demands, a fact that persuaded the authorities that their Robin Hood/rebel stance was a ruse and that money had always been their goal. Or take the behavior of French aristocratic émigrés in London during the French Revolution. In this hotbed of rumor about the imminent restoration of the monarchy and competition to be more-royalist-than-thou, it was vital to convey one's willingness to serve the counterrevolution. Verbal assurances were not enough. Any person who rented an apartment for more than a month was badly regarded; it was better to rent by the week to leave no doubt that one was ready to be called back to France by the counterrevolution.

Not only contemporaries, but also historians routinely use such behavioral indicators to judge the sincerity of public professions of loyalty. Toward the end of World War II, for instance, there was a marked degree of skepticism in occupied France about the prospects for German victory. It might not be safe to express this attitude, but it was reflected in behavior. The proportion of high school students who chose German as a foreign language (or whose parents chose it for them) doubled from 1939 to 1942 and fell rapidly thereafter. Many publishers who eagerly signed up for the right to translate German books chose not to use the option.

Judges and jurors often proceed in the same way. Sometimes, they ask, "Did the accused have a motive for doing X?" hoping that an answer will help them decide whether she in fact did X. In this case, "having a motive" is an objective idea, namely, whether the accused would in some way benefit from doing X. In other cases, more relevant here, it is established that the accused did X and the question is "What was her motive for doing it?" To establish whether a killing was a crime of passion or a cold-blooded action judges and jurors do not mainly look at objective benefits, but try to establish the subjective state of mind of the accused. If the accused claims to have acted in a fit of anger or jealousy and later is shown to have bought the murder weapon ahead of time or to have taken her time over the killing,[5] her credibility is weakened.

Taken individually, each of these techniques may fail. A deputy might not be willing to admit to his wife that he was afraid for his life, or he might claim he was afraid in order to hide a less reputable motive (e.g., taking a bribe). In nineteenth-century India, deathbed statements were seen as unreliable since people sometimes used their dying moments to harm their enemies. In the émigré example, *both* true believers and disbelievers would be motivated to lease by the week, the former to facilitate their return to France when the day arrived and the latter to escape criticism of being defeatist. There are limits, however, on people's ability to weave the tangled web of deceit without revealing their true motives. Hypocrisy, Somerset Maugham said, is a full-time profession. Even Tartuffe slipped in the end. To argue for the sincerity of Henri IV's

---

[5] In a British decision (*R. v. McPherson*) from 1957, Lord Goddard asked rhetorically, "How can it be said that the appellant was acting in a gust of passion when he fired not one shot but four shots, and each shot involved the breaking of the gun to reload and the taking out of cartridges four separate times?"

religious beliefs, his biographer not only quotes the positive evidence of "numerous episodes where his religious spirit manifested itself without any advertising intention" but also argues, "Had there been any hypocrisy, it would have showed its horns on this or that pleasant occasion." Along the same lines we may quote Montaigne:

> Those who counter what I profess by calling my frankness, my simplicity and my naturalness of manner mere artifice and cunning-prudence rather than goodness, purposive rather than natural, good sense rather than good hap – give me more honour than they take from me. They certainly make my cunning too cunning. If anyone of those men would follow me closely about and spy on me, I would declare him the winner if he does not admit that there is no teaching in his sect which would counterfeit my natural way of proceeding and keep up an appearance of such equable liberty along such tortuous paths, nor of maintaining so uncompromising a freedom of action along paths so diverse, and concede that all their striving and cleverness could never bring them to act the same.

While the benefits of misrepresentation may be considerable, the costs can be prohibitive. To some extent, the instrumental profession of motives is self-limiting. Because any given motive is embedded in a vast network of other motives and beliefs, the number of adjustments to be made in sustaining hypocrisy can be crippling. A single false note may be enough for the whole construction to crumble. Many proverbs testify to the irreversibility of the breakdown of trust. Although the folk belief "Who tells one lie will tell a hundred" needs to be severely qualified (Chapter 10), the *unqualified* belief is in fact widely held and serves to some extent as a deterrent for lying. For this reason, among others, Descartes may have been right in saying that "the greatest subtlety of all is never to make use of subtlety."

《《《

Bibliographical Note

The debate on *Erklären* versus *Verstehen* is covered in Part III of
M. Martin and L. McIntyre (eds.), *Readings in the Philosophy of Social
Science* (Cambridge, MA: MIT Press, 1994). The chapter in that volume
by Dagfinn Føllesdal, "Hermeneutics and the hypothetico-deductive
method," argues for a position close to my own. The quote from Weber
is in his essay "The interpretive understanding of social action," in
M. Brodbeck (ed.), *Readings in the Philosophy of the Social Sciences*
(London: Macmillan, 1969), p. 33. The incoherence of anti-Semitic
attitudes is touched on in J. Telushkin, *Jewish Humor* (New York:
Morrow, 1992), which is also my source for other remarks on and by Jews
about their alleged characteristics. The remarks on educational choice are
an implicit polemic against G. Becker and C. Mulligan, "The endogenous determination of time preferences," *Quarterly Journal of Economics*
112 (1997), 729–58. The evidentiary value of deathbed confessions is
discussed in J. F. Stephen, *A History of English Criminal Law* (London:
Macmillan, 1883; Buffalo, NY: Hein, 1964), vol. 1, pp. 447–9. H. Sass,
"Affektdelikte," *Nervenarzt* 54 (1983), 557–72, lists thirteen reasons why a
claim to have committed a crime out of passion might lack credibility.
An outstanding interpretive discussion of motivations in the French wars
of religion is D. Crouzet, *Les guerriers de Dieu* (Paris: Champ Vallon,
1990). Interpretive analyses of the motivations and beliefs of suicide
attackers are found in the essays by S. Holmes, L. Ricolfi, and me in
D. Gambetta (ed.), *Making Sense of Suicide Missions* (Oxford University
Press, 2005). The comment on Henri IV's religious belief is in
J.-P. Babelon, *Henri IV* (Paris: Fayard, 1982), p. 554. Excessive skepticism
about motives is discussed in G. Mackie, "Are all men liars?" in J. Elster
(ed.), *Deliberative Democracy* (Cambridge University Press, 1998).

II

THE MIND

This book is organized around the "belief-desire model" of action. To understand how people act and interact, we first have to understand how their minds work. This is largely a matter of introspection and folk psychology, refined and corrected by the more systematic studies carried out by psychologists and, increasingly, by behavioral economists. The model is vital not only for explaining behavior, but also for assigning praise, blame, or punishment. Guilt usually presupposes mens rea, intentions and beliefs. Strict liability – guilt assigned merely on the basis of the actual consequences of action – is rare. In fact, sometimes we hold people guilty merely on the basis of intentions even when no consequences follow. Attempted murder is a crime. "Witches," declared John Donne, "think sometimes that they kill when they do not, and are therefore as culpable as if they did." "As for witches," wrote Hobbes, "I think not that their witchcraft is any real power; but yet that they are justly punished, for the false belief they have that they can do such mischief, joined with their purpose to do it if they can."

The belief-desire model, although indispensable, is fragile. The methods we use to impute mental states to other people do not always yield stable results. If we want to measure the height of a building, it does not matter whether we do it from the roof downward or from the ground upward. In the determination of beliefs and desires, the outcome may depend on such irrelevant factors. Consider, for instance, the idea that people "maximize expected utility" (Chapter 11). To make it precise, we have to assume that they have a clear and stable idea of the *value* attached to each possible outcome of an action, and of the *probability* they assign to the occurrence of that outcome. Often that assumption is justified, but sometimes it is not.

Consider first the beliefs of the agent. In eliciting the subjective probabilities an individual attaches to an event, a standard procedure is the following. Beginning with a number p, we ask the person whether he would prefer a lottery in which he gains a certain sum of money with probability p or one in which he gains the same amount if the event in question occurs.[1] If he prefers the former, we expose him to a new choice with the probability adjusted downward; if he prefers the latter, we adjust the probability upward. By continuing in this way, we shall ultimately reach a probability p^* such that he is indifferent between a lottery in which he gains the money with probability p^* and one in which he gains it if the event occurs. We can affirm, then, that the revealed or elicited probability he attaches to the event is p^*. In principle, p^* should be independent of the initial p: that is, the elicited probability should be independent of the procedure of elicitation. In practice, this is not the case: a higher p induces a higher p^*. This finding suggests that, to some extent at least, *there is no fact of the matter*, no stable mental state that is captured by the procedure.[2]

Other procedures are even more fragile. Often, scholars impute subjective probabilities to the agents on the assumption that when they know little about the situation they will assign equal probability to each of the possible states of the world. The justification of this procedure is supposed to be the "principle of insufficient reason": if you have no positive grounds for thinking one state of the world more likely than another, logic forces you to assign equal probability to them. But states of the world can be conceptualized and counted in many ways. Suppose you are pursuing a thief and arrive at a fork in the road where three paths

---

[1] We must assume that the event in question is one that, if it occurred, would not affect him personally, such as the discovery of life on other planets. If the event is the victory of his favorite sports team, he might bet money that it will lose so that regardless of what happens he will have something to be pleased about.

[2] This statement is probably too strong. Manipulating the procedure might elicit any probability assignment between 50 percent and 80 percent but none outside that range. In that case, we would be justified in asserting that the subject believes that the event is more likely to occur than not but is not certain that it will. This assessment is far more coarse-grained, however, than what is needed in standard models of decision making.

branch off, two going uphill and one downhill. Since you have no reason for thinking it more likely that he followed one path rather than another, the probability that he took the downhill path should, according to the principle, be one-third. But since you also have no reason for thinking he went uphill rather than downhill, the same probability should be one-half. In this case at least, the principle of insufficient reason is too indeterminate to be of any use in constructing or assigning probabilities.

Consider next the elicitation of preferences. In experiments, subjects have been asked whether they would buy various items (computer accessories, wine bottles, and the like) at a dollar figure equal to the last two digits of their social security number. Thereafter, they were asked to state the maximal price they were willing to pay for the product. It turned out that their social security number had a significant impact on what they were willing to pay. For instance, subjects who had social security numbers in the top quintile were willing to pay on average fifty-six dollars for a cordless computer keyboard, while those in the bottom quintile were only willing to pay sixteen dollars. Although the procedures were supposed to tap or elicit preexisting preferences, the results show that there was nothing there to elicit, no fact of the matter. The numbers owed more to the anchoring provided by the social security numbers than to any "real" preferences.

There is also evidence that people's *trade-offs* among values are highly unstable and may owe as much to procedural artifacts as to an underlying mental reality. Trade-offs can be captured either by *choice* or by *matching* in experiments. Subjects may be given the choice between saving many lives at a high cost per life saved (A) and saving fewer lives at lower cost (B). Alternatively, they may be asked to indicate the cost per life saved that would make them indifferent between saving the larger number of lives at that cost (option C) and option B. Suppose that a given subject states a cost lower than the cost of A. As the person is indifferent between C and B and may be assumed to prefer C to A (because C saves as many lives at lower cost), she should prefer and hence choose B over A. The overwhelming majority of subjects did in fact choose a cost for C below that of A, and yet two-thirds stated that they would choose A over B. The more important value – saving lives – is more salient in choice than in matching, although logically the two procedures should be equivalent.

There are other reasons why we should not always take statements about beliefs and other mental states at face value. Religious beliefs are especially problematic in this respect. In early seventeenth-century England, a prelate such as Bishop Andrewes could at one and the same time claim that the plague was a punishment that God imposed on sinners *and* flee London for the countryside. The belief that by virtue of their divine origin the French kings could heal scrofula by touching the sick person was visibly withering by the end of the eighteenth century, when the traditional formula ("The king touches you; God heals you") was replaced by a subjunctive ("The king touches you; may God heal you"). The eagerness with which the king's court sought out documented proof of successful healings also suggests a belief that was not sure of itself.

For a contemporary example, consider the idea that the behavior of Islamic suicide attackers can be explained, at least in part, by their belief that there is an afterlife to which martyrdom will give them a privileged access. One may ask whether this "belief" is of the same nature as our belief that the sun will rise tomorrow, that is, whether it is used with equal confidence as a premise for action. This is not a matter of certainty versus probability, but of confidence versus lack of it. I may have great confidence in – and be willing to bet on the basis of – a probabilistic belief based on many past occurrences. The belief in the afterlife held by most people is probably not like that. Rather, it may be a somewhat shadowy "quasi-belief," held for its consumption value rather than as a premise for action. If all who claim to believe in the afterlife held the belief with full certainty, or with "confident probability," we would observe many more martyrs than we actually see. Although some believers may be of this type, and suicide attackers may be recruited disproportionately from this subset, I suspect that for many, religion serves as a consolation once the decision has been made rather than as a premise for decision.[3]

---

[3] The idea of religion as "opium of the people" also suggests that it is a consumption good rather than a premise for action. It could, however, be a premise for inaction.

Similarly, people may experience or claim to experience "quasi-emotions" that differ from genuine emotions in that they have no implications for action. Some people who claim to be indignant over third-world poverty and yet never reach for their wallet may enjoy their indignation as a consumption good, because it makes them think well of themselves. Similarly, the visible enjoyment of many who claimed to feel grief (or "quasi-grief") after the death of Princess Diana was inconsistent with the horrible feeling of genuine grief. The appropriate term for their feelings is, I believe, "sentimentality." (The German *Schwärmerei* is even more fitting.) Oscar Wilde defined a sentimentalist as "one who desires to have the luxury of an emotion without paying for it." Whether the payment takes the form of donations to Oxfam or the form of suffering, we can tell from its absence that we are not dealing with the real thing.[4]

A related issue is the immense power of autosuggestion. Once we know that an X is supposed to be a Y, we claim *and believe* that it is obviously a Y. The world's greatest experts on Vermeer were taken in by (what *now* seem to be) obvious forgeries by van Meegeren. Proust refers to the "aptitude which enables you to discover the intentions of a symphonic piece when you have read the program, and the resemblances of a child when you know their kin." A European jazz fan completely changed his high appreciation of Jack Teagarden upon learning that he was not black. If we are well disposed toward a writer, we may read deep meanings into what an impartial reader would consider trivial remarks. We project our expectations on the world and then claim that the world confirms and justifies our beliefs.

The upshot of these remarks is that we should be wary of thinking of beliefs, desires, preferences, emotions, and the like as stable and enduring entities on a par with apples and planets. Later chapters will provide many instances of the elusive, unstable, or context-dependent nature of mental states. This being said, readers will also find statements that may seem to exemplify the kind of pseudoprecision or make-believe rigor I have been

---

[4] A related phenomenon occurs when people take a third-person perspective on themselves. A proverb says, "Virtue does not know itself." Also, one cannot coherently assert one's own naiveté, since the very idea presupposes lack of self-consciousness. And as Nero Wolfe put it, in one of Rex Stout's novels featuring him, "To assert dignity is to forfeit it."

warning against. To proceed beyond qualitative statements that have no definite implications, such as "Agents attach greater weight to present welfare than to future," we have to say something about *how much* more weight they attach to the present. Once we do that, we shall inevitably make statements that make sharper distinctions than what we observe in the behavior of the agents. The trick – more an art than a science – is to know when simplifications illuminate and when they distort.

Some final comments are called for with regard to *unconscious* mental states and mental operations. In this book I shall repeatedly refer to the unconscious workings of the mind. Dissonance reduction (Chapter 1), wishful thinking (Chapter 7), and transmutation of motives (Chapter 4), for instance, are caused by unconscious mechanisms. We may not understand well how they operate, but I find it impossible to deny that they exist. Many have also argued for the existence of unconscious mental *states*. Self-deception, unlike wishful thinking, presupposes that there are unconscious beliefs. Freud thought that we all have a number of unconscious and unavowable desires. There may also be unconscious emotions and prejudices.

To the extent that unconscious mental states have causal efficacy, it should be possible to identify them by their effects. If a denial of a statement is disproportionately strong, for instance, we might infer that it is one that the person in question really, although unconsciously, believes: "Methinks the lady doth protest too much." There is a story (which I have been unable to track down) told about Sigmund Freud, who was invited to meet a prominent person, Dr. X, in the international Jewish movement. During their conversation, Dr. X asked him, "Tell me, Dr. Freud, who in your opinion is the most important Jewish personality in the world today?" Freud answered politely, "Why, I think that must be yourself, Dr. X." When Dr. X replied, "No, no," Freud asked, "Wouldn't 'No' have been enough?" Double negation can be equivalent to affirmation.

One can also identify unconscious prejudices by their effects. In experiments subjects were first asked to classify rapidly (by tapping their left or right knee) each of a list of names into those that are most often considered black (such as Malik and Lashonda) and those that are most often seen as white (such as Tiffany and Peter). Next they were asked to classify rapidly each of a list of words as pleasant in meaning (such as "love" and "baby") or unpleasant (such as "war" and "vomit"). Next, they classified a randomly ordered list that included all of the black names, white names, pleasant words, and unpleasant words. First they were asked to tap their left knee for any black name or unpleasant-meaning word and their right knee for any white name or pleasant-meaning word. Second, the instructions were changed. They were asked to tap their left knee for white names and unpleasant words and their right knee for black names and pleasant words. It took about twice as long to respond to the second task, even though objectively the tasks were of equal difficulty.

Unconscious emotions can often be identified by observers who infer their existence from the characteristic physiological or behavioral expressions. Most of us have heard and many of us uttered the angry statement "I am not angry." Envy can manifest itself in a sharpness of tone and a tendency to adopt a derogatory slant that are obvious to observers but not to the subject. In *Le rouge et le noir* Mme de Rênal discovers her feelings for Julien Sorel only when she suspects that he might be in love with her chambermaid, one emotion (jealousy) thus revealing the presence of another (love).

Self-deception (see Chapter 7) is more problematic in this respect. Suppose I form and then repress the belief that my wife is having an affair with my best friend. Although unconscious, the belief that they are lovers might still guide my actions, for example, by preventing me from going to the part of town where my friend lives and where I might risk seeing my wife visiting him. This may sound like a plausible story, but to my knowledge there is no evidence that unconscious beliefs have causal efficacy. Many arguments for the existence of self-deception rely on (1) the exposure of the person to evidence strongly suggesting a belief he or she would not want to be true and (2) the fact that the agent professes and acts on a different and more palatable belief. To obtain direct evidence for the unconscious persistence of the unpalatable belief one would need to show (3) that it, too, is capable of guiding action, as in the hypothetical example just given. To repeat, I do not know of any demonstration to this effect.

My hunch is that the phenomenon does not exist. It is a pleasant conceit to imagine that my unconscious beliefs could be the handmaiden of my conscious ones, by steering me away from evidence that might undermine them, but it it is no more than an unsupported just-so story. Along equally speculative lines, one could imagine that "the unconscious" is capable of inducing indirect strategies (one step backward, two steps forward), for instance, by making a child hurt herself to get the attention of her parents. These suggestions make the unconscious too similar to the conscious mind, by making it capable of having representations of the future (Chapter 6) and of other people's actions and intentions (Chapter 19). Mental states of which we are unaware may cause spontaneous actions such as answering, "No, no" instead of simply "No," but I do not know of any evidence that they can also cause instrumentally rational behavior.

❲❲❲

Bibliographical Note

Evidence for anchoring of probability assessments is given in A. Tversky and D. Kahneman, "Judgment under uncertainty: Heuristics and biases," *Science* 185 (1974), 1124–31. Evidence for anchoring of preferences is given in D. Ariely, G. Loewenstein, and D. Prelec, "Coherent arbitrariness," *Quarterly Journal of Economics* 118 (2003), 73–105. The reference to Bishop Andrewes is from A. Nicolson, *God's Secretaries* (New York: HarperCollins, 2003), and that to the royal healing from M. Bloch, *Les rois thaumaturges* (Paris: Armand Colin, 1961). A good discussion of sentimentality is M. Tanner, "Sentimentality," *Proceedings of the Aristotelian Society* n.s. 77 (1976–7), 127–47. A large-scale (Internet) experiment on unconscious prejudices is reported in B. Nosek, M. Banaji, and A. Greenwald, "Harvesting implicit group attitudes and beliefs from a demonstration website," *Group Dynamics* 6 (2002), 101–15. For the argument that Freud made the unconscious too similar to the conscious mind, see L. Naccache, *Le nouvel inconscient* (Paris: Odile Jacob, 2006).

Chapter 4
MOTIVATIONS
❀ ❀ ❀

This chapter and the two following ones will be devoted to varieties of motivation. In the present chapter, the discussion is fairly general. In the following, I focus on two specific issues, selfishness versus altruism and temporal shortsightedness versus farsightedness. These two issues complement each other, the latter being as it were the intertemporal version of the former, interpersonal contrast. As we shall see, they are also substantially related, in the sense that farsightedness can *mimic* altruism.

The set of human motivations is a pie that can be sliced any number of ways. Although none of them can claim canonical status, there are four approaches that I have found useful. The first proposes a continuum of motivations, the second and the third both offer a trichotomy, and the fourth a simple dichotomy. The classifications are both somewhat similar and interestingly different, allowing us to illuminate the same behavior from different angles.

From Visceral to Rational

On September 11, 2001, some people jumped to their death from the World Trade Center because of the overwhelming heat. "This should not be really thought of as a choice," said Louis Garcia, New York City's chief fire marshal. "If you put people at a window and introduce that kind of heat, there's a good chance most people would feel compelled to jump." There was no real alternative. Subjectively, this may also be the experience of those who drink seawater when freshwater is unavailable. They may know that drinking even a little seawater starts you down a dangerous road: the more you drink, the thirstier you get. Yet the temptation may, for some, seem irresistible. The craving for addictive substances may also be experienced in this way. An eighteenth-century writer, Benjamin Rush, offered a dramatic illustration: "When strongly urged, by one of his friends, to leave off drinking [a habitual drunkard] said, 'Were a keg of rum in one corner of a room, and were a cannon constantly discharging balls between me and it, I could not refrain from passing before that cannon, in order to get at the rum.' " Sexual desire may also be so overwhelming as to silence more prudential concerns.

Some emotions may also be so strong as to crowd out all other considerations. The feeling of shame, for instance, can be unbearably painful, as shown by the 1996 suicide of an American navy admiral who was about to be exposed as not entitled to some of the medals he was wearing, or by the six suicides in 1997 among Frenchmen who were exposed as consumers of pedophiliac material. Anger, too, may be overwhelmingly strong, as when Zinedine Zidane on July 9, 2006, in the last minutes of the World Cup soccer final, head-butted an Italian opponent to retaliate against a provocation, under the eyes of seventy thousand people in the stadium and an estimated one billion TV viewers worldwide. Had he paused for a fraction of a second to reflect, he would have realized that the action might cost the defeat of his team and the ruin of his reputation.

Except perhaps for the urge to jump from the World Trade Center, it is doubtful whether any of these desires was literally irresistible, in the way a boulder rolling down a hillside might be irresistible to a person trying to stop it in its course. (An urge to fall asleep may be irresistible, but falling asleep is not an action; that is why attempts to do so are self-defeating.) Addicts are somewhat sensible to costs: they consume less when prices go up.[1] People in lifeboats sometimes can prevent each other from drinking sea water. Sexual temptation and the urge to kill oneself in shame are certainly resistible. Because of their intensity, these visceral cravings nevertheless stand at one extreme of the spectrum of human motivations. They have the potential, not always realized, for blocking deliberation, trade-offs, and even choice.

At the other extreme, we have a paradigm – or rather a caricature – of the rational agent who is unperturbed by visceral factors, including emotion. He acts only after having carefully – but no more carefully than

---

[1] That might also be, however, because their budget does not allow them to consume at the same level (Chapter 9).

is warranted under the circumstances – weighed the consequences of each available option against one another. A rational general, chief executive officer, or doctor is concerned merely with finding the best means to realize an objective goal such as winning the war, maximizing profit, or saving a life. Subjective desires and their visceral roots do not enter into the equation. Although we shall see in Chapter 11 that the concept of rationality is much broader than this bloodless idea, it may serve as a benchmark.

An example of the distinction between visceral and rational motivation is provided by the difference between visceral and prudential *fear*. Although it is common to refer to fear as an emotion, it may be only a belief-desire complex. When I say, "I fear it is going to rain," I mean *only* that I believe it is going to rain and that I wish it weren't going to rain. If the "fear" inspires action, as when I take an umbrella to protect me against the rain, it is a paradigm of rational behavior (Chapter 11). None of the characteristic features of the emotions (Chapter 7) is present. Visceral fear, by contrast, may induce action that is not instrumentally rational. It has been calculated, for instance, that 350 Americans who would not otherwise have died lost their lives on the road by avoiding the risk of flying after September 11, 2001. By contrast, it does not seem that the Spanish incurred excess deaths by switching from train to car after the attacks on trains in Madrid on March 11, 2004. It is possible that because of the long run of attacks by Basque Homeland and Freedom (ETA), the population had developed an attitude of prudential rather than of visceral fear toward terror bombings. For them, terrorist attacks may have been just one risk among others, similar to – albeit more dangerous than – the risk of rain.

Between the extremes of the visceral-rational continuum, we find behavior that is partly motivated by visceral factors, yet is also somewhat sensitive to cost-benefit considerations. A man may seek revenge (a visceral desire), yet also bide his time until he can catch his enemy unaware (a prudential concern). If he challenges his enemy to a duel (as required by norms of honor), he may take fencing lessons in secret (a dishonorable but useful practice). If a person is made an offer that is both unfair and advantageous, in the sense that she would be better off taking it than not, she might accept it or reject it, depending on the strength of her interest versus the strength of her resentment.[2] In more complex cases, one visceral factor might counteract another. The desire for an extramarital sexual affair might be neutralized by guilt feelings. An urge to flee generated by fear may be offset or preempted by an urge to fight caused by anger.

Interest, Reason, and Passion

In their analysis of human motivations, the seventeenth-century French moralists made a fruitful distinction among interest, reason, and passion. Interest is the pursuit of personal advantage, be it money, fame, power, or salvation. Even action to help our children counts as the pursuit of interest, since our fate is so closely bound up with theirs. A parent who sends his children to an expensive private school where they can get the best education is not sacrificing his interest but pursuing it. The passions may be taken to include emotions as well as other visceral urges, such as hunger, thirst, and sexual or addictive cravings. The ancients also included states of madness within the same general category because, like emotions, they are involuntary, unbidden, and subversive of rational deliberation. For many purposes, we may also include states of intoxication among the passions. From the point of view of the law, anger, drunkenness, and madness have often been treated as being on a par.

Reason is a more complicated idea. The moralists mostly used it (as I shall use it here) in relation to the desire to promote the public good rather than private ends. Occasionally, they also used it to refer to long-term (prudential) motivations as distinct from short-term (myopic) concerns. Both ideas may be summarized under the heading of *impartiality*. In designing public policy, one should treat individuals impartially rather than favoring some groups or individuals over others. Individuals, too, may act on this motivation. Parents may sacrifice their interest by sending their children to a public school, because they believe in equality of opportunity. At the same time, policymakers as well as private

---

[2] In a case that has been extensively studied (see Chapter 20), rejection entails that the person who made the offer also suffers, a factor that will enhance the resentment motive.

individuals ought to treat outcomes occurring at successive times in an impartial manner by giving each of them the same weight in current decision making, rather than privileging outcomes in the near future. In fact, some moralists argued, a concern with long-term interest will also tend to promote the public good. At the Federal Convention in Philadelphia, for instance, George Mason argued that

> we ought to attend to the rights of every class of people. He had often wondered at the indifference of the superior classes of society to this dictate of humanity & policy; considering that however affluent their circumstances, or elevated their situations, might be, the course of a few years, not only might but certainly would, distribute their posterity throughout the lowest classes of Society. Every selfish motive therefore, every family attachment, ought to recommend such a system of policy as would provide no less carefully for the rights and happiness of the lowest than of the highest orders of Citizens.

Either form of impartiality has degrees. The strength of concern for others tends to vary inversely not only with genealogical distance, but with geographical remoteness. Similarly, even prudent individuals usually give somewhat more weight to the near future than to the more remote, a fact that is only partly explained by their knowledge that they might not live to enjoy the distant future.

As an example of how behavior may be understood in terms of any of these three motivations, we may cite a 1783 letter from New York chancellor Robert Livingston to Alexander Hamilton in which he comments on the persecution of those who had sided with the British during the wars of independence:

> I seriously lament with you, the violent spirit of persecution which prevails here and dread its consequences upon the wealth, commerce & future tranquility of the state. I am the more hurt at it because it appears to me almost unmixed with *purer patriotic motives*. In some few it is a blind spirit of *revenge & resentment*, but in more it is the most *sordid interest*.

The phrases I have italicized correspond to reason, emotion, and interest, respectively. The adjectives are telling: reason is pure, passion is blind, interest is sordid. I return to some implications of these assessments.

Id, Ego, Superego

In his analyses of human motivations, Freud also suggested three basic forms, each of them linked to a separate subsystem of the mind. The three systems are the id, the ego, and the superego, corresponding, respectively, to the pleasure principle, the reality principle, and conscience. The id and the superego represent, respectively, impulses and impulse control, while the ego, "helpless in both directions ... defends itself vainly, alike against the instigations of the murderous id and against the reproaches of the punishing conscience." In a more illuminating statement from the same essay ("The Ego and the Id"), Freud wrote that the ego is "a poor creature owing service to three masters and consequently menaced by three dangers: from the external world, from the libido of the id, and from the severity of the superego." Yet even this formulation does not capture fully what I think is the useful core of Freud's idea. This is the proposition that as the ego is navigating the external world (the reality principle) it also has to fight a two-front war against the impulses from the id (pleasure principle) and the punitively severe impulse control exercised by the superego (conscience).[3]

This proposition is original, profound, and true. What it lacks is a mechanism. Why could not the ego itself exercise whatever impulse control might be needed? Why do morality and conscience so often take the form of rigid rules? Do we need to stipulate the existence of separate and quasi-autonomous mental functions? It took the pioneering work of George Ainslie to provide satisfactory answers to these questions. I discuss his views in Chapter 13. Here I only want to draw attention to the fact that many impulses need to be kept at bay because of the *cumulative* damage they can do if unchecked.[4] On any given occasion, drinking or eating to excess, splurging, or procrastinating (such as failing to do one's

---

[3] To combine two of Freud's metaphors, the ego is like a rider on an unruly horse (the id) who is at the same time ridden by an incubus (the superego).

[4] There is also a fact of cumulative *risk*. The chance of unwanted consequences from unprotected sex may be small on any given occasion, but the lifetime risk might be considerable. On any given trip, the chance of being injured in a car accident while not wearing a seatbelt is small, but the lifetime probability is about 1 in 3.

homework) need not do much harm to the agent. The damage occurs after repeated excesses (or repeated failures). The focus of impulse control, therefore, must not be the individual occasion, since the person can always say to himself or herself that a new and better life will begin tomorrow. Impulse control must address the fact that the impulse will predictably arise on an indefinite number of occasions. The solution arises from reframing the problem, so that failure to control an impulse on any one occasion is seen as a predictor of failure to control it on all later occasions. "Yes, I can postpone impulse control until tomorrow without incurring important harm or risk, but why should tomorrow be different from today? If I fail now, I shall fail tomorrow as well." By setting up an *internal domino effect* and thus raising the stakes, the agent can acquire a motivation to control her impulses that would be lacking if she just took one day at a time. The other side of the coin is that the control must be relentless and, as the Victorian moralists put it, "never suffer a single exception."

Taking Account of Consequences

Finally, motivations may be consequentialist or nonconsequentialist, that is, oriented either toward the outcome of action or toward the action itself. Much of economic behavior is purely consequentialist. When people put aside money for their old age or stockbrokers buy and sell shares, they attach no intrinsic value – positive or negative – to these actions themselves; they care only about the outcomes. By contrast, the unconditional pacifist who refuses to do military service even against the most evil enemy takes no account of the consequences of his behavior. What matters for him is that certain actions are unconditionally forbidden, such as taking a human life. It is not that he is *unaware* of the consequences, as may be the case in emotional action, only that consequences make no difference for what he does.

Public policy may also be adopted on either type of motivation. A policymaker might adopt the principle "Finders keepers" (e.g., in patent legislation), on the assumption that if the person who discovers a new valuable resource is assigned the property right in it, more valuable resources will be discovered. This is a consequentialist argument. A nonconsequentialist argument for the same policy might be that the person who discovers a new resource, whether it be a piece of land or a cure for cancer, has a natural *right* to property in it. For another example, we may consider the speech (XXXI) of Dion Chrysostomos against the practice of the Rhodeans to reuse old bronze statues to honor benefactors of the city: this, he argued, was both to violate the rights of those in whose honor the statues had originally been erected and to discourage potential new benefactors who knew that statues erected in their honor might soon be recycled in favor of someone else. Consequentialist arguments may (seem to) warrant harsh measures toward terrorists even if the steps that are taken violate the nonconsequentialist values associated with human rights and civil liberties.[5]

A special case of nonconsequentialist motivation is the principle that I shall refer to variously as everyday Kantianism, the categorical imperative, or magical thinking: *do what would be best if all did the same.* In one sense this principle is linked to consequences, since the agent does what would bring about the best outcome if everybody else did the same. These are not the consequences of *her* action, however, but of a hypothetical set of actions by her and others. In a given case, acting on the principle could have disastrous consequences for all if others do *not* follow suit. In the international arena, unilateral disarmament is an example.

Another case is the following principle of Jewish ethics. Suppose that the enemy is at the door and says, "Give me one among yourselves to be killed and we shall spare all the others; if you refuse, we shall kill you all." The Talmud requires that in such cases the Jews let themselves all be killed rather than name one to be killed so that others can be saved. If, however, the enemy says, "Give me Peter" under the same conditions, it is acceptable to hand him over. There is not a ban on causing a person to be killed to save others, but on selecting who it shall be. The novel *Sophie's Choice* presents the same dilemma.

---

[5] The parenthetical "seem to" reflects the possible operation of the "psychology of tyranny" (Chapter 2). A classical dilemma of deterrence is that the *hatred* it inspires may in the end more than offset the *fear* it is intended to cause.

Social norms (Chapter 22) offer a further special case of non-consequentialist behavior, with an important twist. Social norms tell people what to do, such as take revenge for an insult or refrain from eating a kid boiled in its mother's milk, not because there are any desirable results to be brought about, but because the action is mandatory in itself.[6] While not taken to *bring about* any outcome, such actions may be seen as undertaken to *prevent* an outcome, namely, being blamed by others for not taking them. We may then ask, however, whether the blamings are also undertaken for similar consequentialist reasons. In general, I shall argue, they are not. Moreover, when people are hurt by the actions of others they retaliate even in one-shot interactions under full anonymity, such as may be obtained in experimental settings. Because the interaction is one-shot, they have nothing to gain in later encounters, and because it is anonymous, they need not fear the blame of third parties. I shall return to these experiments in several later chapters.

Even for a professed nonconsequentialist, consequences may matter if they are important enough. Consider a principle that many would consider an unconditional one, the ban on torturing small children. In a "ticking bomb" scenario, imagine that a necessary and sufficient condition for preventing the detonation of a nuclear device in central Manhattan is to torture a terrorist's small child in her presence. *If* the scenario could be made credible, many nonconsequentialists might acquiesce in the torture. Others would say that since the conditions in the scenario will never obtain in practice, the absolute ban remains in effect. Still others would ban the torture even if the scenario did occur. My task here is not to argue for one of these conclusions, but to make the empirical observation that in real-life situations stakes are rarely so high as to force the nonconsequentialist to consider the consequences of his behavior. It is possible that with more at stake he would abandon his

---

[6] With regard to the rules of kosher food, of which the ban on eating a kid boiled in its mother's milk is only a historical illustration, it was thought for a while that they were justified on hygienic grounds. Today, as far as I have been able to learn, they are recommended on the grounds that it is good for one to do something that is both difficult and pointless. This idea seems to embody the fallacy of by-products that I discuss later: behavior that is justified *merely* by its character-building effects will not even have those. I do not know, though, how many of those who follow the rule do it for this reason.

principles, but since the situation does not arise we cannot tell for certain whether we are simply dealing with a very steep trade-off or with a total refusal to engage in trade-offs.

These four approaches to motivation capture some of the same phenomena. Visceral factors, passions, and the pleasure principle clearly have much in common. The last applies to a wider range of cases, because it involves pain avoidance as well as pleasure seeking. When students procrastinate in doing their homework, it is not necessarily because there is something else they passionately want to do. Often, they are merely taking the path of least resistance. The superego, reason, and nonconsequentialist motivations also have some features in common. Although not all systems of morality are rigid and relentless, some are. Kant's moral theory is a notorious instance. (In fact, his moral philosophy may have originated in the private rules he made for himself to control his impulses, such as his maxim of never smoking more than one pipe after breakfast.) At the same time, morality can rise above rigidity, in individuals not subject to ambiguity aversion. The toleration of ambiguity is, in fact, often said to be the hallmark of a healthy ego. By contrast, the relation among rationality, interest, the ego, and consequentialism is more tenuous. It would be absurd to claim that the hallmark of a healthy ego is the rational pursuit of self-interest.

Wanting and Wishing

We often think of motivations as taking the form of *wanting to bring about* some state of affairs. They may also, however, take the form of *wishing some state of affairs to obtain*. This distinction between wants and wishes is important if we look at the motivational component of emotion (Chapter 7). Emotions can, in fact, be accompanied either by a want to do something or by a wish that something be the case. In anger or *wrath*, A's urge to take revenge on B cannot be satisfied by C's doing to B what A had planned to do or by B's suffering an accident. What matters is not simply the outcome, that B suffer, but that he suffer by A's agency. In sadism, too, what matters is to make the other suffer, not merely that he suffer. By contrast, in *hatred* what matters is that the hated person or group disappear from the face of the Earth, whether this happens by my agency or by someone else's. In *malice*, too, what matters is that the other suffer, not that I make him suffer. In fact, a malicious person may recoil before actively taking steps to make the other suffer, not merely because she is afraid of being seen to do so but because it would be incompatible with her self-image. This is even clearer in *envy*. Many people who would enjoy seeing a rival's losing his possessions and would do nothing to prevent it from happening if they could, would never take active steps to destroy them, even if it could be done without costs or risks to them.[7] A person who would not set her neighbor's house on fire might abstain from calling the fire brigade if she saw it burning.

Wishful thinking (Chapter 7) is based on wishes rather than on wants. In some cases, the agent refrains from the hard work of making the world conform to his desires and adopts instead the easy path of adopting an appropriate belief about the world. If I desire to be promoted but am reluctant to make an effort, I may rely instead on insignificant signs to persuade myself that a promotion is imminent. In other cases, acting on the world is not an option. I may be unable to cause my love to be requited or my sick child to recover. In such cases, I may either engage in gratifying fantasies or face the facts. A further distinction is between cases in which the fantasies have no further consequences for action and those in which they are used as premises for behavior. I may delude myself into thinking that a woman of my acquaintance harbors a secret passion for me and yet not make any overtures to her, either because I am constrained by morality (or self-interest) or because the deluded belief is entertained mainly for its consumption value.[8] The delusion may also be expressed overtly to its object, as happened when a secretary of John Maynard Keynes's told him that she could not help being aware of his great passion for her. Her life was ruined.

---

[7] Some envious people, to be sure, have no such qualms. They may live in a society where little shame attaches to envy or they may just be shameless.

[8] We may note for later reference (Chapter 23) that counterwishful thinking cannot have any consumption value. Hence, when it occurs, it is likely to serve as the premise for behavior.

States That Are Essentially By-Products

A factor that complicates the wish-want distinction is that in some cases I can get X by doing A, but only if I do A in order to get Y. If I work hard to explain the neurophysiological basis of emotion and succeed, I may earn a high reputation. If I throw myself into work for a political cause, I may discover at the end of the process that I have also acquired a "character." If I play the piano well, I may impress others. These indirect benefits are parasitic on the main goal of the activity. If my motivation as a scholar is to earn a reputation, I'm less likely to earn one. To enter a political movement *solely* for the sake of the consciousness-raising or character-building effects on oneself is doomed to fail, or will succeed only by accident. As Proust noted, a musician "may sometimes betray [his true vocation] for the sake of glory, but when he seeks glory in this way, he moves further away from it, and only finds it by turning his back on it." Self-consciousness interferes with the performance. As he also wrote, although "the best way to make oneself sought after is to be hard to find," he would never give anyone advice to that effect, since "this method of achieving social success works only if one does not adopt it for that purpose."

Musical glory or social success falls in the category of *states that are essentially by-products* – states that cannot be realized by actions motivated only by the desire to realize them. These are states that may *come about*, but not be *brought about* intentionally by a simple decision. They include the desire to forget, the desire to believe, the desire to desire (such as the desire to overcome sexual impotence), the desire to sleep, the desire to laugh (one cannot tickle oneself), and the desire to overcome stuttering. Attempts to realize these desires are likely to be ineffectual and can even make matters worse. It is a commonplace among moralists and novelists that intentional hedonism is self-defeating,[9] and that nothing

---

[9] In the final volume of *A la recherche du temps perdu* Proust, probably reflecting on his own life, wrote that the vain search for happiness can nevertheless lead to insights into the human condition that may "offer a kind of joy." The search for states that are essentially by-products can bring them about indirectly, as when a child's instructing someone to laugh causes the person to laugh out loud at this preposterous demand.

engraves an experience so deeply in memory as the attempt to forget it. Although we may *wish* for these states to be realized, we should beware of *wanting* to realize them.

Many people care about *salvation* (in the afterlife) and *redemption* (for wrongs they have done). They may also believe they can achieve these goals by action. To die the death of a martyr in the fight against the infidels may provide the passport to heaven, or so some believe. To fight against the Nazis after having collaborated with them at an earlier stage may redeem the wrongdoing. Yet if these actions are undertaken for the *purpose* of achieving salvation or redemption, they may fail. In Catholic theology, the intention to buy a place in heaven by voluntary martyrdom would be an instance of the sin of simony. Some Islamic scholars make a similar criticism of suicide attackers who are motivated by the belief that they will get a privileged place in paradise. Montaigne writes that when the Spartans "had to decide which of their men should individually hold the honor of having done best that day, they decided that Aristodemus had the most courageously exposed himself to risk: yet they never awarded him the prize because his valor had been spurred on by his wish to purge himself of the reproach he had incurred in the battle of Thermopylae." The French press magnate Jean Prouvost, who had collaborated with the German forces during the occupation of France, tried to redeem himself by writing a large check to the resistance when it became clear that the Germans were losing the war. After Liberation, the High Court granted him a *non-lieu* (a judgment that suspends, annuls, or withdraws a case without bringing it to trial), something the Spartans presumably would not have done.[10]

Push Versus Pull

Why do people leave one country for another? Why do academics leave one university for another? Often, answers are classified as "push versus pull." One may emigrate either because the situation at home is

---

[10] The reason he went free was probably that the resistance needed the money and later found itself obliged to keep the tacit promise of immunity that acceptance of the check implied.

unbearable or because the situation abroad is irresistibly enticing – at least this is a common way of viewing the matter. In many situations, however, it is misleading. Typically, people move because they *compare* the situation at home and abroad and find that the difference is big enough to justify a move, even taking account of the costs of the move itself.[11] Yet it can make sense to distinguish push motives from pull motives, when the former are closer to the visceral end of the continuum and the latter closer to the rational end. People in the grip of strong fear sometimes run away from danger rather than toward safety. The only thought in their mind is to get away, and they do not pause to think whether they might be going from the frying pan into the fire. Depending on the drug, addicts can be motivated either by the pull from euphoria (cocaine) or by the push from dysphoria (heroin). Suicidal behavior, too, may owe more to push than to pull. It is an escape from despair, not a flight to anything.

The operation of social norms (Chapter 22) can also be viewed in terms of push versus pull. The desire to excel in socially approved ways exercises a strong pull on many individuals, whether they strive for *glory* (being the best) or for *honor* (winning in a competition or combat). Other individuals are more concerned with avoiding the shame attached to the violation of social norms. In some societies, there is a general norm that says, "Don't stick your neck out." To excel in anything is to deviate, and deviation is the object of universal disapproval: "Who does he take himself for?" The relative strength of these two motivations varies across and within societies. Classical Athens illustrates the competitive striving for excellence.[12] In modern societies, small towns often show the stifling effects of the hostility to excellence. To risk a generalization, overall the push from shame seems to be a more important motivation than the pull toward glory, which is not to say that the latter cannot be powerful.

---

[11] This formulation presupposes that the cost of moving enters on a par with the benefits of having moved, as determinants of the overall utility of moving. Yet the costs of moving can also enter as *constraints* on the decisions. If the cheapest transatlantic fare costs more than the maximal amount a poor Italian peasant can save and borrow, he will remain in Italy no matter how much better he could do for himself in the United States (Chapter 9).

[12] Aeschylus, for instance, wrote his plays for performance at a dramatic competition. When the young Sophocles defeated him, he was so chagrined that he left Athens for Sicily.

Motivational Conflict

The existence of *competing* motivations is commonplace:

> I need a book so strongly that I am tempted to steal it from the library, but I also want to behave morally.
>
> In the face of a bully I am both afraid and angry: I want to run but also to hit him.
>
> I want all children to have public education, but I also want my child to go a private school to obtain the best education.
>
> I want a candidate who favors legal abortion, but I also want one who favors lower taxes.
>
> I want to smoke, but also to remain healthy.
>
> If I am made an advantageous but unfair offer, "take it or leave it," I want both to reject it because it is unfair and to accept it because it is advantageous.
>
> I want to donate to charity, but also to promote my own interest.
>
> I am tempted to have an extramarital affair, but I also want to preserve my marriage.

How is the conflict among these motivations resolved? A general answer might go as follows. Where the situation is one of "winner takes all," so that no (physical) compromise is possible, the strongest motivation wins.[13] If my concern for my child is stronger than my concern for the schooling of children in general, I will send him or her to a private school. If my pro-choice concern is stronger than my tax-cut concern and no candidate favors both positions, I vote for a pro-choice candidate who proposes to raise taxes. If somebody offers me three dollars out of a common pool of ten dollars, intending to keep the rest for himself, I accept it. If I am offered only two dollars, I reject the offer.[14] When compromise is possible, the stronger motivation has a stronger impact

---

[13] One might, at least in principle, use a probabilistic compromise, by setting up a weighted lottery among the options, using the strength of reasons in their favor as the weights. Some institutions allocate scarce resources on that basis, but I have not encountered any cases of individual motivational conflict that were resolved in this way.

[14] As noted, by rejecting the offer I may also ensure that the proposer gets nothing.

than the smaller one. A smoker may cut down his cigarette consumption from thirty to ten cigarettes a day. As a reflection of the strength of my altruism, I may spend 5 percent of my income on charity.[15]

This answer is not exactly wrong, but it is pretty simplistic, since the idea of "strength of motivation" is more complicated than these quick examples suggest. A motivation may owe its strength to its sheer psychic force; this is the sense in which, for instance, visceral motives are often stronger than what Madison called "the mild voice of reason." A strong motivation may also, however, be one that the agent endorses strongly because of the high value placed on it in her society. Each society or culture is in fact characterized by a normative hierarchy of motivations. Other things being equal, a person would rather perform a given action for motive A than for motive B if A ranks higher in the hierarchy. These are *metamotivations*, desires to be animated by desires of a certain kind.[16] Even though weaker in the visceral sense, they may in the end win out over other motivations.

Interest and passion, notably, often show a certain *deference to reason*.[17] As Seneca said, "Reason wishes the decision that it gives to be just; anger wishes to have the decision which it has given seem the just decision." As there are very many plausible-sounding conceptions of reason, justice, and fairness, it will indeed often be possible to present a decision made in anger as conforming to reason. The trials of collaborators in countries that had been occupied by Germany during World War II were in many cases anchored in a deep desire for revenge. Yet because of their deference to reason, combined with their desire to demarcate themselves from the lawless practices of the occupying regimes, the new leaders presented the severe measures as justice-based rather than emotion-based. A person may have a first-order interest in not donating to charity and a second-order

---

[15] In Chapter 6 I discuss the more puzzling phenomenon of "loser takes all" observed in weakness of will.

[16] The idea of metamotivations is unrelated to the concept of metapreferences. An example of the latter would be a person who had two *different* preference orderings, one for eating over dieting and one for dieting over eating, and a metapreference favoring the latter. Following La Bruyère's insight that "men are very vain, and of all things hate to be thought so," a metamotivation could amount to a preference for preferring dieting to eating on grounds of health over having *the same* preference for dieting on grounds of vanity.

[17] As we shall see in Chapter 12, agents may also show a sometimes excessive deference to *rationality*.

desire for not seeing himself as swayed by interest only. In deference to reason, he may then adopt the philosophy of charity (Chapter 2) that can justify small donations. If others give much he will adopt a utilitarian policy that justifies small donations, and if others give little he will adopt a fairness-based policy that justifies the same behavior.

In these cases, reason has no independent causal role. It only induces an after-the-fact justification for actions already decided on other grounds. The conflict is not resolved, but swept under the carpet. In other cases, the search for a reason-based justification may change behavior. If I adopt a fairness-based policy of charity because others give little and they suddenly begin donating much more generously than before, I have to follow suit. *The same need for self-esteem* that caused me to justify self-interested behavior by impartial considerations in the first place also prevents me from changing my conception of impartiality when it no longer works in my favor. We may imagine that in *King Lear* both Burgundy and France initially fell in love with Cordelia because of her prospects, but that only the former cared so little about his self-image that he was able to shed the emotion when it no longer coincided with his interest. This is a case of interest paying deference to passion rather than to reason, suggesting that passion, or rather this particular passion, ranks above interest in the normative hierarchy. Other passions, such as envy, might well rank below interest. We might then observe efforts to undertake only such envy-based action as may be plausibly presented as interest-based. Actions that cannot be viewed in that light will not be undertaken.

Cognitive dissonance theory predicts that when one motivation is *slightly* stronger than another, it will try to recruit allies so that the reasons on one side become decisively stronger. The unconscious mind shops around, as it were, for additional arguments in favor of the tentative conclusion reached by the conscious mind.[18] In such cases,

---

[18] The converse phenomenon, in which the conscious mind tries to find a reason for a decision reached by the unconscious one, also occurs. A simple example is behavior induced by hypnosis. Or consider the contrived explanations lovers come up with for making frequent phone calls to the object or their affection. This form of self-interpretation or self-misinterpretation should not be confused with transmutation, which occurs before the action, not after it.

"strength" of motivation cannot be taken as given, but should rather, to some extent at least, be seen as a product of the decision-making process itself. Suppose that when buying a car I attach values to differently weighted features (speed, price, comfort, appearance) of each of the alternatives and reach an overall assessment by comparing the weighted sums of the values. I might, for instance, attach overall value of 50 to brand A and of 48 to brand B. Because of the uncomfortable closeness of the comparison, I unconsciously modify the weights so that A becomes a clear winner, with 60 versus 45 as overall value. Before making the purchase, I come across brand C, which with the old weights would have scored 55, but with the new only achieves 50. Had I seen the alternatives in the order C-A-B, I would have chosen C. Because I met them in the order A-B-C, I chose A. Such *path-dependence* undermines the simple idea that motivational conflicts are resolved according to given motivational strength.

On what I called the simplistic view, the decision whether to steal a book from the library might be represented as follows. On the one side of the balance is the benefit of being able to use the book; on the other side, the cost of guilt feelings. What I end up doing depends only on whether the cost exceeds the benefit, or vice versa. But this cannot be right, for suppose someone offered me a "guilt pill" that would remove any painful feelings of guilt for stealing the book. If guilt entered into my decisions merely as a psychic cost, it would be rational to take the pill, just as it would be rational to take a pill that would prevent me from developing a hangover from a planned drinking binge. I submit, however, that most *people would feel just as guilty about taking the pill as they would about stealing the book.*[19] I am not denying that there cannot be, in some sense, a trade-off between morality and self-interest, only that it cannot be represented in this simplistic way.

Here is a more complex case. I wish that I did not wish that I did not want to eat cream cake. I want to eat cream cake because I like it. I wish

---

[19] In Chapter II, I argue that a person who had a short time horizon would, for somewhat similar reasons, refuse to take a "discounting pill" that would make him attach more importance to future consequences of present actions. The general principle illustrated by these two pills is that a rational person would not want to do in two steps what he would not want to do in one step. He might, to be sure, want to do in two steps what he could not do in one.

that I did not like it, because, as a moderately vain person, I think it is more important to remain slim. But I wish I were less vain. *But is that wish activated only when I want to eat cream cake?* In the conflict among my desire for cream cake, my desire to be slim, and my desire not to be vain, the first and the last can form an alliance and gang up (or sneak up) on the second. If they catch me unaware, they may succeed, but if I *understand* that the salience of my desire not to be vain is caused by the desire for cake I may be able to resist them. On another occasion, my desire for short-term gratification and my long-term desire for spontaneity may form an alliance against my medium-term desire for self-control. When more than two motives bear on the choice between two options, the idea of "strength of motivation" may be indeterminate until we know which alliance will be formed.

The seventeenth-century French moralist La Bruyère summarized two forms of motivational conflict as follows: "Nothing is easier for passion than to overcome reason; its greatest triumph is to conquer interest." We have seen that when passion "overcomes reason," it may still want to have reason on its side. Although St. Paul said, "For I do not do the good I want, but I do the evil I do not want," a more common reaction may be to persuade oneself of the goodness or justice of what, in the grip of passion, one wants to do. When passion "conquers interest," it can do so in one of two ways. The agent may, because of the *urgency* that is typical of emotion (Chapter 8), not take the time to find out where her interest lies. Alternatively, the force of emotion may be so strong that she *knowingly* acts against her interest. Such behavior may amount to weakness of will (Chapter 6).

〈〈〈

Bibliographical Note

A theory of visceral motivations is offered by G. Loewenstein, "Out of control: Visceral influences on behavior," *Organizational Behavior and Human Decision Processes* 65 (1996), 272–92. The estimate of "excess car accidents" after September 11, 2001, is from G. Gigerenzer, "Dread risk, September 11, and fatal traffic accidents," *Psychological Science* 15 (2004), 286–7. The lack of similar excess accidents in Spain is documented in A. López-Rousseau, "Avoiding the death risk of avoiding a dread risk: The aftermath of March 11 in Spain," *Psychological Science* 16 (2005), 426–8. The trichotomy interest-reason-passion is analyzed in A. Hirschman, *The Passions and the Interests* (Princeton, NJ: Princeton University Press, 1977); M. White, *Philosophy*, The Federalist, *and the Constitution* (Oxford University Press, 1987); and in my *Alchemies of the Mind* (Cambridge University Press, 1999). George Ainslie's *Picoeconomics* (Cambridge University Press, 1992) provided the lacking mechanisms for Freud's insights. A classic study of push versus pull is D. Gambetta, *Did They Jump or Were They Pushed?* (Cambridge University Press, 1983). I take the arguments of Dion Chrysostomos from P. Veyne, *L'empire gréco-romain* (Paris: Seuil, 2005), p.217. The principle I cite from Jewish ethics is explored in D. Daube, *Collaboration with Tyranny in Rabbinic Law* (Oxford University Press, 1965), and D. Daube, *Appeasement or Resistance* (Berkeley: University of California Press, 1987). I develop the idea of states that are essentially by-products in Chapter 2 of *Sour Grapes* (Cambridge University Press, 1983) and apply it to the question of redemption in "Redemption for wrongdoing," *Journal of Conflict Resolution* 50 (2006), 324–38, and to the question of salvation in "Motivations and beliefs in suicide missions," in D. Gambetta (ed.), *Making Sense of Suicide Missions* (Oxford University Press, 2005). See also L. Ross and R. Nisbett, *The Person and the Situation* (Philadelphia: Temple University Press, 1991), pp. 230–32. I discuss the "deference to reason" in trials of collaborators after World War II in Chapter 8 of *Closing the Books* (Cambridge University Press, 2004). Evidence for change in the weights attached to various features of alternative options is found in A. Brownstein, "Biased predecision processing," *Psychological Bulletin* 129 (2003), 545–68, and J. Brehm, "Postdecision changes in the desirability of alternatives," *Journal of Abnormal and Social Psychology* 52 (1956), 384–9.

Chapter 5
SELF-INTEREST AND ALTRUISM

❀ ❀ ❀

Motivation and Behavior

The contrast between self-interested and altruistic motivations is deceptively simple. As a first approximation, let us understand an *altruistic motivation* as the desire to enhance the welfare of others even at a net welfare loss to oneself, and an *altruistic act* as an action for which an altruistic motivation provides a sufficient reason. If I see you give money to a beggar in the street I call it an altruistic act because it is an action that *could* spring from altruistic motivations, whether or not it actually does.

For a more complex example, consider the experimental findings, discussed several times later, on "altruistic punishment." In these studies, one subject A has the option of punishing another subject B for non-cooperative behavior, at some cost to himself. There is no face-to-face interaction and the two subjects will never meet again. Yet many subjects use the punishment option, causing B to be more cooperative in his later dealings with a third party C. The punishment *could* spring from altruistic motivations, if A anticipates, and is motivated by, the benefit his punishment of B confers on C. In reality, it is more likely to be motivated by a desire for revenge.

There are many instances of such behavior outside the laboratory. In eighteenth-century France, peasants usually granted requests by beggars and vagrants for dinner and lodgings. If a peasant refused, he risked seeing his trees felled, his beasts mutilated, and his house burned down, acts of destruction that produced no benefit to the beggars and involved a risk of being caught. Although there is no reason to believe that they were in fact motivated by a desire to make the peasant take in future beggars, that motivation would be sufficient to explain them. Peasant rebellions in preindustrial England were invariably unsuccessful in their immediate objectives and their leaders were usually punished harshly. Yet by virtue of their nuisance value the rebellions had a long-term success in making the propertied classes behave more moderately than they would have done otherwise.

The reason for defining altruistic motivations in terms of sacrifice of welfare rather than of material goods is to exclude cases like the following. If I pay $100,000 for my child's college education, it may be because my child's welfare is so bound up with my own that the "sacrifice" makes both of us better off.[1] The motivation, although other-regarding, is not altruistic.[2] A case of genuine altruism would be if I sent my child to a public school when I could easily afford a private school and believe it would be better for my child. In doing so I would sacrifice not only my child's welfare but also my own. Similarly, donating to a blood bank (as distinct from giving blood to a close relative) is more likely to spring from genuinely altruistic motives. In practice, though, it may be impossible to tell whether a motivation is altruistic or merely other-regarding.

A further complication arises from the fact that some people *like giving*, because it makes them feel good ("the warm glow effect"). If the warm glow provides the *reason* why they help others or give to them, we would not want to call them altruists. They give because, taking everything into account, giving makes them better off. This is not to say that an altruist might not also feel the warm glow, only that it would not enter into his (unconscious) motives for helping or giving. Once again, however, this distinction might seem impossible to draw in practice. I shall have more to say about it in Chapter 15.

Whatever the problems of identifying altruistic motivations, there is abundant evidence of altruistic *behavior*. The Carnegie Foundation regularly hands out medals to individuals who have saved the lives of others at great risk to themselves. Many people give blood without being

---

[1] It might also be the case that I would have paid the school fees even if they were so high that the expense would make me worse off in welfare terms. In that case, payment of the lower fees is explained by other-regarding motives preempting altruism.

[2] When Marx wrote that the communist society would *be beyond* egoism and altruism rather than based on the latter motivation, he may have meant that any *material* sacrifices people made for each other would not, for similar reasons, entail any sacrifice of *welfare*.

paid for the effort.[3] In Norway, most kidneys for transplantation are donated by relatives of the recipient. The extraction of the kidney carries a medical risk, but there is no monetary reward.[4] Many individuals, especially women, look after their old parents in addition to holding jobs and taking care of their own families. In many countries, more than half of the adult population make regular donations of money for charitable purposes. After the 2004 tsunami, high peaks of giving were observed in many developed countries. In wartime, some individuals try to disguise their disabilities so that they will be allowed to fight. Many soldiers volunteer for dangerous (and some even for suicidal) missions. When people vote in national elections and thus contribute to the viability of democracy, they incur some costs and derive virtually no private benefits. The list could be extended indefinitely.

The reason why we cannot infer the existence of altruistic motivations from altruistic behavior is that other motivations may *mimic altruism*. In the terminology of Chapter 4, we may see altruism as a species of *reason*, which can be effectively simulated either by *interest* or by *passion*. (The word "mimic" or "simulate" may, but need not, imply a conscious effort to deceive others about one's real motivation.) Many people who are little concerned with being disinterested are very concerned with being praised for their disinterestedness. Thus Hume was surely wrong when he claimed that "to love the glory of virtuous deeds is a *sure* proof of the love of virtue" (my italics). Montaigne, by contrast, asserted, "The more glittering the deed the more I subtract from its moral worth, because of the suspicion aroused in me that it was exposed more for glitter than for goodness: goods displayed are already halfway to being sold." At the limit, the only virtuous acts are those that never come to light. The angelic grandmother of Proust's Narrator had internalized this principle so thoroughly that she attributed all her good actions to egoistic motives. To the extent that virtue has this self-effacing character, there may be

---

[3] In fact, it has been argued that nonpayment is important to screen out people with infectious diseases who might donate for money.

[4] In most countries, in fact, the sale of kidneys from living persons is illegal. In this case, the motivation behind the law may be as much to protect destitute individuals against themselves as to protect recipients against low-quality body parts.

more of it than meets the eye. For other reasons, to be sure, there may be less.

Approbativeness and Shamefulness

Montaigne also recognized the rarity of virtue, when he drew a distinction between true and false motivational "coins"– acting for the sake of what is right and acting for the sake of what other people think about you. As the former motivation is rare, policymakers may have to rely on the latter:

> If that false opinion [a concern for what other people think] serves the public good by keeping men to their duty..., then let it boldly flourish and may it be fostered among us as much as it is in our power.... Since men are not intelligent enough to be adequately paid in good coin let counterfeit coin be used as well. That method has been employed by all the lawgivers. And there is no policy which has not brought in some vain ceremonial honours, or some untruths, to keep the people to their duties.

Napoleon echoed the idea when, defending the creation of the Légion d'Honneur in 1802, he said that "by such baubles are men led." (His old soldiers from the republican army reacted strongly against this invention.) *Approbativeness* – the desire to be well thought of by others – is a false coin that may have to substitute for the true coin of altruism and morality. Alternatively, *shamefulness* – the desire not to be thought badly of by others – may serve as the false coin. Social norms may induce people to refrain from actions that they might otherwise have carried out. Abiding by the norm is not enough to make others think well of them, however. Approbation is reserved for *supererogatory* acts, that is, those that go beyond the norm. What is obligatory in one society may be supererogatory in another. In Norway and in the United States, there is a (mild) social norm that a sibling should donate a kidney if one is needed (and suitable) for transplantation,[5] whereas in France such behavior

---

[5] In the United States, doctors often help a potential donor to resist such pressure by telling him or her early on in the process that if requested they are willing to provide a medical excuse for not donating.

might be seen as supererogatory. In certain social circles, donations to charity are mandatory.

These motivations may be illustrated by two contrasting examples from eighteenth-century politics. In the first French Assemblée Constituante (1789–91), the deputies several times sacrificed important interests, ranging from giving up their feudal privileges to declaring themselves ineligible for the first ordinary legislature. Although their motivations were complex, an important component was the desire to be seen as disinterested. In the words of the biographer of one of them, they were "drunk with disinterestedness." Around the same time, in the United States, George Washington repeatedly manifested his fear that others might think he was motivated by private interest. (At the same time, he was aware that too much concern for one's virtue might appear as unvirtuous.) For another pair of illustrations, consider two conceptions of honor. According to one, honor must be *acquired*, through glorious deeds. According to another, honor is assumed as a baseline but can be *lost* through shameful deeds.

Whether approbativeness or shamefulness can mimic altruism depends on the substantive criteria others apply in assessing behavior. Some societies may place high value on – and thus stimulate the expression of – virtues that do not in any systematic way tend to mimic altruism. The desire for honor may induce all sorts of socially wasteful behavior. Napoleon's baubles were intended to encourage soldiers to risk their lives to enhance the glory of France, not to promote the welfare of the French. Some individuals may choose a life of self-abnegation because of the praise their society bestows on religious virtuosi, but hermits and monks are often more focused on the rituals of worship than on their fellow beings. As far as I know, there is no tendency for communities that place a high value on education and learning to generate more altruistic behavior than others. The cult of beauty in modern Western societies stimulates self-centered behavior that would seem to be inimical to the concern for others. In societies subject to what has been called "amoral familism" (Southern Italy has been cited as an example) there are social norms against helping strangers in distress or against complying with the law. Overall, therefore, it is hard to say whether the desire for praise or for blame avoidance tends to mimic altruism.

Transmutations

As discussed in the previous chapter, the original motivation of the agent can also be *transmuted* from interest into reason. The mechanism behind this alchemy is "amour-propre," or *self-love*, the desire for esteem and for self-esteem. Whereas approbativeness and shamefulness, which derive from the desire for esteem, only affect outward behavior, the desire for self-esteem can affect the inner motivations themselves. Most people do not want to see themselves as moved by their personal interest only. Even when acting to satisfy their interest they try to put a non–self-interested gloss on their actions. In the decades before the American Civil War, slavery in the Old South ceased to become a matter of mere interest and turned into a *cause*, defended on grounds of principle. This is a very common type of political ideology. As Marx noted, "One must not form the narrow-minded notion that the petty bourgeoisie, on principle, wishes to enforce an egoistic class interest. Rather, it believes that the *special* conditions of its emancipation are the *general* conditions within which alone modern society can be saved and the class struggle be avoided."

Although it can be hard to tell whether the non–self-interested gloss is sincere or hypocritical, it would be a mistake to think that it is typically the latter. People have, in fact, two degrees of freedom in their efforts to justify their behavior to themselves. On the one hand, there are many *plausible-sounding causal theories* that can be used to support claims that actions benefiting oneself will also benefit others. "Trickle-down" theories of economic growth imply, for instance, that low taxes on the rich will also benefit the poor. On the other hand, there are so many *plausible-sounding normative conceptions* of justice, fairness, or the common good that a person would have to be unlucky or incompetent if she failed to locate one that (according to some plausible-sounding causal theory) coincided with her self-interest. In Chapter 4, I noted that people might select between a fairness-based and a utility-based philosophy of charity to justify low donations.[6] In such cases, people spontaneously and unconsciously gravitate toward a combination of causal theory and normative conception that can justify behavior in line with their self-interest. Although we do not understand how it happens, we know it does happen.

The "mimicking" of altruism need not rest on hypocrisy or transmutation. Self-interested reasoning may generate altruistic behavior by perfectly avowable mechanisms such as choice *behind the veil of ignorance* or reciprocity. In Chapter 5 I cited, as an example of the first, George Mason's argument that the long-term interest of families should induce a concern for the welfare of all classes in society.[7] Similar arguments may apply within the life of a single individual. In societies that have low unemployment but are undergoing rapid structural change, the majority may vote for a party proposing high unemployment benefits if they believe their job is one of those that might disappear. What looks like solidarity may be only a form of insurance.

Reciprocity

Reciprocity can be a simple dyadic relation, as when each party in an ongoing relationship faces the choice between cooperating and not cooperating. One farmer may harvest in August, another in September, and each can benefit from the help of the other. If the farmer whose harvest arrives first solicits the help of the other but then refuses to

---

[6] In this case, the causal theory justifying low donations if others give much is that donations have decreasing marginal utility to the recipients. The fairness-based theory that justifies low donations if others give little does not require a causal premise.

[7] Gouverneur Morris offered a similar argument in the debate over the representation of the states in the Senate: "State attachments and State importance have been the bane of this Country. We cannot annihilate; but we may perhaps take out the teeth of the serpent. He wished our ideas to be enlarged to the true interest of man, instead of being circumscribed within the narrow compass of a particular Spot. And after all how little can be the motive yielded by selfishness for such a policy. Who can say whether he himself, much less whether his children, will the next year be an inhabitant of this or that State." On another occasion Gouverneur Morris was at the receiving end of the same argument. In response to Elbridge Gerry's espousal of Gouverneur Morris's proposal to limit the representation of future western states, Roger Sherman replied: "We are providing for our posterity, for our children & our grand Children, who would be as likely to be citizens of new Western States, as of the old States. On this consideration alone, we ought to make no such discrimination as was proposed by the motion."

reciprocate in September, he is unlikely to receive assistance the following August. A stable relation of mutual assistance is likely to develop that, although it does not rely on feelings of fellowship, may foster them. During World War I, some German and British troops developed a tacit truce, a live-and-let live practice of shelling the adversary less aggressively than they could have.[8] In this case, too, a friendly attitude toward the other side emerged over time, but as a *result* of cooperation, not as its cause.

Descartes described a more complex form of multilateral or indirect reciprocity:

> The reason that makes me believe that those who do nothing save for their own utility, ought also, if they wish to be prudent, work, as do others, for the good of others, and try to please everyone as much as they can, is that one ordinarily sees it occur that those who are deemed obliging and prompt to please also receive a quantity of good deeds from others, even from people who have never been obliged to them; and these things they would not receive did people believe them of another humor; and the pains they take to please other people are not so great as the conveniences that the friendship of those who know them provides. For others expect of us only the deeds we can render without inconvenience to ourselves, nor do we expect more of them; but it often happens that deeds that cost others little profit us very much, and can even save our life. It is true that occasionally one wastes his toil in doing good and that, on the other hand, occasionally one gains in doing evil; but that cannot change the rule of prudence that relates only to things that happen most often.

In direct reciprocity, A helps B if and only if B has helped A. In indirect reciprocity, A helps B if B has helped C. As we shall see in later chapters, a similar distinction applies to "negative reciprocity": A may hurt B if B has hurt A, but also if B has hurt C. The existence of indirect reciprocity suggests that people might behave altruistically in order to develop a *reputation* for having altruistic motivations. Other people will then have to decide whether the behavior reflects genuine altruism or merely a strategic desire to build a reputation for being altruistic

---

[8] Although the high commands tried to stop the practice, it was difficult to monitor.

(Chapter 20). In this case reputation is valued on instrumental grounds, not on intrinsic ones. Whereas approbativeness causes the agent to desire esteem for its own sake, reputation is sought for the material rewards it might yield.

People may also reciprocate in one-shot situations that offer no opportunity for subsequent reward. If A behaves altruistically toward B, B may reciprocate even if both know that they will have no further interaction. The farmer harvesting in August might help the one harvesting in September even though he is planning to emigrate before the next season. One can, to be sure, imagine self-interested reasons for such reciprocation. Perhaps the farmer harvesting early fears that the other will punish him in some way if he does not reciprocate, or third parties on whose assistance he depends might ostracize him. In experimental conditions, however, one can exclude such effects. In the experimental games to be discussed later (Chapters 15 and 20), subjects interact anonymously through computer terminals, thus excluding any face-to-face effects such as shame or embarrassment. Often, the games are also designed so that a given person interacts only once with a given partner.

Even under these stringent conditions, reciprocity is observed. In a Trust Game, one player, the "investor," has the option of transferring anywhere between 0 and 10 of her endowment of 10 monetary units to another player, the "trustee." The experimenter then triples any amount sent, so that if the investor sends 10 the trustee receives 30. The trustee can decide to transfer any amount from 0 to the whole augmented sum (three times what the investor sent) back to the investor. In one experiment, investors transfer on average around two-thirds of their endowment to the trustee, and trustees make on average a slightly larger back transfer. The larger the "forward" transfer, the larger the back transfer. These findings are consistent with a number of motivational assumptions, *except* the hypothesis that both agents are motivated by material self-interest and know each other to be so motivated. On that hypothesis the investor, expecting a zero back transfer, would make a zero forward transfer. Since this outcome is not observed, other-regarding motivations or "social preferences" must be operating. These can fall short of altruism or fairness, since in some experiments trustees send back no more than what they received, yet even this amount is larger than self-interest would dictate.

Moral, Social, and Quasi-Moral Norms

I shall return, in several later chapters, to the implications of this and related experiments. Here I shall only make distinctions among three kinds of "other-regarding" motivations. *Moral norms* include the norm to help others in distress, the norm of equal sharing, and the norm of "everyday Kantianism" (do what would be best if everyone did the same). *Social norms* (Chapter 21) include norms of etiquette, norms of revenge, and norms regulating the use of money. What I shall call "*quasi-moral norms*" include the norm of reciprocity (help those who help you and hurt those who hurt you) and the norm of conditional cooperation (cooperate if others do, but not otherwise). Both social norms and quasi-moral norms are conditional, in the sense that they are triggered by the presence or behavior of other people. Social norms, I shall argue, are triggered when other people can observe what the agent is doing, and quasi-moral norms when the agent can observe what other people are doing.[9] Moral norms, by contrast, are unconditional. What they tell us to do may, to be sure, depend on what others do. If I have a utility-based philosophy of charity, how much good I can do (and hence how much I will give) depends on how much others are giving. The norm itself, however, makes no reference to other donors, only to the recipients.

Two cases of individual responses to water shortage will illustrate the distinction between social and quasi-moral norms. In Bogotá, under the imaginative mayorship of Antanas Mockus, people followed a quasi-moral norm when reducing their consumption of water. Although individual monitoring was not feasible, the aggregate water consumption in the city was shown on TV, so that people could know whether others

---

[9] The two can reinforce each other, when the agent can observe what the observers are themselves doing. If I see you littering, I may not mind your watching me doing the same. If I see you carefully putting your ice cream wrapper in your pocket, however, fairness and fear of disapproval may combine to produce conformity (see also Chapter 22).

were for the most part complying. It appears that enough people did so to sustain the conditional cooperation. People were saying to themselves, "Since other people are cutting down on their consumption, it's only fair that I should do so as well." When there is a water shortage in California, by contrast, it seems that social norms operate to make people limit their consumption. Outdoor consumption such as watering the lawn can of course be monitored not only by neighbors, but also by municipal inspectors. Indoor consumption can be monitored by visitors, who may and do express their disapproval if the toilet bowl is clean.[10] In fact, monitoring of individual behavior also occurred in Bogotá, since children sometimes gave their parents a hard time if they did not economize on water.[11]

Quasi-moral norms can obviously be powerful in inducing altruistic behavior. Do they merely *mimic* altruism or *are* they altruistic motivations? The reason I refer to them as quasi-moral and not as moral is also why I lean to the first answer. The norm of reciprocity allows you *not* to help others in distress unless they have helped you previously. A typical moral norm is to help others in distress unconditionally, even if there is no prior history of assistance. The norm of conditional cooperation allows one to use normal amounts of water if nobody else is reducing consumption, whereas both utilitarianism and everyday Kantianism would endorse unilateral reduction. Moral norms, one might say, are *proactive*; quasi-moral norms, only *reactive*. Another way of expressing the difference is that the feeling of injustice seems to have stronger motivational force than the sense of justice. As we shall see later (Chapter 20), proposals that Responders in an experiment tend to reject

---

[10] Saving water is also a concern in normal times. In New York City, it is achieved by laws fixing the maximal volume of toilet cisterns. In much of Europe, it is established by having toilets with two push buttons dispensing different amounts of water for different uses. The latter system is interesting in that it operates neither on opportunities nor on incentives (Chapter 9), only on the unobservable goodwill of the person.

[11] Experimental findings also suggest this mechanism. In an energy-saving campaign, signs were posted in shower rooms urging students to save energy by turning their shower off as they soaped themselves, and turning it on only to rinse themselves. The signs had minimal effect. When one or two experimental confederates started complying, however, compliance by other shower users increased dramatically. Although the confederates did not say anything to the others, their behavior might serve as a tacit reproach of noncompliers.

as unfair, with the consequence that neither they nor the Proposers get anything, are of the same order of magnitude as what Proposers tend to offer when unconstrained by the fear of rejection.

It would seem that we could identify the operation of genuinely altruistic motives if two conditions are satisfied. First, the action benefiting others is proactive, not reactive. Second, it is anonymous, in the sense that the identity of the benevolent actor is known neither to the beneficiary nor to third parties.[12] We may imagine, for instance, a person sending an anonymous money order to the charity Oxfam or dropping money into the collection box of an empty church. The second example is not as clear-cut as one would want, since the person might be motivated by his belief that God observes him and will reward him. The belief may be illogical (an instance of the "by-product fallacy") but might still be quite common. The first example might seem more unambiguous. Yet even the purest acts of altruism such as anonymous donations to strangers may stem from murky motives. According to Kant,

> it is absolutely impossible to make out by experience with complete certainty a single case in which the maxim of an action, however right in itself, rested simply on moral grounds and on the conception of duty. Sometimes it happens that with the sharpest self-examination we can find nothing beside the moral principle of duty which could have been powerful enough to move us to this or that action and to so great a sacrifice; yet we cannot from this infer with certainty that it was not really some secret impulse of self-love, under the false appearance of duty, that was the actual determining cause of the will. We like to flatter ourselves by falsely taking credit for a more noble motive; whereas in fact we can never, even by the strictest examination, get completely behind the secret springs of action; since, when the question is of moral worth, it is not with the actions which we see that we are concerned, but with those inward principles of them which we do not.

Kant is saying that even if we are not performing before an external audience, we can never know whether we are playing to the *inner*

---

[12] In experiments, the identity of the subject is hidden to the experimenter. In donations to charity, it is hidden to the officials in the charitable organization.

audience. The act of hiding one's virtue that Montaigne found so virtuous cannot be hidden to oneself. As La Rochefoucauld noted, amour propre "always finds compensations, and even when it gives up vanity it loses nothing." As he also said, "If pure love exists, free from the dross of our other passions, it lies hidden in the depths of our hearts and unknown even to ourselves." At best, said Proust, we may be able to learn our true motives from others: "We are familiar only with the passions of others, and what we come to know about our own, we have been able to learn only from them. Upon ourselves, they act only indirectly, by way of our imagination, which substitutes for our primary motives alternative motives that are more acceptable."

Imputing Motivations

In addition to the agent's own motivation, the explanation of her behavior must often appeal to her beliefs about the motivations of others. In forming these beliefs she faces the same hermeneutic dilemma as does the historian or the social scientist. Since she cannot take the professed motivations of others at face value, she can use triangulations of the general kind I discussed in Chapter 3. In addition, she can deploy techniques that only apply to face-to-face interactions. Other people may be able to identify an amateur liar by his body language (or lack of it), since concentration on what he is saying causes him to neglect the gestures that normally accompany spontaneous speech. Also, to verify professed motives one may set a trap for the agent. Whereas historians are unable to trap the individuals they are studying and social scientists are usually prevented on ethical grounds from doing so, an employer, a spouse, or a parent may feel less constrained.

The imputation of motives to others is often tainted by malice. Given the choice between believing that an altruistic action was caused by an altruistic motivation and that it was based on self-interest, we often assume the latter even if there are no positive grounds for the belief. Although such distrust can make sense for prudential reasons (Chapter 26), in many cases this justification is unavailable. Gossip, for instance, seems often to be motivated by what the French moralists, following Augustine, called the *malignity* and *weakness* of human nature.[13] According to La Rochefoucauld, "If we had no faults we should not find so much enjoyment in seeing faults in others." In fact, as he also wrote, our desire to find faults in others is so strong that it often helps us to find them: "Our enemies are nearer the truth in their opinion of us than we are ourselves." Yet, even if our enemies are closer to the truth, they err, too, even if they err less, from the opposite direction. On a scale from 0 to 10, if I am 6, I will think I am 9, and my enemies will think I am 4.

For an analysis of this attitude – sometimes called the "hermeneutics of suspicion" – I can do no better than quote from Jeremy Bentham (translated from his clumsy French):

> Whatever position the King [Louis XVI] takes, whatever sacrifices he makes, he will never succeed in silencing these slanderers: they are a vermin that bad temper and vanity will never fail to nourish in even the most healthy political body. It is first and foremost vanity that is the most prolific source of this injustice. One wants to deal subtly with everything ... and prefers the most contrived assumption to the shame of having suspected that the behavior of a public person might have a laudable motive. If Washington persists in his retirement, it can only be a means to use the road through anarchy to open up the path to despotism. If Necker instead of accepting payment for his services like anyone else pays with his own funds for being allowed to render them, it can only be a sophisticated means to satisfy his greed. If Louis XVI abdicates the legislative power in favor of his people, it can only be as the result of an elaborate plan to take it all back and even more in a favorable moment.

An irony is that the last of the specious accusations cited in this text (written in early 1789) was probably justified by the fall of 1790. One of the king' closest advisers, Saint-Priest, wrote that by that time he had stopped resisting the encroachments of the legislature because "he had convinced himself that the Assembly would be discredited through its

---

[13] I disagree with those who want to explain gossip by its role in enforcing social norms. True, gossip can act as a multiplier on the informal sanctions that sustain social norms, but I believe its origin is more deep-seated.

own errors." Conspiracy theories can be accurate, because conspiracies exist. Yet the tendency to find them may owe less to experience than to a malignant reluctance to admit that public figures might act for good reasons.

❮❮❮

Bibliographical Note

This chapter draws on my "Altruistic motivations and altruistic behavior," in S. C. Kolm and J. M. Ythier (eds.), *Handbook on the Economics of Giving, Reciprocity and Altruism* (Amsterdam: Elsevier, 2006). Other chapters in this volume, notably the introductory essay by Kolm, provide a wealth of empirical information and theoretical analysis. The reference to French beggars is from G. Lefebvre, *La grande peur* (Paris: Armand Colin, 1988), p. 40, and that to English peasant rebellions from E. P. Thompson, "The moral economy of the English crowd in the 18th century," *Past and Present* 80 (1971), 76–136. An analysis of "warm glow" altruism is J. Andreoni, "Impure altruism and donations to public goods: A theory of warm-glow giving," *Economic Journal* 100 (1990), 464–77. On attitudes toward kidney donation, see H. Lorenzen and F. Paterson, "Donations from the living: Are the French and Norwegians altruistic?" in J. Elster and N. Herpin (eds.), *The Ethics of Medical Choice* (London: Pinter, 1994). I take the idea (and the word) of "approbativeness" from A. O. Lovejoy, *Reflections on Human Nature* (Baltimore: Johns Hopkins Press, 1961). The role of disinterestedness in the French Revolution is discussed in B. M. Shapiro, "Self-sacrifice, self-interest, or self-defense? The constituent assembly and the 'self-denying ordinance' of May 1791," *French Historical Studies* 25 (2002), 625–56. For the American parallel, see G. Wood, "Interest and disinterestedness in the making of the constitution," in R. Beeman, S. Botein, and E. Carter II (eds.), *Beyond Confederation: Origins of the Constitution and American National Identity* (Chapel Hill: University of North

Carolina Press, 1987). For the mechanism of transmutation, see my *Alchemies of the Mind* (Cambridge University Press, 1999), Chapter 5. The tit-for-tat example from World War I is taken from R. Axelrod, *The Evolution of Cooperation* (New York: Basic Books, 1984). For the Trust Game, see C. Camerer, *Behavioral Game Theory* (New York: Russell Sage, 2004), Chapter 2.7. On detecting lies, see P. Ekman, *Telling Lies* (New York: Norton, 1992). The passage from Bentham is taken from his *Rights, Representation, and Reform* (Oxford University Press, 2002), pp. 17–18.

Chapter 6
MYOPIA AND FORESIGHT
❈ ❈ ❈

Beyond Gradient Climbing

Freud's pleasure principle (Chapter 4) is the tendency to seek immediate gratification of desires. One manifestation of this tendency is the adoption of the belief one would like to be true rather than the belief that is supported by the evidence. Wishful thinking makes me feel good here and now, even if it may cause me to fall flat on my face later on. Another manifestation occurs in the choice between two actions that induce different temporal utility streams. The pleasure principle dictates the choice of the stream that has the highest utility in the first period, regardless of the shape of the streams in later periods.

More generally, a decision maker, be it an earthworm or a firm, may engage in *gradient climbing*. At any point in time it scans the *nearby* options to see whether one of them yields greater *immediate* benefits than the status quo. The restriction to nearby options is a form of "spatial myopia": out of sight, out of mind. The restriction to immediate benefits is a form of temporal myopia: the pleasure principle. The earthworm scans the environment to see whether any spot nearby is more humid than the one it is currently occupying and moves to that spot if it finds one. The firm scans the "space" of routines that are close to what it is currently doing to find one that promises better short-term performance and adopts it if it finds one. After a while, the earthworm or the firm may come to rest in a place that is superior (in the short run) to all nearby positions. It has attained a *local maximum*.

Human beings can do better. Intentionality – the ability to re-present the absent – enables us to go beyond the pleasure principle and take account of temporally remote consequences of present choices. Planning ahead enables us to make choices that have better consequences than those that would flow from minute-by-minute or second-by-second decisions. In some cases, such farsighted actions may be undertaken to satisfy current needs better, as when an alcoholic forgoes having a drink in a nearby restaurant so that he can buy a whole bottle in a remotely located store at the same price. In other cases, the actions are undertaken to satisfy future needs, as when I save for my old age. Whereas the former kind of foresight is also observed in nonhuman animals, the latter has usually been thought to be beyond their capacity. Some recent evidence suggests, however, that primates may be able to plan on the basis of expected rather than actual needs. Be this as it may, acting on the basis of projected needs is obviously a more sophisticated operation.

Let me give four examples of acting on the basis of temporally remote consequences. The first three examples are also discussed in later chapters.

RECULER POUR MIEUX SAUTER. This French phrase, the rough equivalent of "one step backward, two steps forward," is illustrated by the fundamental fact of economic life that to invest for greater consumption in the future one must consume less in the present. The agent accepts a state that is inferior to the status quo because it is a condition for realizing a superior alternative later on. Needless to say, this makes sense only if (1) the inferior state allows the agent to survive and (2) the gains from the superior state are large enough to justify the loss involved in moving to the inferior state.

WAITING.   Many wines, although good from the time they are bottled, improve with age. To benefit from this fact, the agent has to be willing to reject an option (drinking the wine right away) that is superior to the status quo because the rejection is a condition for realizing an even better outcome later. Again, deferring consumption might not always make sense, for instance, if the agent does not expect to live long enough to enjoy the improved wine. For a more consequential example, consider the choice of spouse. Rather than proposing marriage or accepting a marriage proposal on the first occasion an acceptable candidate appears, one might wait for somebody even better suited. The risk, abundantly illustrated in world literature, is that nobody better suited might come along.

SHOOTING AHEAD OF THE TARGET.   To hit a moving target, one should not aim at where it is, but at where it will be at the time of

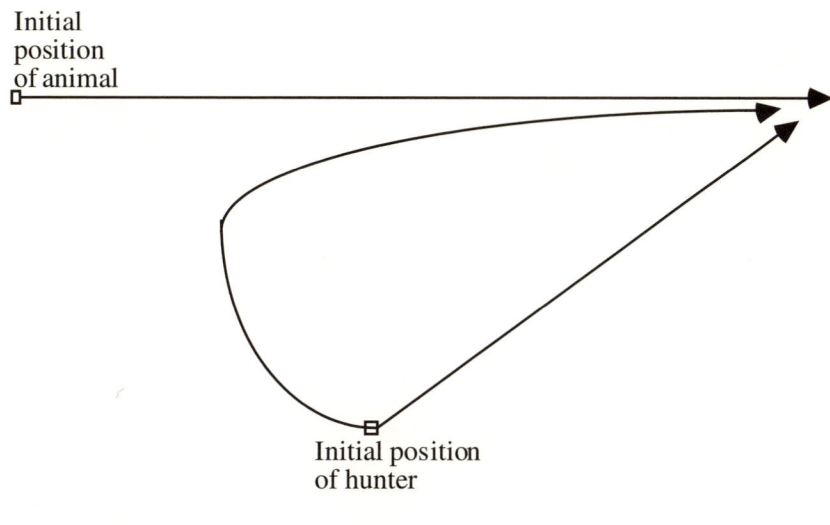

Initial
position
of animal

Initial position
of hunter

FIGURE 6.1

encounter. Similarly, to pursue a moving target, one should aim in a straight line at where the target will be rather than follow the curved path induced by always aiming at its current position.

In Figure 6.1, the hunter, even if he is moving somewhat more slowly than the animal, can catch up with it by going in a straight line toward the point where it will be at some calculable time in the future. If, however, he always aims in the direction of the current position of the animal, following the curved path in the diagram, he will never catch up with it. As we shall see (Chapter 17), natural selection in a changing environment can be viewed in this perspective.

A STRAIGHT LINE IS NOT ALWAYS THE FASTEST WAY. When trying to reach a stationary target, a straight line is not always the most efficient path. In Figure 6.2, the rescuer might impulsively run straight toward the drowning swimmer until she reaches the shoreline and then swim the remaining distance. If she had paused (but not too long!) to reflect, however, she might have realized that as she can run faster than she can swim, she would reach the swimmer faster by taking an indirect path that, although longer on the whole, has a shorter stretch in the water. We behave

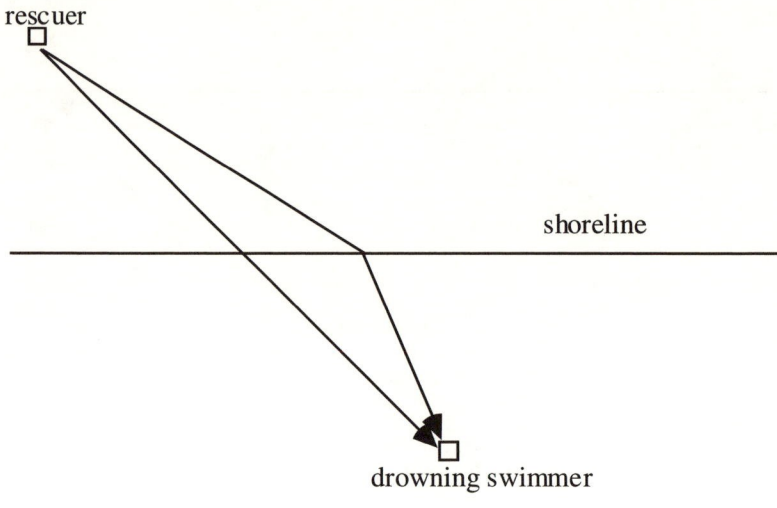

FIGURE 6.2

in this way when we take a turnpike rather than the road that, on the map, seems to be the shorter. In economic planning such "turnpike behavior" is often optimal.

Time Discounting

The existence of the capacity for long-term planning does not imply that it will be used. For perceived long-term consequences to make a difference for present behavior, agents must be *motivated* to take them into account. In the language of psychologists, they must be ready to *defer gratification*. In the language of economists, they must not be subject to excessive *time discounting*.[1] The cognitive and motivational elements are both needed. If future outcomes are shrouded in uncertainty, they cannot motivate present behavior. If they involve risk, their motivating

---

[1] In this book, the phrase "a high rate of time discounting" shall mean that future rewards have a small present value. The phrase "a high discount factor" shall mean that they have a large present value. To illustrate and motivate this seemingly strange terminology, assume that the agent is indifferent between 3 units of reward tomorrow and 2 units today. The future reward is discounted (reduced) by one-third. The discount factor (the number by which we have to multiply the future reward to get its present value) is two-thirds.

force is also attenuated. The ability of future outcomes to shape present behavior is affected both by *the time at which* and by *the probability with which* they will occur. The mechanisms by which they affect choice are, respectively, time discounting and risk attitudes.

As the phrase suggests, time discounting (or myopia) is the tendency to attach less importance to rewards in the distant future than to rewards in the near future or in the present.[2] If given the choice between 100 dollars today and 110 dollars a year from today, most people would prefer the former. This preference could, however, have a number of sources.

> Some people might prefer the early reward because they can invest the funds and withdraw more than 110 dollars in a year's time.

> Others might take the 100 dollars now because they need the money to survive. Getting a bigger sum later has no value if they expect to be dead by then. Or suppose I have the choice between catching fish in the stream with my hands and making a net that will enable me to catch many more fish. Because I cannot catch fish while making the net, however, the opportunity cost of making the net may be so high that I cannot afford it.

> Still others might take the smaller reward because they have a disease that entails a 10 percent chance of dying within a year. More generally, when planning for the future we have to take account of the fact that we know that but not when we shall die.

> If the future sum is an expected reward, involving a 50 percent chance of 130 dollars and a 50 percent chance of 90 dollars, risk aversion might induce a preference for getting 100 dollars with certainty today.

> Finally, some people might prefer the early reward simply because it arrives earlier. This is *pure time discounting*. Just as a big house seen in the distance appears to be smaller than a small house close up, a large sum in the future may appear, subjectively, as smaller than a small sum in the present. In the following, I shall consider only this case.

Is pure time discounting irrational? Suppose a person discounts future rewards very heavily. Rather than getting a college education, which

---

[2] Some individuals, such as pathological misers, may attach more importance to future than to present utility. For them, the time to consume is never quite ripe.

involves a temporary sacrifice of income with a higher income later on, he takes a low-level job with few promotion possibilities immediately after high school. Because he ignores the long-term impact of smoking and high-cholesterol food, he has a short life expectancy.[3] If he does not respect the law on moral grounds, prudential considerations will not deter him from violating it. It is quite likely, in other words, that his life will be short and miserable. If this is not irrational behavior, what is?

In my view, pure time discounting, by itself, is not irrational. It may cause the agent's life to go worse than if she cared more about the future, but that may also be true of selfish motivations. Someone who only cares for herself may end up having a sad and impoverished life, but we should not for that reason say that selfishness is irrational. I discuss these questions in Chapter 11. In this chapter I focus on the proper way to conceptualize time discounting. Several approaches, which have radically different implications, are available.

To model time discounting, decision theorists traditionally assumed that people discount future utility *exponentially*. One unit of utility t periods in the future has a present value of k^t, where $k < 1$ is the per-period discount factor. Exponential discounting has the attractive factor, from a normative point of view, that it allows *consistent planning*. If one stream of rewards has a greater present value than another at one point in time, it will have a greater present value at all other points in time. Hence the agent is never subject to a preference reversal, which is usually (in the absence of reasons for changing one's mind) taken as a hallmark of irrationality.

Empirically, however, the notion of consistent planning makes less sense. Casual observation shows, and systematic observation confirms, that most of us are frequently subject to preference reversal. We often fail to carry out intentions to save, do exercises in the morning, do our piano practice, keep our appointments, and so on. I may call my dentist on March 1 to make an appointment for April 1, only to call and cancel on March 30, saying (untruthfully) that I have to go to a funeral. To account

---

[3] Fifty years ago many people might have "ignored" these consequences in the sense of being unaware of them. While this is less likely today, they may still "ignore" them in the sense of attaching less importance to them in their decisions. Not infrequently, they may also be in a state of "motivated ignorance" (a form of wishful thinking) about the consequences.

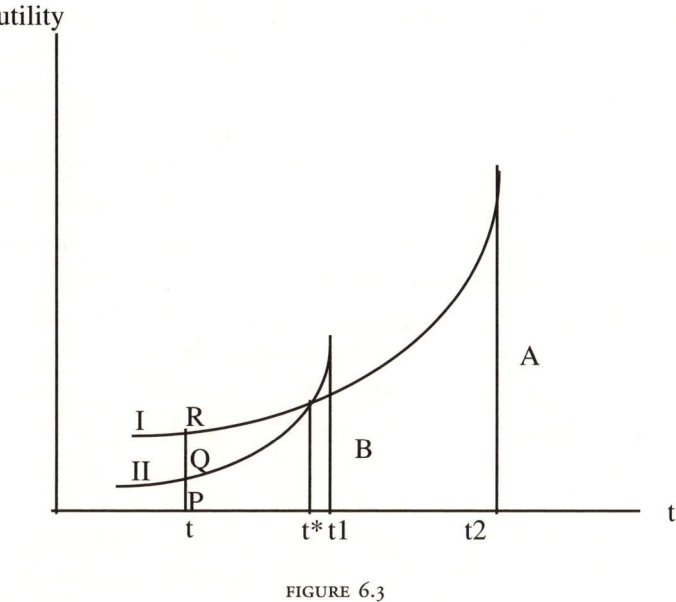

FIGURE 6.3

for these varieties of everyday irrationality (and for a large number of other phenomena) we can replace the assumption of exponential discounting with that of *hyperbolic discounting*.

Suppose that the discounted present value of 1 unit of utility t periods into the future equals $1/(1 + kt)$. (In the example below I assume $k = 1$, but in the more general case, k might be any positive number: the larger it is, the less the agent cares about the future.) Suppose, moreover, that the agent at $t = 0$ faces the choice between a reward of 10 at $t = 5$ and a reward of 30 at $t = 10$. At $t = 0$ the present value of the former is 1.67 and that of the latter is 2.73. An agent that maximizes present value will form the intention of choosing the delayed reward. At $t = 1$ the present value of the earlier reward is 2 and that of the later is 3. At $t = 2$ the values are 2.5 and 3.3; at $t = 3$ they are 3.3 and 3.75; and at $t = 4$ they are 5 and 4.29. At some time between $t = 3$ and $t = 4$, that is, the earlier reward ceases to be the least and becomes the most preferred option *as the result of nothing but the sheer passage of time*. It is easy to see, in fact, that the switch occurs at $t = 3.5$, which is when I call my dentist to cancel the appointment.

This pattern is even easier to see in a diagram. In Figure 6.3, the agent can either choose the small reward B at t1 or wait until t2 and get the larger reward A. The hyperbolic curves I and II represent the present values of these rewards as evaluated at various earlier times. They are in fact *indifference curves* (Chapter 9) that represent the trade-off between the time a reward becomes available and the size of the reward. At time t, for instance, the agent is indifferent between getting reward PQ immediately and getting the small reward at t1, and also indifferent between getting PR immediately and getting the large reward at t2. Since at time t the present value of A is larger than that of B, she will form the intention to choose A. Yet because the hyperbolic curves cross one another at t*, a preference reversal occurs at that time and she chooses B instead.[4]

Pascal's Wager

We can use Pascal's wager to illustrate the relation between exponential and hyperbolic time discounting. Pascal wanted to persuade the freethinking gamblers among his friends that they should bet on the existence of God, since even the smallest chance of eternal bliss would offset the greatest possible earthly pleasures. Pascal's argument harbors many complexities, some of which will concern us in the next chapter. Here I only want to draw attention to a question that Pascal does not mention: does the present (discounted) value of eternal bliss have a finite or an infinite value? If it is finite, the gambler might prefer to take his pleasures on earth rather than wait for the afterlife.

---

[4] There is an alternative, slightly different way of representing hyperbolic discounting. It rests on the intuitive idea that people make a radical distinction between the present and all other times, by attaching more importance to welfare in the current period than to welfare in all later periods. In addition, they differentiate *among* later periods. In a three-period example, writing u_i for experienced welfare in period i, the present value or discounted sum of utility is $u_1 + b(du_2 + d_2u_3)$. There are two discount factors involved. Compared to the present, all future utility, regardless of when it is experienced, is discounted by a factor b. In addition, all future utilities are discounted exponentially by a factor d. The present moment has a visceral salience that makes it stand out compared to all others, whereas later periods gradually lose their motivating power by something more akin to an optical illusion. This pattern, called "quasi-hyperbolic discounting," has in common with hyperbolic discounting proper that it can induce preference reversals. It differs in that the present value of an infinite stream of equal rewards (as in Pascal's wager) has a finite sum. There is some evidence from neurophysiology that quasi-hyperbolic discounting, although introduced only as a useful approximation to hyperbolic discounting, is in fact the more accurate representation.

Suppose for simplicity that each period in the afterlife provides 1 unit of experienced utility; that the person expects to die in n years from the present; and, finally, that he discounts future welfare exponentially by a factor of k ($0 < k < 1$). If God exists and grants him salvation on the basis of his faith, the present value of bliss in the first year after he dies is k^n units of utility, that of the second year k^{n+1}, and so on. As a matter of elementary algebra, this infinite sum ($k^n + k^{n+1} + k^{n+2} \dots$) adds up to a finite sum $k^n/(1-k)$. Conceivably, at least, this sum might be inferior to the present value of n years of hedonistic living on Earth. By contrast, if the agent is subject to hyperbolic discounting the infinite sum $1/(n+1) + 1/(n+2) + 1/(n+3) \dots$ increases beyond any given finite value, implying that if we compare present values any earthly pleasure will ultimately be overtaken by the bliss of salvation. Even if the latter is multiplied by a small probability (as small as you wish) that God exists, the product will still increase beyond any finite number.

Suppose, however, that Pascal's interlocutor is regularly exposed to opportunities to gamble. When considered ahead of time, he prefers to attend mass rather than gamble, because the former will ultimately make him believe and assure him an expectation of infinite bliss. By the logic of hyperbolic discounting, however, the imminence of the opportunity to gamble will induce a preference reversal. He will form the intention to gamble just one more time and then start going to mass. With St. Augustine, he will say, "Give me chastity and continence, but not yet." Next week, the same reasoning will apply. Thus the very structure of time discounting that ensures that eternal bliss has the greater present value will also prevent the gambler from taking the steps to achieve it.

Weakness of Will

As this example shows, hyperbolic discounting may illuminate the classical problem of weakness of will (WW). A weak-willed (or *akratic*) person is characterized as follows:

1. The person has a reason for doing X.
2. The person has a reason for doing Y.

3. In the person's own judgment, the reason for doing X is weightier than the reason for doing Y.
4. The person does Y.

Emotions, in particular, are often held to have the capacity for inducing action against the better judgment of the agent. When Medea in Euripides' play is about to kill her children, she says, "I know indeed what evil I intend to do. But stronger than all my after thoughts is my fury." In Ovid's version of the play, she says, "An unknown compulsion bears me, all reluctant down. Urged this way or that . . . I see the better and approve it, but I follow the worse."

These utterances, like the four statements used to characterize weakness of will, are all ambiguous or underspecified in that there is no mention of *when* they are supposed to be true. Let us define a *strict conception of weakness of will* as follows:

1. The person has a reason for doing X.
2. The person has a reason for doing Y.
3. The person does Y, judging *at the moment of action* that the reason for doing X is weightier than the reason for doing Y.

Imagine a person who has resolved to quit smoking and goes to a party where she is offered a cigarette. She accepts the offer, knowing as she does so that she should not. A person on a diet may accept an offering of dessert knowing as he does so that it is not a good idea. Although there is nothing impossible about this conception of weakness of will, it runs into two empirical problems. It would be hard to establish that the action and the "better judgment" coexisted at the very same moment, rather than that the judgment changed a split second before the action. Also, nobody to my knowledge has specified the causal mechanism by which the desire to do Y acquires greater causal efficacy than the desire to do X.

To bypass these problems we may define a *broad conception of weakness of will*, which allows the agent's judgment that he should do X and the choice of Y to occur at different moments:

1. The person has a reason for doing X.
2. The person has a reason for doing Y.

3. In the person's own calm and reflective judgment, the reason for doing X is weightier than the reason for doing Y.
4. The person does Y.

Socrates denied that WW in the strict sense was possible. Aristotle, too, came close to suggesting the same thing. He allowed for WW in the broad sense, citing as an example a person whose judgment at the time of action is under the influence of alcohol. Suppose I go to the office party, have too many drinks, offend my boss, and make amorous advances to his wife. At the time, these actions seem the perfectly natural thing to do. Yet ahead of time, had anyone suggested I might act in this way, I would have rejected it as inconsistent with my calm, reflective judgment. If I had been persuaded that my judgment might be dissolved in alcohol, I would have stayed away. After the fact, I might bitterly regret my behavior.

This case, shown in Figure 6.4, is a case of *temporary preference reversal*, not of WW in the strict sense. There are at least three mechanisms that may bring about such changes. One is *temporal proximity*, as explained in the discussion of hyperbolic discounting. Another is *spatial proximity*, as illustrated by the phenomenon of cue dependence. This mechanism explains, for instance, many cases of relapse among addicts. Even after years of abstinence, an environmental cue traditionally associated with drug use may trigger relapse. Merely seeing drug paraphernalia on TV may be sufficient. The resolve to go on a diet may be undermined by the sight of the dessert trolley coming around. In these cases, too, the agent chooses according to her conception *at the moment of choice* of what she most prefers, all things considered. Finally, *passions* are capable of inducing temporary preference change, by virtue of the fact that they usually have a short half-life (Chapter 8). They may

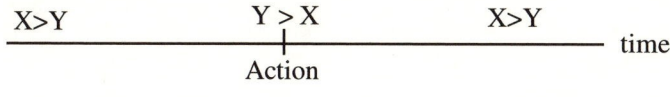

FIGURE 6.4

also induce preference reversal by causing the agent to pay less attention to the remote future.[5]

We may extend this idea to include temporary (and motivated) changes in the agent's *beliefs*. On this very broad conception, weakness of will can also result from self-deception (or wishful thinking). Having decided ahead of a party to have only two drinks in order to be able drive home safely, a person might, under the influence of his desire for a third drink, tell himself, against the weight of the evidence, that it will not make a difference to his driving skills.[6] His preference (for safe driving) remains unchanged, but his belief about the conditions under which he can drive safely has changed. He might also, of course, undergo a temporary preference change, if he decides that having a good time at the party is so important that it offsets the risks (which he may perceive accurately) of drunk driving.

❮❮❮

Bibliographical Note

For evidence that primates may be able to plan for future (not currently experienced) needs, see N. Mulcahy and J. Call, "Apes save tools for future use," *Science* 312 (2006), 1038–40. Two source books on time discounting and other aspects of intertemporal choice are G. Loewenstein and J. Elster (eds.), *Choice over Time* (New York: Russell Sage Foundation, 1992),

[5] In fact, the preference reversal caused by hyperbolic time preferences may be mimicked by emotionally induced changes in the discounting factor associated with exponential time preferences. Suppose the agent faces the choice between two options, A and B, which offer the respective rewards (2, 5, 6) and (5, 4, 1) in three successive periods. With a one-period discounting rate of 0.8 (and a two-period rate of 0.64), the present values of the two options (as assessed in the first period) are respectively, 9.84 and 8.84. With a one-period discounting rate of 0.6 (and a two-period rate of 0.36), the values are 7.16 and 7.96. Not surprisingly, the agent ceases to prefer the option with the better long-term consequences when emotions cause him to pay less attention to the future.

[6] By contrast, if he is concerned with being stopped by the police rather than with having an accident, it is harder to make himself believe that the third drink will not cause the blood alcohol content to go beyond the legal limit. As I argue in the next chapter, even wishful thinking is (somewhat) subject to reality constraints.

and G. Loewenstein, D. Read, and R. Baumeister (eds.), *Time and Decision* (New York: Russell Sage Foundation, 2003). I discuss Pascal's wager at greater length in "Pascal and decision theory," in N. Hammond (ed.), *The Cambridge Companion to Pascal* (Cambridge University Press, 2004). The neurophysiological evidence for quasi-hyperbolic time discounting is in S. McClure et al., "Separate neural systems evaluate immediate and delayed monetary rewards," *Science* 306 (2004), 503–7. Modern discussions of weakness of will take off from D. Davidson, "How is weakness of the will possible?" in his *Essays on Action and Events* (Oxford University Press, 1980). I comment on his ideas in "Davidson on weakness of will and self-deception," in L. Hahn (ed.), *The Philosophy of Donald Davidson* (Chicago: Open Court, 1999). Motivated belief formation is discussed in D. Pears, *Motivated Irrationality* (Oxford University Press, 1984). I discuss the link between weakness of will and preference reversal at greater length in "Weakness of will and preference reversal," in J. Elster et al. (eds.), *Understanding Choice, Explaining Behavior: Essays in Honour of Ole-Jørgen Skog* (Oslo Academic Press, 2006).

Chapter 7
BELIEFS

❧ ❧ ❧

What Is It to "Believe" Something?

To understand the role of beliefs in generating action, we have to understand their nature, their causes, and their consequences. As I mentioned in the introductory remarks to Part II, it is not always clear what it means to "believe" that something is the case, for example, that there is a life after death. Many of the great religious figures have written about their constant struggle with doubt. In their believing moments, was their faith as simple and unconditional as that of someone who has never known doubt? Did the followers of Communism who "believed" that the party can do no wrong really *believe* it?[1] How can we tell the difference between the congenital pessimist who tends to believe the worst and the prudent decision maker who merely acts *as if* the worst-case scenario were true?

Also, in everyday language "belief" suggests less than full endorsement. I *believe* it will rain tomorrow, but I also know I might be wrong. I do not merely believe that I am married; I *know* it. In philosophical analyses, knowledge is usually defined as justified true belief, a belief that stands in a particular relation both to the world (it is true) and to the body of evidence the agent possesses (it is justified). Yet neither of these features of knowledge captures the subjective certainty that often underlies the phrase "I know" in ordinary discourse. This certainty is not simply the limit of 97% probability, 98%, 99%, 99.9%, and so forth. It is qualitatively different from anything short of certainty.[2]

---

[1] After the fall of Communism, a woman from the former East Germany said at a public meeting that her generation had been raised from childhood on to conform, to stay in line. A long-term schizophrenia had *hollowed them out* as people. So, this woman said, now she could not just suddenly "speak openly" or "say what she thought." She did not even really know precisely what she thought.

[2] Matters are a bit more complicated. When people are confronted with very high numerical probabilities, such as 99.9 percent, two different mechanisms (in the sense of Chapter 2) may be triggered: the difference between uncertainty and high probability is either neglected or exaggerated. (Similarly, very low probabilities are either neglected or exaggerated.) This complication does not arise, however, in the example of the certainty effect given in the text.

This "certainty effect" shows up in the following experiment. One group of subjects was asked to express their preferences over various options. (Numbers in parentheses indicate the proportion of subjects preferring a given option.)

> A 50% chance to win a three-week tour of England, France, and Italy (22%).
> A one-week tour of England, with certainty (78%).

Another group was given the following options:

> A 5% chance to win a three-week tour of England, France, and Italy (67%).
> A 10% chance to win a one-week tour of England (33%).

Members of the first group tend to prefer the "England only" option because it is available *for sure*. Once it is deflated by the same probability as the alternative, the latter looks more attractive. Soldiers who are asked whether they will volunteer for highly dangerous missions may have disproportionately fewer hesitations than those who are asked to volunteer for suicide missions. The former may also, of course, be subject to wishful thinking ("It won't happen to me"), which has no purchase on the latter.

Four Cognitive Attitudes

Even setting aside these problems, the idea of belief remains ambiguous. We may distinguish among four cognitive attitudes to the world, with decreasing strength. First is the mode of *certainty*. Second is the mode of *risk*, in which agents assign probabilities, whether based on past frequencies or their own judgment, to each of a set of mutually exclusive and jointly exhaustive outcomes. Third is the mode of *uncertainty*, in which people know the set of mutually exclusive and jointly exhaustive outcomes but find themselves unable to attach any (cardinal) probabilities to them.[3] Finally is the mode of *ignorance*, in which both the

---

[3] They may be able to assign ordinal probabilities, that is, to say that one outcome is more likely to occur than another, without being able to say how much more likely.

range of possible outcomes and their probability of occurrence are unknown or incompletely known. In the memorable words of former Defense Secretary Donald Rumsfeld, we are facing not only known and unknown quantities, but also "unknown unknowns."[4]

I focus on certainty and risk, not because these are always the appropriate cognitive attitudes, but because they are the most common ones. Even when people have no grounds for having *any* belief on a given topic, they often feel irresistibly compelled to form an opinion – not a specific opinion (as in wishful thinking), but *some opinion or other*. This propensity is to some extent determined by cultural factors. Albert Hirschman has said that most Latin American cultures "place considerable value on having *strong opinions* on virtually *everything* from the *outset*." In such societies, to admit ignorance is to admit defeat. But the tendency is really universal. Montaigne said that "many of this world's abuses are engendered – or to put it more rashly, all of this world's abuses are engendered – by our being schooled to be afraid to admit our ignorance and because we are required to accept anything which we cannot refute." The intolerance of uncertainty and ignorance flows not only from pridefulness, but from a universal human desire to find meanings and patterns everywhere. The mind abhors a vacuum.

A particular version of the tendency to find meaning in the universe is to impute *agency* to events that might as plausibly or more plausibly be due to chance. Under the old regime in France, the population could never accept that nature only was responsible for its misery. In a dearth of grain the general assumption was that hoarders had been driving the price up even if the actual cause was a bad harvest. Sometimes, the lack of grain was even explained in terms of the desire of the elites to starve the people, as part of ongoing class warefare. According to article 22 of the Hamas Charter, Jews were "behind the French Revolution, the Communist revolution and most of the revolutions we heard and hear about, here and there. With their money they formed secret societies, such as Freemasons, Rotary Clubs, the Lions and others in different parts of the

---

[4] More complex cases are also possible. I might be able to assign probabilities to some outcomes, while being unable even to specify others.

world for the purpose of sabotaging societies and achieving Zionist interests. With their money they were able to control imperialistic countries and instigate them to colonize many countries in order to enable them to exploit their resources and spread corruption there." This conspiratorial or paranoid cast of mind is largely immune to refutation, since believers in a conspiracy theory will find it *confirmed* by lack of evidence or even by contrary evidence, which they interpret as signs of the devilishly clever nature of the conspirators.

These error-generating mechanisms rely in one way or another on *motivation*. Yet error can also arise from *ignorance*. The point seems obvious but is actually a bit subtle. Darwin noted, for instance, that "ignorance more frequently begets confidence than does knowledge." Ignorance together with confidence is a good recipe for error. Conversely, when the circle of light expands, so does the surrounding area of darkness, inducing greater humility. Experiments suggest in fact that incompetence not only causes poor cognitive performance, but also the inability to recognize that one's competence is poor. The incompetent are doubly handicapped.

Yet there is another possibility, namely, that "the dangerous thing" is "a *little* knowledge" rather than ignorance. Montaigne wrote that "there is an infant-school ignorance which precedes knowledge and another doctoral ignorance which comes after it"; Pascal said the same thing at greater length. With the acquisition of more information, one becomes first more confident but ultimately less. I conjecture that the Montaigne-Pascal hypothesis is more valid than Darwin's. It is not our increased *level* of knowledge but our *increased* level that causes the mind to leap ahead of itself and generate more confidence than the data warrant.

Subjective Assessments of Probability

Probability judgments can stem from observation of objective frequencies or be purely subjective evaluations.[5] When the agent can draw

---

[5] In a deeper analysis, the first (objective) method boils down to the second (subjective) one, since to be useful objective data always need a subjective interpretation. For many practical purposes, though, the distinction is clear and useful.

on a large number of observations of similar situations, the frequentist method can yield good results. If I plan to have a picnic on my birthday next month and need to form an opinion about the likely weather, the best I can do is probably to look up the weather statistics for the same day in previous years. But if I need to form an opinion about the weather tomorrow, the best single predictor is today's weather. It is not, however, the only predictor. Past records can tell me whether sunny weather on that day is a rare or normal event. If it is rare, today's sunny weather loses some of its predictive value. I may consult the barometer on my wall to see whether the air pressure is rising or falling or look at the evening sky, the flight of the swallows, and so on.

To integrate all this information into an overall probability judgment about tomorrow's weather is a difficult task. Most of us are not very good at it. Often, the problem is not lack of information, but an abundance of it, combined with the lack of a formal procedure for integrating it into an all-things-considered opinion. Some people, though, are better than most of us at integrating vast and diffuse information with varying degrees of relevance into an overall assessment. They possess the elusive but crucial quality of *judgment*. Successful generals, businesspeople, and politicians tend to have it – that is why they succeed. A good central banker needs to have it, but most economists do not.[6] The best the rest of us can do is to recognize that we do not have it and learn not to trust our intuition. I may learn, for instance, that I often distrust people for reasons that, when I come to understand them, are irrelevant. ("He looked like a bully I knew in fifth grade.") Hence I may come to distrust my distrust.[7]

We tend to think, however, that judgment is possessed not only by successful generals, politicians, and businesspeople, but also by trained

---

[6] Writing about Alan Greenspan (*New York Times*, October 28, 2005), Paul Krugman noted that while distrusting formal models he had "the ability to divine from fragmentary and sometimes contradictory data which way the economic wind was blowing."

[7] Knowing that one may be subject to bias is one thing; being able to correct it is another. Studies show that deliberate attempts to debias one's judgment are of little value, since one easily falls into the traps of insufficient correction, unnecessary correction, or overcorrection. One may learn to distrust one's judgment, but it is harder to improve it. If one were able to, there might be no need to.

experts. In complicated matters of diagnosis or prognosis, such as identifying psychotic individuals or assessing how likely it is that a person who requests early release from prison will commit a second offense, we trust the expert. Because of their experience, experts are sensitive to telltale signs that untrained observers might ignore or whose significance they might not understand. Moreover, when different pieces of evidence point in different directions, experts can draw on their experience to decide which, in any given case, should be given most weight. This at least is how we think about experts. As most of us consider ourselves experts in some domain or other, if nothing else in predicting the behavior of our boss, spouse, or children, we have a great deal invested in this image of the superior cognitive skills of the expert.

Unfortunately, *this image is thoroughly false*. In many studies the diagnostic or prognostic performance of experts has been compared with the performance of a simple mechanical formula based on a few variables. Essentially, this amounts to comparing objective (frequentist) methods and subjective ones. The weights assigned to the variables are derived by statistical techniques that assign the weights most likely to predict observed outcomes. Almost without exception, the formula performs at least as well as the expert and usually better.[8] In a study of the diagnosis of progressive brain dysfunctioning based on intellectual testing, to cite only one example, a formula derived from one set of cases and then applied to a new sample correctly identified 83 percent of the new cases. Groups of experienced and inexperienced clinicians correctly identified 63 percent and 58 percent, respectively. Moreover, experts often disagree strongly with one another. In another study, highly experienced psychiatrists who viewed the same psychiatric interview could not agree on the patient's diagnosis, motivations, or feelings. Some psychotherapists use responses to ambiguous inkblots as cues to diagnoses. It appears, however, that the patients are as ambiguous to them as the inkblots to the patients.

---

[8] This superiority remains even if we simply assign equal weights to all variables!

Some Errors of Statistical Inference

Experts no less than laypersons often go wrong because they ignore obvious or not-so-obvious principles of statistical reasoning. In one study, subjects were given a description of a young man with long hair and a habit of reading poetry and asked whether they thought it more likely that he was an orchestra violinist or a truck driver. Most said he was more likely to be a violinist, thus ignoring the *base rate* of the two groups, that is, the absolute number of individuals in each. There are so many more truck drivers than orchestra violinists in the nation (and so much variation among truck drivers) that the poetic young man is in fact more likely to drive a truck.

Another source of mistakes in belief formation is *selection bias*. Patients in dialysis centers are often surprisingly reluctant to be on the waiting list for a kidney transplantation. One reason is that all the transplanted patients they ever see are those for whom the operation failed so that they had to go back on dialysis. Montaigne was citing a bias of this kind when he referred to Diagoras as being "shown many vows and votive portraits from those who have survived shipwrecks and . . . then asked, 'You, there, who think that the gods are indifferent to human affairs, what have you to say about so many men saved by their grace?' – 'It is like this,' he replied, 'there are no portraits here of those who stayed and drowned – and they are more numerous!' " Similarly, a psychiatrist who claims that "no child abusers ever stop on their own" neglects the fact that if any does he is unlikely to have met them.

Israeli air force leaders made a less obvious mistake when assessing the relative efficacy of reward and punishment in the training of pilots. Noting that the performance of pilots improved when they were punished for a bad performance but not when they were rewarded for a good one, they concluded that punishment was more efficient. In doing so, they ignored the phenomenon known as *regression to the mean*. In any series of events that are fully or partly determined by chance, there is a tendency for an extreme value on one occasion to be followed by a less extreme value on the next. Tall fathers get sons who are shorter than they, and bad pilot performances are followed by less bad ones, independently of reward and punishment. When athletes who have done exceptionally well in one season do less well the next, fans and coaches often say they have been spoiled by success, when what we observe may only be regression to the mean.

The gambler's fallacy and its (nameless) converse offer another example. The purchase of earthquake insurance increases sharply after an earthquake but then falls steadily as memory fades. As do gamblers who make the mistake of believing that red is more likely to come up again if it has come up several times in a row, the purchasers form their beliefs by using the *availability heuristic*. Their judgment about the likelihood of an event is shaped by the ease with which it can be brought to mind, and recent events are more readily available than earlier ones. The decay of emotion over time (Chapter 8) might also be a factor. Conversely, people living in areas that are subject to frequent floods often believe that a flood is less likely to occur in year n + 1 if one has occurred in year n. As do gamblers who make the mistake of believing that red is less likely to come up again if it has come up several times in a row, they form their beliefs by relying on the *representativeness heuristic*. They believe, or act as if they believe, that a short sequence of events is likely to be representative of a longer sequence in which it is embedded.

People often fail to grasp the relation between random processes and the distribution of outcomes. During the Second World War, many Londoners were certain that the Germans systematically concentrated their bombing in certain parts of their city, because the bombs fell in clusters. They did not understand the basic statistical principle that random processes tend to generate clustering, and that bombs falling in a neat gridlock pattern would have been stronger evidence of deliberate target selection. A fact that never fails to surprise those who have not come across it before is that in a group of as few as twenty-three people, the probability that two of them have the same birthday (day and month) is more than 50 percent.

Magical Thinking

Consider next various forms of *magical thinking*, that is, the tendency to believe one can exercise a causal influence on outcomes that are actually outside one's control. People will, for instance, place larger bets on a coin that has not yet been tossed than on a coin that has already been tossed and for which the outcome has been concealed. In Proust, the Narrator's friend Robert Saint-Loup was subject to "a sort of superstitious belief: that the fidelity of his mistress to him might depend on his to her." Also, people may fail to grasp the distinction between *causal and diagnostic relevance.* In one experiment, subjects who were led to believe that the length of time they could hold their arms in painfully cold water was the best indicator of longevity held their arms in the water longer than those not given this (false) information.[9] Also, using their own behavior as a predictor of how others will act, people may choose the cooperative strategy in a Prisoner's Dilemma as if they could somehow bring it about that others cooperate too. In one experiment, cooperating subjects who were asked to predict the choice of their interaction partner as well as that of a nonpartner who was matched with another person were more likely to predict (and had greater confidence in their prediction) cooperation by their interaction partner than the nonpartner.[10]

Calvinism offers an example of this kind of magical thinking (Chapter 3). Given the Calvinist belief in predestination, there would seem to be no reason for a Calvinist not to indulge in all sorts of worldly pleasures, which by assumption cannot affect their fate after death. Max Weber claimed that Calvinism nevertheless made its followers adopt an ascetic lifestyle, not to gain salvation but to acquire the subjective certainty of being among the elect. We may read him as saying that the Calvinists confused the causal and diagnostic relevance of their behavior. This is made quite explicit in a letter circulated by English Baptists in 1770: "Every soul that comes to Christ to be saved . . . is to be encouraged. . . . The coming soul need not fear that he

---

[9] This distinction between cause and symptom is not always evident. As late as 1959, the great statistician R. A. Fisher, assuming a genetic trait that predisposed the individual both to smoking and to cancer, argued that smoking was diagnostic of lung cancer rather than its cause. (It is true that he was in the pay of tobacco companies at the time.) Or consider the finding, discussed in Chapter 2, that the longer an individual has been out of work the less likely it is that he will find a job in a given time span. The duration of unemployment might be simply diagnostic of employability, or it could make a causal contribution (through demoralization, etc.) to the chances of finding employment.

[10] This discrepancy allows us to exclude that the imputation of cooperative behavior to the interaction partner could have been due merely to the "false consensus effect" (Chapter 23).

is not elected, for none but such would be willing to come." If God has chosen me to be among the elect, he will also *cause me to will* certain kinds of behavior.

These errors (and many others that have been extensively documented) are for the most part "cold" or unmotivated mistakes, similar in some respects to optical illusions. Other errors, or "hot" mistakes, arise because the beliefs of the agents are *motivated*, that is, unduly influenced by their desires. As we shall see in Chapter 11, a causal influence of desires on beliefs is not intrinsically irrational. A desire can provide a reason for investing a specific amount of resources in information acquisition. The information thus obtained may serve as a reason for holding a certain belief. Although the desire does not provide a reason for holding the belief, it enters into a rational complex of belief formation. What drives in the wedge between the initial desire and the final belief is the fact that the outcome of the search for information is, by definition, not known at the time the decision to search is made.

Motivated Belief Formation

The influence of desires on beliefs I just cited is, uncontroversially, consistent with rationality. A more controversial idea was provided by Pascal's wager. As I explained in the last chapter, Pascal argued that an agent who believes that there is a nonzero probability, however small, that God exists, should for the purely instrumental reason of maximizing expected value try to acquire a firm belief (in the mode of certainty) that God exists because, if he does exist, that belief will ensure eternal bliss. The premises for the argument are (1) that certain belief is certain to provide salvation and (2) that the instrumental origin of the belief does not detract from its efficacy for salvation. Although both premises may be dubious from a theological point of view, this need not concern us here. The question is whether this "decision to believe" is a rational project. In one sense it is not: I cannot decide to believe at will the way I can decide to raise my arm at will. One might, however, use an indirect strategy. By acting *as if* one believed, Pascal argued, one will end up believing. The mechanism by which this might happen is, however, somewhat unfathomable.[11]

There are other cases in which one might want to acquire a belief one believes to be false, because of the good consequences of holding it. If I want to cut down on my drinking but find myself insufficiently motivated by the risk of becoming an alcoholic, I may desire to believe that the risk is larger than I now believe it to be. By and large, however, there is no reliable technology for acquiring such beliefs. Unless the process has a *self-erasing component*, by which the origin of the belief in the desire to acquire it is eliminated from the conscious mind, the desire is likely to remain a mere wish.

In the "uncontroversial" case, the agent's desire induces a certain level of information gathering that will in turn induce some belief or other. In the "controversial case" the desire induces specific behavior that will in turn induce a specific belief the agent wants to hold. Both are indirect strategies. I now turn to beliefs that are *directly* shaped by motivation. This can come about in one of two ways, corresponding to two basic features of motivations: arousal and content. Just as we say that the stone broke the ice by virtue of its weight, not of its color, we may say that a motivation affects belief not by virtue of its content, but by virtue of the accompanying arousal level. Moderate physiological arousal can improve the quality of belief formation, by focusing attention and stimulating the imagination. "When a man knows he is to be hanged in a fortnight," Dr. Johnson said, "it concentrates his mind wonderfully." Beyond a certain level of arousal, however, cognition deteriorates. In states of extreme hunger, stress, fear, or addictive craving, it is hard to think straight because the arousal makes it difficult to keep previous reasoning steps in mind. Presumably, mental concentration is blunted when the hanging is but one day away. In scholastic aptitude tests a very strong motivation to get it right may actually cause one to get it wrong, just as a shooter's strong desire to hit the target may cause her hands to shake so that she misses.[12] In

---

[11] For reasons explained later, dissonance reduction is not a plausible mechanism.

[12] And it does not help to tell oneself, or be told, to relax, since the state of being relaxed, like the state of sleep, is essentially a by-product.

the next chapter I argue that because of the urgency of many emotions, they may cause the agent to bypass the normal machinery of rational belief formation. Thus beliefs may be *shaped by motivation* yet not be *motivated*, because the agent has no particular desire to believe they are true. Arousal *clouds* the mind but does not *bias* it in favor of any particular belief.

Rationalization

Content-generated beliefs are of two main varieties. As I noted earlier, the agent may be motivated to hold *some belief or other* on a given topic, because of a need for closure or an intolerance of admitting ignorance. Alternatively, he may be motivated to hold some *specific* belief, such as the belief that his spouse is being faithful to him.[13] The most important mechanisms generating this variety are rationalization, wishful thinking, and self-deception. The difference between the first and the last two lies in the relation to behavior. In rationalization, the behavior occurs first and the belief follows. (This not to say that the beliefs, once adopted, may not induce further behavior.) In wishful thinking and self-deception, we observe the opposite sequence.

As an example of rationalization, consider a standard "cognitive dissonance" experiment. Two groups of subjects are asked to write an essay offering arguments for the position on the pro-life versus pro-choice issue that they do *not* favor. The subjects in one group are paid a considerable sum of money for participating, whereas the others are asked to do so as a favor to the experimenter. After writing the essay, those in the second group but not those in the first display a more favorable attitude toward the position they have been arguing for. The explanation, plausibly, is that all the subjects desire to have a *reason* for what they are doing. Members of the first group can simply cite the money as their reason.[14]

---

[13] Or, as in the case of Othello, unfaithful. Such "countermotivated beliefs" were briefly mentioned in Chapter 2 and are further discussed in Chapter 23.

[14] Punishment for *not* participating would also be a sufficient reason. This explains why citizens under Communism might consistently have a system of double bookkeeping without their inner rejections being undermined by their overt enthusiasm.

Members of the second group can cite their (adjusted) beliefs as the reason why they argue the way they do.[15]

A French proverb says, "Who has offended, cannot forgive." If I have unjustly harmed another person, I may be unable to admit to myself that I am at fault. Instead, I will seek out a fault in the other person that justifies or at least excuses my behavior. Rapists will say, "She dressed provocatively," an excuse that is sometimes endorsed by the courts. Those who engage in anti-Semitic violence will come up with a story that since Jews owe their success to immoral or illegal means, they deserve to be punished. That the behavior induces the beliefs rather than the other way around is clear from the amazing flexibility of rationalization. As noted in Chapter 3, the rhetoric of anti-Semitism includes the characterization of Jews as subhuman "vermin" as well as claims about Jewish omnipotence in history.

Wishful Thinking

Let me turn to wishful thinking and self-deception. These two ill-understood phenomena have in common that a desire that p be the case causes the belief that p is the case. In wishful thinking this is a simple one-step process: the wish is the father of the thought. The evidence is not so much denied as ignored. As a result, the wishfully formed belief might happen to be the very same one that would be justified by the evidence, had it been consulted.[16] Self-deception as usually

---

[15] In Pascal's wager, the reason for acting as if one believed is so overwhelmingly strong – the prospect of eternal bliss – that the believer need not look for another explanation of his behavior.

[16] Ignoring this point could be a source of irrational belief formation. Because it is often easy to detect the operation of motivated belief formation in others, we tend to disbelieve the conclusions reached in this way, without pausing to see whether the evidence might in fact justify them. Until around 1990 I believed, with most of my friends, that on a scale of evil from 0 to 10 (the worst), Communism scored around 7 or 8. Since the recent revelations I believe that 10 is the appropriate number. The reason for my misperception of the evidence was not an idealistic belief that Communism was a worthy ideal that had been betrayed by actual Communists. In that case, I would simply have been victim of wishful thinking or self-deception. Rather, I was misled by the hysterical character of those who claimed all along that Communism scored 10. My ignorance of their claims was not entirely irrational. On average, it makes sense to discount the claims of the manifestly hysterical. Yet even hysterics can be right, albeit for the wrong reasons. Because I sensed and still believe that many of these fierce anti-Communists would have said the same regardless of the evidence, I could not believe that what they said did in fact correspond to the evidence. I made

conceived involves four steps: first, the evidence is considered; second, the appropriate belief is formed; third, this belief is rejected or suppressed because it is inconsistent with our desire; and last, the desire causes another and more acceptable belief to be formed in its place. Self-deception is a paradoxical phenomenon, whose existence and even possibility have been called into doubt, so let me begin with the simpler issue of wishful thinking.

Before suggesting a mechanism by which wishful thinking is brought about, let me first state that, unlike what is the case for self-deception, it is impossible to deny its existence. One may deny that it occurs in high-stake situations or that it affects aggregate behavior such as stock markets or elections, but not that it occurs. If nothing else, world literature would testify to its existence. Moreover, many wishfully formed beliefs serve as premises for *action*, and hence are more than mere "quasi-beliefs." Some smokers who fool themselves into believing that smoking is not dangerous, in general or for them specifically, would have quit or tried to quit had they held more rational beliefs.[17] Overconfident individuals, who wishfully believe they are more capable than they really are, may embark on ventures they would otherwise have avoided. People who fool themselves into thinking they are as successful as others may lose a spur to improve themselves. A common mechanism is the following. First, a person is motivated to believe he is successful. Second, he finds some areas in his life in which he does in fact do well. Third, he enhances the importance of those areas to be able to tell himself that he is successful overall. Finally, he relaxes his efforts to succeed in other walks of life.

To navigate in life, it is instrumentally useful to have accurate beliefs. At the same time, beliefs may be intrinsically pleasant or unpleasant, that is, cause positive or negative emotions. If told that I have cancer, I can seek treatment, but the belief will also make me feel horrible. In Freud's language, those governed by the reality principle seek accurate beliefs, whereas those subject to the pleasure principle seek pleasant beliefs. This

---

the mistake of thinking of them as a clock that is always one hour late rather than as a broken clock that shows the right time twice a day.

[17] As in the case of alcohol, quitting might require the irrational belief that smoking is *more* dangerous than it actually is.

distinction applies only to beliefs in the strict sense, not to quasi-beliefs. People who form unrealistic beliefs about receiving a big monetary prize for their achievements yet do not spend the prize money before they have received it are at worst subject to a harmless form of the pleasure principle. In the more noxious variety, their conviction that they will receive the prize actually causes them to go into debt.

Belief formation can also have costs. If beliefs are formed because of their intrinsic benefits, the cost is that I forgo instrumental benefits. This cost depends both on the outcome that will occur if the motivated belief is false, compared to what would happen if it is true, and on the probability that it is false. I shall refer to these as the *outcome component* and the *probability component* of the costs. Conversely, beliefs that are formed to provide instrumental benefits may have the cost that I forgo intrinsic ones. I shall discuss cases in which rational belief formation has short-term intrinsic costs and long-term instrumental benefits, while the motivated belief has short-term intrinsic benefits and long-term instrumental costs. In doing so, I shall contrast the explanations of motivated belief formation proposed by economists and psychologists to argue that we need to build on both.

Economists focus on *costs*. Some have argued, for instance, that workers form motivated beliefs about job safety according to whether the benefit of holding the belief exceeds the cost. If the psychological benefit of suppressing one's fear of a particular activity exceeds the cost due to increased chances of accident, the worker will believe the activity to be safe. The implication is that the agent unconsciously scrutinizes the evidence to see whether she can afford to adopt the promotivated belief. It is assumed, furthermore, that there are no constraints on belief formation: the worker can believe whatever she chooses irrespective of the information available to her. I think this is the wrong model, not only because it has no place for constraints but also because costs enter in the wrong way. The benefits of motivated beliefs occur now and the possible costs later. For the argument to go through, we have to assume that the unconscious mind is capable of making such intertemporal trade-offs. As I argued in the introduction to this Part, there is no evidence for this idea.

A more plausible idea, in my opinion, is that wishful thinking is triggered *by the known outcome component of the costs*. When there is little at stake, the agent may form a belief without considering the probability component of the costs, that is, without considering the evidence. There is no trade-off, but a two-step process. First, the agent considers the stakes. If they are low, he adopts the more pleasant belief. If they are high, he considers the evidence and, if necessary, gathers more of it. What it means that the stakes are "low" will, of course, vary across individuals. All one can say is that for a given individual and other things being equal, wishful thinking is more likely when the stakes are low.

Psychologists focus on *constraints*. An agent who begins smoking may be tempted to form the wishful belief that smoking is not dangerous, or at least not dangerous for her. In doing so, however, she may be constrained by her prior beliefs about the dangers of smoking. The first time a person does badly on an exam, he may tell himself a story about bad luck, but if the same outcome occurs on the next four occasions the story is less likely to work if he fails for a sixth time. Or consider the example of the expensive Broadway show tickets that I introduced in Chapter 1. If I have paid seventy-five dollars for the ticket but the show is lousy, my recollection of what I paid is likely to be too vivid to be subject to wishful downward revision. Given the intangible and multidimensional nature of aesthetic appreciation, it is easier to adjust my evaluation of the show upward. Similarly, although there is evidence both that likely events are seen as more desirable and that desirable events are perceived as more likely, the latter effect is more heavily constrained than the former.

In an instructive experiment, subjects expected to participate in a history trivia game with a given person either as their partner or as their opponent. After exposure to a sample of the person's performance, in which he got a perfect score, those who expected the person to be their partner (and therefore wished him to have high ability) judged him as better at history than those who expected him to be their opponent (and who therefore wished him to have low ability). At the same time, subjects were clearly constrained by the nature of the information they received, since even subjects expecting him to be their opponent judged him as better than average. A limitation of the experiment is that it did not offer the subjects an opportunity to *act* on these beliefs, with the potentially costly consequences that might follow from underestimating an opponent. For all we know, they might be mere quasi-beliefs.

In the examples just given, wishful thinking is constrained by prior factual beliefs. In other cases, it may be constrained by plausible causal beliefs. Wishful thinking often involves "telling oneself a story," the idea of a story being closely related to the idea of a mechanism that I discussed in Chapter 2. The plethora of mechanisms makes it easier to find some story or other that will justify any belief one might want to be true. I may dismiss an unwelcome rumor with the proverb "Rumors often lie" and embrace a welcome one by the proverb "Rumors rarely lie." Or suppose I read in the application material for a school of social work that emotional stability is highly desirable for people in that profession. If my mother left the workforce to take care of me when I was born, I may bolster my belief in my stability by telling myself a story that children benefit from the full-time attention of their parents. If she kept her job and sent me to day care, I may instead adopt a story that children benefit from being with other children and from having parents who have professional fulfillment outside the home.[18] If my favorite soccer team does badly, I can maintain my belief in its superiority if the other team won by (what can be construed as) a fluke event. "If the ball hadn't been deflected by the referee, the wing player would have received the pass in a position to score." If my horse finishes second, I can maintain my belief in my betting skills by saying that it "almost won." In an even more blatantly irrational piece of wishful thinking, if I put money on 32 and 33 comes up, I can also say that I "almost won" even if the two numbers are far from each other in the roulette wheel.[19]

Sometimes, however, there is no readily available and plausible story. Suppose a person places his money on 24. The number that did come out was 15, which is adjacent to 24 on the number wheel; hence his belief in his gambling skills is confirmed. Probably he would have considered

---

[18] As a matter of fact, no consistent differences are found in the later development of children brought up in these two environments.

[19] At the same time, people may be more disappointed if their number is close to the winning number. Some national lotteries offer small "consolation prizes" to those who "almost won."

other outcomes, such as 5, 10, and 33, also confirmations, because they are nearby on the wheel. Also he could have taken the outcomes 22, 23, 25, and 26 as confirmations because their numerical value is closer, or the numbers 20, 21, 26, and 27 because they are adjacent on the table. Thus 13 out of 37 possible outcomes could be taken as confirmations of his betting ability. But that also means that there are 24 outcomes for which no simple story is available. If one of these occurs, even a person prone to wishful thinking and highly motivated to adopt a specific belief might have to face the facts.

Self-Deception

Consider now the thorny issue of self-deception. In everyday life people appear to deceive themselves about such things as their weight, their health, their drinking habits, their tendency to procrastinate, or the faithfulness of their spouses. In one typical scenario, they receive information suggesting that something is wrong and then fail to take further steps to reach a more definite conclusion. Looking in the mirror, I see that I am overweight but it is hard to tell by how much. By abstaining from going on the scales, I can tell myself that it is probably only a few pounds that I can lose anytime I want to. A woman feels a lump in her breast but fails to make an appointment with her doctor to determine whether it is benign or malign. In such cases, self-deception is facilitated by lack of precise knowledge. The woman does not first conclude that she probably has cancer and then suppress the belief. Rather, she suspects she *might* have cancer.

This case, which I shall treat as paradigmatic, is characterized by the following features.

1. The initial suspicion of cancer takes the form of a low-probability belief.
2. It is accompanied by a firm belief that if she does in fact have cancer and does nothing about it, the outcome is almost certainly fatal.
3. It is also accompanied by the firm belief that if she has cancer and does something about it, the outcome may nevertheless be fatal and that even if it is not, the treatment will be very unpleasant.

4.   The woman does not, at any point, ask herself whether the pain of the treatment (compared to the pain of an untreated disease) offsets the differential mortality risk.

5.   Instead, she simply abstains from seeing her doctor to find out whether she has cancer.

In this example, the crucial features are (1) and (3). Because the initial belief is a low-probability one, the costs of rearranging it are small. The woman can easily focus on many stories she will have heard about harmless lumps and needless scares. *Yet in the absence of feature (3), she has no motivation to reshape her beliefs.* If she knew that there were a costless and painless treatment that would be certain to cure her, she would have no motivation not to see her doctor. There is no known form of irrationality that would favor the tendency to block *costless* avoidance of low-probability disasters, for example, by turning a low subjective probability into a zero probability.

Self-deception thus conceived does not involve the simultaneous entertainment of two contradictory beliefs, one held consciously and the other unconsciously. When the initial probability assessment is replaced by another, the former *disappears for good* rather than being relegated to the unconscious. Many writers consider this contradiction to be the central feature of self-deception. This need not be the case, however. The self-deceptive person is not (or not necessarily) like the person who hates to see cats yet finds that to look away from them he first has to notice them. He is more like a person who sees a shadow in the dark that might be a cat but that could easily be something else. His aversion to cats can be satisfied by first reinterpreting the shadow and then not moving closer to see whether it is in fact a cat.

I doubt psychology or philosophy can do much better than literature in bringing self-deception alive for us. In *Swann's Way*, Proust describes how Swann reflects "on the time when people had described Odette [his mistress] to him as a kept woman" and on how incongruous that description seemed compared to the Odette he knew. By a train of associations he came to think of his banker and reminded himself to draw some money to help her out of some material difficulties.

Then, suddenly, he wondered if this was not precisely what was meant by "keeping" her . . . and if one could not apply to Odette . . . those words which he had believed so irreconcilable with her – "kept woman." He could not study this idea in greater depth, because an attack of that mental laziness which in him was congenital, intermittent, and providential, happened at that moment to extinguish all light in his intelligence, as abruptly as, later, when electric lighting had been installed everywhere, one could cut off the electricity in a house. His mind groped for a moment in the darkness, he took off his glasses, wiped the lenses, passed his hand over his eyes, and saw the light only when he found himself in the presence of an entirely different idea, namely that he ought to try to send six or seven thousand francs to Odette next month instead of five, because of the surprise and pleasure it would give her.

❰❰❰

Bibliographical Note

Evidence for many of the findings reported here can be found in the following source books: D. Kahneman, P. Slovic, and A. Tversky (eds.), *Judgment Under Uncertainty* (Cambridge University Press, 1982); D. Bell, H. Raiffa, and A. Tversky (eds.), *Decision Making* (Cambridge University Press, 1988); T. Connolly, H. Arkes, and K. R. Hammond (eds.), *Judgment and Decision Making* (Cambridge University Press, 2000); D. Kahneman and A. Tversky (eds.), *Choices, Values, and Frames* (Cambridge University Press, 2000); T. Gilovich, D. Griffin, and D. Kahneman (eds.), *Heuristics and Biases: The Psychology of Intuitive Judgment* (Cambridge University Press, 2002); C. Camerer, G. Loewenstein, and M. Rabin (eds.), *Advances in Behavioral Economics* (New York: Russell Sage, 2004); I. Brocas and J. Carillo (eds.), *The Psychology of Economic Decisions*, vols. 1 and 2 (Oxford University Press, 2003, 2004). The greater tendency to impute cooperation to partners then to nonpartners is documented in L. Messé and J. Sivacek, "Predictions of others' responses in a mixed-motive game: Self-justification or false consensus?" *Journal of Personality and Social Psychology* 37 (1979), 602–7. The double incompetence of the ignorant is documented in J. Kruger and D. Dunning, "Unskilled and unaware of it," *Journal of Personality and Social Psychology* 77 (1999), 1121–34. A sophisticated study of the unreliability of the judgments of some experts ("hedgehogs") and the somewhat more reliable judgments of others ("foxes") is P. Tetlock, *Expert Political Judgment* (Princeton, NJ: Princeton University Press, 2005). For the data about earthquakes and floods, see P. Slovic, *The Perception of Risk* (Sterling, VA: Earthscan, 2000). For the (il)logic of conspiracy theories, see B. Keeley, "Of conspiracy theories," *Journal of Philosophy* 96 (1999), 109–26. On theories of famine see S. Kaplan, "The famine plot persuasion in eighteenth-century France," *Transactions of the American Philosophical Society* 72 (1982), and F. Ploux, *De bouche à oreille: Naissance et propagation des rumeurs dans la France du XIXe siècle* (Paris: Aubier, 2003). A study of conspiratorial thinking is R. Hofstadter, *The Paranoid Style in American Politics* (Cambridge, MA: Harvard University Press, 1964). Its role in the Middle East is the topic of D. Pipes, *The Hidden Hand: Middle East Fears of Conspiracy* (New York: St. Martin's Press, 1998). My comments on how two economists (George Akerlof and Matthew Rabin) and one psychologist (Ziva Kunda) treat motivated belief formation are further elaborated in "Costs and constraints in the economy of the mind," in I. Brocas and J. Carillo (eds.), *The Psychology of Economic Decisions*, vol. 2 (Oxford University Press, 2004). The best overview of self-deception is a special issue of *Behavioral and Brain Sciences* 20 (1997), organized around an article by A. Mele, "Real self-deception."

Chapter 8

EMOTIONS

❀ ❀ ❀

The Role of the Emotions

Emotions enter human life in three ways. At their most intense they are the most important *sources of happiness and misery*, far overshadowing hedonic pleasures and physical pain. The radiant love of Anne Elliott at the end of *Persuasion* is unsurpassable happiness. Conversely, the emotion of shame can be utterly devastating. Voltaire wrote, "To be an object of contempt to those with whom one lives is a thing that none has ever been, or ever will be, able to endure."

Shame also illustrates the second way in which emotions matter, namely, in their *impact on behavior*. In Chapter 4, I cited several cases in which people killed themselves because of the overpowering emotion of shame. In this chapter I shall mainly discuss the *action tendencies* that are associated with the emotions. The extent to which these tendencies are translated into actual behavior will concern us in later chapters.

Third, emotions can matter because of their impact on *other mental states*, notably on beliefs. When a desire for a certain state to obtain is supported by a strong emotion, the tendency to believe that it does obtain can be irresistible. As Stendhal says in *On Love*, "From the moment he falls in love even the wisest man no longer sees anything *as it really is*. . . . He no longer admits an element of chance in things and loses his sense of the probable; judging by its effect on his happiness, whatever he imagines becomes reality." In *A la recherche du temps perdu* Proust pursues the same theme over hundreds of pages, with more variations and twists than one might have thought possible.

What Are the Emotions?

Before considering each of these aspects of emotion in more detail, I need to say something about *what emotions are* and *what emotions there are*. There is no agreed-upon definition of what counts as an emotion, that is, no agreed-upon list of sufficient and necessary conditions. There is not even an agreed-upon list of necessary conditions. Although I shall discuss a large number of common features of the states that we understand, preanalytically, as emotions, there are counterexamples to all of them. For any such feature, that is, there are some emotions or emotional occurrences in which it is lacking. We may think that action tendencies are crucial to emotion, but the aesthetic emotions provide a counterexample. We may think that a "short half-life," that is, a tendency to decay quickly, is an essential feature of emotion, but in some instances unrequited romantic love (such as that of Cyrano de Bergerac) or the passionate desire for revenge can persist for years. We may think that emotions are triggered by beliefs, but how do we then explain that people can get emotionally upset by reading stories or watching movies that are clearly fictitious? Many other examples could be given of allegedly universal features that turn out to be lacking in some cases.[1]

In light of this problem, the natural response is to deny that "emotion" is a useful scientific category. In the language of philosophers, emotions do not seem to form a *natural kind*. In spite of their difference, whales and bats, qua mammals, belong to the same natural kind. Whales and sharks, in spite of their similarity, do not; nor do bats and birds. Anger and love have in common the capacity for clouding and biasing the mind, but this similarity does not make them into a natural kind. To see how such reasoning by analogy can go astray, we may notice that the intake of amphetamines and romantic love produce many of the same effects: acute awareness, heightened energy, reduced need for sleep and food, and feelings of euphoria. Yet nobody would claim, I assume, that the two states belong to the same natural kind.[2]

For the purpose of social-scientific explanation, this conundrum can be left unresolved. We can focus on occurrences of emotions in which a certain number of features are regularly observed and ask how these can help us to explain behavior or other mental states. The fact that in other

---

[1] For diagnostic purposes, one might stipulate that a mental state is an emotion if it has (say) eight or more of twelve defining features. For explanatory purposes, however, this is unsatisfactory.

[2] They may, however, recruit some of the same neural circuitry.

occurrences that intuitively count as emotions some of these features are lacking is interesting from a conceptual point of view but does not detract from their explanatory efficacy in cases where they are present. The features I want to draw attention to are these:

- *Cognitive antecedents.* Emotions are triggered by beliefs, often by the agent's acquiring of a new belief. Emotions may also have other causal conditions (we are more readily irritated when we are tired), but the presence of these will not by themselves cause the emotion to occur, any more than a slippery road will cause a car accident.
- *Physiological arousal.* Emotions go together with changes in heart rate, electrical skin conductance, bodily temperature, blood pressure, respiration, and numerous other variables.
- *Physiological expressions.* Emotions go together with characteristic observable signs, such as bodily posture, voice pitch, flushing and reddening (from embarrassment), smiling or baring the teeth, laughing and frowning, weeping and crying, and white or red anger (as manifested in pallor and blushing, respectively).
- *Action tendencies.* Emotions are accompanied by tendencies or urges to perform specific actions. Although these tendencies may not lead to actual behavior, they are more than dispositions – they are forms of incipient behavior rather than mere potential for behavior.
- *Intentional objects.* Unlike other visceral phenomena such as pain or hunger, emotions are *about* something. They may have "propositional objects" ("I am indignant that . . .") or nonpropositional objects ("I am indignant with . . .").
- *Valence.* This is a technical term for the pain-pleasure dimension of the emotions as we experience them. As noted, the valence might range from the glowing happiness of Anne Elliott to the crushing shame of the exposed consumers of pedophiliac material.

Do not emotions, as do the colors, also have specific qualitative *feelings*? Shame and guilt, for example, seem to *feel* different in a way that cannot be reduced to the fact that shame is more intensely unpleasant. There is evidence that one could insert an electrode into my brain and make me feel sad, embarrassed, or afraid even though I would not be able to identify either a cause or an object of the feeling. Important as this aspect may turn out to be for our understanding of emotion, it is not yet well enough understood to suggest specific causal hypotheses.

What Emotions Are There?

I shall list and briefly describe some two dozen emotions, without claiming that this classification is superior to the many others that have been proposed. My aim is to provide some understanding of the emotions that have either intrinsic or causal importance in social life, not to try to satisfy the (legitimate) concerns of emotion theorists. In particular, I shall have nothing to say about which emotions are "basic" and "nonbasic."

One important group of emotions are the *evaluative emotions*. They involve a positive or a negative assessment of one's own or someone else's behavior or character.[3] If an emotion is triggered by the behavior of another person, that behavior may be directed either toward oneself or toward a third party. These distinctions yield ten (or eleven) emotions altogether:

- *Shame* is triggered by a negative belief about one's own character.
- *Contempt* and *hatred* are triggered by negative beliefs about another's character. Contempt is induced by the thought that another is inferior, hatred by the thought that he is evil.
- *Guilt* is triggered by a negative belief about one's own action.
- *Anger* is triggered by a negative belief about another's action toward oneself.
- *Cartesian indignation*[4] is triggered by a negative belief about another's action toward a third party.
- *Pridefulness* is triggered by a positive belief about one's own character.
- *Liking* is triggered by a positive belief about another's character.
- *Pride* is triggered by a positive belief about one's own action.

[3] Emotions triggered by negative assessments of oneself always have negative valence. Those caused by negative assessments of others are more ambiguous in this respect.

[4] The emotion was first identified by Descartes, who added the important qualification that when the agent *loves* the third party the reaction is anger rather than indignation.

- *Gratitude* is triggered by a positive belief about another's action toward oneself.
- *Admiration* is triggered by a positive belief about another's action toward a third party.

Second, there is a set of emotions generated by the thought that someone else is in the deserved or undeserved possession of some good or bad.[5] The target of these emotions is neither individual action nor individual character, but a state of affairs. Following Aristotle's discussion in the *Rhetoric*, we may distinguish six (or seven) cases.

- *Envy* is caused by the deserved good of someone else.
- *Aristotelian indignation* is caused by the undeserved good of someone else.[6] The closely related emotion of *resentment* is caused by the reversal of a prestige hierarchy, when a formerly inferior group or individual emerges as dominant.
- *Sympathy* is caused by the deserved good of someone else.
- *Pity* is caused by the undeserved bad of someone else.
- *Malice* is caused by the undeserved bad of someone else.
- *Gloating* is caused by the deserved bad of someone else.

Third, there are positive or negative emotions generated by the thought of good or bad things that have happened or will happen to one – *joy* and *grief*, with their several varieties and cognates. As many have observed, bad events in the past may also generate positive emotions in the present, and good events negative emotions. Thus in the main collection of proverbial sayings from antiquity, the *Sentences* of Publilius Syrus, we find both "The remembrance of past perils is pleasant" and "Past happiness augments present misery."

All the emotions discussed so far are induced by beliefs that are (or may be) held in the mode of certainty. There are also emotions – *hope*, *fear*, *love*, and *jealousy* – that essentially involve beliefs held in the modes

---

[5] I include "nonundeserved" under the heading of "deserved." Thus when someone wins the big prize in the lottery I shall say that it is deserved, somewhat contrary to ordinary usage.

[6] Although Aristotle's term for this emotion is usually translated by "indignation," it should be clear how it differs from Cartesian indignation.

of probability or possibility. These emotions are generated by the thought of good or bad things that may or may not happen in the future, and of good or bad states of affairs that may or may not obtain in the present.[7] By and large, these emotions require that the event or state in question be seen as more than merely conceivable; that is, there must be a nonnegligible chance or a "downhill causal story" that it might actually occur or obtain. The thought of winning the big prize in the lottery may generate hope, but not the "uphill" thought of receiving a large gift from an unknown millionaire. These emotions also seem to require that the event or state fall short of being thought to be certain. If I *know* that I am about to be executed, I may feel despair rather than fear. According to Stendhal, love withers away both when one is certain that it is reciprocated and when one is certain that it is not. According to La Rochefoucauld, jealousy may disappear the moment one *knows* that the person one loves is in love with somebody else.

Some emotions are generated by *counterfactual* thoughts about what might have happened or what one might have done. *Disappointment* is the emotion that occurs when a hoped-for positive event fails to materialize.[8] *Regret* is the emotion that occurs when we realize we could have made a hoped-for positive event occur if we had made a different choice. The positive counterparts of these emotions (caused by the non-occurrence of negative events) are sometimes referred to as *elation* and *rejoicing*, respectively. (In everyday language, the two are usually blurred under the heading of *relief*.) Whereas disappointment and elation involve comparisons of different outcomes caused by different states of the world for a given choice, regret and rejoicing involve comparisons caused by different choices within a single state. In some cases, negative events can be imputed to either source. If I get wet on my way to work I may either

---

[7] Emotions may also, perhaps more rarely, be generated by uncertainty about the past. After the downfall of the former German Democratic Republic, many citizens required access to their security files to find out whether any of their friends and relatives had informed on them. More poignantly, some wanted to find out whether their personal failures (not getting a promotion or being dropped by a lover) were due to their own failings or to other people's being instructed by the state security services to ostracize them.

[8] Near-misses generate stronger emotions; thus silver medalists in Olympic competitions report less happiness than do bronze medalists.

ascribe it to a chance meteorological event or to the fact that I did not take an umbrella. Although I might prefer the first framing, this piece of wishful thinking might be subject to reality constraints (Chapter 7) if I had just heard a forecast of rain before leaving the house.

Emotions and Happiness

The role of emotions in generating happiness (or misery) suggests the idea of a "gross national happiness product." The usual measures of economic performance are, of course, more objective. Yet objectivity in the sense of physical measurability is not what we ultimately care about. The reason we want to know about economic output is that it contributes to *subjective* welfare or happiness. Moreover, happiness can stem from sources that do not lend themselves to any kind of objective quantitative measurement. In 1994, when Norway hosted the Olympic Winter Games, the country had to build new arenas for the events and housing for the participants, at considerable cost. On the revenue side one could include the money spent by visitors to the country and by spectators of the events, as well as the income generated by these constructions in the future. Economists who have carried out these calculations do not believe that the games broke even. I feel utterly certain, however (but of course cannot prove), that if we include the emotional benefits to the Norwegian population, the games ran a huge surplus. The unexpectedly large number of Norwegian gold medalists created a mood of collective euphoria, which was all the greater *because* the victories were so unexpected. The "objective" number of victories owed a great deal of its impact to the element of subjective surprise.[9] More recently, the victory of the French soccer team in the 1998 World Cup as well as its defeat in 2002 generated feelings of euphoria and dejectedness that owed much of their intensity to the fact of surprise.

---

[9] Suppose that the prior probability of a victory is p and that the satisfaction derived from a victory is proportional to $1/p$ (because the surprise is greater when p is low). In this special model of surprise, the *expected* satisfaction of victory is independent of the probability of victory. In general, the impact of surprise is going to be more complex.

In general, it is difficult to compare the emotional components of welfare or well-being with other components. That positive emotions at their most intense contribute more to happiness than does simple hedonic welfare proves nothing, unless we know how often the intense episodes occur. Also, we do not understand whether and to what extent the propensity for emotional highs goes together with the propensity for emotional lows. If it does, is a life in steady contentment more happy overall than one that alternates between euphoria and dysphoria? As Montaigne noted, the answer depends on the occasions offered by the environment. "If you say that the convenience of having our senses chilled and blunted when tasting evil pains must entail the consequential inconvenience of rendering us less keenly appreciative of the joys of good pleasures, I agree. But the wretchedness of our human condition means that we have less to relish than to banish." The ideal of extinguishing the emotions that one finds in many ancient philosophies, notably Stoicism and Buddhism, emerged in societies where the environment may have offered more occasions for emotions with negative valence. Writing during the wars of religion that were devastating France, Montaigne may have been in the same situation.

Emotion and Action

The mediating link between emotion and action is that of an action tendency (or action readiness). We may also think of an action tendency as a temporary preference. Each of the major emotions seems to have associated with it one (or a few) such tendencies (see Table 8.1).

Although anger and Cartesian indignation induce the same action tendency, that of anger is stronger. Experiments show that subjects are willing to incur a larger cost to hurt somebody who hurt them than to hurt somebody who hurt a third party. After the end of World War II, Americans were often more eager to punish Nazis who had mistreated American prisoners of war than those were responsible for the Holocaust. An exception, which confirms the principle, were the Jewish members of the Roosevelt administration.

TABLE 8.1

Emotion	Action Tendency
Anger or Cartesian indignation	Cause the object of the emotion to suffer
Hatred	Cause the object of hatred to cease to exist
Contempt	Ostracize; avoid
Shame	"Sink through the floor"; run away; commit suicide
Guilt	Confess; make repairs; hurt oneself
Envy	Destroy the envied object or its possessor
Fear	Flight; fight
Love	Approach and touch the other; help the other; please the other
Pity	Console or alleviate the distress of the other
Gratitude	Help the other

The emotions of anger, guilt, contempt, and shame have close relations to moral and social norms. Norm violators may suffer guilt or shame, whereas those who observe the violation feel anger or contempt. The structures of these relations differ as shown in Figure 8.1.

Social norms, further discussed in Chapter 22, are mediated by exposure to others. That is why the suicides mentioned in the beginning of this chapter occurred only when the shameful actions became public knowledge. As I argued in Chapter 5, moral norms differ in this respect.[10]

Some of the action tendencies appear to aim at "restoring the moral balance of the universe." Hurting those who hurt you and helping those who help you are, seemingly, ways of *getting even*. This may be true in some cases. Yet prospect theory (Chapter 12) implies that "Two eyes for an eye" may be a better description of the action tendency of anger than "An eye for an eye."[11] Although many acts of gratitude may be performed simply to rid oneself of a debt, others may stem from a genuine feeling of goodwill toward one's benefactor. The moral-balance view is more

[10] I suspect that violations of quasi-moral norms trigger the same emotions as do violations of moral norms, but my intuition is not robust.

[11] Thus in response to the killing of 365 Lebanese Muslims a Lebanese woman said that "at this moment I want the [Moslem militia] . . . to go into offices and kill the first seven hundred and thirty defenseless Christians they can lay their hands on." In *The Civil War in France* Marx cites a newspaper letter from a priest taken hostage by the communards in which he says that "a decision has been taken to execute two of the numerous hostages they hold for every new execution" (by the government forces). Seneca observed, finally, that "a wrong not exceeded is not revenged."

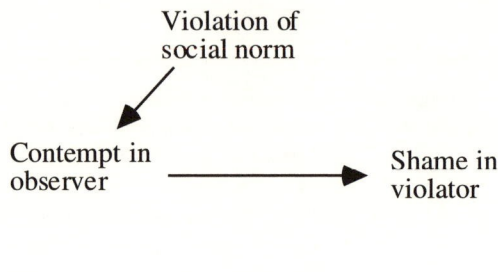

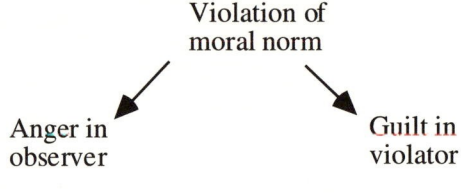

FIGURE 8.1

compelling in the case of guilt, where the action tendency of making repairs is explicitly restorative. Moreover, when the agent cannot undo the harm she has done, she can restore the balance by harming herself to an equal extent. If I have cheated on my income taxes and discover that the IRS does not accept an anonymous money order for the amount I owe, I can restore the balance by burning the money instead.

Emotional action tendencies do not merely induce a desire to act. They also induce a desire *to act sooner rather than later*. To put this idea in context, let me distinguish between *impatience* and *urgency*. I define impatience as a preference for early reward over later reward, that is, some degree of time discounting. As I noted in Chapter 6, emotions may cause an agent to attach less importance to temporally remote consequences of present action. I define urgency, another effect of emotion, as a preference for early action over later action. The distinction is illustrated in Table 8.2.

In each case, the agent can take one and only one of two actions, A or B. In case 1, these options are available at the same time, in cases 2 and 3 at successive times. In case 2, the rewards (whose magnitude is indicated by the numbers) occur at the same later time, in cases 1 and 3 at successive later times. Suppose that in an unemotional state, the agent chooses B in all cases, but that

TABLE 8.2

t1	t2	t3	t4
A	3		
B		5	

Case 1: *Impatience*

A		3	
	B	4	

Case 2: *Urgency*

A		3	
	B		6

Case 3: *Impatience and/or urgency*

in an emotional state he chooses A. In case 1, the choice of A is due to emotionally induced impatience. In case 2, it is due to emotionally induced urgency. In case 3, it could be due to either or to the interaction of the two.

Impatience, a much-discussed issue, was a central topic of Chapter 6. Although urgency is less frequently discussed, I believe it can be quite important. In particular, the urgency of the emotions provides one of the mechanisms by which they may affect belief formation. As we shall see in Chapter 11, rational belief formation requires an optimal gathering of information. Rather than going by the evidence already at hand, a rational agent will gather additional evidence before acting if the decision to be made is sufficiently important and the cost of waiting sufficiently small. Urgent emotions are often triggered in situations in which the cost of waiting *is* high, that is, in the face of acute physical danger. In such cases, acting quickly without pausing to find out more is of the essence. But when an important decision could be improved by waiting, an emotion-induced desire for immediate action can be harmful. As Seneca said, "Reason grants a hearing to both sides, then seeks to postpone action, even its own, in order that it may gain time to sift out the truth; but anger is precipitate." The proverb "Marry in haste, repent at leisure" suggests both the impetus of emotion and the unfortunate consequences of inability to resist it.[12]

---

[12] The curtailments of civil liberties enacted by several Western governments in the wake of September 11, 2001, are a good test case. Did they illustrate the need to act rapidly in the presence of an imminent danger, or were they a panicky reaction that, by making these governments appear

Earlier, I mentioned that not all emotions have a short half-life. Usually, nevertheless, emotions do decay quite rapidly with time. In some cases, this is simply due to the fact that the situation that triggered them ceases to exist. When I have gotten safely away from the bear that was threatening me, fear is no longer warranted. More often, though, emotion wanes as memory fades, by the sheer passage of time. Anger, shame, guilt, and love rarely persist with the intensity they had at the onset of emotion. After September 11, 2001, for instance, the number of young American men who expressed an interest in serving in the army increased by 50 percent, but there was no marked increase in actual enlistment. These facts are consistent with the hypothesis that the initial surge of interest was due to emotion, which then abated during the several months required for the enrollment process. There was almost no increase in the interest in serving among young women, a fact that has no obvious explanation.

This being said, people are often unable to anticipate the decay of their emotions. When in the grip of a strong emotion, they may believe, wrongly, that it will last forever and may even lose any sense of the future. If the suicidal individuals I have referred to had known that their shame (and the contempt of the observers) would abate, they might not have killed themselves. If young couples knew that their love for each other might not last forever, they would be less willing to make binding commitments and in particular to enter into a "covenant marriage" from which it is more difficult to exit.

Let me conclude on this point by pointing to an interaction between two emotion-induced phenomena: preference reversal and clouded belief formation. On a rosy view, these two might cancel one another: because of the preference reversal one wants to act contrary to one's calm and reflective judgment, but because of the clouded belief one is unable to carry out the intention. More frequently, I believe, the two will reinforce each other. Vengeance is an example. The risk is minimal if I do not take revenge for an affront; greater if I take revenge but bide my time; and maximal if I take revenge immediately without any concern for the risks. Montaigne made a similar observation: "When we punish any injuries

---

even more odious in the eyes of their enemies, made further attacks more rather than less probable? Compare also the remarks on the "psychology of tyranny" in earlier chapters.

we have received, philosophy wants us to avoid choler, not so as to diminish our revenge but (on the contrary) so that its blow may be weightier and better aimed; philosophy considers violent emotion to be an impediment to that." Yet that is to ignore the paradox that if we do not feel emotion, we may not want revenge, and if we do feel it, we may not be able to carry out the revenge effectively.

Emotion and Belief

Emotion can affect belief formation directly as well as indirectly. The direct effect produces biased beliefs, the indirect effect low-quality beliefs. One form of bias is illustrated in Stendhal's theory of *crystallization*. The origin of the term is as follows: "At the salt mines of Hallein near Salzburg the miners throw a leafless wintry bough into one of the abandoned workings. Two or three months later, through the effect of the waters saturated with salt which soak the bough and then let it dry as they recede, the miners find it covered with a shining deposit of crystal. The tiniest twigs no bigger than a tom-tit's claw are encrusted with an infinity of crystals, scintillating and dazzling." The analogy with love is clear: "From the moment you begin to be really interested in a woman, you no longer see her *as she really is*, but as it suits you to see her. You're comparing the flattering illusions created by this nascent interest with the pretty diamonds which hide this leafless branch of hornbeam – and which are only perceived, mark you, by the eyes of this young man falling in love."

In a French proverb I have cited earlier and shall cite again, we easily *believe what we fear*. This, too, is a form of bias. In addition to the fact that we naturally (even in nonemotional states) tend to give excessive importance to low-probability risks (Chapter 12), feelings of visceral fear may also cause us to believe that dangers are greater than they actually are. When we walk in a forest at night, a sound or a movement may trigger fear, which then causes us to interpret as fearsome other sounds or movements that we had previously ignored. The fear "feeds on itself." We may also think of this as "the Othello effect." I shall have more to say about it in Chapter 23.

The urgency of emotion acts on the gathering of information prior to belief formation rather than on the belief itself. The result is a low-quality belief, based on a less than optimal amount of information, but not a belief that is biased for or against any particular conclusion that the agent would like to be true. In practice, though, the two mechanisms tend to go together and reinforce each other. The agent initially forms an emotion-induced bias, and the urgency of emotion then prevents her from gathering the information that might have corrected the bias. As we saw in the previous chapter, wishful thinking is to some extent subject to reality constraints. Counterwishful thinking, too, is constrained in this manner. Hence if the agent had gathered more information, it might have been difficult to persist in the biased belief.

I should repeat, though, that it may not be rational to gather large amounts of information if the opportunity cost of doing so is high. If you spend too much time trying to decide whether the shape on the path is a stick or a snake, you may end up dead. It should also be added that in nonemotional states, there is a tendency to *disregard* opportunity costs and to pay more attention to out-of-pocket expenses (Chapter 12). Faced with a possible risk, an agent might be dissuaded from taking extensive precautions because of their direct cost, while not giving enough weight to the fact that inaction might also be costly. In some circumstances, therefore, the urgency of emotion might provide a useful corrective to this irrational tendency. At the same time, to repeat, urgency and low-quality beliefs can create problems rather than solve them.

Emotions and Transmutation

Because of the normative hierarchy of motivations (Chapter 4), people may be ashamed of their emotions. Envy, for instance, is not an emotion most people acknowledge having. When Iago says, "If Cassio do remain, he hath a daily beauty in his life that makes me ugly," he is being unusually, perhaps implausibly frank. The most common reaction to one's own perceived envy is a mental shrug of the shoulders. One registers a painful feeling of inferiority, has a fleeting destructive desire, and then moves on. Sometimes, however, the emotion may be so strong that it cannot be ignored. At the same time, it cannot be acknowledged. The solution to the conflict is that envy is transmuted into righteous indignation, by means of a suitable rewriting of the script. I can tell myself a story in which the other obtained the envied object by illegitimate and immoral means, and perhaps at my expense, thus transmuting the envy into Aristotelian indignation or anger.

In Chapter 7, I discussed motivated belief formation. As Figure 8.2 shows, this phenomenon may be embedded in the process of *motivated motivation* that I considered in Chapter 4. For the agent to be able to adopt a motivation that he is not ashamed of, cognitive rewriting may be necessary.

This metamorphosis of envy into righteous indignation can also occur in a more direct manner. Envy is not only shameful: it is painful. The belief that someone else succeeded where I could have succeeded, too, had I made more of an effort, can be intensely unpleasant. To alleviate the pain, I can adopt a similar story about the disreputable causes of the other person's success. Guilt can also be hard to bear, notably if one is subject to pridefulness. Prideful individuals will easily be able to come up with a story blaming their victim instead of themselves: "Those whom they injure, they also hate" (Seneca). This pattern seems common, for instance, in Renaissance princes, ancient tyrants, and other overbearing

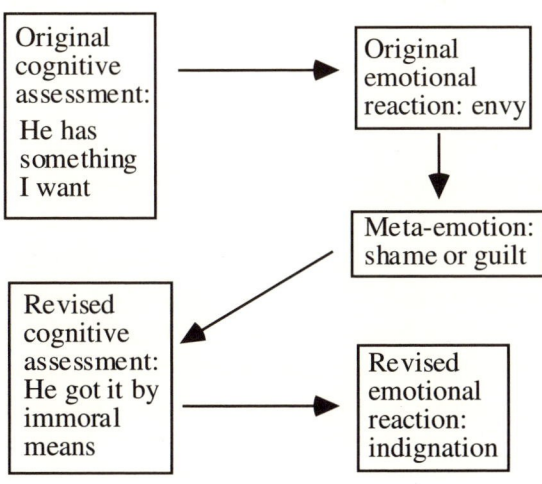

FIGURE 8.2

individuals. The concern with self-image may also cause regret avoidance. For some individuals, admitting to themselves that they made a
mistake is so painful that they would rather pursue an unprofitable
activity than write it off, as rationality would dictate. This is the "sunk-
cost fallacy," also sometimes referred to as "the Vietnam fallacy" or "the
Concorde fallacy." I shall have more to say about it in Chapter 12.

Culture and Emotions

Are all emotions universal? If not, are there some universal emotions?
I answer a firm yes to the second question, and a tentative yes to the first.

It seems clear that some emotions are universal. There are half a dozen
emotions – happiness, surprise, fear, sadness, disgust, and anger – that
have facial expressions people recognize across cultures. If one believes, as
I do, that social norms exist in all societies, the emotions that sustain
them – contempt and shame – must also be universal. One might imagine
a society in which people felt anger when offended, but no (Cartesian)
indignation when they observed offenses toward a third party. I find it
hard to believe that such a society could exist, but I may be wrong. If love
is universal (see later discussion), would not jealousy be too?

It is said that the Japanese have an emotion, *amae* (roughly rendered as
helplessness and a desire to be loved), that does not exist in other
societies. It has also been argued that ancient Greece was a "shame
culture" that differed from modern "guilt cultures," that romantic love is
a modern invention, and that the feeling of boredom (if that is an
emotion) is of recent origin. One cannot exclude, however, that the
allegedly absent emotions may have existed but not been conceptualized
by members of the society in question. An emotion may be recognized as
such by an external observer, but not acknowledged by the members of
that society. In Tahiti, a man whose woman friend has left him will show
the behavioral symptoms of sadness but will state only that he is "tired."
In the West, the *concept* of romantic love is a relatively recent one, dating
from the age of the troubadours. Prior to that time, there was only
"merry sensuality or madness." Yet it is possible, and in my opinion
likely, that the *experience* of romantic love occurred even when the

society did not have the concept of that emotion. Individuals can be in love without noticing it, and at the same time their emotion may be obvious to observers, whether from their own society or from another. The ancient Greeks displayed a cluster of guilt-related reactions – anger, forgiveness, and reparations – that point to the presence of the emotion even if they did not have a word for it. The way people think about emotions may be culture specific, even if the emotions themselves are not.

One should add, though, that when a certain emotion is not explicitly conceptualized, it may also have fewer behavioral manifestations. La Rochefoucauld wrote that "some people would never have fallen in love if they had never heard of love." Guilt, too, may be more common in societies where people are told from an early age that they ought to feel guilty on this or that occasion.

❮❮❮

Bibliographical Note

The best book on emotion is N. Frijda, *The Emotions* (Cambridge University Press, 1986). I draw heavily on his work in *Alchemies of the Mind* (subtitled *Rationality and the Emotions*) (Cambridge University Press, 1999), where the reader can find further references to the concepts discussed here. The idea of urgency, as distinct from impatience, is an addition to the framework of that book. Sustained discussions of the role of emotions in explaining behavior include R. Petersen, *Understanding Ethnic Violence: Fear, Hatred, and Resentment in Twentieth-Century Eastern Europe* (Cambridge University Press, 2002), and Chapter 8 of my *Closing the Books: Transitional Justice in Historical Perspective* (Cambridge University Press, 2004).

III

ACTION

Although I shall largely use "action," "behavior," "decision," and "choice" as synonymous terms, it is sometimes useful to distinguish among them. The broadest category is *behavior*, understood as any bodily movement whose origin is internal to the agent, not external (as when he is carried away by a landslide). *Action* is intentional behavior, caused by the desires and beliefs of the agent. Thus reflex behaviors are not actions; having an erection is not an action (but it may be induced by one, such as taking Viagra); falling asleep is not an action (but may be induced by taking a sleeping pill). An action may or may not be preceded by a conscious *decision*. When I drive to work along my usual route I do not consciously decide to turn right here and left there, although each action is intentional or goal-oriented. The very first time or times I drove to work, however, the actions were preceded by explicit decisions. In fact, they were preceded by an explicit *choice* among alternative paths. Although all choices are decisions, the converse is not true. When I decide to pick up the book I have been reading, I need not have any explicit alternative in mind. I see the book on the table; the sight reminds me that I have enjoyed reading it; and I decide to pick it up. No choice is involved.

The most important feature of this conceptual landscape is perhaps that *not all decisions lead to actions*. One may decide not to do something, for example, not to save a drowning person if the intervention would be at some risk to oneself. If the person drowns and no third parties are involved, I have no causal responsibility for the outcome. I may have a moral and, in some countries, a legal responsibility, but that is another matter.[1] But suppose there is a third party present or, as in the Kitty Genovese case, many parties. If the third party observes that I am in a position to help the drowning person and that I do not, he or she might reasonably draw the inference that the situation is less serious than it would otherwise have seemed and, as a result, also abstain from helping. In that case, my decision to do nothing would have caused another person to decide to do nothing. Thus decisions can have causal efficacy even when they do not generate an action.

Much of Part III is organized around rational-choice theory. As I explained in the Introduction, I have come to be more skeptical of rational-choice explanation of action (or inaction!) than I used to be. Yet although much behavior is irrational, in one way or another, there is a sense in which rationality remains primary. Human beings *want* to be rational. We do not take pride in our lapses from rationality. Rather, we try to avoid them or correct them, unless our pridefulness prevents us from recognizing them.

《《《

---

[1] In the United States, there is no duty to be a Good Samaritan, except under narrowly circumscribed conditions. In Continental Europe, "non-assistance to a person in danger" can be severely punished if the risk to the Samaritan of helping is small compared to the danger of the person in need of help. Some American legal scholars argue that the American law is more efficient, since a general duty to assist would create an incentive for potential rescuers to avoid locations where rescues are likely to be needed, because of the threat of liability. This may or (more likely) may not be so; what does seem certain is that the American system did not come into being for efficiency reasons, nor did it come into being for other reasons and then continue in effect because of its efficiency properties.

Chapter 9

DESIRES AND OPPORTUNITIES

❀ ❀ ❀

Doing One's Best

To characterize behavior, we sometimes say, "He did the best he could." If we unpack this sentence, it contains two elements: desires and opportunities. Desires define what, for the agent, counts as "the best." Opportunities are the options or means that the agent "can" choose from. This characterization may also serve as a rudimentary rational-choice *explanation* of the behavior. If we ask, "Why did he do it?" the answer "It was the best he could do" may be fully sufficient. In many cases, more is needed to provide a satisfactory rational-choice explanation. In particular, we may need to appeal to the *beliefs* of the agents and not merely to desires and opportunities. These complications will concern us in Chapter 11. Here, I discuss how far the simple desire-opportunity framework can get us.[1] I shall also suggest that the framework is sometimes not as simple as it might appear, since desires and opportunities are not always (as is sometimes assumed) independent of each other.

There is another, equivalent way of looking at the matter. In understanding behavior, we may begin with all the abstractly possible actions the individual might undertake. The action that we actually observe can be seen as the result of two successive filtering operations. The first filter is made up of all the *constraints* – physical, economic, legal, and others – that the agent faces. The actions consistent with all the constraints constitute the opportunity set.[2] The second filter is a mechanism that determines which action within the opportunity set will actually be carried out. Here, I am assuming that the agent chooses the action that will have the best consequences, as assessed by his desires (or preferences). In later chapters, we shall consider other second-filter mechanisms.

---

[1] In doing so, I adopt the implicit premise that the set of options the agent *believes* to be available to him coincides with the "objective" opportunity set.

[2] When I refer to legal constraints, I do not mean the effect of laws in making certain actions more costly than others (that belongs to the second filter), but to their effect in making them possible or impossible. I cannot vote at times other than election days or get married outside the legally determined venues.

The filter approach suggests the following question: what if the constraints are so strong that there is nothing for the second filter to work on? Can it happen that the constraints uniquely determine one and only one action that is consistent with all of them? The rich and the poor alike have the opportunity to sleep under the bridges in Paris, but the poor may have no other opportunity.[3] For a poor consumer, economic and calorific constraints might jointly determine a unique bundle of goods.[4] Those who defend the idea of *structuralism* in the social sciences may be understood as saying that constraints typically are so strong as to leave very little or no scope for choice.[5] *Why* this should be so, however, remains mysterious. One cannot argue, for example, that the rich and powerful make sure that the poor and oppressed have no other option than to work for them, since this statement presupposes that the rich and powerful, at least, do have a choice.

In some cases, the desire-opportunity approach is incomplete. I may have the opportunity to perform the action that will best realize my desire, such as choosing the right answer on a test or hitting the target in a rifle contest, but not the *ability* to identify which action that is. In some cases, one might trace the inability to an earlier stage, in which the agent lacked either the opportunity or the desire to acquire the ability. In other cases, the inability follows from hard psychophysiological constraints. I may have both the desire and the opportunity to choose the action that maximizes my long-term welfare, but not the ability to determine, on the spot, which action that is. When economists and mathematically minded political scientists try to determine what is optimal behavior in a given situation, they often need many pages of complicated mathematics to spell it out. Some individuals might never, regardless of how much training they receive, be able to carry out these calculations, or not without expending more effort than the task is worth, or more time than is available.

---

[3] If the opportunity set is described in finer grain, the poor may have the choice as to which bridge to sleep under. This is a general point: for any description of the options one may be able to specify a situation in which the agent has only one feasible option, but for any situation one may find a description under which there is more than one.

[4] Typically, however, there are several strategies for surviving at subsistence level. Unlike the choice of which bridge to sleep under, these often differ in nontrivial ways. One of the flaws in Marx's labor theory of value stems from his failure to understand this fact.

[5] Another, unrelated idea of structuralism was considered in Chapter 1.

Opportunity Explanations

Even when behavior is the joint result of desires and opportunities, *variance* in behavior over time may be largely explained by opportunities. Alcohol consumption is, in general, determined both by the strength of people's desire to drink, compared to their other desires, and by what they can afford. When alcohol prices rise steeply, for instance, in wartime, consumption falls sharply.

One explanation could be in terms of indifference curves (Figure 9.1). Suppose that the consumer has to allocate her income between alcohol and some bundle of ordinary consumption goods. The relative prices and her income are initially such that she faces the opportunity set inside the triangle OAA'. Assuming she spends all her income, we can limit ourselves to the

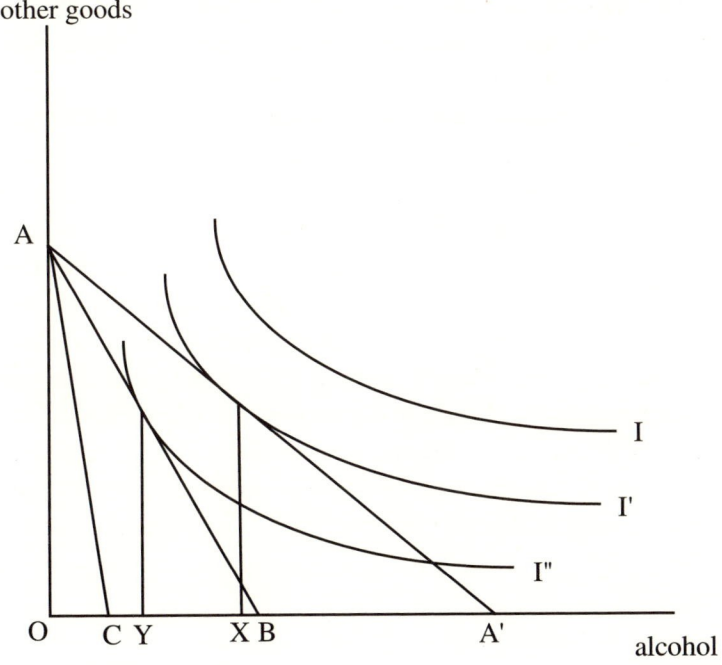

FIGURE 9.1

budget line AA'.[6] The strength of her desires for alcohol versus the consumption bundle is shown in the shape of the *indifference curves* I, I', and I''. The term reflects the idea that the consumer is indifferent among all the combinations of alcohol and other goods that lie on any given curve, while preferring any combination on a higher curve to any on a lower curve.[7] To choose the best among the options available to her, the consumer must pick the point on the budget line that is tangent to an indifference curve, since this will be the highest among the curves that include a combination she can afford. In Figure 9.1, this yields alcohol consumption OX.

Suppose now that the price of alcohol goes up so that the consumer faces the budget line AB. As the point of tangency has moved to the left, the consumer will now consume OY. We could carry through the same reasoning if a further price increase shifts the budget line to AC. Yet even if we know nothing about the shape of the indifference curves, we can predict that in this situation the consumer will not consume more than OC, which would be the case if she spent all her income on alcohol. The opportunity set by itself can explain a great deal of the variance over time. The second filter, in fact, could be anything – optimizing behavior, an irresistible craving for alcohol, custom, or whatever – the consumer would still be severely restricted by the first filter.

I chose this particular example to discuss the question of allegedly "irresistible" desires, such as the desire of drug addicts, heavy smokers, or alcoholics for the substance to which they are addicted. Are drugs more like insulin, which a diabetic will buy at any price, or more like sugar, of which consumers routinely purchase less when the price goes up? As proof that they are more like sugar, one often cites the fact that drug consumption goes down when prices go up. Yet as we have seen, that might simply be due to the inability of the addict to consume beyond his budget. (The diabetic, too, might be unable to purchase the insulin he needs if the price goes up.) Thus it seems that the fall of alcohol consumption during wartime is often due to

---

[6] I ignore, in other words, that the person might work overtime, make her own liquor, or buy smuggled goods. In policy applications, these issues are important.

[7] The shape of the curves corresponds to the fact that the more alcohol the agent is currently consuming, the more alcohol she needs to compensate (and remain at the same level of welfare) for a given cut in the consumption bundle.

its unavailability, leaving the question of irresistible versus resistible desires unresolved. We do know on other grounds, however, that alcohol consumption *is* price sensitive. Even when consumers can afford to maintain their previous level of consumption at higher prices, they do not.

Another argument is sometimes offered to show that opportunities have greater explanatory force than desires. Some economists claim that all individuals have essentially the same desires and preferences: only opportunities differ. Although it might appear as if people differ in their taste for classical music, observed consumption differences are (it is claimed) simply due to the fact that some individuals have more "musical consumption capital," and hence get more pleasure from classical music, than others. A trained ear, to be sure, is more akin to an ability than to an opportunity, but it is an ability that depends on the opportunity to acquire it. The desire to acquire the ability is assumed to be the same in everyone. The last statement, however, reveals a weakness in the argument. Today, the access to classical music on the radio is essentially costless, even taking account of opportunity costs (you can listen while you do other things). Since not everybody desires to acquire a trained ear, the explanation must be found in the subjective inclination to acquire it, which is a function (among other things) of how classical music strikes different *untrained* ears.

Other Ways in Which Opportunities Are More Important Than Desires

Opportunities are more basic in one fundamental respect: they are easier to observe, not only by social scientists, but also by other individuals in society. In military strategy, a basic dictum is that one should plan on the basis of the opponent's (verifiable) opportunities, not on his (unverifiable) intentions.[8] If we have reason to believe that the opponent *might* have hostile intentions, the dictum can lead to worst-case assumptions: the opponent will hurt us if he can.[9] The situation is complicated by the

---

[8] Overestimations of Soviet or Iraqi military might remind us, however, that even opportunities can be hard to verify.

[9] Even when we have no reason to think that another nation is currently harboring hostile intentions, contingency planning for future scenarios can occur. Deeply buried inside the U.S. Department of Defense there is probably a plan about how to invade Canada.

fact that our belief in the hostile intentions of the opponent may be grounded in a perception that *he* believes we have the means and perhaps the intention of hurting him. In this morass of subjectivity, objective opportunities may seem to provide the only firm basis for planning.

Still another reason why opportunities may appear more fundamental than desires has to do with the possibility of influencing behavior. It is usually easier to change people's circumstances and opportunities than to change their minds.[10] This is a cost-benefit argument about the dollar effectiveness of alternative policies – not an argument about relative explanatory power. Even if the government has a good theory, allowing for explanation as well as prediction, it may not allow for much control, since the elements on which it can act may not be the causally important ones. Suppose that weak economic performance can be traced back to risk-averse businesspeople and to strong unions. The government may be fully convinced that the mental attitude of managers is the more important cause yet be unable to do anything about it. By contrast, as the Reagan and Thatcher years showed, unions can be broken by government action.

For an important example, consider suicidal behavior. To commit suicide, the desire to kill oneself is not enough: one must also find the means to do it. The high suicide rate among doctors, for instance, may be due in part to their easy access to lethal drugs, which are the favored means of suicide in this group.[11] Although the government may try to limit suicidal intentions, by providing help lines or persuading the media to play down the reporting of suicides, which can trigger suicide by contagion, the most effective results are obtained by making access to the means of suicide more difficult.[12] Policies include barriers that make it more difficult to jump from bridges or tall buildings, more rigorous control of certain prescription drugs, restrictions on the sale of handguns, the replacement of lethal carbon monoxide by natural gas in kitchen

---

[10] In addition, as argued later, the best way to change their minds may be to change their circumstances.

[11] Contrary to a widespread belief, police officers' easy access to guns does not make them more suicide prone than others.

[12] When suicide rates fell radically in Britain in the 1970s, the change was initially attributed to the helplines established by the Samaritan Centres but later explained by the shift from lethal coal gas to the less lethal natural gas in domestic ovens.

ovens, and the installment of catalytic converters that reduce the carbon monoxide emissions in motor vehicle exhaust. In the future, we may see the banning of "suicide help" Internet sites. Even the simple switch from bottles to blister packs has contributed to the reduction of the number of suicides from paracetamol poisoning. Reducing the maximal number of tablets in individual preparations or prescriptions may also reduce the likelihood of severe poisonings. In France, but not in the United Kingdom, the content of each pack of paracetamol has been legally limited to eight grams. This is thought to be one reason why severe liver damage and deaths after paracetamol poisonings are less common in France than in the United Kingdom.

To be sure, a determined individual will usually find a way. When one common means of taking one's life is removed, the ensuing drop in the suicide rate may to some extent be a temporary one. Yet in some cases at least, the effect seems to have been lasting, as one would expect. If the urge to kill oneself is fleeting rather than firmly anchored, it might be gone by the time one manages to get hold of a suitable means.[13] Hence merely *delaying* (rather than blocking) access to means could be effective in preventing impulsive suicides. The requirement of a waiting time before the purchase of a handgun could reduce suicide as well as homicide rates.[14]

Varieties of Desire-Opportunity Interactions

A more complex example of desire-opportunity interactions may be taken from Madison's analysis of factions in *The Federalist*. He argued that in the regime that would prevail in a direct democracy (which would necessarily be small) or in a small representative republic, *factions* would have both the motive and the means to cause mischief. On the one hand, "a common passion or interest will, in almost every case, be felt by the

[13] I do not think the increased *cost* of locating a means could deter suicide. There may be cost-benefit considerations involved in a decision to kill oneself, such as weighing the pain the agent will inflict on others against his or her own relief from pain, but the cost of finding an appropriate means will not, for a determined individual, make a difference.

[14] As a matter of fact, most of the American states that impose a waiting period before the purchase of a handgun do so to give the authorities time to see whether the prospective buyer has a criminal record or a history of mental illness, not to create a cooling-down period for the buyer.

majority of the whole." On the other hand, the small number of citizens provides the opportunity for the majority to act oppressively against the minority, for the reason that they can more easily meet together. By contrast, in a large republic it is "less probable that a majority of the whole will have a common motive to invade the rights of other citizens; or, if such a common motive exists, it will be more difficult for all who feel it to discover their strength, and to act in unison with each other." In this transposition of the desire-opportunity argument from the individual to the collective level, it takes on a somewhat different form. Although, Madison thought, institutional design is ineffective in changing individual motives, it can change the likelihood that a majority of individuals will share the same motive. While institutional design cannot strictly speaking affect the opportunity of the members of a factious majority (should one nevertheless exist) to act in concert, it can reduce their *ability* to do so by making it less likely that they will know about each other's existence. Prior to the age of opinion polls, there must in fact have been innumerable occasions on which a silent majority failed to recognize itself as such.

Madison's argument is, as it were, double-barreled: not only will a large republic prevent factious majorities from arising, but it will also prevent concerted action. In Tocqueville's *Democracy in America* we find a large number of arguments with this "not only" structure. Consider for instance his discussion of the impact of slavery on slaveowners. In the first place, slavery is unprofitable, compared to free labor. "The free worker receives wages, the slave receives an upbringing, food, medicine, and clothes; the master spends his money little by little in small sums to support the slave; he scarcely notices. The workman's wages are paid all at once and seem only to enrich the man who receives them; but in fact the slave has cost more than the free man, and his labor is less productive."[15] But "the influence of slavery extends even further, penetrating the master's soul and giving a particular turn to his ideas and tastes." Because work is associated with slavery, the southern whites scorn "not only work itself but also enterprises in which work is necessary to success." They lack both the

---

[15] This argument is uncharacteristically opaque. A simpler argument is that except for certain branches of agriculture slavery is unprofitable because it creates no incentive for slaves to apply themselves to their work.

opportunities and the desire to get rich: "Slavery ... not only prevents the white men from making their fortunes but even diverts them from wishing to do so." If Tocqueville is right, the classic debate over the economic stagnation of slave societies is spurious. There is no need to ask whether lack of investment desires or lack of investment opportunities provides the correct explanation: both sides could be right.

The arguments made by Madison and Tocqueville have a common structure: one and the same third variable shapes both desires and opportunities, which jointly shape action (or prevent it, as the case may be). In the abstract, there are four possibilities (plus and minus signs indicate positive and negative causal effects) (see Figure 9.2).

Case (A) is illustrated by Madison's analysis of direct democracies or small republics. Case (B) is exemplified by his argument in favor of large republics and by Tocqueville's analysis of the effects of slavery on the slaveowner.

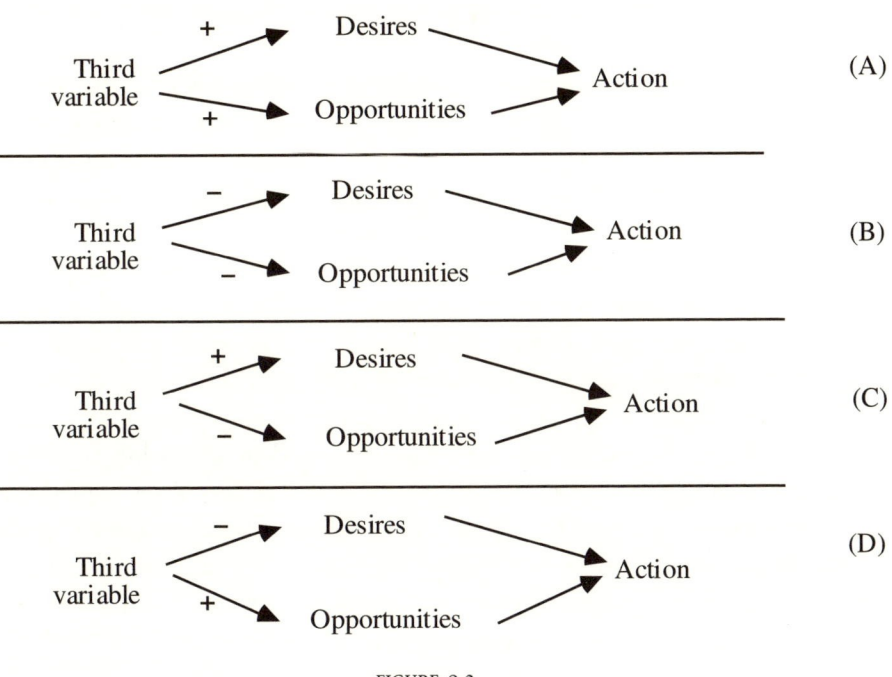

FIGURE 9.2

Case (C) is observed in the many cases in which lack of resources has the dual effect of increasing the incentive to improve one's situation and of reducing one's opportunity to do so. Although it is said that "necessity is the mother of invention," that is true only to the extent that hardship increases the motivation to innovate. But since innovation often requires resources (which might therefore be called "the father of invention"), the motivation by itself may not lead anywhere. Innovation often requires costly investments with an uncertain and delayed payoff – but this is exactly what firms on the brink of bankruptcy cannot afford. Prosperous firms can afford to innovate but may not bother to do so. As the economist John Hicks said, "The greatest of all monopoly profits is a quiet life."

Similarly, while the desire to emigrate is enhanced by poverty in one's home country, the same poverty may block access to the means of emigration because of the costs of travel. Until the early nineteenth century, emigrants to the United States could use their bodies as collateral. Their future employers would pay the trip in exchange for a period of indentured servitude. Today, smugglers of humans can rely on fear of the Immigration and Naturalization Service to prevent illegal immigrants from reneging on their promise to repay travel costs out of their income from labor in the receiving country. But when the Irish fled their famine in the 1840s, the poorest stayed home to die.

A further instance of case (C) is found in the study of peasant rebellions: although the poor peasants have the greatest incentive to rebel, they may not have the resources to do so. Participation in collective action requires the ability to take time off from productive activities, which is precisely what the impoverished peasant cannot afford. The middle peasants who have managed to save a bit can afford to join a rebellion, but their motivation is less acute. Marx argued that civilization arose in the temperate zones because only there did the desire for improvement meet with opportunities for improvement. Where nature is too lavish there is no desire, and where it is too scanty there are no opportunities. As this example shows, there may be a range of resources within which both desires and opportunities are sufficiently developed to generate action, but a priori nothing can be said about how wide or narrow it is, or whether it even exists.

We have seen an instance of case (D) in Chapter 2. The upper part of Figure 2.1 shows how Tocqueville argued that democracy (by the intermediary of religion) inhibited the desire to engage in the disorderly behavior for which democratic institutions such as freedom of the press and freedom of association provided an opportunity. A more commonplace observation by Tocqueville relies on the conjunction of (C) and (D), with young or old age as the third variable: "In America most rich men began by being poor; almost all men of leisure were busy in their youth; as a result, at the age when one might have a taste for study, one has not the time; and when time is available, the taste has gone."[16]

Desires and opportunities may also affect each other directly: consider first case (E) in Figure 9.3. In Chapter 2 I touched on some of the ways in which opportunities can affect desires: people may end up desiring most what they can get or prefer what they have to what they do not. Again we may quote Tocqueville on slavery: "Is it a blessing of God, or a last malediction, this disposition of the soul that gives men a sort of depraved taste for the cause of their afflictions?" This mechanism suggests a further reason for thinking opportunities more basic than preferences. Opportunities and desires jointly are the proximate causes of action, but at a further remove only opportunities matter since they also shape desires. The mechanism of "adaptive preference formation" (a form of dissonance reduction) ensures that no option outside the opportunity set is preferred to the most preferred option within it.

One might ask whether this mechanism *matters* for behavior, since, by definition, options that are not in the opportunity set will not be chosen.[17] Suppose the agent initially ranks options in the order A, B, C, D

---

[16] A different mismatch is expressed in the French saying "Si jeunesse savait, si vieillesse pouvait" (literally: If the young knew, if the old could), which implies that two requirements for action, the knowledge of what to do and the energy to do it, never occur together. A Norwegian proverb has a different twist: "Middle age is when you are old enough to know better and young enough to do it nevertheless."

[17] The adaptation could matter for the *welfare* of the agent, by providing peace of mind. This effect is ambiguous, however, since the self-poisoning of the mind associated with many cases of "sour grapes" or "sweet lemons" (such as the Broadway shows I discussed in Chapter 1) may, in a broader perspective, detract from welfare.

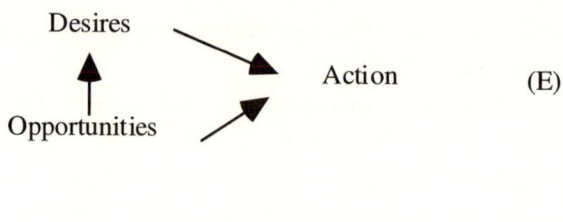

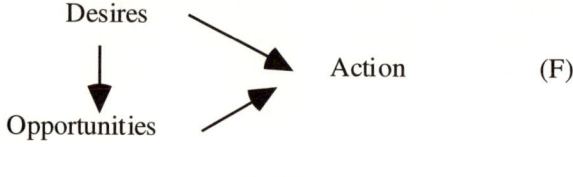

FIGURE 9.3

and then learns that A is unavailable. By adaptive preference formation, she now ranks them in the order B, A, C, D. She will choose B, as she would have had her preferences remained the same. Suppose, however, that the new ranking is C, B, A, D, inducing the choice of C. This might occur through a process of "overadaptation" to the limited opportunities. Tocqueville claimed this was a peculiar characteristic of the Frenchman: "He goes beyond the spirit of servitude as soon as he has entered it." More likely, we are dealing with a general tendency observed in many status societies. Also, the new preference ranking might be B, C, D, A. If beautiful women reject my advances, I may console myself by the thought that by virtue of their narcissism they are actually the least desirable partners.

Consider finally case (F), in which the opportunity set is shaped by the agent's desire. This may come about either by intentional choice, which I consider in Chapter 13, or by an unintentional causal mechanism. As I noted in Chapter 4, the desire for states that are essentially by-products may interfere with the opportunity to bring them about. The mechanism could be intrapsychic, as in the self-defeating desire to fall asleep, or interpersonal, as in the following example. In one university department where I taught there was a tacit rule that any faculty member who visibly wanted to become chair would thereby ruin the opportunity of attaining that position. In his career, Tocqueville illustrated both sides of that proposition. In an early stage, his political ambitions were frustrated because he was too visibly ambitious (as a saying has it, "Who enters the conclave as Pope, leaves it as cardinal"). In later life, commenting on his success in the elections to the Constituent Assembly in 1848, he wrote that "nothing makes for success more than not desiring it too ardently."

《《《

Bibliographical Note

The idea of "irresistible desires" is effectively demolished by G. Watson, "Disordered appetites: Addiction, compulsion, and dependence," in J. Elster (ed.), *Addiction: Entries and Exits* (New York: Russell Sage, 1999). The claim that individuals have the same preferences and only differ in the opportunities they face is notably associated with G. Stigler and G.Becker, "De gustibus non est disputandum," *American Economic Review* 67 (1977), 76–90. The idea of adaptive preferences and notably of overadapation to constraints is due to P. Veyne, *Le pain et le cirque* (Paris: Seuil, 1976) (partial translation in *Bread and Circuses* [New York: Penguin, 1982]). The decline in the (overall) suicide rate that followed the switch from coal gas to natural gas in Britain is documented in N. Kreiman, "The coal gas story," *British Journal of Social and Preventive Medicine* 30 (1976), 86–93. The extent to which reduced access to one means of suicide induces greater use of other means is discussed in C. Cantor and P. Baume, "Access to methods of suicide: What impact?" *Australian and New Zealand Journal of Psychiatry* 32 (1998), 8–14. Madison's use of the opportunity-desire distinction is analyzed by M. White, *Philosophy*, The Federalist, *and the Constitution* (New York: Oxford University Press, 1987). I discuss Tocqueville's use of the distinction in Chapter 4 of *Political Psychology* (Cambridge University Press, 1993).

Chapter 10
PERSONS AND SITUATIONS
❀ ❀ ❀

Shame and guilt, or contempt and anger, differ in that the first emotion in each pair targets a person's *character* and the second some *action* by the person (Chapter 8). Similarly, pridefulness rests on the belief that one is a superior person, and pride on the belief that one has performed some outstanding deed. But when we blame or praise an action, is it not because we believe it reflects the agent's character? To what other factor could it be ascribed?

When Folk Psychology Goes Wrong

This book is not about praise or blame, but about the *explanation* of behavior. In this context, the question is the power of character to explain action. People are often assumed to have personality traits (introvert, timid, etc.) as well as virtues (honesty, courage, etc.) or vices (the seven deadly sins, etc.). In folk psychology, these features are assumed to be stable over time and across situations. Proverbs in all languages testify to this assumption. "Who tells one lie will tell a hundred." "Who lies also steals." "Who steals an egg will steal an ox." "Who keeps faith in small matters, does so in large ones." "Who is caught red-handed once will always be distrusted." If folk psychology is right, predicting and explaining behavior should be easy. A single action will reveal the underlying trait or disposition and allow us to predict behavior on an indefinite number of other occasions when the disposition could manifest itself. The procedure is not tautological, as it would be if we took cheating on an exam as evidence of dishonesty and then used the trait of dishonesty to explain the cheating. Instead, it amounts to using cheating on an exam as evidence for a trait (dishonesty) that will also cause the person to be unfaithful to a spouse. If one accepts the more extreme folk theory that all virtues go together, the cheating might also be used to predict cowardice in battle or excessive drinking.

People often make strong inferences from the austere private conduct of others. A member of the French Academy reportedly voted for de Gaulle because of the dignity of his private life, with the tacit premise that someone who would betray his wife is also likely to betray his country. In Vietnam, Communist leaders were able to win "the minds and the hearts of the population" because of their incorruptible personal style, in stark contrast to the less self-denying organizers from other political groups. Among the Mafiosi, having affairs is thought to be a sign of a disorderly and weak character.

To some extent, folk psychology is self-fulfilling. If people *believe* that others will predict their behavior in a situation of type A on the basis of their behavior in a situation of type B, they will act in situation B with situation A in mind. If the belief in a link between private and public morality is widespread (and known to be so), it creates an incentive for politicians to behave honestly in private life, assuming that any mis-behavior would be made known to the electorate. Or suppose that it is widely believed that people have the same rate of time discounting in all situations. If they care too little about their futures to take care of their bodies, they are also (according to folk psychology) likely to break a promise to realize a large short-term gain. Hence to be able to make credible promises about mutually profitable long-term cooperation, one should also cultivate a slim and healthy appearance.

To a larger extent, however, *folk psychology is demonstrably false.*[1] If one can eliminate the effects of folk psychology itself, so that there is no incentive to live up to expectations of cross-situational consistency, little consistency is found. Parents who only observe the behavior of their children at home are routinely surprised to learn that they are much more well behaved at school or when visiting the homes of classmates. Moreover, interventions to improve behavior in the family do not lead to improved adjustment at school, compared to that of control groups that received no intervention.[2] In laboratory experiments, most people (about

---

[1] Not only folk psychology: social scientists who argue that agents signal through their behavior whether they are "good types" or "bad types" also overestimate consistency.

[2] There is a twist to these findings. The children of parents who complied with the advice of the interventiontists did better at school than the children of noncompliant parents, a fact cited by some

two-thirds of the subjects) can be induced to behave heartlessly, to the point of imposing (what they believe to be) severe electrical shocks (about 450 volts) on a confederate of the experimenter. Yet there is no reason to believe that their behavior is due to an underlying trait of sadism, cruelty, or indifference to the suffering of others; in fact, many of the subjects who behaved in this way were upset and torn by what they were doing. Children are much more willing to wait for a larger delayed reward when both that reward and a smaller one that could be obtained immediately are hidden from sight. Any academic will know other academics who are conscientious in their research, but less so in their teaching or in their administrative tasks. Being talkative at lunch turns out to be poorly correlated with talkativeness on other occasions. A person may procrastinate in cleaning up the house but never on the job.[3]

In an essay "On the inconstancy of our actions," Montaigne contrasts the behavior of the younger Cato with that of ordinary humans such as he: "Strike one of [Cato's] keys and you have struck them all; there is in him a harmony of sounds in perfect concord such as no one can deny. In our cases on the contrary everyone of our actions requires to be judged on its own: the surest way in my opinion would be to refer each of them to its immediate circumstances, without looking farther and without drawing any firm inference from it." As he also notes, "if [a man] cannot bear slander but is resolute in poverty; if he cannot bear a barber-surgeon's lancet but is unyielding against the swords of his adversaries, then it is not the man who deserves praise but the deed."

Let me give some examples from art and artists. Proust wrote that "one might have thought" that the young men in *Le temps retrouvé* who were paid for inflicting pain on the customers of Jupien's brothel must be "fundamentally bad, but not only were they wonderful soldiers during

in support of the spillover from home to school. Yet the finding may be due simply to the fact that compliance is inheritable. Parents who conscientiously follow the instructions of an interventionist are more likely to have children who conscientiously follow the instructions of a teacher.

[3] In a letter to the ethicist Randy Cohen (*New York Times Magazine*, January 15, 2006) an academic asked whether the fact that an untenured colleague claimed discounts at the Faculty Club to which he was not entitled warranted a vote against him for tenure "because of his dishonesty and its potential extension to his research." Cohen said no, on the grounds that "people who behave badly in some situations often behave well in others."

the war, true 'heroes,' they had just as often been kind and generous in civil life." Commenting on the apparent contradiction between Swann's "exquisite dissimulation of an invitation to Buckingham Palace" and his boast that the wife of a lower functionary had visited Mme Swann, he wrote that

> the main reason was (and this is one that holds for all of humanity) that even our virtues are not extraneous, free-floating things which are always at our disposal; in fact they come to be so closely linked in our minds with the occasions for acting on which we feel they should be deployed that, if we are required to engage in some different activity, it can take us by surprise, so that we never even think that it too might entail the use of those very virtues.

The jazz musician Charlie Parker was characterized by a doctor who knew him as "a man living from moment to moment. A man living for the pleasure principle, music, food, sex, drugs, kicks, his personality [*sic*] arrested at an infantile level." Another great jazz musician, Django Reinhardt, had an even more extreme present-oriented attitude in his daily life, never saving any of his substantial earnings, but spending them on whims or on expensive cars, which he quickly proceeded to crash. In many ways he was the incarnation of the stereotype of "the Gypsy." Yet you do not become a musician of the caliber of Parker and Reinhardt if you live in the moment *in all respects*. Proficiency takes years of utter dedication and concentration. In Reinhardt's case, this was dramatically brought out when he damaged his left hand severely in a fire and retrained himself so that he could achieve more with two fingers than anyone else with four. If these two musicians had been impulsive and carefree across the board – if their "personality" had been consistently "infantile" – they could never have become such consummate artists.

After 1945, the Norwegian novelist Knut Hamsun, who had collaborated with the Nazis during the war, underwent psychiatric observation to determine whether he was mentally capable of being tried (he was eighty-six years old at the time). When the psychiatric professor asked him to describe his "main character traits," he replied as follows:

> The so-called naturalistic period – Zola and his time – wrote about persons with main character traits. They had no use for nuanced psychology. People

had one dominant capacity that governed their actions. Dostoyevsky and others taught us all something different about people. From the very beginning I do not think there is a single person in any of my writings with this dominant and unitary capacity. They are all without so-called character – they are divided and fragmented, not good not bad, but both. Nuanced and changing in their mind and in their actions. This is no doubt how I am myself. It is very possible that I am aggressive, and that I have a little of the other traits the professor suggested – vulnerable, suspicious, selfish, generous, jealous, righteous, logical, sensitive, a cold nature. All these would be human traits, but I cannot give any of them the preponderance in myself.

In Chapter 14, I shall pursue the question of character or "lack of character" in works of fiction. Here I shall only note that Hamsun does not refer to the possibility that he might be, for instance, consistently generous in one type of situation and consistently selfish in another. I now turn to this issue.

The Power of the Situation

"Being impulsive with money" and "being dedicated to one's music," "being talkative at lunch," or "being conscientious in one's research" are also, of course, character traits. They are, however, situation-specific or *local traits* rather than global personality features that manifest themselves across the board in all situations. Contrary to folk psychology, systematic studies find very low levels of cross-situational consistency for character traits. Although correlations exist, they are typically so low that they cannot be detected "by the naked eye." Psychopaths may exhibit uncaring behavior across the board,[4] and the younger Cato may have been consistently heroic, but for the great majority of individuals who fall between these extremes such consistency is not to be expected. The more extreme idea of folk psychology, according to which all virtues go together, has not been as thoroughly tested, perhaps because it seems so obviously implausible. Yet it may still have a grip on the mind, as shown

---

[4] Since an intelligent egoist who cared about the future would often have an interest in *mimicking* concern for others (Chapter 5), the ultimate explanation of psychopathic behavior might be excessive discounting of the future.

by our confidence in the medical skills of doctors who have good "bedside manners." In classical antiquity, the idea that excellence in one arena was an infallible predictor or "index" of excellence in others was common. Psychologists refer to this as a "halo effect."

Often, therefore, the explanation of behavior is found in the *situation* rather than in the *person*. Consider for instance the fact that some Germans acted to rescue Jews from the Nazi regime. On a "characterological" theory, one would assume that the rescuers had an altruistic personality type that nonrescuers lacked. It turns out, however, that the factor with the strongest explanatory power was the "situational" fact of *being asked* to rescue someone. The causal link could arise in two ways. On the one hand, it is only by being asked that one can obtain the *information* that is needed to act as a rescuer. On the other hand, the face-to-face situation of being asked might trigger acceptance because of the *shame* one would feel if one refused.[5] The first explanation assumes altruism but denies that it is sufficient to explain the behavior. The second denies altruism and substitutes social norms for moral norms. On either account, what differentiates rescuers from nonrescuers is the situation in which they find themselves rather than their personality.

The Kitty Genovese case is another real-life example of the power of the situation. It is implausible to stipulate, on the basis of their inaction, that all the witnesses to her murder were callous and indifferent to human suffering. Rather, many of them may have thought that someone else was going to call the police, or that since nobody was doing anything about it the situation was not as serious as it might seem ("probably just a domestic dispute"), or that the inaction of the others suggested that direct intervention might be risky.[6] These lines of reasoning become more plausible the greater the number of passive bystanders. Thus in one experiment, subjects heard a confederate of the experimenter feigning an

---

[5] Similarly, the success of telethons in making people give money does not rest on their appeal to altruistic motives but to the fact that they are accompanied by a knock on the door by someone making a face-to-face request. In this case, the information-based explanation is clearly inadequate.

[6] People who were afraid of intervening physically to protect the victim from her assailant might still have called the police. At the time, however, the police did not accept anonymous calls, so that bystanders might have been afraid of getting into trouble. In other situations of this kind the option of calling the police may be unavailable.

epileptic seizure over the intercom system. When subjects believed they were the only listener, 85 percent intervened to help; when they believed there was one other listener, 62 percent intervened; when they believed there were four others, 31 percent intervened. In another experiment, 70 percent of lone bystanders intervened but only 7 percent did so when sitting next to an impassive confederate. With two naive subjects, the victim received help in 40 percent of the cases. Thus not only does the chance that any *given* bystander will intervene go down when there are more of them, but the chance that *some* bystander will intervene also falls with the number of bystanders.[7] In other words, the dilution of the responsibility to intervene caused by the presence of others occurs so fast that it cannot be offset by the greater number of potential interveners.

In another experiment, theology students were told to prepare themselves to give a brief talk in a nearby building. One-half were told to build the talk around the Good Samaritan parable(!), whereas the others were given a more neutral topic. One group was told to hurry since the people in the other building were waiting for them, whereas another was told that they had plenty of time. On their way to the other building, subjects came upon a man slumping in a doorway, apparently in distress. Among the students who were told they were late, only 10 percent offered assistance; in the other group, 63 percent did so. The group that had been told to prepare a talk on the Good Samaritan was not more likely to behave as one. Nor was the behavior of the students correlated with answers to a questionnaire intended to measure whether their interest in religion was due to the desire for personal salvation or to a desire to help others.[8] The situational factor – being hurried or not – had much greater explanatory power than any dispositional factor.

---

[7] This is at least the general tendency in the numerous experiments of this kind that have been carried out. In the one just cited (the epileptic seizure heard over the intercom) it turns out that if we assume that the other listeners were real, naive subjects who received the same information (and not simply confederates or fictions created by the experimenter), the chance that at least one of them would intervene is roughly constant, that is, around 85 percent. In the case of five subjects (the main subject and the four listeners), the chance that any one of them would abstain from intervening is 0.69. The chance that all of them would abstain is $(0.69)^5$, or 0.156, yielding a likelihood of 0.844 that at least one would intervene.

[8] Just like the subjects who were induced to inflict electrical shocks, many of those who hurried by the man in distress were themselves visibly distressed by the encounter.

It would not be accurate to subsume this analysis under that of the previous chapter, by saying that the students in the "hurry" category behaved the way they did because of a *time constraint*. Their constraint was not an objective or "hard" one, and in fact 10 percent of the students in this group did offer assistance. Rather, the situation shaped behavior by affecting the salience of competing *desires*. The face-to-face request enhances the strength of other-regarding motives, whereas being told to hurry diminishes it. Being able to *see* the reward that is imminently available makes it more attractive compared to one that will only be available with a delay, just as the sight of a beggar in the street can trigger generosity that the abstract knowledge of poverty would not. Kitty Genovese situations change both the perceived costs and perceived benefits of helping. The desire to comply with instructions by an impassive experimenter that "you must continue" to administer apparently painful and possibly fatal electrical shocks overrules the desire not to inflict pain needlessly.

There is no general or common mechanism by which a situation can affect behavior. Situations range from face-to-face demands to rescue Jews to the most trivial events, such as when finding a quarter in the coin return slot of a pay phone lifts one's mood and makes one help a stranger (in reality a confederate of the experimenter) retrieve a bunch of papers dropped on the sidewalk. The important lesson from these observations, in real life and in the laboratory, is merely that *behavior is often no more stable than the situations that shape it.* A person may be talkative at lunch when he can relax with long-standing colleagues and be tongue-tied with strangers. A person may consistently give to beggars but otherwise not give a thought to the poor. A person may invariably be helpful in situations in which nobody else can help, and invariably passive in the presence of other potential helpers. A man may be consistently aggressive and make biting remarks to his wife, yet be calm and generous to other people. His wife, too, may display the same dual behavior. His aggression triggers hers, and vice versa.[9] If they rarely see the spouse interact with other adults, for example, at the workplace, they may believe that he

---

[9] Metaphorically speaking, they are in a "bad psychological equilibrium." Yet aggression need not be a "best response" to aggression (as required by the game-theoretic notion of equilibrium), only a psychologically intelligible one.

or she is intrinsically aggressive rather than merely aggressive in the situation defined by their presence.

The Spontaneous Appeal to Dispositions

To pursue the last example, marital therapists often try to make the spouses who seek their help switch from character language to action language. Rather than saying, "You are a bad person," thereby leaving little room for hope or change, they should make an effort to say, "You did a bad thing." The latter phrasing leaves open the possibility that the action in question might have been triggered by specific situational factors, such as a provocative remark by the other spouse. One reason (among many) why therapists often have little success in reframing conflicts in this way is that people spontaneously privilege character-based explanations of behavior over situation-based ones. If we learn that somebody has contributed to a "gay rights" ad, we tend to assume that the person *is* gay or liberal rather than that he *was asked* in a way that made it hard to refuse. When interviewing a job candidate, we tend to explain what the person says or does in light of the dispositions we (overconfidently) impute to him or her, rather than to the special nature of the interview situation. Language itself reflects the dispositional bias. Adjectives that apply to actions ("hostile," "selfish," or "aggressive") can usually also be applied to the agent, whereas there are few characterizations of actions that also apply to situations ("difficult" is an exception).

Psychologists refer to the inappropriate use of dispositional explanation as the *fundamental attribution error*, that is, explaining situation-induced behavior as caused by enduring character traits of the agent. When subjects were asked to predict behavior of the theology students who encountered a distressed individual, they (wrongly) thought that people whose religion was based on a desire to help others would be more likely to act as a Good Samaritan and (again wrongly) that being in a greater or lesser hurry would make no difference at all. Other subjects overpredicted infliction of electrical shocks in the absence of the specific situational factors in the original experiment, thus revealing their belief in a dispositional explanation. When an instructor assigns a student the task of writing a pro-Castro essay, other students, knowing how it was assigned, still interpret the essay as manifesting a pro-Castro attitude. When students were asked to volunteer for tasks with either low or high remuneration, and low or high numbers of volunteers resulted, observers, knowing the pay differential, nevertheless predicted that *all* volunteers were more likely than nonvolunteers to volunteer for a nonpaying cause. The observers, in other words, attributed the action of volunteering to a disposition to volunteer rather than to the reward structure of the situation.

People in some societies seem less prone than those in others to the fundamental attribution error. Experiments indicate that compared to Americans, Asians ascribe more importance to the situation and less to personal dispositions in explaining behavior. Real-life situations, too, display this difference. Thus in 1991, an unsuccessful Chinese physics student shot his adviser, several fellow students, and then himself. In the same year, an American postal employee who had lost his job shot his supervisor, several fellow workers and bystanders, and then himself. Both events were widely reported in English and in Chinese newspapers, the former consistently explaining them in dispositional terms ("disturbed," "bad temper," "mentally unstable") and the latter in situational terms ("easy access to guns," "had just lost his job," "victim of pressure to succeed"). Other findings confirm this difference. It might be due, however, to the fact that situational factors actually play a greater role in generating behavior of Asians. Rather than being better at overcoming the dispositional bias, they may have less of a bias to overcome, or both of these factors might operate.

Overcoming the fundamental attribution error can be liberating. First-year college students who are told that most freshmen do poorly but that their grades subsequently improve, in fact do somewhat better in later years than those who are not given this information. The latter are more likely to impute their poor performance to their low ability than to the unfamiliar and distracting college environment. Not believing they can do better, they are less motivated to try. When oppressed groups shed the essentialism of their oppressors – the idea that women, blacks, or Jews are intrinsically inferior – they can more easily shed their shackles.

Is the fundamental attribution error hot or cold – a motivated mistake or more along the lines of an optical illusion? To the extent that motivation enters into the process of attribution, there is no reason why it should consistently lead us to overemphasize dispositions. On self-serving grounds, we should attribute our success to our enduring character traits, and our failures to unfortunate circumstances.[10] If the French moralists are to be believed, we should attribute the successes of others to their good luck and their failures to their dispositions.[11] On cognitive grounds, the tendency to favor the person over the situation may be an instance of a more general tendency to pay more attention to the moving foreground than to the static background. It follows that the error should be less common in cultures in which more evenhanded attention is paid to foreground and background, as seems to be the case in Asian cultures.

The Rehabilitation of the Person

The findings I have described undermine what one might call "crude essentialism" in the study of personality. It is simply not true that people *are* aggressive, impatient, extroverted, or talkative across the board. At the same time, the findings do not imply that the situation is all-powerful in explaining behavior. Rather, we have to decompose "the" character into a set of *contingent* response tendencies. Instead of characterizing a person as altruistic, we might describe him or her by the phrase "helps when asked, but does not volunteer to help," or by the phrase "helps when unstressed, but is neglectful when stressed." Each of these phrases might characterize one aspect of a person and thus underwrite a more subtle form of essentialism. A person might scold a spouse for never cleaning up around the house ("you're lazy") or for never cleaning up unless asked to ("you're thoughtless"). In the latter case, the spouse might be proactive rather than

---

[10] Sometimes, though, we may be motivated to impute our failures to our character. A gambler or an alcoholic may be happy to tell himself that he "just cannot help it" in order to have an excuse for persisting.

[11] Sometimes, though, we may be motivated to impute the successes of others to their character *flaws*. Anti-Semitism relies on the myth that Jews succeed because their immoral character makes them willing to adopt any means to get ahead.

reactive in other matters, such as monitoring the health of the children in the family. There would be no across-the-board trait of reactiveness.

In this perspective, explanation of behavior rests on the particular situation plus the person-specific relation between situations and behavioral propensity. One person might be highly aggressive with individuals over whom he has power, but exceptionally friendly with those who have power over him, whereas another person might show the opposite pattern. If we observe both of them behaving in a friendly manner, we might be tempted to conclude that they both *are* of a friendly disposition. As should be clear by now, however, the similarity of behavior might be due to differences in situation and in response contingencies that exactly cancel each other.

《《《

Bibliographical Note

The "tendency to overestimate the unity of personality" was clearly stated by G. Ichheiser, "Misunderstandings in human relations: A study in false social perception," *American Journal of Sociology* 55 (1949), Supplement. Recent work deemphasizing "character" derives from W. Mischel, *Personality and Assessment* (New York: Wiley, 1968). The present exposition relies heavily on L. Ross and R. Nisbett, *The Person and the Situation* (Philadelphia: Temple University Press, 1991), and on J. Doris, *Lack of Character* (Cambridge University Press, 2002). The references to Communist organizers in Vietnam and to Mafiosi are from, respectively, S. Popkin, *The Rational Peasant* (Berkeley: University of California Press, 1979), and D. Gambetta, "Trust's odd ways," in J. Elster et al. (eds.), *Understanding Choice, Explaining Behavior: Essays in Honour of Ole-Jørgen Skog* (Oslo: Academic Press, 2006). The reference to the effects of intervention is from J. R. Harris, *No Two Alike* (New York: Norton, 2006). The willingness to inflict electrical shocks is described in a classic study by S. Milgram, *Obedience to Authority*

(New York: Harper, 1983). Information about the two musicians is found in R. Russell, *Bird Lives: The High Life and Hard Times of Charlie (Yardbird) Parker* (New York: Charterhouse, 1973), and M. Dregni, *Django: The Life and Music of a Gypsy Legend* (Oxford University Press, 2004). The statement by Hamsun is translated from G. Langfeldt and Ø. Ødegård, *Den rettspsykiatriske erklæringen om Knut Hamsun* (Oslo: Gyldendal, 1978), p. 82 The use of behavior as an "index" in antiquity is discussed by P. Veyne, *Le pain et le cirque* (Paris: Seuil, 1976), pp. 114, 773; see also P. Veyne, "Pourquoi veut-on qu'un prince ait des vertus privées?" *Social Science Information* 37 (1998), 407–15. The "character-ological" explanation of the willingness to rescue Jews is argued by K. Monroe, M. C. Barton, and U. Klingemann, "Altruism and the theory of rational action: Rescuers of Jews in Nazi Europe," *Ethics* 101 (1990), 103–22. The "situationist" explanation is argued by F. Varese and M. Yaish, "The importance of being asked: The rescue of Jews in Nazi Europe," *Rationality and Society* 12 (2000), 307–24. In a game-theoretic analysis of the Kitty Genovese case, A. Dixit and S. Skeath, *Games of Strategy*, 2nd ed. (New York: Norton, 2004), pp. 414–18, argue that we should expect the chances that *anyone* will intervene to go down when the number of potential interveners goes up. A skeptical note about the tendency to infer dispositions from behavior is sounded in J. L. Hilton, S. Fein, and D. Miller, "Suspicion and dispositional inference," *Personality and Social Psychology Bulletin* 19 (1993), 501–12. The contrast between Americans and Asians is summarized in R. Nisbett, *The Geography of Thought* (New York: Free Press, 2004). What I call the "rehabilitation of the person" is argued in W. Mischel, "Towards an integrative science of the person," *Annual Review of Psychology* 55 (2004), 1–22.

Chapter 11
RATIONAL CHOICE
❀ ❀ ❀

The Structure of Rational Action

Rational-choice theorists want to explain behavior on the bare assumption that agents are rational. This assumption includes the hypothesis that agents form rational beliefs, including beliefs about the options available to them. There is no need, therefore, to classify the determinants of behavior as either subjective (desires) or objective (opportunities). Rational-choice theory is subjective through and through.

The structure of rational-choice explanation is laid out in Figure 11.1. An action is rational, in this scheme, if it meets *three optimality requirements*: the action must be optimal, given the beliefs; the beliefs must be as well supported as possible, given the evidence; and the evidence must result from an optimal investment in information gathering. In Figure 11.1 the arrows have a double interpretation, in terms of causality as well as of optimality. The action, for instance, should be caused by the desires and beliefs that make it a rational one; it is not enough to do the right thing by fluke. Similarly, a belief is not rational if it is the outcome of two oppositely biased processes that exactly cancel

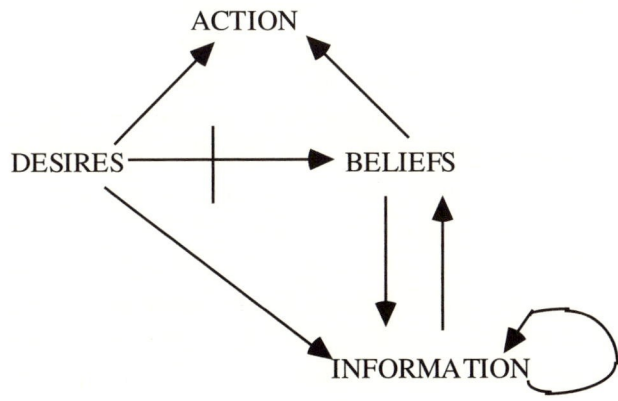

FIGURE 11.1

191

each other. To take an example, smokers as well as nonsmokers process information about the dangers of smoking in ways that make them believe these are greater than in fact they are. At the same time, smokers are subject to a self-serving bias that makes them discount the risks. If as a result they form the same belief as an unbiased observer would hold,[1] that does not prove they are rational. In one of the most influential discussions of rationality in the social sciences, Max Weber made the mistake of inferring "process rationality" from "outcome optimality" when he wrote that

> for the purposes of a typological scientific analysis it is convenient to treat all irrational, affectually determined elements of behavior as factors of deviation from a conceptually pure type of rational action. For example a panic on the stock exchange can be most conveniently analyzed by attempting to determine first what the course of action would have been had it not been influenced by irrational affects; it is then possible to introduce the irrational components as accounting for the observed deviations from this hypothetical course. Similarly, in analyzing a political or military campaign it is convenient to determine in the first place what would have been a rational course, given the ends of the participants and adequate knowledge of all the circumstances. *Only in this* way is it possible to assess the causal significance of irrational factors as accounting for the deviation from this type.

Although Weber was right in thinking that deviation from the rational course of action is a sufficient condition for irrationality to be at work, he erred in asserting (in the phrase I have italicized) that it was a necessary one. A similar mistake is involved in asserting that instinctive fear reactions are rational, when all that can be said is that they are *adaptive*. When I see a shape on the path that may be either a stick or a snake, it makes sense to run away immediately rather than gathering more information. It seems that human beings are in fact hardwired to do so. This flight behavior is not rational in the strict sense, since it is not produced by the machinery of rational decision making, yet it mimics rationality in the sense of being the very same behavior that that machinery

---

[1] As a matter of fact, the second bias of the smokers does not fully compensate for the first.

would have produced had it been brought to bear on the situation. When the opportunity costs of gathering information (Chapter 12) are high, a rational agent will not collect much of it. Yet often the flight tendency is not caused by such calculations, but preempts them.[2]

Preferences and Ordinal Utility

Spelled out more fully, the first optimality requirement is that the action must be the best means of satisfying the agent's desires, given his beliefs about the available options and their consequences. What is "best" is defined in terms of "betterness" or preference: the best is that than which none is better, as judged by the agent. There is no implication that the desires be *selfish*. The confusion of rationality and egoism is a crude error, although one that is facilitated by the practice of some rational-choice theorists. Nor do we need to require that desires be *stable*, not even in the minimal sense of excluding temporary preference changes. An agent who under the influence of emotion or drugs prefers A to B acts rationally in choosing A, even if she under other circumstances prefers B to A. A case in point (see Chapter 6) occurs when the weight the agent assigns to future consequences of present choice is diminished as the result of such influences.

For the analysis to get off the ground, the notion of "best" has to be well defined. Two conditions ensure that this will be the case.[3] First, preferences have to be *transitive*. Suppose there are three options, A, B, and C. If a person thinks A is at least as good as B and B at least as good as C, he should also think A at least as good as C. If transitivity fails, for instance if the person strictly prefers A to B, B to C, and C to A, he may not have a "best" option. Moreover another person can exploit this fact, by offering the agent a move from a less preferred to a more preferred option in return for a sum of money. Since preferences cycle, this

---

[2] In rats, the delay between the unthinking response and the reflective one is about 10 milliseconds.

[3] I ignore the technical condition that the set of options has to be compact and closed. Compactness is violated if for any feasible option there is one that is better, and closure if the limit of a sequence of feasible options is not itself feasible.

operation can be repeated indefinitely, bringing about the person's ruin by a series of stepwise improvements.[4]

This situation can arise if the agent ranks the options by "counting aspects." Suppose I prefer one apple to another if it is better in at least two out of three aspects, such as price, taste, and perishability. If apple A beats apple B in price and taste, apple B beats apple C in price and perishability, and apple C beats apple A in taste and perishability, transitivity is violated. Although this possibility is relatively unimportant in individual choice, in which it merely reflects the failure of a rule of thumb, we shall see (Chapter 25) that it is more significant in collective choice.

A different problem arises when indifference fails to be transitive. I may be indifferent between A and B and between B and C, because the differences within each pair are too small be noticeable, but prefer C to A because there is a detectable difference between them. There is an option that is "best," namely, C, but it is still possible to make the agent worse off by making her a series of offers – exchanging C for B and B for A – that she has no reason to refuse and hence might well accept. What justifies calling an agent with intransitive preferences irrational is not so much the lack of a "best" option, but the fact that she may accept offers that make her worse off.

To ensure that the idea of "the best" is always a meaningful one we must also require that preferences be *complete*: for any two outcomes the agent should be able say whether he prefers the first to the second, prefers the second to the first, or is indifferent between them. If he is unable to make any of these three responses, he may not be able to determine which option is the best. I say more about incompleteness toward the end of the chapter. Here, I only want to note that unlike lack of transitivity, a lack of completeness is not any kind of failure. Suppose I want to give an ice cream to the one of two children who will enjoy it most. For *me* to have a preference over the two options, I would have to be able to compare *their* levels of preference satisfaction were they given the ice cream. Often, however, this is an impossible task. The failure to carry it

---

[4] For another way of "improving oneself to death," see note 1 to Chapter 18.

out is not a failure, in the sense that I could have done better, but reflects simply a fact of life.

For many purposes, transitivity and completeness of preferences are all we need to identify the rational action. It is often convenient, however, to represent preferences by numbers, often called *utility values*, that are assigned to the options. To ensure this possibility we impose a further condition on preferences: *continuity*. If each option in a sequence A1, A2, A3, . . . , is preferred to B and the sequence converges to A, then A should be preferred to B; if B is preferred to each option in the sequence, B should be preferred to A. A counterexample is provided by "lexicographic preferences": a bundle of two goods A and B in quantities (A1, B1) is preferred to another bundle (A2, B2) if and only if either A1 > A2 or (A1 = A2 and B1 > B2). In this preference ranking, the bundles (1.1, 1), (1.01, 1), (1.001, 1), . . . , are all preferred to (1, 2), which is preferred to (1, 1). Loosely speaking, we may say that the first component of the bundle is incomparably more important than the second, since no extra amount of good B can offset even the smallest loss of good A.[5] Or, more simply, no trade-off is possible. Hence these preferences cannot be represented by indifference curves. Whereas lexicographic preferences rarely if ever apply to ordinary consumption goods, they can matter for political choices. A voter may prefer candidate A to candidate B if and only if A has a stronger pro-life attitude on abortion *or* if they have the same attitude on that issue and A proposes lower taxes than does B. For such voters, the "sacred value" of life may not be traded off against the secular value of money.

If the agent's preferences are complete, transitive, and continuous, we can represent them by a continuous utility function u that assigns a number u(A) to each option (A). Instead of saying that a rational agent chooses the best feasible option, we may then say that the agent *maximizes utility*. In this phrase, "utility" is a mere shorthand for preferences with certain properties. To see this, we may note that the only requirement for a function u to represent a preference order is that A is preferred to B if and only if u(A) > u(B). If u is always positive, $v = u^2$

---

[5] The intuitive notion of incomparability may, therefore, be spelled out in two distinct ways: as incomplete preferences or as discontinuous preferences.

can also represent the same preference order, although v assigns larger or (for $u < 1$) smaller numbers than u. The absolute numbers have no significance; only their relative or *ordinal* magnitude has. Hence the idea of "utility-maximization" does not imply that the agent is engaged in getting as much as possible of some psychic "stuff." It does, however, exclude the kind of value hierarchy embodied in lexicographic preferences. These cannot, in fact, be represented by a utility function.

Cardinal Utility and Risk Attitudes

Often, agents face *risky* options, that is, choices that may, with known probabilities, have more than one possible outcome. Intuitively, it would seem that a rational agent would choose the option with the greatest *expected utility*, an idea that incorporates the utility of each outcome as well as its probability of occurrence. She would first, for each option, weigh the utility of each consequence by its probability and add up all the weighted utilities, and then choose the option with the greatest sum.

Ordinal utility does *not* allow us, however, to spell out this idea. Suppose there are two options, A and B. A can produce outcome O1 or O2 with probabilities 1/2 and 1/2, whereas B can produce outcome O3 or O4 with probabilities 1/2 and 1/2. Assume now a utility function u that assigns values 3, 4, 1, and 5 to O1, O2, O3, O4, respectively. The "expected ordinal utility" of A is 3.5 and that of B is 3. If instead we use the function $v = u^2$, the numbers are 12.5 and 13. Each function represents preferences as well as the other, and yet they single out different options as "the best." Clearly, this approach is useless.

It is possible to do better, but at some conceptual costs. The approach associated with John von Neumann and Oskar Morgenstern shows that one can assign the options utility values that have a *cardinal* and not merely ordinal significance. An instance of a cardinal value assignment is temperature. Whether we measure temperature in Celsius or Fahrenheit does not affect the truth value of the statement "the average temperature in Paris is higher than the average temperature in New York." (If temperatures were measured ordinally, this statement would not make sense.) By contrast, the truth value of the statement "It is twice as hot in Paris as in New York" *does* depend on the choice of scale. Yet although the truth value of this particular statement about intensities is scale sensitive, others are not. The truth value of the statement "The temperature difference between New York and Paris is greater than that between Paris and Oslo," for instance, does not depend on the choice of scale. Similarly, we can construct cardinal measures of utility that reflect – among other things, as we shall see – the intensity of preferences and not merely the ordinal ranking of options. These enable us to compare the utility gain (or loss) of going from x to (x + 1) to that of going from (x + 1) to (x + 2), that is, to talk about increasing or decreasing marginal utility – concepts that are meaningless for ordinal utility measures.

The technical details of the construction need not concern us, as the basic idea is simple and sufficient for present purposes. We begin by assuming that agents have preferences not simply over options, but over *lotteries* of options (including the "degenerate lotteries" that consist of getting a basic option for sure). For any given set of basic options or "prizes," a lottery specifies, for each prize, the probability of obtaining it, the probabilities adding up to 1. Agents are assumed to have complete and transitive preferences over such lotteries. Preferences are also assumed to obey an "independence axiom": the preference between two lotteries p and q is unaffected if they are both combined in the same way with a third lottery r. The "certainty effect" cited in Chapter 7 and further discussed in Chapter 12 violates this axiom.

Finally, preferences are assumed to exhibit a form of continuity, defined as follows. Suppose the basic options include a best element A and a worst element B. We assign them, arbitrarily, utility numbers 1 and 0. Continuity means that for any intermediate option C there is a probability p(C) that would make the agent indifferent between getting C for certain and engaging in a lottery that would give him A with probability p(C) and B with probability 1−p(C).[6] We then define the *cardinal utility* u(C) as equal to p(C). This number, to be sure, is

---

[6] *Identifying* this probability raises the problems of anchoring cited in the introduction to Part II.

arbitrary because the end-point utilities are. Suppose we assign utility numbers M and N to A and B, respectively (M > N). We then define the utility of C as the expected utility of the lottery:

$$pM + (1-p)N = Mp + N - Np = (M-N)p + N.$$

The class of utility functions that arise in this way is much smaller than the class of ordinal utility functions.[7] It is easy to see that if option X has greater expected utility than Y according to one function, it will also have greater expected utility according to any other. Thus we can assert, without ambiguity, that a rational agent maximizes expected utility.

Cardinal utility functions have the important property of being *linear in probability*. Let us introduce the notation XpY, meaning a lottery that offers probability p of getting X and 1 − p of getting Y. Using the 1 – 0 end-point scale, the utility u(X) equals the probability q at which the agent is indifferent between X and the lottery AqB. Similarly, the utility u(Y) equals the probability r at which he is indifferent between Y and the lottery ArB. XpY, therefore, offers the utility equivalent of a chance p of getting A with probability q and a chance 1 − p of getting A with probability r. The utility of XpY, therefore, is pq + r(1 − p), which is p times the utility of X plus (1 − p) times the utility of Y. For instance, the utility of the probabilistic combination of a 3/5 chance of getting X and a 2/5 chance of getting Y is 3/5q + 2/5r.

Somebody could make the following objection. Suppose a farmer has the choice between two crops: the traditional variety that is equally likely to produce a good or a mediocre harvest, depending on the weather, and a modern variety that is equally likely to produce an excellent crop or a poor one. Suppose the cardinal utilities are 3 and 2 for the old crop, 5 or 1 for the new one. Since the expected utility of the new crop is larger, that is what the farmer ought to choose. But – the objection might go – does this not disregard the fact that the farmer might be risk averse and unwilling to accept any option that might lead to a utility level as low as 1? The objection involves double-counting, however, as risk aversion is

---

[7] Any two such functions are in fact related to each other as are the Celsius and Fahrenheit temperature scales, which assign different values (corresponding to M and N in the text) to the temperatures at which water boils and freezes.

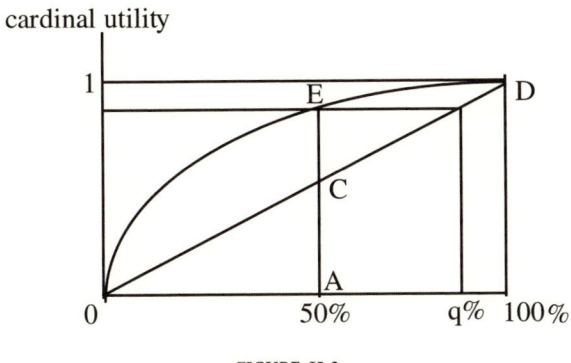

FIGURE II.2

already incorporated in the construction of the cardinal utilities. Assuming that A, B, and C take the values of 100, 0, and 60, u(C) might well be 0.75 for a risk-averse person, implying that she is indifferent between getting 60 for certain and a lottery that leaves her with a 25 percent chance of getting nothing and a 75 percent chance of getting 100. A similar argument applies to the assignment of cardinal utility values to physical amounts of the crop.

For another illustration, consider the allocation of child custody (see Figure 11.2). The horizontal axis can be understood in two ways, as involving either a physical division of custody (percentage of the time spent with the child) or a probabilistic division (the chance of being awarded full custody in a court of law). The cardinal utility of equal time sharing is AE, which is greater than the utility AC of a 50 percent chance of full custody. (Here we appeal to the fact that cardinal utility is linear in probability.) The reason is that most people in this situation display risk aversion. They are willing to accept joint custody because a 50 percent risk of not being able to see the child at all is intolerable. It is only if a parent believes that his or her chance of getting full custody is greater than q percent that litigation is preferable to joint custody. If there is a considerable amount of custody litigation it is not because parents are risk lovers, but because wishful thinking makes them exaggerate their chance of being awarded custody.

Risk Aversion and Decreasing Marginal Utility

The preceding exposition, while accurate, could be misleading. There is a tendency in part of the literature to blur the distinction between risk aversion and decreasing marginal utility. To develop this point, I need to introduce a concept that is intuitively meaningful, although it has not (so far) lent itself to measurement. This is the idea of the *intrinsic utility* of a good, reflecting the intensity of preferences of the agent. Introspection tells us compellingly that some goods or experiences are immensely enjoyable, others merely satisfying, still others mildly annoying, and some downright dreadful. To represent the difference between them merely in terms of ordinal preferences – "I prefer heaven to hell, just as I prefer four apples to three" – is clearly to use a very impoverished notion of welfare or utility. The fact that there is no reliable way of assigning numbers to intrinsic levels of satisfaction or dissatisfaction does not prove that the idea is meaningless, any more than our inability to quantify and compare the levels of satisfaction of different individuals shows that the idea of interpersonal comparison of welfare is meaningless.

The idea that many goods have decreasing marginal utility may be understood in this perspective. For a poor person, the first dollars have great utility, but then each successive extra dollar becomes worth less in subjective terms. Every smoker knows that the first cigarette in the morning is the best one, and that you enjoy each cigarette more if you pace yourself and do not smoke too frequently. Smoking a cigarette, in fact, has two effects: producing enjoyment in the present and reducing the enjoyment of future cigarettes.

The second effect does not, however, have to be negative. Consider again the child custody case. For a parent, one afternoon with the child every other weekend may provide more frustration than satisfaction. An afternoon every weekend is more than twice as satisfying, because the stronger emotional bonds created by more frequent encounters make each of them more satisfying. At the other end of the time spectrum, the extra satisfaction of being with the child seven days a week rather than six

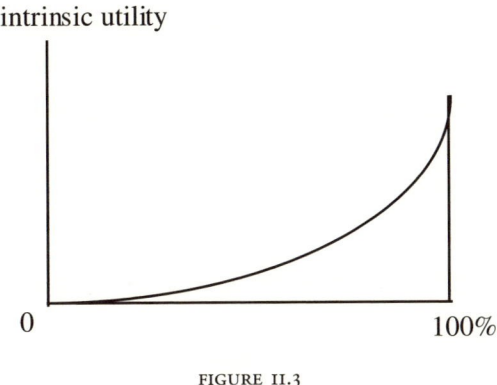

intrinsic utility

0   100%

FIGURE 11.3

exceeds the extra satisfaction of six days rather than five, because full custody provides the benefits of unconstrained planning. Being with the child, in fact, has increasing marginal (intrinsic) utility, as shown in Figure 11.3.

Here, the interpretation of the horizontal axis is percentage of the time spent with the child. For the reasons just given, each extra hour is more valuable than the preceding one. *This statement is perfectly compatible with the analysis underlying* Figure 11.2. The marginal utility of time spent with the child may be decreasing if utility is understood as cardinal utility, but increasing if it is understood as intrinsic utility. The fact that only the first part of this statement has a measurable interpretation does not imply that the second is meaningless.

While cardinal utility functions are always generated by two underlying psychological factors, risk attitudes and intrinsic utility, these cannot be measured separately. We cannot tell in any rigorous way whether the curve OED in Figure 11.2 is derived from risk neutrality combined with decreasing marginal intrinsic utility of time spent with the child or from risk aversion combined with increasing marginal intrinsic utility of time spent with the child. In a given case, intuition may tell us that the one or the other interpretation is more plausible. For some parents, time spent with the child may be experienced the way it is by many grandparents: it is good in small doses but soon becomes exhausting. At the same time, these parents may not worry much about the risk of not spending any time at all with the child (risk neutrality). Other parents might differ in both respects, generating the same cardinal utility function. To repeat, or re-repeat, these statements cannot (so far) be made rigorous, but they make obvious sense.[8]

Rational Beliefs

This concludes the discussion of the first component of a rational choice: choosing the best means to realize one's desires, given one's beliefs. Clearly, this is only a necessary condition for rationality, not a sufficient one. If I want to kill my neighbor and believe the best way of killing someone is to make a puppet representing him and stick a pin through it, I act rationally (as far as this first component goes) if I make a puppet representing my neighbor and stick a pin through it. Barring special circumstances, however, that belief is hardly rational.[9]

Rational beliefs are those that are shaped by processing the available evidence using procedures that, in the long run and on average, are most likely to yield true beliefs. Suppose we want to form a belief about the likelihood of rain on November 29, one week from today. We can probably not do much better than look up the statistics of rainfall in earlier years and assume that the (expected) future will be like the past. But as November 29 approaches, current rainfall may make us modify our expectations. If it often rains in November and we experience day after day with unclouded skies, we might infer the existence of a high-pressure system that makes rain on November 29 somewhat less likely.

This process of belief revision is often called *Bayesian learning* (named after the eighteenth-century minister Bayes). Assume that we have an initial ("prior") subjective probability distribution over different states of

---

[8] Hence the analogy with temperature scales is only partly valid. These scales measure *only* the intensity of temperature. Cardinal utility functions measure the joint result of intensity of preference and risk attitudes.

[9] Belief in witchcraft may be self-fulfilling, if the cursed person believes in the efficacy of the curse and simply loses the will to live. In that case, the observed efficacy of the curse might make belief in witchcraft rational, even if (as with the theory of action at a distance) the agent cannot specify the mechanism by which it works. It could also make witchcraft punishable on the basis of its actual consequences rather than, as suggested by Donne and Hobbes (see introduction to Part II), on the basis of mens rea only.

the world. In the example just given, the prior distribution was derived from past frequencies. In other cases, it might be a mere hunch. On the basis of my intuition, I might assign, for instance, probability 60 percent to the prime minister's (PM's) being competent and 40 percent to his being incompetent. We can then observe the actions he takes in office and their outcomes, such as the rate of growth of the economy. Suppose we can form an estimate about the likelihood of these observations *given the competence* of the PM. With a competent PM we have an 80 percent expectation of a good outcome, with an incompetent only 30 percent. Bayes showed how we can then update our initial probabilities concerning the PM's competence, *given the observations*.

Assume that there are only two possible outcomes, good or bad, and that we observe a good one. If we write $p(a)$ for the probability that a obtains and $p(a \mid b)$ for the *conditional probability* that a obtains given that b obtains, we have assumed that $p(\text{PM is competent}) = 60\%$, $p(\text{PM is incompetent}) = 40\%$, $p(\text{good outcome} \mid \text{PM is competent}) = 80\%$, and $p(\text{good outcome} \mid \text{PM is incompetent}) = 30\%$. We seek to determine $p(\text{PM is competent} \mid \text{good outcome})$. We use the letters a and b to denote, respectively, competence and good outcome. We then note first that

$$p(a \mid b) = p(a \,\&\, b)/p(b) \qquad\qquad (*)$$

In words, the conditional probability $p(a \mid b)$ equals the probability that both a and b obtain, divided by the probability of b. This follows from the more intuitive idea that $p(a \,\&\, b)$ equals $p(b)$ multiplied by $p(a \mid b)$. Dividing both sides of this equation by $p(b)$, we get equation $(*)$.

Using equation $(*)$ again, but with a and b reversed, we have

$$p(b \mid a) = p(a \,\&\, b)/p(a)$$

or, equivalently,

$$p(a \,\&\, b) = p(b \mid a) \cdot p(a)$$

Substituting the latter expression in $(*)$, we obtain

$$p(a \mid b) = p(b \mid a) \cdot p(a) / p(b) \qquad\qquad (**)$$

Now, there are two ways for b (the good outcome) to occur, with a competent PM or with an incompetent PM. Drawing on the fact that the probability that one of two mutually exclusive events will occur is the sum of the probabilities for each event, we can thus write

$$p(b) = p(b \& a) + p(b \& \text{not-a})$$

which, by the reasoning in the paragraph following (*), is equivalent to

$$= p(b \mid a) \cdot p(a) + p(b \mid \text{not-a}) \cdot p(\text{not-a})$$

If we substitute this expression for p(b) into (**), we obtain *Bayes's theorem*:

$$p(a \mid b) = p(b \mid a) \cdot p(a)/[p(b \mid a) \cdot p(a) + p(b \mid \text{not-a}) \cdot p(\text{not-a})]$$

Plugging in the numerical probabilities on the right-hand side of this equation tells us that $p(a \mid b) = 80\%$, that is, that the observation of a successful outcome raises the likelihood that the PM is competent from 60% to 80%. A second and a third positive observation would raise it to 91% and then to 97%.[10] If another person initially estimated $p(a) = 0.3$ rather than 0.6, three successive positive observations would raise her estimate first to 0.53, then to 0.75, and finally to 0.89. Hence it may not matter much whether the initial hunches are unreliable, since as more and more information comes in the updated beliefs become more and more trustworthy. Over time, initial differences of opinion can be swamped by new evidence.[11] For future reference (Chapter 23), we also

[10] In this reasoning we rely on prior beliefs of two kinds, a "foreground belief" concerning the type of the PM and a "background belief" about the likelihood that a PM of a given type will produce a good outcome. While the background belief remains constant throughout, the foreground belief is revised as we receive new information. We might also move the foreground to the background, and vice versa, if what interests us is whether competent politicians are in fact able to shape economic outcomes or whether these are mainly affected by random or exogenous factors. We might then begin with a foreground belief about the likelihood that good politicians produce good outcomes and a background belief about the competence of a given politician. If observation shows that the economy fares badly under the stewardship of a politician assumed to have a high likelihood of being a competent type, we might assign increased likelihood to the hypothesis of random or exogenous influences.

[11] For the convergence to occur, the successive pieces of new information must be statistically independent of each other. In the textbook example of Bayesian belief formation, a person draws balls from an urn known to be equally likely to contain either 80 percent black and 20 percent white balls or 20 percent black and 80 percent white in order to determine how likely it is that the one or the other obtains. Since the draws are random and the balls are put back into the urn after each draw, the outcome of each draw is independent of the previous ones. In political situations such as the one described in the text, it may be much more difficult to verify independence. Also, convergence presupposes that the underlying situation remains the same or at least does not change

note that each new piece of information has less of an impact than the previous one.

Optimal Investment in Information-Gathering

The third component of a rational action is the optimal investment of resources – such as time or money – in acquiring more information. As shown in Figure 11.1 there are several determinants of this optimum. First, how much information it is rational to acquire depends on the desires of the agent.[12] For instance, an agent who does not care much about rewards in the distant future would not invest much in determining the expected lifetime of a durable consumption good. More obviously, it makes sense to gather more information before making an important decision such as buying a house than when choosing between two equally expensive bottles of wine. In the latter case, one should perhaps just decide by flipping a coin, if the expected cost of determining which is the better exceeds the expected benefit (based on a prior knowledge of the quality range of equally priced wines) from drinking the better wine rather than the inferior one.

Desires and prior beliefs jointly determine the expected benefits from new information. It is sometimes possible to tell with great precision how many additional lives will be saved by doing a specific test for cancer or, translated to the level of the agent, how likely it is that his or her life will be saved. The value of life depends on how the agent goes about trading off life against other desired ends. By one calculation, a premium of about $200 per year was required to induce men in risky occupations such as coal mining to accept one chance in a thousand per year of accidental death. Hence at the time this calculation was done, the value of a life was about $200,000.[13] The expected costs of new information, which

---

too fast. If the environment changes rapidly, the process of updating beliefs resembles that of aiming at a moving target (Chapter 6).

[12] Wishful thinking, in which "the wish is the father of the thought," is clearly irrational. By contrast, there is nothing irrational about the process shown in Figure 11.1, in which the desires are, as it were, the grandfather of the beliefs.

[13] There are many pitfalls in making such calculations, but the general point is impossible to deny: we all attach a finite value to our lives. If we did not, we would not engage in all the enjoyable or profitable risky activities that we do.

are determined by prior beliefs, can also sometimes be ascertained with precision. To detect intestinal cancer, it is common to perform a series of six inexpensive tests on a person's stool. The benefits of the first two tests are significant. However, for each of the last four tests the costs of detecting an additional case of cancer (not even curing it) were found to be $49,150, $469,534, $4,724,695, and $47,107,214, respectively.

The optimal search for information may also depend on the results of the search itself (this is represented by the loop in Figure 11.1). When a new medical product is being tested, there is a prior decision to provide the medication to one group and withhold it from another for a certain period. If it becomes evident early on, however, that the product is spectacularly successful, it would be unethical to withhold it from the control group. The same argument applies to a single rational agent. Suppose I am out in the woods plucking berries. I know that berries tend to grow in clusters, so I am prepared to spend some time looking before I start plucking. If I am lucky and find an abundant patch right at the beginning, I would be foolish to keep on looking.

We may view the gathering of information as a *shadow action* that accompanies the primary action. Before deciding what to do, we have to decide how much information to collect. Sometimes, *the shadow action and the primary action may coincide*, at least partially. Suppose the leaders of a country are weighing whether to go to war against another country. Germany's invasion of France in 1940 can serve as an example. To make the final decision whether to attack, information was crucial. The leaders needed to know the objective capacities of the prospective enemy, as well as "the organization, customs and habits of the enemy's army" (from the German manual *Duties of the General Staff*). Much of this information could be gathered by conventional means, including spying. However, to determine the *morale* of the enemy – their fighting spirit – there was no other option than actually fighting them.

Indeterminacy

These last examples – plucking berries and planning for war – will also help us see the *limitations* of rational-choice theory, or rather one of its

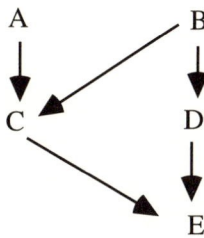

FIGURE II.4

two limitations. As an explanatory tool, the theory can fail in one of two ways. On the one hand, it may fail to yield unique predictions about what, in a given situation, people will do. On the other hand, people may fail to live up its predictions, whether unique or not. The second failure, *irrationality*, is the topic of the next chapter. The first, *indeterminacy*, is the topic of the following remarks.

An agent may be unable to identify the best element in the feasible set, for one of two reasons. A consumer may be *indifferent* between two options that are equally and maximally good. In trivial cases, this happens when the options are indistinguishable, as when a consumer faces the choice between two identical cans of soup in the supermarket. In nontrivial cases, two options might differ along several dimensions so that the differences exactly offset each other. The nontrivial case is rare, perhaps nonexistent. If offered a choice between two cars that differ in price, comfort, appearance, speed, and so on, I might not prefer either to the other without, for that matter, being indifferent between them. If I were, a five-cent discount on one car should induce a preference for that option. Intuition suggests that this is unlikely to happen.

In fact, the consumer's preferences may be *incomplete*. Suppose I have inspected five car models, A, B, C, D, and E, and rank them as shown in Figure II.4 (arrows standing for the preference relation). My inability to compare C and D does not matter, since I am not going to buy either of them anyway. By contrast, my inability to compare A and B leaves me in a pickle. True, I might try to gather more information, but how do I know it is worth the trouble? I return to this point shortly. First, however, let me point to another and probably more important source of incomplete preferences. Typically, option preferences are induced by outcome preferences. I prefer one option because I prefer its outcome, that is, its expected utility, compared to that of other options. If the situation is one of uncertainty or ignorance rather than risk (Chapter 7), however, I may not be able to compare the outcomes.[14] In the immortal words of Dr. Johnson, "Life is not long, and too much of it must not pass in idle deliberation how it shall be spent: deliberation, which those who begin it by prudence, and continue it with subtlety, must, after long expence of thought, conclude by chance. To prefer one future mode of life to another, upon just reasons, requires faculties which it has not pleased our Creator to give to us."[15]

A further indeterminacy arises in the difficulty of determining the optimal investment in information gathering. When I am out plucking berries in unknown territory, how long should I keep looking for a dense cluster and when should I begin plucking? Unless I find a rich patch right away, it makes sense to spend some time looking around. At the same time, I do not want to keep looking until nightfall, because then I shall certainly go home with an empty basket. Between the lower and the upper bounds on the time one should spend looking, there may be a large interval of indeterminacy. A different problem arises in the case of planning for war. If the primary decision and the shadow decision coincide, the planner is doomed to remain in a state of (at least partial) uncertainty. Rational-choice theory cannot guide us well in these situations. The theory is helpful in highly structured situations about which a great deal is known, such as testing for cancer, but less so in unknown environments.

Whereas spending less time than the lower bound and more than the upper bound would be irrational, no choice the agent makes *within* this

---

[14] In decision making under uncertainty, I may be able to compare options if the worst outcome of one option is better than the best outcome of another. In decision making under ignorance, even this modest comparability is unavailable.

[15] I might, however, "conclude by chance" and then invent the "just reasons," for instance, by giving greater weight to the attributes on which the chosen option is clearly superior. This can have undesirable consequences. Suppose I have the choice between going to law school and going to forestry school. Being unable to make a reason-based choice, I go to law school more or less by chance and justify the decision retrospectively by giving more weight to the income dimension of the two careers. With these newly induced preferences, I might go on to make other decisions that differ from those I would have made on the basis of my pre-choice preferences.

interval can be characterized as irrational. One might therefore, perhaps, think about dropping the idea of rationality in favor of that of *non-irrationality*. This revised version of the theory would allow us to make sense of a greater range of behavior but have less predictive power. Most practitioners of the theory would, I believe, be reluctant to revise the theory along these lines. What attracts them to the theory in the first place is precisely that it holds out the promise of generating *unique* predictions. It does so by virtue of the elementary mathematical fact that any "well-behaved" utility function defined over a "well-behaved" opportunity set attains a maximal value for a unique member of that set. The interaction between opportunity set and indifference curves in Figure 9.1 offers a good example of the compelling simplicity of this idea, "doing as well as one can."

The most important source of belief indeterminacy arises in strategic interaction, when each agent has to form beliefs about what others are likely to do on the basis of *their* beliefs, knowing that they are going through similar reasoning with regard to his. In some cases, further considered in Chapter 19, the reward structure does not allow the agents to converge to a commonly held set of beliefs.

Rationality Is Subjective Through and Through

Let me conclude the discussion of rational-choice theory by emphasizing again its *radically subjective nature*. One might, to be sure, take the word "rational" in an objective sense, implying that a rational agent is one who makes decisions that *make his life go better* as judged by objective criteria such as health, longevity, or income. Used in this way, however, the idea would not have any explanatory power. As I have emphasized, *consequences* of a decision cannot explain it. Only the mental states that precede the decision enable us to *explain* the actions as optimal from the point of view of the agent rather than to *characterize* them as useful or beneficial from the point of view of an external observer (or of the agent at a later time).

Suppose I suffer from a severe inability to defer gratification, that is, from being unable to take account of future consequences of present behavior. And suppose scientists came up with a discounting pill, which would increase the weight of future rewards in present decisions. If I take the pill, my life will go better. My parents will be happy I took the pill. In retrospect, I will be grateful that I did. But if I have a choice to take the pill or not, I will refuse if I am rational. Any behavior that the pill would induce is already within my reach. I could stop smoking, start exercising, or start saving right now, but I do not. Since I do not want to do it, I would not want to take a pill that made me do it. Similarly, a selfish person would refuse an "altruism pill" and, even more compellingly, an altruistic person a "selfishness pill." If I love my family and am willing to sacrifice some of my hedonic welfare for their sake, I would refuse a pill with the two-step effect of lowering theirs, just as I would refuse any option (e.g., buying an expensive meal for myself) that produced the same effect in one step.

To sharpen the argument, assume that a person consumes x today and y tomorrow, and that her one-period discount rate is 0.5 (she is indifferent between one unit of utility tomorrow and one half-unit today). Assume for simplicity that $u(x) = x$ and $u(y) = y$. The discounted presented value of her consumption stream is $x + 0.5y$. Suppose the person learns that tomorrow she is going to suffer from pain that will reduce the utility of her consumption by a factor of 0.5. The discounted present value of consumption now is $x + 0.25y$. If a rational agent is offered a costless aspirin that will eliminate the pain, she would clearly take it, thus restoring the original present value. If she took a pill that induced a discounting rate of 1 (but did not take the aspirin) the outcome would be the same in the sense that in either case, she would be indifferent between the two-period stream and a period-one utility of $x + 0.5y$. Since the agent would take the aspirin and since its effect is the same as that of the discounting pill, why would she not take the latter? The reason is that the choice of the discount pill is constrained by the need for the pill-induced consumption to be superior to nonpill consumption *as judged by prepill preferences*. There is no similar constraint on the aspirin choice, because there is no difference between pre-aspirin and post-aspirin preferences. Even without the aspirin I prefer being able to be free of pain tomorrow. When that state becomes part of my repertoire, I choose to bring it about. By contrast, the utility stream induced by the discounting pill is already in my repertoire, but I choose not to bring it about.[16]

Choices, in other words, need to be seen through the eyes of the agent. A myopic person who loses his glasses may be prevented by his myopia from finding them. He is "trapped."[17] Similarly, a rational agent may find himself in a "belief trap" that leaves him stuck with a false belief, namely, if the believed costs of testing the belief are too high. Thus women who practice genital mutilation may be caught in a belief trap. The Bambara of Mali believe that the clitoris will kill a man if it has contact with the penis during intercourse. In Nigeria, some groups believe that if a baby's head touches the clitoris during delivery, the baby will die. In Poland it has been widely believed that anyone who drinks when using disulfiram (Antabuse) implanted under the skin will die. As a matter of fact, implanted disulfiram is pharmacologically inert. The false belief might nevertheless deter people from testing it.

The *rationality* of beliefs is a completely different matter from that of their *truth*. Whereas truth is a feature of the relation between the belief and the world, rationality is a feature of the relation between the belief and the evidence possessed by the agent. Although rationality may require the agent to invest in new information, the investment is always constrained by its expected (that is, *believed*) costs and benefits. If gathering more information is believed to have high *opportunity* costs, as in the face of a possible imminent danger, it may be rational to

---

[16] With hyperbolic discounting, an agent might accept a discounting pill. Using the numerical example from Chapter 6, suppose that the effect of the pill is to lower the value of k from 1 to 0.3. At the time the smaller reward becomes available, its present value is simply 10 (no discounting). The present value of the larger reward of that time is $30/(1 + 0.3.5) = 12$. Hence precommitment in the form of taking the pill will enable the agent to act in accordance with his calm and reflective judgment, thus preventing weakness of will (in the broad sense). This statement remains true even if he has to buy the pill, as long as its cost (in utility terms) is less than 2. It also remains true if precommitment has the effect of reducing the value of the delayed reward (perhaps the discounting pill has the side effect of reducing the capacity for enjoyment), as long as the loss is less than 5. These facts might be relevant if for the discounting pill we substitute psychotherapy.

[17] If offered his glasses, he would put them on. I have argued that if offered the discounting pill, he would not take it. The difference is that he can already do without the discounting pill anything he could do if he took it, whereas there are many things he cannot do without his glasses that he could do if he put them on.

abstain from the investment. If it is believed to have high *direct* costs, as in testing the belief about the fatal effects of drinking while using implanted disulfiram, only an irrational person would make the investment. More generally, many beliefs must be taken at face value secondhand, since if we were to test them all we would never get on with our lives.

Any choice-based explanation of behavior is subjective. Not all subjective explanations assume, however, the transparency of the agents to themselves and the relentless search for optimality that are the hallmarks of rational-choice explanations. In the next chapter I shall canvass a number of explanations that depart from rational-choice theory on one or both accounts.

❲❲❲

Bibliographical Note

I discuss the relation between reason (in the sense of Chapter 4) and rationality in my inaugural lesson at the Collège de France, *Raison et raisons* (Paris: Fayard, 2006). For more about Weber and rationality, see my "Rationality, economy, and society," in S. Turner (ed.), *The Cambridge Companion to Weber* (Cambridge University Press, 2000). A classic exposition of utility theory is found in R. D. Luce and H. Raiffa, *Games and Decisions* (New York: Wiley, 1957). The original work by J. von Neumann and O. Morgenstern, *The Theory of Games and Economic Behavior*, 2nd ed. (Princeton, NJ: Princeton University Press, 1947), is still worth consulting. An outstanding exposition of rational-choice theory (and its problems) is R. Hastie and R. Dawes, *Rational Choice in an Uncertain World* (Thousand Oaks, CA: Sage, 2001). I discuss the child custody example at greater length in Chapter 3 of *Solomonic Judgments* (Cambridge University Press, 1989). An excellent elementary presentation of Bayesian theory is R. Winkler, *An Introduction to Bayesian Inference and Decision* (Gainesville, FL: Probabilistic Publishing, 2003). My argument that a rational person would not take the discounting pill has been influenced by exchanges with Gary Becker and Peter Diamond; see also O. J. Skog, "Theorizing about patience formation: The necessity of conceptual distinctions," *Economics and Philosophy* 17 (2001), 207–19. I take the idea of a belief trap from G. Mackie, "Ending footbinding and infibulation: A convention account," *American Sociological Review* 61 (1996), 999–1017. A useful study of the importance of intelligence in preparing for war is E. R. May, *Strange Victory: Hitler's Conquest of France* (New York: Hill & Wang, 2000). I owe the information about the use of implanted disulfiram in Poland to W. Osiatynski, *Alcoholism: Sin or Disease?* (Warsaw: Stefan Batory Foundation, 1997), and the data about its ineffectiveness to J. Johnsen and J. Mørland, "Depot preparations of disulfiram: Experimental and clinical results," *Acta Psychiatrica Scandinavica* 86 (1992), 27–30.

Chapter 12
RATIONALITY AND BEHAVIOR
❀ ❀ ❀

Ignoring the Costs of Decision Making

The idea of rationality has a strong normative appeal. We *want* to have reasons – desires and beliefs in light of which the action appears as rational – for what we do. In fact, our desire to act for a reason – our deference to rationality – can be so strong as to induce irrational behavior.[1] We may define *hyperrationality* as the propensity to search for the abstractly optimal decision, that is, the decision that would be optimal if we were to ignore the costs of the decision-making process itself. These costs are of three kinds: (1) the cost of the means of deciding, (2) the cost of the side effects of deciding, (3) the opportunity costs of deciding, that is, the value of the other things one might have done instead of going through the decision process. Let me illustrate them briefly.

Hyperrationality through neglect of (1) could arise in *comparison shopping* when the (expected) savings from finding the lowest price is less than the money spent on transportation traveling from store to store. Tourists in the South of France cross the border to Spain to buy cheap cigarettes as if gasoline were free. Neglect of (2) could induce hyperrationality in contested child custody cases. The court may try to promote the interest of the child by determining which parent is more fit for custody.[2] Once that issue has been settled, the court has a good reason for awarding custody to that parent. In the juridico-psychological process of ascertaining relative fitness, however, incalculable damage may be done to the child. A more rational procedure, given the aim to be achieved, might be to flip a coin or retain the traditional presumption of maternal custody.

---

[1] Acting for *a* reason should not be confused with acting according to reason, as that idea was defined in Chapter 4. The person who chooses according to his or her self-interest acts for a reason, but not according to reason. Conversely, the person who acts on the categorical imperative acts according to reason, but not for a reason (see note 15 to this chapter). Readers who find the last statement counterintuitive probably have a different understanding from mine of what it means to "act for a reason."

[2] The "best interest of the child" is in fact the criterion used in most child custody laws.

Neglect of opportunity costs is illustrated in an observation by Dr. Johnson in a conversation with Boswell about which subjects children should be taught first: "Sir, it is no matter what you teach them first, any more than what leg you shall put into your breeches first. Sir, you may stand disputing which it is best to put in first, but in the mean time your breech is bare. Sir, while you are considering which of two things you should teach your child first, another boy has learnt them both."[3] Again, flipping a coin may be more rational. Or consider the doctor who arrives at the scene of an accident and has to decide what steps to take. Although he obviously needs to examine the patient, his behavior is self-defeating if he spends so much time on it that the patient dies under his hand ("The operation was successful, but the patient died"). Others may have had the experience, when plucking berries, of looking so long for the best place that by the time they find it night is falling. Even when the savings from comparison shopping exceed the transportation costs, the behavior might still be irrational because of the value of the lost time.

Some Canonical Principles of Rationality

By a "puzzle" I shall here understand observed behavior that seems recalcitrant to rational-choice explanation. Although some puzzles may, on closer inspection, lose their puzzling character, many do not. Experiments and real-life behavior show numerous instances of behavioral patterns that violate the canons of rationality. In the following selective list of these canonical principles, I begin with the more fundamental and proceed to the more specific. I limit myself to individual choices; anomalies in interactive choices are discussed in Part V. The list may be supplemented by some of the cognitive anomalies I discussed in Chapter 7.

1. In a choice between acting and doing nothing, a rational agent will not act if the expected utility costs of acting exceed the expected utility benefits.
2. In the choice between evils, a rational agent will choose the lesser evil.

---

[3] Johnson, being a Shakespeare scholar, may have had in mind the King's remark in *Hamlet* (3.3): "Like a man to double business bound I stand in pause where I shall first begin, and both neglect."

3. A rational agent assigns the same weight to opportunity costs and to direct costs.

4. A rational agent will never prefer having a subset of a set of options to having the full set.

5. If a rational agent prefers X to a glass described as half-full she should also prefer X to one described as half-empty.

6. In a game of pure chance, a rational gambler will not, when placing her bets, pay attention to the outcomes of previous gambles.

7. When deciding whether to persist in a project or scrap it, a rational investor will pay attention only to the present value of future utility streams from these two options.

8. If at time 1 a rational agent forms a plan to carry out action X at time 2, she will do X at time 2 unless either her desires or her beliefs have changed in the meantime.

9. In a risky choice, a rational agent will choose means according to the expected outcome, not only according to the best-case (or worst-case) scenario.

10. In a market of rational agents, the rate of return on all assets should be (approximately) the same.[4]

11. If a rational agent chooses A from the set (A, B, C), she will also choose A from the set (A, B).

12. A rational agent will not act on an effect to suppress the cause (she will take antibiotics rather than aspirin to cure pneumonia).

13. If a rational agent prefers getting reward X with certainty to getting reward Y with probability q, she will also prefer getting X with probability p to getting Y with probability pq (the independence axiom of cardinal utility theory).

14. If a rational agent does X when she knows that circumstance C obtains (or intends to do X when C is expected to obtain) and does X when circumstance C does not obtain (or intends to do X when C is not expected to obtain), she should do or intend to do X even when she is ignorant about the circumstances.

15. A rational agent will never make an offer if its acceptance will reveal information that makes the deal have negative expected value.

---

[4] There are two reasons why the equality can be expected to be only approximate. First, external shocks will always induce deviations from equality. Second, risk aversion may induce lower values (and therefore higher rates of return) on highly volatile assets.

16. If an offense induces a desire for vengeance, the offended person will, if rational, bide his time until he can strike back with maximal chance of success or with minimal risk for himself.[5]

17. If challenged to a fencing duel, a rational agent will take fencing lessons if he has to take up the challenge.

18. Before asking for another person's hand in marriage, a rational agent will gather information about the other's behavioral and emotional propensities.

Violations of the Canon

These normatively compelling principles are, it turns out, routinely violated. Examples (with numbers matching those of the principles they violate) follow.[6]

1. *The paradox of voting.* Since no national election has ever been won by a single vote, an individual vote makes no difference to the outcome and may entail considerable trouble for the voter. Yet people do vote in large numbers.[7]

2. *More pain preferred to less.* Subjects of an experiment were exposed to two sequences of highly unpleasant noise. Both sequences involved exposure to thirty-five seconds of high-level noise. In the first, this exposure was followed by fifteen seconds of gradually decreasing (but still unpleasant) noise. When asked which sequence they would prefer to undergo again, subjects chose the one that was unambiguously less pleasant.

---

[5] Some might be tempted to replace "or" with "and" in this sentence. Except by fluke, however, one cannot maximize two objectives at the same time. To be more precise, the agent would seek the optimal feasible mix of the two goals, as represented by an opportunity set and a family of indifference curves (Chapter 9).

[6] Many of the examples have been cited in previous chapters and summarized here for convenience. They are from various sources: proverbs, classical authors, thought experiments, laboratory experiments, and real-life observations. Examples in the first three categories are, however, based on well-established theories that are surveyed later in the chapter.

[7] The paradox arises when the sole aim of the voters is to put a candidate into office or a proposal into effect. It need not arise when the aim is to contribute to the vitality of the democratic system or to give a "mandate" to a candidate, since in these cases votes matter even if they are not pivotal. Yet even when the motivation is to support democracy the explanation may lie in one of the nonrational mechanisms discussed later.

3. *The lawn-mowing paradox.* In a small suburban community, Mr. H. mows his own lawn. His neighbor's son would mow it for twelve dollars. He would not mow his neighbor's same-sized lawn for twenty dollars.

4. *The Christmas club puzzle.* In this system, customers deposit a monthly sum at low or no interest, which they can only withdraw at Christmas. The option of earning normal interest and costless withdrawal at will is also open to them.

5. *The credit card paradox.* When credit cards were introduced, the credit card lobby preferred that any difference between cash and credit card customers be labeled as a cash discount rather than as a credit card surcharge. Although the two descriptions are logically equivalent, consumers were more likely to use the cards if the difference was described as a cash discount.

6. *Two gamblers' fallacies.* If red has come up five times in a row, about one-half of gamblers believe that it is more than 50 percent likely to come up black next time. The other half believes it is less than 50 percent likely to come up black.

7. *The sunk-cost fallacy.* "To terminate a project in which $1.1 billion has been invested represents an unconscionable mishandling of taxpayers' dollars" (Senator Denton, November 4 1981). This fallacy is also sometimes referred to as "the Concorde fallacy," after the costly Anglo-French Concorde airplane project, or "the Vietnam fallacy," after the U.S. reluctance to disengage from Vietnam. If you buy tickets for an event and heavy snowfall makes it burdensome to get there, you might still go even though you would have refused the tickets had they been offered to you free.

8. *The dentist puzzle.* On March 1 I make an appointment with the dentist for April 1. On March 30 I call her to say that because of a (fictitious) funeral in the family I cannot keep it. Except for the sheer passage of time, no change has occurred in the interval. In particular, the pain from toothache is the same.

9. *Best- and worst-case scenarios.* Cancer patients in late stages often overestimate their chance of survival. Rather than palliative therapy to relieve their pain, they choose aggressive and painful chemotherapy with few benefits. When asked how much they would pay to reduce the likelihood of a low-probability disaster, people are willing to pay as much to have it reduced to one chance in 1 million as to have it reduced to one chance in 10 million.

10. *The equity premium puzzle*. Historically, the yield on stocks is vastly higher than the yield on bonds. A person who invested one dollar in stocks on January 1, 1928, would on January 1, 1998, have a portfolio worth eighteen hundred dollars, Somebody who invested a dollar in bonds would have a portfolio worth fifteen dollars. The puzzle is why this discrepancy has not led to a rise in the value of stocks to bring the return on stocks closer to the return on bonds.

11. *Effect of irrelevant alternatives*. If each of two options A and B is superior to the other along one of two relevant dimensions, people may find it hard to choose and instead decide to gather more information about the options. If a third option C, which is (1) inferior to A along both dimensions and (2) inferior to B on one dimension and superior on another, is introduced, there is a tendency to choose A without further search.

12. *The cold-water puzzle*. In an experiment, subjects who were led to believe that the length of time they could hold their arms in painfully cold water was the best indicator of longevity held their arms in the water longer than those not given this (false) information.

13. *The certainty effect* (Chapter 7). In experiments, a majority prefer to win a one-week tour of England with certainty to a 50 percent chance of winning a three-week tour of England, France, and Italy, but a majority also prefer a 5 percent chance of the second option to a 10 percent chance of the first.

14. *The disjunction effect*. If subjects in an experiment expect to win in a future gamble and are asked whether they will agree to take part in a further gamble, they tend to say yes. If they expect to lose, they are likely to state the same intention, If they do not know whether they will win or lose, they are less likely to do so. The same effect is observed in one-shot Prisoner's Dilemmas: a person is more likely to cooperate if he knows that the other cooperated than if he knows he defected, and – this is the disjunction effect – *even more likely* to cooperate if he is ignorant of the other's choice.

15. *The Winner's Curse*. In this experiment, subjects are asked to bid for a piece of land and told that the seller knows its exact value, whereas they know only that the value falls within a certain range, with all numerical values in that range equally likely. Buyers are also told that if they acquire the piece of land, it will be worth 50 percent more to

them than to the seller, because they will be able to exploit it more efficiently. If an offer is accepted, rational buyers should be able to infer *from that fact* that the expected value to them of the land is less than what they bid. If the values range from 0 to 1,000 and a bid of (say) 600 is accepted, the buyer can infer that the real value to the seller is between 0 and 600, with an expected value of 300. Hence its expected value to the buyer would be 450, which is less than what he offered to pay. Since the same argument can be made for any bid that is accepted, rational buyers should never make a bid. Yet in experiments (which were inspired by real cases) nobody fails to make a bid.

16. *Rush to vengeance.* A proverb has it that "vengeance is a dish that is best served cold." Another says that "delay in vengeance gives a heavier blow." Presumably, both arose in reaction against vengeance in hot blood, thus testifying to the existence of that phenomenon.

17. *Disregard for efficiency.* Montaigne wrote that "the honor of combat consists in rivalry of heart not of expertise; that is why I have seen some of my friends who are past masters in that exercise choosing for their duels weapons which deprived them of the means of exploiting their advantage and which depend entirely on fortune and steadfastness, so that nobody could attribute their victory to their fencing rather than to their valor."

18. *Marry in haste, repent at leisure.* This dictum applies not only to marriage in the literal sense. When people fall in love with a house, they are sometimes so eager to sign the contract that they fail to discover hidden flaws that surface later.

Alternatives to Rational-Choice Theory

To account for these puzzles, there is now available a wide repertoire of alternatives to rational-choice explanation. Before discussing them individually, let me list the key mechanisms in the alternative accounts I shall consider (with the puzzle numbers in parentheses). Some puzzles are listed more than once, because they may plausibly be accounted for in more than one way.

- Loss aversion (3, 5, 7, 10)
- Nonprobabilistic weighting of outcomes (13)

- Hyperbolic discounting (4, 8)
- Heuristics (2, 6)
- Wishful thinking (9, 12)
- Inability to project (15)
- The desire to act for a reason (11, 14)
- Magical thinking (1, 12, 14)
- The categorical imperative (1)
- Emotions (3, 7, 14, 18)
- Social norms (1, 3, 16, 17)

In current thinking, the most prominent mechanisms are probably loss aversion and hyperbolic discounting. In my opinion, emotions are an even more important source of irrational behavior, whether they operate directly or through the intermediary of social norms. Although emotions can upset rationality in many ways, the most important is perhaps by inducing urgency.

LOSS AVERSION is defined with respect to a reference point, on the assumption that people attach value to changes from a given baseline rather than to the end states obtaining after the change. The reference point is typically taken to be the status quo, although subjects may be induced to choose other reference points. Loss aversion is the tendency for people to attach larger value (in absolute terms) to a loss from the reference level than to a same-sized gain.[8] Empirically, the ratio is found to be about 2.5 to 1, which I assume in the following. Another important property of the value function is that it is concave for gains and convex for losses, meaning that each extra unit of gain is valued less than the previous one, and each extra unit of loss is less painful than the previous one.

Two of the puzzles can be explained by the simple fact that losses loom larger than gains. To resolve the lawn-mowing puzzle, we need only observe that loss aversion predicts that opportunity costs and

---

[8] Assuming that goods (including money) have decreasing marginal utility, standard rational-choice theory also predicts that losses will count more heavily than equal-sized gains from the same baseline. The magnitude of the effect, however, is typically much smaller. Also, standard utility theory implies that the utility gain of moving from A to B equals the utility loss of moving from B to A, since these differences are simply derived by comparing the utility *levels* of the two states.

out-of-pocket expenses are valued very differently. Since the value to the homeowner of a gain of twenty dollars is equivalent to the value of a loss of eight dollars, he prefers forgoing the gain to paying twelve dollars out of his pocket. The same reasoning could explain the credit card puzzle.

The resolution of the equity premium puzzle requires an additional premise, namely, that people choose their mix of bonds and stocks within a short time horizon. Since the return on stocks is volatile whereas bonds yield a steady income year in, year out, we can view the holding of stocks as accepting a risky gamble. Suppose we offer a person a bet on stocks that gives her a 50 percent chance to win \$200 and a 50 percent chance to lose \$100, with the fixed return to bonds as the reference point. If we assume loss aversion, this is captured by saying that the value of money is equal to x for x > 0 and equal to 2.5x for x < 0. Since the value of a loss of \$100 is equal (in absolute terms) to a gain of \$250, the prospect of a gain of \$200 cannot compensate her for the equally likely prospect of a loss of \$100. She will, therefore, reject the offer. Suppose now that we offer her a package of two such bets, to be carried out in successive periods. This compound gamble amounts to a 25 percent chance of gaining \$400, a 50 percent chance of gaining \$100, and a 25 percent chance of losing \$200. If we multiply the loss by 2.5 to make it comparable to the gains and calculate the expected value,[9] it is easily shown to be 25. The person will, therefore, accept the compound gamble. Empirical studies suggest that investors do tend to reevaluate their portfolios too frequently, a myopic practice that induces them to invest too little in stocks and too much in bonds.[10]

The resolution of the sunk-cost puzzle appeals only to the curvature (convexity or concavity) of the value function. Let us consider the following example. A family pays \$p for tickets to a game to be played sixty

---

[9] Since prospect theory assumes that the decision weights differ from probabilities, this calculation is only approximately correct. Neither this simplification nor the assumption of a linear value function matters for the conclusion of the analysis.

[10] The term "myopic" does not have the same meaning here as it has in analyses of time discounting (Chapter 6). It does not refer to the way the agent calculates the present value of future streams of income, but to the tendency to make successive decisions separately rather than "bundling" them together in one overall choice. Such "decision myopia," as we might call it, could also operate in other contexts. Thus when people try to control hyperbolic discounting by "bunching" successive choices together (Chapter 13), their success may depend on the number of choices they include.

miles way. On the day of the game there is a snowstorm. They decide to go anyway but note in passing that had the tickets been given to them, they might have stayed home. Writing v for the value function for gains, the value of going to the game is $v(g)$. Writing v^* for the value function for losses, the value of losing \$p is the negative number $v^*(-p)$. The cost of enduring the snowstorm is c. We assume that $v(g) = -v^*(-c)$, implying that if the family had received the tickets free they would have been indifferent between staying home and going to the game in a snowstorm. But since they have already paid \$p, they prefer to go. To see this, note first that because of the convexity of v^*, $v^*(-(c + p)) > v^*(-c) + v^*(-p)$.[II] This can be rewritten as $v^*(-(c + p)) - v^*(-c) > v^*(-p)$, which on the assumption just stated is equivalent to $v^*(-(c + p)) + v(g) > v^*(-p)$. Since the left-hand term in the last inequality is the net gain or loss from going to the game and the right-hand term the loss from not going, they prefer to go.

NONPROBABILISTIC WEIGHTING OF OUTCOMES.   Loss aversion follows from an influential alternative to rational-choice theory called *prospect theory*. Another implication of that theory is that people tend to weigh outcomes differently than expected utility theory asserts. According to that theory, utility is linear in probabilities (Chapter 11). Prospect theory, by contrast, argues that people are most sensitive to changes in probability near the natural boundaries of 0 (impossible) and 1 (certain). The certainty effect illustrates the nonlinearity around 1. The creators of prospect theory, Daniel Kahneman and Amos Tversky, cite the following example (which they attribute to Richard Zeckhauser) of the non-linearity around 0:

> Suppose you are compelled to play Russian roulette, but are given the opportunity to purchase the removal of one bullet from the loaded gun. Would you pay as much to reduce the number of bullets from four to three as you would to reduce the number of bullets from one to zero? Most people feel that they would be willing to pay much more for a

---

[II] Since this is a comparison of two negative numbers, the inequality states that the former is closer to zero, that is, smaller in absolute terms.

reduction of death from 1/6 to zero than for a reduction from 4/6 to 3/6. Economic considerations [that is, expected utility theory] would lead one to pay more in the latter case, where the value of money is presumably reduced by the considerable probability that one will not live to enjoy it.

HYPERBOLIC DISCOUNTING was discussed in Chapter 6. Here, let me simply note the close link between puzzles (8) and (4). The reason people join Christmas clubs is presumably that they know that if they put their savings in a normal account with the intention of keeping them there until Christmas, they will change their mind and take them out again.

HEURISTICS.   Heuristics (rules of thumb) can lead people astray. The gambler's belief that the roulette wheel has a memory may stem either from the representativeness heuristic ("It is time for red to come up") or from the availability heuristic ("Red is on a roll"). The preference for the more unpleasant noise stems from the use of a "peak-end" heuristic, according to which past experiences are valued according to how they were at their best (or worst) and how they were at the end, not by their overall pleasantness or unpleasantness. This heuristic would cause people to prefer the experience that is objectively the worst, since it has a better end than the other and the same peak.

WISHFUL THINKING. The phenomenon of wishful thinking was discussed in Chapter 7. It may be triggered by a simple desire, as when people in well-paid risky occupations downplay the risks they are running. It is even more likely to occur when the desire stems from a strong emotion, as when terminal cancer patients choose treatment whose only effect is to make them suffer more. Wishful thinking induced by the desire for a long life may also be at work in the cold-water puzzle.

INABILITY TO PROJECT.   In a number of situations, people make bad decisions because of their inability to project themselves into the future. By this I mean the lack of ability to imagine what oneself or others would have reasons to believe, or incentives to do, in future situations that depend on one's present choice. The Winner's Curse can be explained by this inability. For another example, consider President Chirac's disastrous calling of anticipated elections in June 1997. The reason his coalition lost may be that the voters understood that if he wanted early elections, it was because he knew something they did not and that made him believe that he would lose if he waited. By calling early elections, he revealed what he knew, or at least revealed *that* he knew something unfavorable, and therefore gave them a reason to vote against him. The polls told him he would win, but *polls are unlike elections* since holding a poll does not reveal anything to the respondents about the beliefs of the person who commissioned it.[12]

THE DESIRE TO ACT FOR A REASON. I cited several instances of this mechanism at the beginning of this chapter. In puzzle 11, the desire causes the agent to modify her behavior upon the introduction of an option that is unambiguously inferior to one of the options she already possesses.[13] In other cases, adding options may prevent the agent from making any decision at all. Behavior similar to that of Buridan's ass, which starved to death because it could not decide which of two identical haystacks to eat, has been confirmed in real-life settings. A psychologist who set up stalls on Broadway selling jam found that when stalls had a large variety of brands bypassers looked at more of them but purchased fewer, compared to stalls with few varieties. With more options it is more difficult to say to oneself, unhesitatingly, "This is the best." Those who need to base their choice on sufficient reasons will abstain from choosing.

As suggested by puzzle 14, to act for a reason one needs to *have* a reason, not merely to *know* that one has a reason. Thus suppose I know that exactly one of p or q is the case, but I do not know which. If p is the case, I have a reason to do X. If q is the case, I also have a reason to do X.

---

[12] In Part V I discuss Chirac's behavior as an instance of what I call the "younger sibling syndrome."

[13] This phrasing is somewhat misleading, since in experiments it is not the *same* subjects who are exposed first to the choice set (A, B) and then to set (A, B, C), but two different groups of subjects allocated at random to one of them. The natural interpretation of the finding, however, is that the subjects in the (A, B, C) group *would have behaved* as subjects in the (A, B) group had they been exposed only to the two options. The "modification," therefore, refers to a counterfactual baseline, not to an actual one. This remark applies to many of the experiments cited in this book.

Hence I know that whatever is the case, I have a reason to do X, but since I do not know *which* reason, I abstain from X. Puzzle 14 offers an example of this anomaly.[14] For another example, consider the fact that in older English law an accused would be acquitted if the evidence left it uncertain whether he had committed theft or embezzlement, although he would have been convicted if either charge had been proven. To be convicted he would have to be found either guilty of p or guilty of q. Being found guilty of (p or q) would not be sufficient. Another response to the predicament might be to postpone the decision. Suppose that the U.S. government is debating whether to establish a trade relationship with another country in which there is an upcoming presidential election. If the pro-U.S. candidate wins, the United States will have sufficient reasons to establish relations. If the anti-U.S. candidate wins, the United States will have (another set of) sufficient reasons to pursue the same policy. Yet the United States might wait until after the election before announcing its policy. Under some circumstances, this might be a costly but needless delay.

MAGICAL THINKING.   The mechanism of magical thinking (Chapter 7) could explain behavior in the cold-water puzzle. It may also explain some cases of the disjunction effect. If people are more likely to cooperate in the Prisoner's Dilemma when they do not know whether the other person cooperated or defected, it may be because they believe, magically, that by cooperating they can bring about the cooperation of the other. "Being like me, he will act like me." Voting intentions, too, may be shaped in this way. If I believe, irrationally, that my voting is not merely a predictor of others' voting but somehow makes it more likely that they will vote, the increased efficacy of my action makes voting appear rational.

THE CATEGORICAL IMPERATIVE.   There is a close relation between this last instance of magical thinking, the categorical imperative, and (an everyday version of) Kant's categorical imperative, according to which

---

[14] Along similar lines, the maximal amount people are willing to pay for a lottery between two options has been shown to be less than the maximum they are willing to pay for the least attractive of the options.

one should do A rather than B if we would all be better off if all did A than if all did B. Acting on the categorical imperative is, however, irrational. Rationality tells me to choose as a function of what will happen if *I* do A rather than B.[15] The categorical imperative tells me to choose as a function of what will happen if *everybody* does A rather than B. In a national election, even those who are not subject to magical thinking might "abstain from abstaining" by the thought "What if everybody did that?"

EMOTIONS. To compare emotion-based behavior with rational behavior, we may modify Figure 11.1 to include (in the heavily drawn lines) the impact of emotion on each of the elements of the scheme (see Figure 12.1).

It has been argued that emotions may affect *action* directly, in cases of weakness of will (Chapter 6). Medea, when killing her children to take revenge on Jason, knows *as she is doing so* that she is acting against her better judgment. I noted my reservations about that idea, but it cannot be excluded. Emotions affect *desires* in two ways. First, by virtue of the associated action tendency they may cause a temporary preference

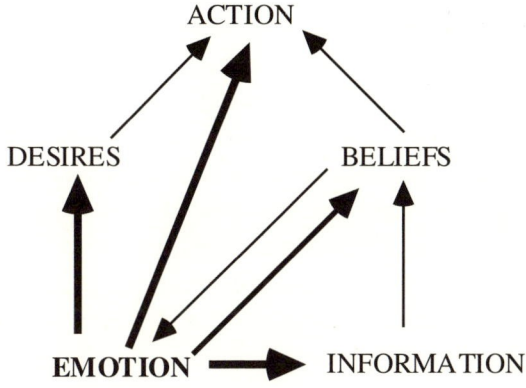

FIGURE 12.1

[15] Rationality does not tell me to choose as a function what will happen *to me* if I do A rather than B (see Chapter 11). It is compatible with some forms of other-regarding morality, but not with the one represented by the categorical imperative.

change. If the situation imposes a delay between the time at which the decision to act is made and the time of acting, the action may never be undertaken. An example cited in Chapter 8 was the way the increased expressions of interest after September 11, 2001, in serving in the army did not lead to increased enlistment. If action can be taken immediately, it may sometimes be reversed later when the emotion abates. Thus among the two hundred thousand men who deserted the Union Army during the American Civil War, presumably out of fear, 10 percent returned voluntarily. In some cases, however, action taken on the basis of emotion-induced temporary preferences is irreversible (a lobster-trap situation). When young men and women enlist in a guerrilla movement in a moment of enthusiasm and later want to leave it, they may find that this option is closed to them. Second, emotions may induce a temporary increase in the rate of time discounting, thus making previously less preferred options with bad long-term consequences appear to be preferable.

Emotions can affect *beliefs* directly by the mechanisms of wishful thinking and counterwishful thinking. The emotion of pridefulness – based on the belief that one is a superior kind of person – will resist the acknowledgment that one has made a mistake. This may explain, in some cases at least, vulnerability to the sunk-cost fallacy.[16] Pridefulness may also explain why people tend to blame their victims:[17] since their self-image does not allow them to admit guilt, they find a fault in the other that not only justifies what they did to him but motivates further injurious behavior. As in the sunk-cost fallacy, the unwillingness to admit a past mistake may lead to worse consequences than that mistake itself. As for emotions and counterwishful thinking, we shall see several examples in Chapter 23 of fear-induced panics.

Finally, by virtue of the urgency of emotions (Chapter 8) they may interfere with the optimal acquisition of *information* and hence also affect beliefs indirectly. Anger (puzzle 16) and love (18) make us do things

---

[16] In this context, it is interesting that animals do not seem to commit the sunk-cost fallacy: perhaps it is because they do not have any self-image to care about.

[17] As I note toward the end of Chapter 15, there is also a tendency to blame the victim of an action committed by a third party, as when people other than the rapist blame the victims of rape. Here the mechanism is not pridefulness, but a belief or tacit assumption that since the world is fundamentally just the victim must somehow have deserved her fate.

we would not have done had we had a more rational policy of information gathering. An observation by Seneca may help us pull some of these strands together: "Anger is altogether unbalanced; it now rushes farther than it should, now halts sooner than it ought." Often, the urgency induces a neglect of the temporally remote effects of the options, by virtue of the fact that *the determination of long-term consequences is itself time-consuming*. Hence the truncation of the time horizon need not be due to higher discounting of known consequences, but to the fact that some consequences do not even appear on the mental screen of the agent.

SOCIAL NORMS.   The emotions of contempt and shame play an important role in sustaining social norms (Chapter 21). The rush to vengeance may be due to the urgency of anger, but it could also be due to a social norm that brands as a coward anyone who delays avenging himself. The refusal of duelers to choose the weapons with which they are most proficient is also sustained by the fear of being thought excessively concerned with mere survival rather than with honor. Finally, the lawn-mowing puzzle might be explained by the operation of social norms rather than by loss aversion. A resident would not think of mowing his neighbor's lawn because there is a social norm in suburban communities against an adult doing such tasks for money. It simply *is not done*. Voting, too, may reflect the operation of social norms if the act of voting is visible to others and they disapprove of nonvoters. Voting in large anonymous elections is more plausibly seen as the result of *moral* norms, which may themselves have irrational aspects (see earlier discussion).

❝❝❝

BIBLIOGRAPHICAL NOTE

A critical assessment of rational-choice theory from a perspective somewhat different from the present one is found in D. Green and I. Shapiro, *Pathologies of Rational Choice Theory* (New Haven, CT: Yale

University Press, 1994), usefully supplemented by J. Friedman (ed.), *The Rational Choice Controversy* (New Haven, CT: Yale University Press, 1996). For the idea of rationality as a norm, see D. Føllesdal, "The status of rationality assumptions in interpretation and in the explanation of action," in M. Martin and L. McIntyre (eds.), *Readings in the Philosophy of the Social Sciences* (Cambridge, MA: MIT Press, 1994). I argue for the hyperrationality of the "best interest of the child" principle in Chapter 3 of *Solomonic Judgments* (Cambridge University Press, 1989). A useful discussion of some related issues is J. Wiener, "Managing the iatrogenic risks of risk management," *Risk: Health, Safety and Environment* 9 (1998), 39–82. Most of the subsequent puzzles are discussed in articles reprinted in the source books listed in the bibliographical note to Chapter 7. Exceptions are puzzle 1, for which see A. Blais, *To Vote or Not to Vote: The Merits and Limits of Rational Choice Theory* (Pittsburgh: University of Pittsburgh Press, 2000); puzzle 2, for which see D. Kahneman, "Objective happiness," in D. Kahneman, E. Diener, and N. Schwartz (eds.) *Well-Being: The Foundations of Hedonic Psychology* (New York: Russell Sage, 1999); puzzles 16 and 17, for which see Chapter 3 of my *Alchemies of the Mind* (Cambridge University Press, 1999); and puzzle 18, for which see the discussion in Chapter 8. Most of the alternatives are canvassed in the same source books, except for wishful thinking (Chapter 7), emotions (Chapter 8), and social norms (Chapter 21). It should be noted that the certainty effect is closely related to the very first puzzle that was explicitly presented (in 1953) as a challenge to rational-choice theory, the "Allais paradox." The "Chirac puzzle" is discussed, together with many similar examples, in A. Smith, *Election Timing* (Cambridge University Press, 2004). The claim that animals do not commit the sunk-cost fallacy is defended in H. Arkes and P. Ayton, "The sunk cost and Concorde effects: Are humans less rational than lower animals?" *Psychological Bulletin* 125 (1999), 591–600. The example of the jam sales on Broadway is taken from S. Iyengar and M. Lepper, "When choice is demotivating: Can one desire too much of a good thing?" *Journal of Personality and Social Psychology* 79 (2000), 995–1006. The reference to embezzlement and theft in old English law is from J. F. Stephen, *A History of English Criminal Law* (London: Macmillan, 1883; Buffalo, NY: Hein, 1964), vol. 3, p. 153. The findings about reenlistment in the Union Army are from D. Costa and M. Kahn, "Deserters, social norms and migration," forthcoming in *Journal of Law and Economics*. Evidence about heightened time discounting induced by emotion is offered in D. Tice, E. Braslasvky, and R. Baumeister, "Emotional distress regulation takes precedence over impulse control," *Journal of Personality and Social Psychology* 80 (2001), 53–67.

Chapter 13

RESPONDING TO IRRATIONALITY

❀ ❀ ❀

Second-Best Rationality

In the last two chapters I have considered the ideal of rational behavior and the frequent lapses from rationality. These lapses, however widespread and frequent, are not inevitable. If we understand our propensity to make mistakes, we can and do take precautions to make us less likely to make them again, or at least limit the damage if we do. As I have said repeatedly, we *want* to be rational. We may think of these precautionary strategies as a form of imperfect or *second-best rationality*. They should be distinguished from simple *learning*, which occurs when the propensity simply fades away as a result of improved insight. It has been reported, for instance, that when people realize that voting is, in one sense, pointless, they are less likely to vote.[1] Cognitive fallacies that are akin to optical illusions can also be overcome by learning. Just as we all learn to ignore the appearance of a stick that looks broken in water, some gamblers presumably learn the hard way that the dice have no memory. I am concerned here, however, with propensities that persist over time.

To cope with our tendencies to behave irrationally, we may use either intrapsychic strategies or extrapsychic devices (*precommitment*). I shall first illustrate how these techniques are used to counteract hyperbolic discounting and the inconsistent behavior it generates, and then discuss their use to control emotional and addictive behavior. These various strategies are not necessarily rational, but many of them are.

---

[1] Students of economics, in particular, seem to behave in this way.

Future Selves as Allies

An agent who is subject to hyperbolic discounting and knows it is *sophisticated*. Unlike the naïve agent who finds himself changing his mind over and over again without understanding the underlying mechanism, the sophisticated agent both is aware of her propensity and deplores it. Anticipating future situations in which she will face the choice between an early small reward and a delayed larger reward, she would like to make herself choose the latter despite her propensity to choose the former. In some cases, she may treat her "future selves" as allies in a common effort to overcome temptations. In other cases, she may treat them as adversaries and try to limit the damage they can do to her "present self." This language, to be sure, is metaphorical, but it will be demetaphorized.

Consider first the case in which the choice between an early small and a delayed large reward can be expected to arise over and over again. The agent can then make herself go for the delayed reward by *bunching* (or *bundling*) the choices.

Let me illustrate by an example from a time I was living up in the hills close to the university where I was teaching. Every day I took my bike to get to campus and back. The return trip involved some steep uphill climbing, so that every day I faced the temptation to get off the bike and walk rather than forcing myself to pedal. When I set out from campus I was firmly committed to staying on the bike all the way, but in the middle of the climb a seductive thought would often occur to me, "Why not walk today, and resume biking tomorrow?" Then, fortunately, a further thought occurred, "What is so special about tomorrow? If I yield to temptation today, does not that predict that I will do so again tomorrow, and the day after, and so on?" The last thought enabled me to stay on the bike.

This intrapsychic device involves a *reframing* of the situation. Rather than thinking about future trips home as involving *a series of choices*, I began to see them as *a choice between two series*: always biking up the hill and always walking the bike. By telling myself that my behavior on one occasion was the best predictor of my behavior on the next occasion, I set up an internal domino effect that raised the stakes and made me go for the delayed reward of improved health rather than for the early reward of relief from discomfort. Referring to Figure 6.1, it can be shown, in fact, that if we place many pairs of rewards identical to A and B on the horizontal line and then form two curves, one for the sum of the present-value curves of all the small rewards and one for the sum of the present-value curves of all the large rewards, the latter curve will lie above the former at the time the first choice has to be made, provided that the number of successive choices to be made is large enough.[2] In other words, bundling the choices can make the option of always going for the larger reward preferable to always going for the smaller reward. To be sure, choosing the smaller reward today and the larger reward on all future occasions is even better, but by assumption this option is not in the opportunity set of the agent.[3]

Can this assumption be justified? *Is* my behavior today a good predictor of my behavior tomorrow? In cases that involve a genuine causal effect, this may be true. Biking today will keep my muscles strong so that I can also bike tomorrow.[4] In my case, however, I relied on magical thinking rather than on causal efficacy. Just as many people vote or give to charity under the influence of the thought "If not me, who?" what kept me on the bike was the thought "If not now, when?" Or more

[2] For an illustration, suppose that the present value of 1 unit of utility at time t in the future is $1/(1 + t)$ and that the agent is twice exposed to the choice between a small reward of 3 and a large of 10. The small rewards become available at times 0 and 6, the large ones at times 3 and 9. At time 0, the present value of the first large reward is $10/(1 + 3) = 2.5$, which is less than the present (instantaneous) value of the small reward. If the choice is made on the basis of this comparison only, the small reward will be chosen. The same choice, for identical reasons, will be made at time 6. As the sum of the present values of the two small rewards is $3 + 3/(1 + 6) \cong 3.43$ and the sum of the present values of the two large rewards is $10/(1 + 3) + 10/(1 + 9) = 3.5$, bunching will make the agent prefer the two large rewards.

[3] If the agent suffers from "decision myopia" (Chapter 12), the bunching may not work. Suppose, namely, that the agent bundles his choices well ahead of the time when the first reward becomes available. At the time of bunching, the present value of the stream of large rewards is greater than that of the stream of small rewards, and the agent firmly intends to wait for the first large reward. As he moves closer in time to the moment when the first reward becomes available, this intention may or may not survive. This preference reversal is not due to hyperbolic discounting per se, but to decision myopia.

[4] For an analogy, suppose that by voting I could influence many others, who would otherwise have abstained, to cast a vote as well. Note that on this assumption, no magical thinking is involved, only a causal multiplier effect.

elaborately: "There is nothing special about today. If I get off the bike, the causes that made me do it will also operate tomorrow and induce the same behavior. If I do not make an effort now, I never will." In the absence of a genuine causal effect, however, the conclusion does not follow. If I *can* stay on the bike today but decide to get off, I can also stay on it tomorrow. Although false, the reasoning is compelling and, I believe, extremely widespread. It shows that we can enlist one form of irrationality (magical thinking) to combat another (hyperbolic discounting).[5]

To work well, such strategies may have to be framed as binary choices: always doing it or never doing it. For many people, abstention is easier than moderation. Boswell noted that "Johnson, though he could be rigidly *abstemious*, was not a *temperate* man either in eating or drinking. He could refrain, but he could not use moderately." The same problem arises if instead of limiting consumption on each occasion one tries to limit the number of occasions on which one may indulge. The stratagem of laying down in advance what will count as a legitimate occasion is easily eroded. When people resolve not to drink alcohol before dinner, they may find themselves scheduling dinner earlier and earlier. The rule of drinking wine only at restaurants, never at home, may cause one to dine out more frequently. Kant's rule of smoking only one pipe after breakfast (Chapter 4) was not unambiguous enough to give him full protection, since as time passed he bought himself bigger and bigger pipes. When feasible, the rule "Never do it" may be the only one that can be stably upheld. Since this policy is not feasible with regard to eating, obesity may be more recalcitrant than are addictions to private rules.

The binary choice framing can, however, induce absurdly rigid behavior. Suppose I have told myself never to suffer a single exception to the rule of brushing my teeth every night. On a given occasion I find myself without a toothbrush and decide to walk five miles in a blizzard to buy one. To sustain the decision, I tell myself that if I break the rule on that occasion, I will be on a slippery slope leading to rule violations for

---

[5] In voting, the effect of magical thinking is to help us overcome the propensity to socially harmful rational behavior rather than to counteract irrationality.

ever more trivial reasons, and soon there will be no rule at all and my teeth will fall out. Some people construct very elaborate systems of this kind, in which failure to follow one rule predicts failure with regard to other rules as well, thus raising the stakes even more.[6] Because private rules may have these stultifying effects, they sometimes provide a remedy worse than the disease. In Freudian language (Chapter 4), the rigid impulse control exercised by the superego could do more damage than the impulses from the id.

Future Selves as Adversaries

Consider now the case in which the agent confronts the choice between rewards (or punishments) at one of several future dates. (Unlike the previous case, the choice is only supposed to arise once.) The agent may then adopt the intrapsychic device of responding strategically to the known propensity of "future selves" to discount the future hyperbolically. Suppose I am a "hyperbolic procrastinator" who always put things off until tomorrow, and then, when tomorrow arrives, puts them off again until the day after tomorrow. Once I understand that I am subject to this propensity, my optimal behavior changes. Suppose that I can carry out a given unpleasant task in any of three periods, and that the cost of doing so goes up with time. If I am naive, I may tell myself that I will perform the task tomorrow. If I am sophisticated, I know that tomorrow I will delay until the last period. The understanding that the cost will in fact be very high unless I perform the task right away may induce me to do exactly that.[7]

---

[6] They may believe, erroneously (Chapter 10), that cross-situational consistency will induce cross-situational triggering of breakdowns.

[7] For an illustration, suppose that the present value of 1 unit of utility at time t in the future is $1/(1 + t)$ and that I will suffer increasingly by delaying my visit to the dentist: if I go today I suffer a pain of -2.75, tomorrow it will be -5, and the day after -9. From today's perspective, the present values are, respectively, -2.75, $-5/(1 + 1) = -2.5$, and $-9/(1 + 2) = -3$. Hence it might seem that the optimal choice from today's perspective is to postpone the visit until tomorrow. However, being sophisticated I know (today) that tomorrow the present value of going tomorrow will be -5 and that of going the day after $-9/(1 + 1) = -4.5$, inducing a preference to wait until the day after. Since today, however, I prefer going today to going the day after tomorrow, I go today.

In this case, being sophisticated helps. In other cases, being naive may be better. Suppose you can have a reward in any one of three successive periods and that the rewards increase with time. An example might be a person who has been offered a bottle of wine that improves with time up to the third year, and then deteriorates. A naive person may form the intention to wait until the third period, and then change her mind and drink the wine in the second period. A sophisticated person will know that he is never going to wait until the third period, so that he effectively only faces the choice between the first-period reward or the second-period reward. In that choice, the early reward may win out.[8] Some alcoholics report being subject to a similar kind of reasoning: "I know I am going to yield to temptation, so I might as well do it right away." Also, naive smokers who quit for the first time may hold out longer than sophisticated smokers who have tried several times and know the odds against succeeding. Although backsliding in addiction need not be due to hyperbolic discounting, the general point is the same: if you can predict that you will deviate from your best plan, you may end up deviating even more from it or earlier than if you are unaware that you will fail.

Extrapsychic Devices

In practice, sophisticated planning against one's future selves is probably less important than bunching strategies and the precommitment devices to which I now turn. These involve affecting the external world, in ways that cannot be instantly and costlessly undone, for the purpose of making it less likely that one will choose the earlier, smaller reward in the future. Five strategies stand out: *eliminating* the choice of the early reward from the feasible set, *imposing a penalty* on the choice of the early reward,

---

[8] For an illustration, suppose that the present value of 1 unit of utility at time t in the future is $1/(1 + t)$ and that I can benefit more and more by delaying my consumption of a bottle of wine: if I drink it this year I derive a pleasure of 2.75, next year it will be 5, and the year after 9. From today's perspective, the present values are, respectively, 2.75, $5/(1 + 1) = 2.5$ and $9/(1 + 2) = 3$. Hence it might seem that the optimal choice from the first year's perspective is to drink the wine the year after next. However, being sophisticated I know (this year) that next year the present value of drinking it next year will be 5 and that of drinking it the year after $9/(1 + 1) = 4.5$, inducing a preference to drink it the next year. Since in the first year, however, I prefer drinking it the first year to drinking it next year, I drink it today.

adding a premium for the choice of the delayed reward, *imposing a delay* between the choice and the actual delivery of the reward, and *avoiding cues* that might trigger preference reversal. Saving behavior can illustrate the first four options. If I begin saving for Christmas but find myself taking money out of my savings account instead of keeping it there, I may join a Christmas savings club that will not allow early withdrawals (Chapter 12). Alternatively, I may put my savings into a high-interest account that carries a penalty for early withdrawal, thus combining premium and penalty. If I want to save for my old age, I may set up a delay between a decision to dissave and the moment the funds become available, by investing in illiquid assets rather than in stocks or bonds. The fifth option is illustrated by the person whose craving for dessert is triggered by visual cues. The trick is to go to a restaurant where they do not wheel around the dessert trolley, so that one has to order from the menu. We may contrast this with a person who has a dessert problem because of hyperbolic discounting. For him, the best option is to go a restaurant where he has to order dessert at the beginning of the meal.

People who sign up for weekly physical exercises often drop out after a week or two. To prevent this, they may (in theory at least) sign a contract with the fitness center to pay twice the normal fee up front and receive a fraction back each time they show up. People who sign up for weight loss programs may have to pay a deposit that they get back only if they lose a stipulated amount of weight, sometimes with the rider that if they fail, the deposit will be donated to the person's most disliked political cause. When I set out to give the lectures that resulted in the present book, I precommitted myself by telling my students that I would give them a draft chapter at the end of each week. If I had failed to live up to that promise, I would have suffered the cost of their mild ridicule. If I am afraid I might cancel my appointment with the dentist when the time approaches, I can authorize him to bill me twice the regular amount if I fail to show up. In the case of wine that will improve with time, you may ask the seller to store it for you to protect yourself against premature gratification. If you are afraid that you might read the last novel by your favorite crime writer too quickly, skimming paragraphs to get to the dénouement, you might buy a book-on-tape version (and a player with no fast-forward function) that leaves you no choice but listening to every word.

The examples in the last two paragraphs involve precommitment against two kinds of temptation. On the one hand there is *procrastination*, including failures to save, to seek painful treatments, to do physical exercise, or to write up a manuscript. On the other hand, there is *premature gratification*, such as drinking wine too early or skipping pages in a book. These temptations stem directly from hyperbolic discounting. Nothing but the sheer passage of time is involved. In a further category of cases, *excessive behavior*, hyperbolic discounting may interact with other, visceral motivations. These include overeating, compulsive gambling, and addictive behavior. It may be hard to know, in such cases, whether preference reversal is due to the discounting structure or to other factors. A decision to fast that is made on a full stomach may dissolve as the person again begins to feel hungry. A decision to stop smoking may be eroded by the sight of another person lighting up a cigarette. This is the phenomenon of *cue dependence* – cravings that are triggered by visual cues associated with the consumption of the addictive substance. A decision to stop gambling that is induced by the guilt feelings of the gambler toward her family may unravel once the emotion fades in strength (Chapter 8). It may also be hard to tell whether we are dealing with procrastination or with visceral factors. A decision to take medication regularly may be undermined by the decline of the strong emotions that caused the patient to see a doctor in the first place.

Once the agent understands that he is subject to these other mechanisms, he may precommit himself to forestall their operation. To prevent his resolve to diet from being undermined by hunger, he may take a pill that attenuates the craving for food. More drastically, he may have his jaws wired so that he can only take in liquid sustenance. If he knows that his desire for dessert is cue dependent, he will not go to restaurants where they present a dessert trolley.[9] Former heroin addicts will stay away from the places where they used to consume the drug.

---

[9] If we compare this case with the one in which dessert had to be ordered at the beginning of the meal, we can see that they both involve protecting oneself against the effects of the *proximity of temptation*, be it spatial or temporal.

Ex-gamblers learn not to go to a casino "just to watch others play." If the agent can predict that her anger will fade so that she will not want to punish the offender, she might carry out the punishment immediately. This behavior was observed in Belgium after the war. On the basis of their experience from World War I, many Belgians believed that after a while the popular willingness to impose severe sentences on the collaborators would give place to indifference. Hence they wanted the trials to proceed as quickly as possible, before their emotions faded.

In fighting addiction, the strategy of imposing costs on oneself is very common. When General de Gaulle wanted to quit smoking, he told all his friends about it, to increase the costs of backsliding. In a cocaine addiction center in Denver, doctors are offered the opportunity to write a self-incriminating letter to the State Board of Medical Examiners confessing to drug use and asking that their license be revoked. The letter is automatically mailed if the patient tests positive for cocaine use. Some former alcoholics try to stay dry by taking disulfiram, a drug that has the effect of making the user violently ill if he takes a drink.[10]

Self-imposed delays can also be effective in resisting cravings. To prevent myself from impulse drinking, I may store my liquor in a safe with a timing device. Alternatively, I may adopt a policy of having no liquor at home so that I have to go to a store to get it. The disulfiram technique in fact combines the imposition of costs with delays, since once you have taken the pill you have to go two days without taking it before you can drink without getting sick. The cocaine addiction center, too, combined costs with delays. It allowed people to break out of the compact by submitting a notarized declaration of withdrawal from the arrangement. There was a two-week delay. Anyone who submitted a request for withdrawal could retrieve the incriminating letter after two weeks. But if during the two weeks' interim, the withdrawal was rescinded, then it would require another two weeks' notice. Although many of the patients invoked the withdrawal procedure, none went two weeks without revoking the revocation.

---

[10] The most common form is by oral intake, which works by causing the consumption of alcohol to make you sick. The (physically inefficacious but psychologically efficacious) implantation under the skin is less common.

The concern with precommitment against time inconsistency and excessive behavior is relatively recent. The classical writers on the topic focused on precommitment against *passion*, taken in a wide sense that also includes intoxication and psychotic states.[11] In *The Odyssey*, Homer offered what has become the standard example of precommitment: Ulysses binding himself to the mast so that he would be unable to respond to the song of the Sirens. In *On Anger*, Seneca wrote, "While we are sane, while we are ourselves, let us ask help against an evil that is powerful and oft indulged by us. Those who cannot carry their wine discreetly and fear that they will be rash and insolent in their cups, instruct their friends to remove them from the feast; those who have learned that they are unreasonable when they are sick, give orders that in times of illness they are not to be obeyed." In Mme de Lafayette's novel *La Princesse de Clèves*, the princess flees the court to avoid the temptation of responding to the overtures of the duc de Nemours; even later, when her husband is dead and she is free to remarry, she stays away. "Knowing how circumstances affect the wisest resolutions, she was unwilling to run the risk of seeing her own altered, or of returning to the place where lived the man she had loved." In Stendhal's novel *Lucien Leuwen*, Mme de Chasteller takes care to see Lucien only in the company of a chaperone, to make it prohibitively costly to give in to her love for him.

These strategies are quite common. When people burn their bridges, it may be for strategic reasons (Chapter 19), but sometimes they do it to prevent themselves from giving in to fear. I may stay away from the office party because I know from past experience that I am likely to have a drink or several, and that because of its disinhibitory effect alcohol will induce aggressive or amorous behavior that I will later regret. Alternatively, I may decide to take my spouse along, to raise the cost of such behavior. Merely *resolving* not to drink (or not to get emotional if I do) is less likely to be effective, given "the power of the situation" (Chapter 10). Similarly, controlling anger by the intrapsychic device of counting to ten before talking back or lashing out presupposes a detachment that tends

---

[11] The phenomenon, briefly mentioned in the text, of precommitting oneself while being in the grip of passion and fearful that it will abate is much less common.

to be lacking in the heat of the moment. A general advice of self-help is in fact to "break the chain early" rather than to rely on self-control in the face of temptation or provocation. As Mark Twain said, "It is easier to stay out than get out." For an extreme case, I refer to a *New York Times* headline (April 5, 1996): "Texas Agrees to Surgery for a Molester: Soon to Leave Prison, Man Wants Castration to Curb His Sex Urge."

Delay strategies might seem to hold out the best promise for dealing with emotion-based irrationality. Since emotions tend to have a short half-life, any obstacle to the immediate execution of an action tendency could be an effective remedy. As I note later, public authorities do indeed count on this feature of emotion when they require people to wait before making certain important decisions. It is rare, however, to observe people imposing delays on *themselves* for the purpose of counteracting passion. The requisite technologies may simply be lacking. One example, however, is the "covenant marriage" offered by three American states (Arkansas, Arizona, and Louisiana), an optional form of marriage that is harder to enter and harder to leave than the regular marriage. Typically, a couple who have entered a covenant marriage can be granted a divorce only after two years of separation, as compared to a normal waiting time of six months. The small minority (less than 1 percent of marrying couples) who use this option presumably do so to signal their commitment to each other and to protect themselves against short-lived passions and temptations.

Precommitment often involves the help of other individuals, organizations, or public authorities. These need, however, to be independent from the agent issuing the precommitment instructions, since otherwise he might revoke them. To fight his opium addiction, Samuel Coleridge hired a man to oppose by force his entrance into any druggist's shop. When the man tried to restrain him, Coleridge said, "Oh, nonsense. An emergency, a shocking emergency has arisen – quite unlooked for. No matter what I told you in times long past. That which I *now* tell you, is – that, if you don't remove that arm of yours from the doorway of this most respectable druggist, I shall have a good ground of action against you for assault and battery." Similarly, Mao Tse-tung gave orders that any orders he might issue after taking sleeping pills were to be ignored. When, after having taken the pills, he ordered his aide to send an invitation to the American table tennis team to visit China (the beginning of Chinese-American relations) and the aide asked him, "Do your words count?" he answered, "Yes, they do. Do it quickly. Otherwise there won't be time."

Organizations are more reliable tools for self-binding. The cocaine clinic in Denver and the Christmas clubs offer self-binding options that the individuals could not have come up with on their own and that were deliberately designed to help them to overcome their problems[12] *and* to prevent them from rescinding their instructions. In Norway, the Law of Psychic Health Protection allows individuals to commit themselves *voluntarily but irreversibly* to a three-week treatment in a psychiatric institution. It seems, however, that the system does not work, because doctors have the right but not the duty to retain individuals once they are in the clinic. To make it effective, patients would have to be allowed to sue their hospital if, at their request, it released them prematurely.

In 1996, the state of Missouri began a self-exclusion program for compulsive gamblers. Anyone who signs up for a self-exclusion list is banned for life from entering any of Missouri's casino riverboats. If she tries to ignore the ban and gamble on one of Missouri's riverboats anyway, she is to be removed from the boat, and "the licensee shall cooperate with the commission agent in reporting the incident to the proper prosecuting authority and request charges be filed . . . for criminal trespassing, a class B misdemeanor." Self-excluded gamblers are to be denied any winnings if they somehow manage to go aboard a riverboat, gamble, and win. The state can also take a more active role, by imposing delays on abortion, gun purchase, or divorce (and marriage!) and by allowing consumers a three-day or week-long waiting period during which they can cancel purchases made in a moment of enthusiasm. These are, however, instances of *state paternalism*, not of *state-assisted self-paternalism*.

Sometimes, political constitutions are understood as precommitment devices, or a form of *collective self-paternalism*. John Potter Stockton, writing in 1871, said that "constitutions are chains with which men bind

---

[12] Safes with timing devices, by contrast, were not made to help people fight their drinking problems.

themselves in their sane moments that they may not die by a suicidal hand in the day of their frenzy." Another common metaphor is that constitutions are ties imposed by Peter when sober on Peter when drunk. Bicameralism is often cited as an example of political precommitment: by having all legislation pass through two houses, one creates time for impulsive passions to cool down and reason (or interest!) to regain the upper hand. Imposing delays on constitutional amendments has been justified by the same argument. If precommitment is understood as *self-binding*, however, the extension from the individual to the collective case, and from the intragenerational to the intergenerational case, is quite dubious. Rather than a community's binding itself, we find majorities binding minorities and the present generation binding the future. Moreover, since constitutions are typically written in turbulent times, framers or founders are often themselves in the grip of passion. Being "drunk," they may not see the need to take precautions against drunkenness. Thus on September 7, 1789, when the French Assemblée Constituante was debating whether to write unicameralism or bicameralism into the constitution, the deputy Adrien Duquesnoy wrote the following entry into his journal: "If one can be allowed to make a probability assessment, it seems clear that the majority of the assembly will never vote for the two chambers. This outcome may have great disadvantages, but the situation is such, and the minds are so exalted, that no other is possible; perhaps it will be possible to make a change in a few years. One will come to understand that a unique assembly, in a nation as extremely impetuous as ours, can produce the most terrible effects."

‹‹‹

Bibliographical Note

The intrapsychic device of bundling or bunching the options has been extensively discussed by G. Ainslie, notably in *Picoeconomics* (Cambridge University Press, 1992). An attempt to provide rational foundations for such "private rules" is R. Bénabou and J. Tirole, "Willpower and personal rules," *Journal of Political Economy* 112 (2004), 848–86. The discussion of decision myopia draws on O.-J. Skog, "Hyperbolic discounting, willpower, and addiction," in J. Elster (ed.), *Addiction: Entries and Exits* (New York: Russell Sage Foundation, 1999). Strategic responses by sophisticated individuals who are aware of their propensity to discount the future hyperbolically are discussed by T. O'Donoghue and M. Rabin, "Doing it now or later," *American Economic Review* 89 (1999), 103–24. The idea of precommitment or self-binding to cope with one's irrational propensities is discussed in T. Schelling, "Egonomics, or the art of self-management," *American Economic Review: Papers and Proceedings* 68 (1978), 290–4, and in several of his later publications. I have discussed it in *Ulysses and the Sirens*, rev. ed. (Cambridge University Press, 1984); in *Ulysses Unbound* (Cambridge University Press, 2000); and in "Don't burn your bridge before you come to it: Ambiguities and complexities of precommitment," *Texas Law Review* 81 (2003), 1751–88. A book-length treatment of the failure to take prescribed medications is G. Reach, *Pourquoi se soigne-t-on* (Paris: Editions de Bord de l'Eau, 2005). The story about Coleridge is found in Thomas de Quincy, *Confessions of an Opium Eater* (London: Penguin Books, 1968), p. 145. The story about Mao Tse-tung is found in J. Chang and J. Halliday, *Mao: The Unknown Story* (New York: Knopf, 2005), 580–1. Whereas in *Ulysses and the Sirens* I was enthusiastic about the idea of constitutions as precommitment devices, I recanted in *Ulysses Unbound*.

Chapter 14

SOME IMPLICATIONS FOR TEXTUAL INTERPRETATION

❧ ❧ ❧

In a common view, the scientific enterprise has three distinct parts or branches: the humanities, the social sciences, and the natural sciences. For some purposes, this is a useful way of carving up the field of science, but for other purposes a rigid distinction may prevent cross-fertilization. In Part IV, I shall argue that the social sciences can benefit from the biological study of human beings and other animals. In this chapter I argue that the humanities and the social sciences have more in common than is usually assumed. In particular, I shall try to show that *interpretation* of works of art and *explanation* are closely related enterprises. To understand a work of art is to explain it in terms of the antecedent mental states of its creator. A *successful* work of art is one that can be given a rational-choice explanation. At the same time, I shall argue against what one might call "interpretation by consequences," a phrase that will be clarified later on. The account I shall offer does not cover all art forms. Even within literature, to which I shall limit myself, it makes sense only for classical (pre-1850) novels and plays, defined by the tacit convention that the events and characters that are described *could have been real.*[1]

Consider first rationality as a motive of the *characters* in fiction or plays. A classical problem in literary criticism is why Hamlet delays taking revenge for his father's death. Many explanations have been offered. Some of them appeal to irrationality, in terms of weakness of will or clinical depression. There is, however, also a simple rational-choice account. Although Hamlet initially believes what his father's ghost told him about Claudius, he later decides to *gather more information* by

---

[1] An early example of a violation of this convention occurs toward the end of Ibsen's *Peer Gynt* (1867), when Peer is afraid of drowning and the "strange passenger" tells him that "one does not die in the middle of the fifth act."

staging a play to "catch the conscience of the king." Once the reactions of the king have confirmed his belief, however, he lacks an *opportunity* to realize his desire, which is to make Claudius burn in hell forever. Although he has an occasion to kill Claudius while he is praying, doing so would according to contemporary theology ensure Claudius salvation rather than damnation. Later, he kills Polonius behind a curtain, *wrongly but not irrationally* believing him to be the king. Given the information he had, his belief that it was the king hiding behind the curtain was rational. Moreover, he had no reason to gather *more* information, since he could reasonably assume that someone hiding behind the curtain in the queen's presence would be the king.

I do not claim that this is the right interpretation (in fact I have not yet said what it means for an interpretation to be "right"). My point is simply that the three episodes I have mentioned are prima facie consistent with the idea that Hamlet is rationally pursuing the goal of avenging his father's murder. Another question is whether the idea is consistent with Hamlet's repeated self-accusations for lacking the resolve to take revenge. Many commentators interpret these famous monologues as a sign of weakness of will and view the two first episodes as based on self-deceptive excuses for inaction. (The third episode is harder to square with this view.) Now, although weakness of will and self-deception violate the canons of rationality, they are perfectly *intelligible* (Chapter 3). When dealing with the internal development of the work of art, intelligibility rather than rationality is the most useful idea for the task of interpretation.

In contrast to the internal point of view, we may take the external point of view of the author. To the question "Why does Hamlet delay his revenge until the fifth act?" we might answer, "The death of the king must take place at the end of the play."[2] This is a matter of dramaturgical construction, not of psychology. By itself, this answer would not be satisfactory. If Shakespeare had dragged out the revenge by a series of arbitrary events or ad hoc coincidences, simply for the purpose of having

---

[2] Unlike the words Ibsen puts in the mouth of "the strange passenger" (see previous note), Shakespeare could not have had Hamlet say, "I cannot kill the king until act V."

it occur at the end of the play, we would have deemed it an authorial failure. More pointedly, it would have been a case of *authorial irrationality*.

Authorial rationality is like the rationality imputed to God. Like God, the author is setting in motion a process in which each event can be *explained twice over*, first causally and then teleologically. I take this idea from Leibniz, who wrote that there are

> two kingdoms, one of efficient causes, the other of final, each of which separately suffices in detail to give a reason for the whole, as if the other did not exist. But neither is adequate without the other when we consider their origin, for they emanate from one source in which the power that makes efficient causes, and the wisdom which rules final causes, are found united.

God's aim is to create the best of all possible worlds. Specified to include the temporal dimension, the idea can be understood as the *best of all possible sequences*. Although the transition from one state of the universe to the next occurs by ordinary physical causality, the initial state and the laws of causality have been chosen so as to maximize the overall perfection of the sequence.

If we limit ourselves to the classical drama or the classical novel, the author's task is to develop the plot through what the characters say and do, often in response to one another. The aim is to do so in a way that maximizes aesthetic value. Thus each action or statement by a character can be explained twice over, both as a reaction to previous actions and statements (or external events) and as a generator of surprise, tension, and ultimately tension resolution in the reader. The first explanation rests on the intelligibility of the characters, the second on the rationality of the author, in a sense I shall now try to clarify.

The fact that authors often make many drafts before they are satisfied, or before they lay down their pens, is irrefutable evidence that they are engaged in a process of *choice* and that they possess explicit or implicit criteria for *betterness*. The fact that these drafts typically involve *small* variations suggests that they are aiming at a *local maximum* of whatever form of betterness they are striving for. However, the difference between an author and someone who is merely climbing along a gradient is that the former's *creativity* goes beyond mere choice.[3] The reason why the creation of a work of literature cannot be reduced to rational choice is that the number of meaningful word sequences is too large for one person to scan them all and select "the best." Although a "rational creator" may try to make the problem more tractable by deliberately excluding some sequences (this is one of the functions of meter and rhyme in verse), too many options will usually remain for choice to be a feasible selection mechanism. Instead, the author will have to rely on his or her unconscious associative machinery.

Rational creation is therefore largely about getting the second decimal right or, to shift the metaphor, about climbing to the top of the nearest hill. In yet a further metaphor, this is a left-hemisphere task. The right-hemisphere task of getting the first decimal right, or finding a hill that towers over the others, is not within the scope of rationality. Yet even reduced to the task of fine-tuning, authorial rationality matters. As suggested by the phrase "a minor masterpiece," it may be better to find the top of a low hill than to remain on the slopes of a taller one. Without implying any comparative judgment, *Chronicle of a Death Foretold* and *Look Homeward, Angel* can serve to illustrate the two possibilities.

Let me enumerate and then discuss some demands that rationality imposes on the author. First, the acts and utterances of the characters have to be intelligible. Second, the author has to meet the twin requirements of *fullness* and *parsimony*. Third, the work has to flow *downhill*, in the sense of minimizing the appeal to accidents and coincidences. Fourth, it has to offer a psychologically gratifying pattern of the buildup and resolution of tension.

Intelligibility can be absolute or relative, and if relative, global or local. The question of absolute intelligibility is whether *any* human being could behave in this way. The question of relative global intelligibility is whether the behavior of a fictional person is consistent with his or her overall character as displayed earlier in the work. The question of relative

---

[3] For the same reason, attempts to find rational-choice explanations of technical change are bound to fail.

local intelligibility is whether the behavior of a fictional person is consistent with his or her behavior in similar situations earlier in the work. Whereas the requirements of absolute and of relative local intelligibility are crucial constraints on authorial rationality, that of relative global intelligibility is not. If anything, the respect for the latter constraint may be seen as an aesthetic flaw.

In some cases, absolute intelligibility may be violated by excess of rationality. Consider again Euripides' Medea or Racine's Phèdre, both equally lucid about their self-destructive passions. They are portrayed as being subject to weakness of will in the strict sense, knowing that what they are doing is contrary to the all-things-considered judgment they hold *at the very moment of acting*. Although passion causes them to deviate from that judgment, it does not affect it. Racine's Hermione is a more credible character. Because her judgment is clouded by her emotions, she is self-deceptive rather than weak willed. My suggestion – it is nothing more than that – is that the simultaneous presence of extreme emotion and full cognitive lucidity goes against what we know about human nature.

Whereas too much rationality can be unintelligible, irrationality can be perfectly intelligible. What can be more intelligible than the reaction of M. de Rênal in Stendhal's *Le rouge et le noir* when, in the face of strong signs that his wife is having an affair with Julien Sorel, he chooses to believe in her fidelity? The wish is the father of the thought. More paradoxical are cases in which the desire that one's wife be faithful causes the belief that she is *not*, against the evidence. In *Othello*, "Trifles light as air are to the jealous confirmation strong as proofs from holy writ." The first is a case of short-circuiting, the second one of wire crossing (Chapter 3).

Relative intelligibility, which is violated by a person in a play or a novel who acts "out of character," raises different problems. First, we must take account of arguments by psychologists that character traits tend to be *local* rather than global (Chapter 10). Whereas many authors (Hamsun mentions Zola) subscribe to the folk psychology that assumes cross-situational consistency, good authors (he mentions Dostoyevsky) do not. The latter may disappoint readers who expect characters to behave "in character," but these are not the intended audience of the work. As we shall see shortly, even good authors may be constrained by the flawed psychology of their readers, but the belief in global traits is not one they should respect. Readers have a right, however, to expect local consistency. If the author paints himself into a corner, so that the only way to develop the plot as planned is to allow for a character to act in a locally inconsistent manner, he is violating his implicit contract with the readers. A plot should develop as water seeks its natural downhill course, not by the author's forcing it to run uphill.

Let me illustrate this idea by some of Stendhal's marginal comments in the manuscript of his unfinished and posthumously published novel *Lucien Leuwen*. Stendhal has the eponymous hero fall in love with a young widow, Mme de Chasteller. His feelings are reciprocated, but he does not dare to reach out to her. The very delicacy of mind that makes him superior to "the most accomplished Don Juan" and hence capable of inspiring love also makes him inferior to any "less well-bred young Parisian" who would instantly know how to handle the situation. To move the plot forward, Stendhal needs to bring them together but does not quite know how to do it. He writes in the margin: "Upon which the chronicler says: one cannot expect a virtuous woman to give herself absolutely; she has to be taken. The best hunting dog can do no more than bring the game within gunshot. If the hunter doesn't shoot, the dog is helpless. The novelist is like the dog of his hero." The comment strikingly illustrates the need for the behavior of characters in a novel to be "in character."

Stendhal does eventually manage to engineer a situation in which the love of Lucien and Mme de Chasteller for each other can be shown and understood, and yet not be declared. But his difficulties do not end there. Stendhal's plan for the novel followed the dialectical Hollywood recipe: boy meets girl, boy and girl break up, boy and girl reunite. As we just saw, he had problems getting the thesis established. To produce the antithesis, Stendhal uses the ridiculous and manifestly teleological device of making Lucien believe that Mme de Chasteller, whom he has seen daily at close quarters, has suddenly given birth to a child. But what really stumped him was the synthesis. Although we do not know why he never got around to writing the third part in which the lovers would be reunited, one conjecture is that their union would not be plausible. In the second part of the novel, after the breakup, Lucien turns into a bit of a cynical rake, fundamentally honest by the lax standards of the July Monarchy but certainly very different from the awkwardly delicate person with whom Mme de Chasteller had fallen in love. Stendhal may have decided that having her love the transformed Lucien would violate relative intelligibility.

Aristotle wrote that "the story . . . must represent one action, a complete whole, with its several incidents so closely connected that the transposition or withdrawal of any one of them will disjoint and dislocate the whole. For that which makes no perceptible difference by its presence or absence is no real part of the whole." We may read this passage as expressing the two aesthetic ideals of *fullness* and *parsimony*. The reader is entitled to think that the author has presented her with all the information she needs to understand the development of the plot.[4] Conversely, she is entitled to expect that if the author tells her that it was raining when a character left his house, it is because the premise of rain will be needed later on, and entitled to believe that a speech attributed to a character is intended to tell us something about the person or to serve as a premise for the action of other characters.[5]

Earlier, I referred to the "downhill" character of a good plot, using acting "in character" as an example. More generally, good plots should not turn on unlikely events, accidents, and coincidences. In *Middlemarch*, the encounter between Raffles and Mr. Bulstrode – a crucial element in the development of the story – is so contrived that it detracts from the

---

[4] To be sure, potentially relevant details may deliberately be left out to leave some room for the imagination of the reader. Rational creation is compatible with (and may even demand) some blanks to be filled out by the reader. If, however, the artist overestimates the imagination of her audience, her effort will be deemed a failure. Suppose a novelist tries to suggest the temperamental incompatibility of a hero and heroine by making the street numbers of the houses in which they live mutually prime, that is, having no common divisors. Barring special circumstances, she cannot reasonably count on the reader's being able to pick up that fact.

[5] To be sure, redundancy is not always to be eschewed, since it can serve an aesthetic function. To convey boredom, redundancy may be more effective than a mere authorial statement. Yet even then, there would be a point when the repetition would bore the *reader* rather than evoking the boredom of the character.

otherwise seamless progression of the novel. Accidents may, to be sure, have their place in a novel. The accidental death of a parent may trigger or shape the unfolding of a plot, as may the death of both parents in the same accident. But if the plot requires their deaths in *two* separate accidents, credulity is strained. The convenient death of a spouse that allows the hero or heroine to marry his or her real love is also a sign of blamable authorial laziness.

The psychology of readers is not, however, finely attuned to probability theory. Suppose the author has the choice between getting from A to B in a plot in two steps or in six steps. For specificity, suppose that the two steps require events that will occur with likelihood 0.9 and 0.2, respectively, whereas each of the six events will occur with likelihood 0.75. Assuming the events in each sequence to be independent of each other, the two-step sequence is more likely to occur (0.18 versus 0.178), yet only the six-step sequence will be seen as having the desirable downhill property. The overall plausibility of a scenario depends much more on the plausibility of its weakest links than on the number of links. I believe the author should respect this particular quirk of the readers, since it prevents him from resorting to facile but unlikely coincidences.

Even a downhill stream may have many twists and turns before it winds somewhere safe to sea. If it did not, observing its course would not provide much of an experience. The author is obliged, therefore, to provide the necessary surprises for readers and viewers, and obstacles for the characters, to keep audience interest alive. The repertoire of stratagems is huge, too huge to be surveyed or even to be classified. Some of them are closely linked with the genre. Within the theater, comedy, drama, and tragedy have different means at their disposal. Whereas comedy often relies on *misunderstandings* to generate tensions, drama and even more so tragedy may rely on *ignorance*. As misunderstandings are dissipated, felicity ensues; as ignorance is lifted, disaster occurs. Novelists can add their own voices to those of the characters to generate uncertainty, as long as they do not deliberately mislead the readers.

I am now in a position to say what I mean by the "right interpretation" of a text. As I stated at the outset, this is a question of explanation. Since all explanations are causal (including those that cite intentions as causes) and since a cause must precede its effect, it follows that *actual* audience perceptions of the work are strictly irrelevant. Intended perceptions, by contrast, can be part of the explanation. Among the antecedent causes of the work, the authorial intention is not all that matters. Unconscious attitudes of the author may also influence it. Thus Jules Verne's *L'île mystérieuse* may have been shaped by his antiracist intentions as well as by his racist prejudices. For the sake of brevity, however, I shall limit myself to conscious intentions.

An interpretation of a work of literature, then, is a claim that important features of the work can be traced back to decisions that the author made for the purpose of enhancing the aesthetic value of the experience that some specific audience could be expected to derive from the work. To make a claim of this kind, literary critics must proceed just as other scholars do. They can appeal to drafts, when they exist, and to statements by the author about the work, Stendhal's marginalia, for example. They can appeal to other works by the same author, to see whether a similar pattern of choices is observed. They can refer to contemporary works, to distinguish the conventions that frame choices from the choices themselves. They can draw on other contemporary sources to determine the audience expectations that may have constrained the author.

In doing all this, their method is in no way different from that of other historians. As other historians do, they face the problem that the data are essentially finite, because the past is not amenable to experiments. And as other historians do, they can try to minimize the temptations of "data mining" by triangulating old sources, looking for new sources, and drawing out novel implications of their interpretation to be tested against evidence. They may differ from other historians in that their interpretation more often, although not invariably, goes together with *value judgments*. Did the author succeed, or approach closer to succeeding than to failing, in his or her aim of creating a local maximum of aesthetic value? Some writers, to be sure, do not have this aim. They may only be concerned with making money or writing propaganda, goals that have different rationality requirements. But if one can make out a plausible case for the hypothesis that the author had mainly aesthetic pretensions, it make sense to ask, as with any other aim, how well they were realized.

Earlier, I said that authorial failures may be intelligible. Authors, I have argued, are under a double pressure: they need to make the plot move on, and to do so through intelligible actions and statements by the characters. We may blame them if they sacrifice the latter goal to the former – that is, if they sacrifice causality to teleology – but we can still *understand* why they do so. Even if causally implausible, Hamlet's procrastination could be made to seem teleologically intelligible in the light of Shakespeare's need to delay his vengeance until the end of the play. This, too, would be a piece of interpretation. Although obviously very different from an interpretation of the delay in terms of Hamlet's psychology and circumstances, it does answer the same question: why the delay? Although in a good work of literature everything can be explained twice over, imperfect works may only allow for one interpretation.

Let me conclude by citing an example of how interpretation may violate or ignore the demands of explanation. Several recent writers have claimed that Fanny Price in *Mansfield Park* is scheming and strategic, and that her seeming modesty is merely a stratagem deployed to win Edmund Bertram. They also argue, moreover, that her very name suggests "sex for money." These claims *fail two tests of intentionality*. First, there is no evidence in the novel for imputing scheming intentions to Fanny Price. Although her modesty is in fact rewarded, that *consequence* of her behavior cannot explain it.[6] Second, there is no evidence for imputing to Jane Austen an intention to make readers view Fanny Price as a semi-prostitute. Although the text may cause these associations to be produced in some modern readers, the writers in question offer no evidence that Austen intended her readers to associate "Fanny" with the heroine of the pornographic novel *Fanny Hill* or "Price" with payment for sex. These "interpretations by consequences" have much in common with functional explanations in the social sciences. They rely on arbitrary methods that are constrained not by facts but only by the limits of

---

[6] Also, the hypothesis of a mercenary Fanny Price cannot account for her rejection of a marriage proposal from the better-situated Henry Crawford.

ingenuity of the scholars who propose them. In Part IV, however, we shall look at some more respectable varieties of "explanation by consequences."

⟪⟪⟪

Bibliographical Note

The general approach I take in this chapter is often accused of embodying an "intentional fallacy." I agree with the responses of N. Carroll to this criticism, notably in "Art, intention and conversation," in G. Iseminger (ed.), *Intention and Interpretation* (Philadelphia: Temple University Press, 1992), and in "The intentional fallacy: Defending myself," *Journal of Aesthetics and Art Criticism* 55 (1997), 305–9. In "Hermeneutics and the hypothetico-deductive method," in M. Martin and L McIntyre (eds.), *Readings in the Philosophy of the Social Sciences* (Cambridge, MA: MIT Press, 1994), D. Føllesdal offers an interpretation of *Peer Gynt* along similar lines, except that this play is not constrained by the convention that the events and characters that are described could have been real. I owe the observation that Hamlet's delay may have been due to dramaturgical concerns to E. Wagenknecht, "The perfect revenge – Hamlet's delay: A reconsideration," *College English* 10 (1949), 188–95. I discuss the idea of works of art as local maxima in Chapter 3 of *Ulysses Unbound* (Cambridge University Press, 2000). That chapter also includes a fuller discussion of Lucien Leuwen. The idea of downhill versus uphill plots is inspired by D. Kahneman and A. Tversky, "The simulation heuristics," in D. Kahneman, P. Slovic, and A. Tversky (eds.), *Judgment Under Uncertainty* (Cambridge University Press, 1982). The interpretations of *Mansfield Park* that I criticize are those of J. Heydt-Stevenson, "'Slipping into the ha-ha': Bawdy humor and body politics in Jane Austen's novels," *Nineteenth-Century Literature* 55 (2000), 309–39, and of J. Davidson, *Hypocrisy and the Politics of Politeness* (Cambridge University Press, 2004).

IV

LESSONS FROM THE NATURAL SCIENCES

The various scientific disciplines may stand in one of two relations to one another: *reduction* or *analogy*. Reduction takes the form of explaining phenomena at one level in the hierarchy of sciences in terms of lower-level phenomena (see Figure IV.1).

Reductionist programs tend to be controversial. For a long time, many biologists vehemently claimed that the reduction of biology to chemistry could not possibly work – but it did. From Emile Durkheim onward many have argued that social science cannot possibly be reduced to psychology. A central claim in the present work is that it can.

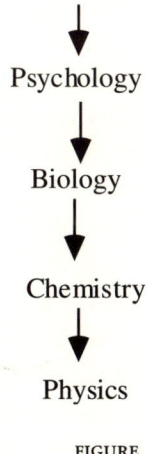

Sociology, economics, political science, anthropology

Psychology

Biology

Chemistry

Physics

FIGURE IV.I

Between these two reductions there is the reduction of psychology to biology. The relevant biological disciplines are genetics, physiology, developmental biology, and evolutionary biology. The first two study proximate causes of the structure and behavior of organisms, the last two remote causes in the history of the individual organism or of the species. The study of structure and the study of behavior are related, in that structure provides both opportunities for behavior and constraints on behavior. The fact that we have two kidneys and only need one allows us to donate one to a sibling for transplantation and makes it possible for social norms mandating or banning that practice to arise. Yet the reason we have two kidneys is not to allow transplantations from living donors. Many structures exist because of what they allow us to do, but this is not an example. Often, however, it is hard to tell whether the enabling effects of a structure are accidental or explanatory.

The relevance of biology for the social sciences ought to be obvious, since their domains overlap. Yet many social scientists resist biological explanations on the ground that they are "reductionist." This is a strange accusation for those who believe, as I do, that reductionism is the engine of progress in science. Yet if "reductionism" is prefixed by "premature," "crude," or "speculative," the objection can be well founded.

Premature reductionism is observed when scholars who are convinced of the ultimate feasibility of moving from higher-level to lower-level explanations try to do so before the requisite measurement techniques, concepts, and theories are in place. A classical example is Descartes's mechanistic physiology, on which Pascal commented in the following terms: "Descartes. We must say summarily: 'This is made by figure and motion,' for it is true. But to say what these are, and to compose the machine, is ridiculous. For it is useless, uncertain, and painful." Today, those who propose algorithms for pattern recognition and automatic translation may be in a similar situation. The tasks of recognizing a human face and of detecting nonsensical sentences that we perform effortlessly are, so far, beyond the capacity of artificial systems.

Crude reductionism is observed when scholars try to explain specific behavior in biological terms rather than explaining the *capacity* or *tendency*, which in a given case may or may not be used or realized, for such behavior. Trying to explain political behavior in terms of the "territorial imperative" found in lower animals is an example. Another is the idea that the practice of weightlifting can be explained as the outcome of sexual selection, analogous to the feathers of the peacock or giant antlers in deer. Many other cases could be cited.

Speculative reductionism is observed when scholars produce "just-so" stories that provide an account of how given behavior *could* have emerged, without showing that it *did* emerge in that way. Sociobiology and the closely related field of evolutionary psychology abound with examples, as when scholars argue that self-deception has evolved because of its evolutionary benefits or that postpartum depression in women has evolved as a bargaining tool (Chapter 17).

To say that bad reductionism is bad is not very illuminating. The desire to reduce complex phenomena to simpler may take simplistic forms, but so can any research strategy in science. Overwhelmingly, the history of science shows that reductionism is a progressive and antireductionism an obstructionist force in science. History also shows the risk of using *analogies* between one scientific discipline and another to generate hypotheses. In itself, the use of analogies is harmless: scientific hypotheses are to be judged by their descendants (testable implications), not by their ancestors. Yet when analogical thinking leads scholars to privilege one kind of hypothesis over others, the result often ends up in the cabinet of horrors of scientific thought. The analogy with society and biological organisms, for instance, has been used to support the idea that societies, like organisms, are self-regulating entities with built-in homeostatic correction mechanisms (e.g., revolutions). In the nineteenth century, scholars debated what, in society, would correspond to the *cell* in the organism, without asking themselves whether there was any reason to expect any analogy at all. Other writers have used physical rather than organic analogies and looked for the social equivalent of Newton's laws or the force of gravity. Scholars who argue that the social sciences can have an impact on the object they study routinely invoke Heisenberg's uncertainty principle, as if the profundity of his principle could turn their truism into something equally profound.

In Chapter 15 I consider some findings from physiology and brain science that hold out the promise of offering reductionist accounts of phenomena such as fear, trust, and "jumping to conclusions." In Chapters 16 and 17 I discuss the theory of natural selection, which has been put to the double use of reduction *and* analogy. I argue that while some reductionist attempts are plausible, others are premature, crude, or speculative. The use of natural selection as an analogy for social phenomena has a more dubious value. One reason why, in Chapter 16, I set out the mechanisms of natural selection in a manner that may seem excessively detailed in a book about social science (yet much too superficial to serve as an exposition of the subject) is to show that nothing remotely comparable exists in the social world. Hand waving by social scientists about "social selection" and "social evolution" is too lacking in precision and focus to be taken seriously.

⟨⟨⟨

BIBLIOGRAPHICAL NOTE

For criticisms of speculative sociobiology and evolutionary psychology, see P. Kitcher, *Vaulting Ambition* (Cambridge, MA: MIT Press, 1987), and D. Buller, *Adapting Minds* (Cambridge, MA: MIT Press, 2005). For an argument that the neuroscientific approach to behavior is premature and an explicit defense of a "black-box" approach, see J. R. Staddon, *Adaptive Dynamics: The Theoretical Explanation of Behavior* (Cambridge, MA: MIT Press, 2001). A survey of biological metaphors in the study of society is J. Schlanger, *Les métaphores de l'organisme* (Paris: Vrin, 1971).

Chapter 15
PHYSIOLOGY AND NEUROSCIENCE

❀ ❀ ❀

The search for the physiological (often neurophysiological) basis for complex human behavior has been carried to a new pitch in recent years, largely as a result of new measurement and observation techniques. There is little doubt that this line of investigation has a great future, even though some current exercises may be premature, crude, or speculative. I shall mention three sets of findings that seem particularly relevant to the purposes of this book.

Fear

In Chapter 8 I asserted that emotions typically are triggered by *beliefs*, or cognitive antecedents. I get angry if I believe that your bumping into me was intentional, reckless, or negligent, but not if I believe it was an accident caused by a third party's bumping into you or by a sudden movement of the train. In Proust's *La prisonnière*, the feelings of jealousy in the Narrator wax and wane with his beliefs about what Albertine may have been up to during the periods he let her out of his sight. One might ask, however, whether emotions are not sometimes caused by mere *perceptions* that, unlike beliefs, are not "about" anything. Descartes thought, for instance, that surprise or astonishment "can happen before we know in the least whether this object is suitable to us or not."

Neurophysiological work on fear (in rats) confirms this idea. There are two different pathways from the sensory apparatus in the thalamus to the amygdala (the part of the brain that causes visceral as well as behavioral emotional responses). Confirming the traditional view that emotions are always preceded and triggered by a cognition, one pathway goes from the thalamus to the neocortex, the thinking part of the brain, and from the neocortex onward to the amygdala. The organism receives a signal, forms a belief about what it means, and then reacts emotionally. There is also, however, a direct pathway from the thalamus to the amygdala that bypasses the thinking part of the brain entirely. Compared to the first pathway, the second is "quick and dirty." On the one hand, it is faster. In a rat it takes about twelve milliseconds (twelve one-thousandths of a second) for an acoustic stimulus to reach the amygdala through the thalamic pathway, and almost twice as long through the cortical pathway. On the other hand, the second pathway differentiates less finely among incoming signals. Whereas the cortex can figure out that a slender curved shape on a path through the wood is a curved stick rather than a snake, the amygdala cannot make this distinction. Yet from the point of view of survival, the cost of reacting to a stick as if it were a snake must have been much smaller than the cost of the opposite mistake.

It is not known whether these findings from the study of fear generalize to other emotions. Conjecturally, something of the sort might also be true of anger. When exposed to something that could be an attack, the opportunity cost of waiting to find out whether it is one might be very high. Natural selection might well have hardwired a tendency to "shoot first; ask later." If I do lash out and later find out that I was in fact not the victim of an attack, I might nevertheless invent a story to justify my behavior. This rather subtle mechanism, linked to our need for self-esteem and summarized in the proverb "Who has offended, cannot forgive," would interact with a neurophysiological mechanism that we share with animals that lack the need for self-esteem. This is likely to be the pattern of many findings from physiology and neuroscience. Near-automatic reactions that we share with other species may be subject to the self-serving interpretations and elaborations that are unique to human beings. These rationalizations are not trivial, since they may cause us to persist in aggression rather than admit that we were at fault.

Another finding from the same research program suggests an alternative to Freud's theory of memory suppression. Rape victims or combat soldiers sometimes have no conscious memory of their experience. Is the nonremembering (the need for this neutral term will be apparent shortly) a motivated process, as Freud thought, or one in which motivations play no role at all? The answer may turn on the relation between stress and the formation (or nonformation) of memory. Mild stress enhances memory of the stressful event, but strong and prolonged stress may raise the level of adrenal steroids to the point where the hippocampus (the part of the brain where conscious memories are formed) is adversely affected. Rather than being repressed, memories of the traumatic event may not have been formed at all. This conclusion, if correct, does not imply that the traumatic event left no psychic traces at all. Suppose you have a car accident and the horn gets stuck. Later, the sound of a horn becomes a conditioned fear stimulus, goes straight to the amygdala, and elicits bodily responses that typically occur in danger. The panic emotion, again, is triggered by a perception rather than by a belief.

Trust

Anticipating the discussion of *trust* in Chapter 21, let me cite three thought-provoking experimental findings. All rely on a Trust Game (TG) between two players, an "investor" and a "trustee." The investor receives a certain endowment, part or all of which he may transfer to the trustee. The experimenter then makes the transfer fructify, so that the trustee receives several times the amount that was transferred. The trustee, finally, decides whether to make a "back transfer" to the investor and, if he does, how generous to be. In some experiments, the investor also has the option of punishing the trustee if the back transfer is deemed insufficiently generous. If both players are rational, are self-interested, and know each other to be so, no transfers will take place in anonymous one-shot interactions, yet in experiments positive levels of transfers and of back transfers are the rule. Another variant of the TG will be further considered in Chapter 21. Here I shall only mention some findings that relate the behavior of investors to their hormonal state and to the activation of pleasure centers in their brains.

The first experiment studies investment size as a function of the presence or absence of the hormone oxytocin. The hormone was known to stimulate prosocial behavior in rodents and to promote the release of breast milk in human females, but the finding that it also promotes prosocial behavior, or trust, in humans came as a surprise. When receiving the hormone, the percentage of investors who transferred their whole endowment to the trustee increased from 21 percent to 45 percent. Three further findings are intriguing. First, trustees who received the hormone did not make larger back transfers. Second, investors given the hormone had the same beliefs about the trustworthiness of trustees (i.e., expectations about back transfers) as those not given the hormone. Third, when investors knew the back transfers were generated by a random mechanism with the same distribution of payoffs as when they played against a real person, oxytocin made no difference for the size of transfers.[1] The natural interpretation is that the hormone affected the behavior by making the investors less "betrayal averse" rather than by making them less risk averse. The importance of betrayal aversion is also confirmed by other experiments that do not rely on physiological manipulations.

The second experiment, which allowed investors to punish ungenerous trustees, studied what went on in their brains as they were punishing. In this TG, the investor had the choice between transferring his whole endowment of 10 monetary units (MUs) to the trustee and transferring nothing. If he made a transfer, it was quadrupled by the experimenter, leaving the trustee with a total of 50 MU – an original endowment of 10 plus the 40 generated by the investment. The trustee then had the choice between transferring 25 of the 50 back to the investor and transferring nothing. The three possible outcomes, in other words, were (10, 10), (25, 25), and (0, 50) (see Figure 15.1).

In addition, after the trustee made his decision both players received an additional endowment of 20 MU. The investor could use his endowment to punish the trustee, in either of two conditions. In a "costly" condition, the investor could attach up to 20 "punishment points" to the trustee; each point caused the investor to lose 1 MU and the trustee to lose 2 MU. Thus by punishing maximally, the investor could ensure that the payoff of the trustee was reduced from 70 (50 + 20) to 30, while his

---

[1] Actual investor payoffs in TGs against a real trustee were used to determine payoff distributions they are told to expect when playing against a random mechanism. Assuming that subjects in the TG have *rational expectations*, that is, correct beliefs about the payoff distributions they can expect to receive, they face the same distributions in both conditions. This assumption might be questioned.

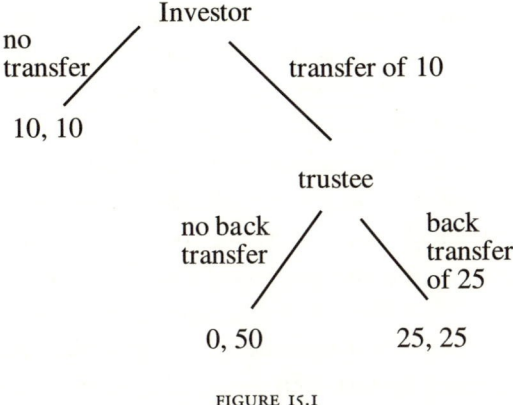

FIGURE 15.1

own was reduced from 20 to 0.[2] In a "costless" condition, only the trustee was affected by the punishment.

All of fifteen investors but one consistently chose to make transfers. The experiment was manipulated so that each investor played against seven trustees, of whom three made the back transfer while four kept all for themselves. These selfish trustees were the focus of the experiment. After a trustee had announced his decision to keep all for himself, the investor had one minute to deliberate and decide whether he wanted to punish the trustee and how severely. During this period his brain was scanned to detect activities in the various regions that might be relevant. One region, the caudate nucleus, is closely linked to the processing of rewards. Another, the prefrontal and orbitofrontal cortex, is linked to the integration of separate cognitive process, for example, to trade-offs between costs and benefits. In each of these regions the pattern of activities confirmed the hypothesis about the motivation for punishment that I shall now go on to state.

In both the costly and the costless conditions there was a correlation between activation of reward-related circuits and the actual monetary punishment that was imposed. This correlation could mean either that

---

[2] In the sums actually paid to the subjects, each point corresponded to 0.1 Swiss franc. The sum seems trivial, but other experiments show that in games of this kind qualitatively the same results obtain when the stakes are at the level of a monthly salary. These results are mostly obtained by using first-world research grants to carry out experiments in third-world countries.

the decision to punish induces satisfaction or that the expected satisfaction from punishment induces the decision to punish. To distinguish between the two hypotheses the experimenters considered eleven subjects who imposed the maximal feasible punishment in the "costless" condition. Among these subjects, those whose reward circuits were more highly activated also imposed more severe punishments in the "costly" condition. As they got more of a kick from punishing, they were willing to spend more on it, thus supporting the second hypothesis. This interpretation is also confirmed by the fact that the cortex was more highly activated in the costly condition, when subjects had to trade off the material costs and psychic benefits of punishment against each other, than in the costless condition.

This finding seems to confirm the "warm glow" theory of this particular form of altruistic behavior (Chapter 5). The punishment, while altruistic in the indirect behavioral sense of benefiting third parties at some material cost to the agent, is not generated by altruistic motivations. It is too early to tell whether the results will hold up, and whether they generalize to direct forms of altruism (giving money to the poor) or to third-party punishment (A's punishing B for unjustly harming C). The impartiality of third-party punishment might not generate the sweet satisfaction that is provided by retaliation for a personal affront. What seems clear, nevertheless, is that science is now offering the means for deciding between competing motivational hypotheses that elude simple introspection. If punishment is motivated by the expected pleasure of punishing, this aim cannot be the conscious goal of the agent. Except sadists, people punish because they believe the other *deserves* it. To take an even more clear-cut example, it is conceptually incoherent to think that people's conscious motivation for giving to the poor could be *solely* the warm glow from giving, since the glow is parasitic on the belief that one is doing something good for others, not for oneself. States that are inaccessible to consciousness might now become accessible to brain scans.

Inflicting punishment differs from *observing* a deserved punishment. In a third experiment, a subject was brain scanned while watching a painful shock being inflicted on two persons (confederates of the experimenter) who had interacted with the subject in a Trust Game, one of them behaving fairly and one unfairly. When the subject observed the fair player being punished, the brain scan showed activation of pain-related brain areas ("I feel your pain"). Observing the punishment of unfair players caused less activation in pain-related areas but increased activation in pleasure-related areas ("Schadenfreude"). (An important but unexplained finding was that women felt more pain and less pleasure than men when unfair subjects were punished.) Schadenfreude is a kind of vicarious anger: A derives pleasure from observing B punishing C when C has harmed A. It would be interesting to investigate brain activities in vicarious indignation: would A derive as much pleasure from observing B punishing C when C has harmed D? Also, one might compare vicarious anger with direct anger: how does the pleasure from observing B punishing C when C has harmed A compare to the pleasure from A punishing C when C has harmed A? These elementary emotions, well known from fiction, plays, and poetry, now seem to be within the grasp of science.

Filling In

Readers who use spell checkers will know that the program is capable of "guessing" or "filling in" what might be missing from a misspelled word. Sometimes, it produces the wrong word, which (if unchecked) can have comical or even disastrous effects, but by and large it is a reliable and useful tool. The brain, too, has this capacity for filling in the gaps in experience. A circular figure with small gaps in it will be seen as a complete or closed circle. If there are many gaps it may not literally be seen as a complete circle, but we still perceive the visible parts as lying on an invisible circle. In the top part of Figure 15.2, we "see" the circles under the rectangles, but when the rectangles are removed, as in the bottom part, the circles also disappear.

Filling in is an everyday phenomenon. The other day I was walking in Levallois-Peret, just outside Paris proper, and saw a street sign that I read as "Rue Auguste Blanqui." I wondered why, in this affluent and presumably conservative neighborhood, one would name a street after the most violent nineteenth-century French revolutionary. When I looked more closely, I saw it was "Rue Aristide Briand," named after an impeccably respectable French statesman. What happened, obviously, was that my mind noticed the first letter of the name and the surname as

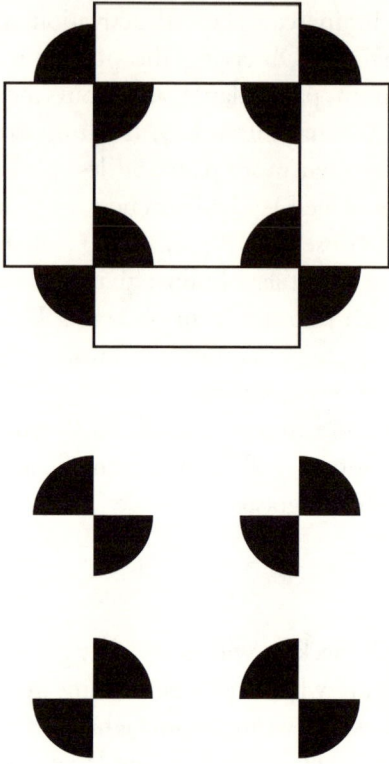

FIGURE 15.2

well as the rough length of each name, and, because I am much more familiar with Blanqui than with Briand, inferred that I was seeing a street sign commemorating him. It is not that I interpreted these signs by consciously filling in the missing letters one way or another: the filling in happened unconsciously and my conscious experience was that of *seeing* the two complete words. On another occasion, I was looking for a bakery ("*boulangerie*") and noticed a sign for a store of that designation, only to discover that what I'd seen was the second half of "Restaurant de l'Orangerie." Unlike the Blanqui-Briand case, this may have been a case of *motivated misperception* rather than merely the brain's making its "best guess" on what it was seeing.

Making one's best guess could also be called "jumping to conclusions." The brain does it all the time, luckily for us. Filling-in mechanisms, like spell checkers, are useful; in fact, indispensable. However, sometimes the search for patterns turns into an obsessional search for meaning. The brain is a natural conspiracy theorist. More accurately, according to some theories, the right hemisphere of the brain has the function of imposing a coherent framework on all the information with which we are constantly bombarded. This might explain some cases of "anosognosia," or denial of illness by sufferers. Rather than a *motivated* phenomenon, as a Freudian account would suggest, the denial might simply be the best guess of the spell checker in the brain. More likely, it seems, the phenomenon could be due both to motivational and to nonmotivational mechanisms.

I suspect that the "filling-in" and "meaning-bestowing" activities of the brain are at work not only in the subjects scientists study, but in many scholars as well. I am not saying that there is no difference between the conspiracy theories of Hamas on the one hand and postmodern literary criticism, functional explanation, or psychoanalysis on the other, only that they all seem to be animated by the need to find meaning and coherence over and above what can be justified by the facts at hand. In the case of scientific hypotheses, shortcuts and extrapolations cannot be justified and explained by the need to take immediate action, as they can often be in everyday life. Rather they reflect the deep unease we feel when we are unable to assign meaning to the world, whether or not we are called to act upon it. The need for cognitive closure and the intolerance of admitting ignorance (Chapter 7) also reflect this unease, as does the hyperrationality exhibited by those who invest more in making a rational decision than what is at stake in the decision itself (Chapter 12). The tendency to "blame the victim" is a further example. Assuming that the world is fundamentally just, so that people "get what they deserve," we tend to devalue and derogate victims of purely chance events, even the selection by lot for military service; indeed, the victims themselves tend to do so.

❬❬❬

BIBLIOGRAPHICAL NOTE

The discussion of fear relies on J. LeDoux, *The Emotional Brain* (New York: Simon & Schuster, 1996). The impact of oxytocin on trust is shown in M. Kostfeld et al., "Oxytocin increases trust in humans," *Nature* 435 (2005), 673–6. The idea of betrayal aversion is confirmed by I. Bohnet and R. Zeckhauser, "Trust, risk and betrayal," *Journal of Economic Behavior and Organization* 55 (2004), 467–84. The study of trust and revenge is by J. F. de Quervain et al., "The neural basis of altruistic punishment," *Science* 305 (2004): 1254–8. The study of trust and Schadenfreude is by T. Singer et al., "Empathic neural responses are modulated by the perceived fairness of others," *Nature* 439 (2006), 466–9. A stimulating guide to "filling-in" phenomena is V. S. Ramachandran and S. Blakeslee, *Phantoms in the Brain* (New York: Quill, 1998), explaining how Ramachandran's initial hostility to Freudian explanations of anosognosia was replaced by the belief that an element of unconscious denial must be present; see also N. Levy, "Self-deception without thought experiments," at au.geocities.com/neil_levy/Documents/articles/Self-deception.pdf. The "blame the victim" findings are in S. Rubin and A. Pepau, "Belief in a just world and reaction to another's lot," *Journal of Social Issues* 29 (1973), 73–93.

Chapter 16
EXPLANATION BY CONSEQUENCES AND NATURAL SELECTION

❀ ❀ ❀

Reinforcement

All explanation is causal explanation. We explain an event by citing its cause. Causes precede their effects in time. It follows that we cannot explain an event, such as an action, by its consequences. If, however, the explanandum is a *pattern* of recurrent behavior, the consequences of that behavior on one occasion can enter into the causes that make its occurrence on a later occasion more likely. There are two main ways in which this can happen: by *reinforcement* and by *selection*. I shall focus on the second, since it is the more important for my purposes, but begin with some words about the first.

If the consequences of given behavior are pleasant or rewarding, we tend to engage in it more often; if they are unpleasant or punishing it will occur less often. The underlying mechanism could simply be conscious rational choice, if we *notice* the pleasant or unpleasant consequences and *decide* to act in the future so as to repeat or avoid repeating the experience.[1] Often, however, the reinforcement can happen without intentional choice. When infants learn to cry because the parents reward them by picking them up when they do, there is no reason to think that they first consciously note the benefits from crying and then later cry at will to get them. When older children throw a tantrum to get their way, parents can usually tell that it is not a genuine one.

Reinforcement learning has been extensively studied in laboratory experiments on animals. One typically offers the animal the opportunity to press a lever, or one among several levers, and rewards the presses

---

[1] Recall, however, that we are not always very good at noticing which of two experiences was the more painful (puzzle 12 in Chapter 12).

271

either as a function of the number of lever presses since the last reward or as a function of the time passed since the last reward. In either case, the function can be deterministic or probabilistic. In *fixed-ratio* schedules, the animal receives a reward after it has pressed a lever a fixed number of times, whereas in *variable-ratio* schedules the number of presses needed to produce a reward varies randomly. In either case, each press produces a "reward point" that is added to previous points. In *fixed-interval* schedules a press will produce a reward a given time after the last reward was offered, whereas in *variable-interval* schedules the time before a new reward is made available varies randomly. In either case, the timing of the reward is independent of the number of presses. Each schedule of reinforcement produces, after some learning time, a specific and stable pattern of behavior, which, moreover, will be extinguished in a specific pattern once the reinforcer (the reward) is removed. For instance, responses that are learned by rewarding every lever press (a special case of a fixed-ratio schedule known as continuous reinforcement) are extinguished more quickly than those learned on a random variable-ratio schedule. Intuition might suggest the opposite, since continuous reinforcement would seem to produce a stronger habit, but, as sometimes happens, intuition is wrong.

The relevance of these findings outside the laboratory depends on the purpose. If the aim is to *shape* action, for example, in a classroom situation, in a gambling casino, or in the workplace, a designer may (more or less freely) impose a reward schedule to generate desired behavior. For instance, variable-interval schedules are often used to shape behavior, as when a teacher announces a policy of random quizzes. On the variable-ratio schedule that operates in many gambles, it is easier to establish the behavior if the first reward occurs early on.[2] As casino and race track managers lack the technology for sucking in novices by offering them big wins, they have to rely on the fact that by the laws of chance some gamblers will have beginner's luck.[3] Con-man operations, however, often rely on

---

[2] It is also easier to establish when the gambling technology allows for the possibility of near-wins. Although each of the near-wins is less reinforcing than an actual win, there are more of them.

[3] Their good luck, in this case, is their bad luck, and the casino's good luck.

the deliberate inducement of early wins by the mark. In the classroom and the casino, the reward schedules operate "behind the back" of the students or gamblers, in the sense that they do not shape the behavior by explicit incentives but rather, as in the case of the crying infant, by an unconscious process. By contrast, when managers pay employees once they achieve a set target (a fixed-ratio schedule) or on a monthly basis (a fixed-interval schedule), they are simply setting up an incentive system. Since the behavior of the employees can be adequately explained by the *expected* reward, there is no need to appeal to *actual* reward.

If the aim is to *explain* behavioral patterns by their actual consequences, the reward schedules are relevant only if they occur naturally and, moreover, are so opaque that they do not create explicit incentives. This does not often seem to happen with the two fixed schedules. In everyday life, the sheer number of responses is rarely decisive for reward. It is not the number of friendly smiles I give my friends that shapes their behavior toward me, but the consistency and the appropriateness of my smiling. In natural settings, rewards that arrive every so often, such as my paycheck, are rare. The two variable schedules are more important. A person who plays "hot and cold" (a variable-ratio schedule) with a member of the opposite (or the same) sex may induce a stronger attraction than someone who invariably displays friendly behavior. A variable-interval schedule arises when you try to reach someone on the phone and the line is busy. You know that sooner or later you will get through by redialing, but you do not know when. This situation induces a pattern of steady redialing that would not be the unique prediction of rational-choice theory. That theory could predict any number of patterns, depending on the caller's beliefs about how long the conversation of the other person is likely to last. It seems unlikely, however, that people have stable beliefs about such matters.

The response pattern generated by reinforcement is not, in general, the one that would be produced by conscious, rational choice. Suppose for instance that an animal has the choice between pressing either of two levers, one that rewards on a variable-ratio schedule and one that rewards on a variable-interval schedule. The rational pattern, which will maximize overall reward, is to press the variable-ratio lever most of time, to accumulate reward points, while visiting the variable-interval lever from time to time to see whether a new reward has become available. This is not, however, the pattern produced by reinforcement learning. Instead, the animals press the variable-interval level much more often than is optimal. In doing so, they equalize the *average* rewards to pressing the one or the other level rather than, as rationality would dictate, equalizing the *marginal* rewards. For other schedule combinations, reinforcement learning sometimes mimics rational choice, but not in any consistent manner. If there is any nonintentional mechanism capable of reliably simulating rationality, we shall have to look for it elsewhere.

Differential Reproductive Fitness

The most frequently cited mechanism is that of natural or social *selection*. In Part III of the book I discussed how we can explain behavior by assuming that *agents adapt to their environment*, in a more or less rational manner. In a radically different perspective, we may try to explain behavior by assuming that *agents are selected by the environment*. Although selection can be the work of an intentional agent, as when domestic dogs are bred to be docile or laboratory rats to become more intelligent, many selection mechanisms rest on causal processes that involve no intentional agent.

In particular, *differential survival* of organisms based on their behavioral patterns may lead to optimal behavior (optimal for reproduction) in the population even in the absence of any optimizing choices or intentions. Suppose that 10 percent of the organisms in a population of 100 organisms forage so efficiently that they leave on average 10 offspring that survive to adulthood, whereas the remaining 90 percent leave only 5. If the behavior of the parents is (by whatever mechanism) transmitted to the offspring, the next generation of adult organisms will include a fraction of $100/550 = 2/11 \sim 18$ percent that displays the more efficient behavior. Over the course of a few more generations, virtually all organisms will display it. If we ask *why* it is universally displayed, the answer is that it has better consequences.[4] This mechanism works across generations. Unlike reinforcement learning, it does not modify the

---

[4] Better than what? This question will concern us shortly.

behavior of any given individual, only the typical behavior of successive generations of individuals.

Natural Selection

The theory of natural selection spells out this story in great detail. Here, I shall present a simplified or "classical" version of the theory, which is sufficient for my purposes. I want to show, in particular, how natural selection differs from intentional choice and a fortiori from rational choice. Natural selection is an optimizing mechanism, but only in a weak sense. I also want to lay the groundwork for the argument in the next chapter that *social* selection is unlikely to produce even this weak form of optimizing.

The fitness of an organism, measured by the number of its (reproducing) offspring,[5] is jointly determined by its environment and its physiological and behavioral properties, or *phenotype*. Its *genotype* is the set of instructions that, again jointly with the environment, determine the phenotype. These instructions are encoded in long DNA molecules, which have many properties in common with a written language. The letters of DNA are four molecules (nucleotides) called T, A, G, and C. The words or *codons* of DNA are triplets of nucleotides, with each triplet containing instructions for assembling one of the twenty amino acids that are the basic building blocks of the proteins in the organism. Since there are sixty-four triplets (sixty-one if we exclude three that have a different function), more than one of them may code for the same amino acid. A *gene* is a segment of DNA that codes for one particular protein.

The organisms that forage more efficiently first appeared as the result of a random mutation of the genome. In the classical picture of evolution, mutations were supposed to result from small random errors in the duplication of genetic material that takes place in the process of reproduction. There are several types of small mutations: deletion of a nucleotide, insertion of a nucleotide, or substitution of one nucleotide

---

[5] Fitness in the reproductive sense differs from ecological fitness, as measured by life span. Although ecological fitness is usually a means to reproductive fitness, the two can also diverge, as when parents risk death to defend their brood.

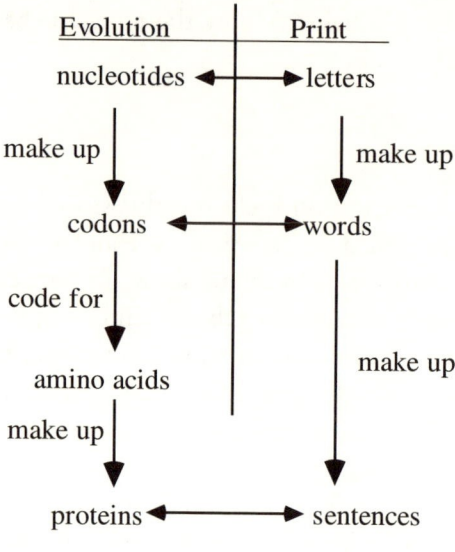

FIGURE 16.1

for another. In this simplified exposition, I shall refer only to the third and most common one. Although it is now understood that mechanisms such as gene duplication can produce macromutations, I shall stick with the classical picture for the time being.

Within this picture, the way in which mutations contribute to evolution may be clarified by means of an analogy with the three-layered structure of a printed sentence. Figure 16.1 shows the similarities between the two cases.

When a book is being reset from the first edition, poor concentration of the typesetter may cause some deviations from the original text. We may think of these as the substitution of one letter for another, turning for instance "hand" into "land" or "pand." The errors are random in the specific sense that they are unrelated to the content of the book. Similarly, mutations are random in the sense that their likelihood of occurrence is unrelated to the nature of the phenotypic changes they will induce. Certain letters may be changed more frequently than others, if the typesetter has difficulties distinguishing "m" from "n." The second edition of some books may contain more errors than others, for instance if the typesetter was drunk. Similarly, mutation rates can be affected by mutagenic agents.[6]

Misprints in a book or in any written message usually have a negative impact on the content, sometimes (literally) fatally. The displacement of a comma, for instance, may be a matter of life and death.[7] Similarly most mutations have harmful consequences for the organism in which they occur, meaning that they reduce its reproductive fitness. Occasionally, however, a mutation may occur that increases the fitness of the organism, just as an accidental failure to reproduce the text of the first edition might provide more accurate or updated information. At the next step in the argument, however, the analogy breaks down. A favorable mutation is going to be more heavily represented in the next generation, since the organism in which it occurred will have more offspring and mutations are transmitted to the offspring. By contrast, there is no mechanism by which a book that accidentally corrects the mistakes of the first edition will tend to sell better.

In typographical errors, any letter may be replaced by any other. The new word is not constrained to be a meaningful one; "hand" is as likely to be replaced by "pand" as by "land." In mutations, too, any of the nucleotides in a triplet can be replaced by any other nucleotide. By contrast, not any amino acid can emerge from any other by a single nucleotide mutation. Some protein changes can occur in this way, but others cannot. It is always possible, however, to go from one amino acid to another by successive point mutations. The process is a bit like the family game in which a given word is to be transformed by one-letter replacements into another, subject to the constraint that all intermediate words are in the dictionary. You can go from HAIR to HAIL in one step, and from HAIR to DEAN in four steps (HAIR to HEIR to HEAR to DEAR to DEAN), but I am fairly sure that no number of steps will take you from HAIR to LYNX unless you go outside the dictionary.

---

[6] Radiation for instance can cause mutations; that is why X-ray scanning to detect cancer may cause cancer by inducing mutations.

[7] Since I have not found an equivalent English example, I illustrate this claim by two Norwegian sentences: "Vent, ikke heng ham" and "Vent ikke, heng ham," meaning, respectively, "Wait; do not hang him" and "Do not wait; hang him."

In the corresponding "mutation game" all sixty-four codons are in "the dictionary," except for three that serve as "periods" (terminating the protein). Although these three "stop codons" preclude some one-step triplet changes, the constraint is too weak to block multistep changes. Thus you can go from the amino acid methionine to tryptophan in two steps, either from ATG to TTG (leucine) to TGG or from ATG to AGG (glycine) to TGG.[8] In addition, there are pathways involving more than two steps, such as ATG-ACG-TCG-TGG.

Imagine now a more complicated family game than the one usually played and suppose that each word is embedded in a sentence, and that the substituted word must not only be in the dictionary, but yield a meaningful sentence.[9] Now, there are *two constraints* on acceptable letter replacements. Suppose the initial sentence is "I tend my looks." Replacing it with "I mend my looks" respects both the meaning constraint and the dictionary constraint. Replacing it by "I send my looks" respects only the dictionary constraint. Replacing it by "I send my tooks" respects neither. If "I send my looks" is further changed into "I send my books," both constraints are satisfied. To get to that (meaningful) sentence from the initial (meaningful) one by one-letter substitutions, we had to go outside the set of meaningful sentences.

Natural Selection Generates Local Maxima

The biological analogy is clear. An amino acid resulting from a nucleotide substitution is embedded in a protein. Since proteins are vital for the organism, they have to be biologically viable (the analogue of meaningfulness for sentences). If any intermediary protein in the pathway from the initial form to the final one is nonviable, it cannot be fixed in the population *since the organism in which the mutation to that protein first*

---

[8] I have chosen this example because these two amino acids are the only ones coded for by a single triplet. Each of the other acids has two or four codons. Thus the phrase "a path from amino acid X to amino acid Y" should, for the present purposes, be read as "a path from a given codon for X to one of the codons for Y."

[9] This kind of language game was practiced by a French group of writers known as the Oulipo movement. The best known of them, Georges Perec, wrote a whole novel, *La Disparition*, in which the letter "e" was nowhere used.

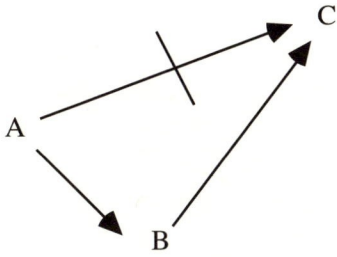

FIGURE 16.2

occurred will not leave any descendants who could take the next step. Even if the final form of the protein would increase fitness compared to that of the first stage, that fact cannot generate any evolutionary pressure at intermediate stages. If *all* feasible pathways from the first to the final stage would, at some point, require the organism to adopt the indirect strategy of "one step backward, two steps forward," the final form could never be reached. Since the majority and probably the vast majority of mutations are deleterious, this situation is quite plausible. In simplified form (disregarding multiple pathways), the structure is shown in Figure 16.2. Three different proteins confer different degrees of fitness (measured vertically). The structure of the genetic code allows for single-nucleotide mutations from A to B and from B to C, but not from A to C.

Natural selection (in this classical picture) is constrained to small incremental improvements. The organism climbs along a fitness gradient until it reaches a *local maximum*, defined as a state in which all further one-step changes would reduce fitness. Although there may be higher peaks in "the adaptive landscape," these will not be attainable by one-step changes. This process differs from intentional choice in three respects. Recall from Chapter 6 that by virtue of their intentionality, human beings are capable of (1) using indirect strategies, (2) waiting, and (3) aiming ahead of a moving target. We have just seen that natural selection is incapable of (1). As for (2), consider Figure 16.3.

The structure of the genetic code allows for single-nucleotide mutations from A to B and from A to C, but not from B to C. If a mutation from A to B occurs, the population is stuck in the (low-level) local

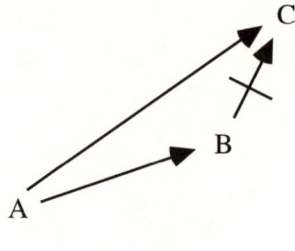

FIGURE 16.3

maximum B, since a one-step mutation to the global maximum C is blocked. There is no mechanism that would favor a mutation to C rather than B. Unlike intentional agents, natural selection is *opportunistic*, grabbing any chance for an improvement while being incapable of *waiting* until the optimal change occurs.

As for (3), populations are adapting to an environment that is constantly changing. If the changes are regular, for instance, seasonal or diurnal, they adapt to the changes. If a one-shot event occurs, such as a sudden climate change, behavior that was at a local fitness maximum prior to the change may become suboptimal, so that mutations that previously would have been deleterious are favorable. If the change is protracted, as when the climate cools or warms over a long period of time, this process may never reach a new local maximum. The population will track the changes in the environment with an efficacy that depends on the relative speed of the two processes. The amazingly fine-tuned adaptations observed in animals and plants suggest that animals adjust to the environment much faster than the latter itself changes. Yet the organisms will always lag somewhat behind, since they cannot *anticipate* changes in the environment. By contrast, human beings may become aware of future changes such as global warming and take precautions against them before they actually occur or, if they result from human behavior, prevent them from occurring.

The environment of a population is made up, among other things, of populations from other species to which it may stand in a prey-predator relation. As prey, it may evolve better evasive strategies; as predator, better hunting strategies. Just as the individual fox and hare are chasing each other across the fields, so do the species Fox and Hare chase each other over generations. But whereas the logic of natural selection precludes the Fox from anticipating where the Hare is going to be a few millennia hence, some predators are able to intersect the flight path of the prey. Similarly, the locally maximizing process of natural selection has produced the capacity for global maximization found in human beings.

Mutations are both an input to and a product of natural selection, since the rate at which they occur may be shaped by the effects on fitness. There are several mechanisms involved. In a bacterial population that is constantly exposed to new antibiotics, strains with higher mutation rates may be favored. This is a special case of the more general idea that in a changing environment, "immutable" populations will become extinct. At the same time, very high rates of mutation can lead to loss of valuable genetic information and to extinction. In between, there is an optimal rate. In a constant environment, there is a trade-off between the benefits of a low mutation rate and the cost of the "proofreading" and repair mechanisms that are needed to maintain the low rate.

This "classical picture" is simplistic in a number of ways that would have to be spelled out if this were a biology textbook. Since it is not, I shall only assert that the more complicated picture modifies but does not invalidate the claim that natural selection tends to get stuck in a "local maximum trap." Large mutations do occur, and some of them may be responsible for developments that would not have been possible through small point mutations. Also, inferior forms are not eliminated instantly by competition. In Figure 16.2, the mutation to B does not necessarily produce an organism that is unviable in the strict sense of being unable to survive or to reproduce. Some organisms in state B might survive to produce organisms in state C. In Figure 16.3 some organisms in state A might survive the competition from the more efficient organisms in state B long enough for a mutation to state C to occur. Whether the global maximum occurs is a matter of the relative speed of two processes: the extinction of inferior varieties and the rate at which favorable mutations occur. There is no mechanism, however, that could mimic, *in a systematic way*, the capacity of intentional beings to preempt, to wait, or to use indirect strategies.

From the tendency of natural selection to produce optimizing behavior or optimal structures through gradient climbing we should not conclude that all observed features of organisms are optimal. For one thing, as already mentioned, there might be a *lag*, if the population has not caught up with changes in the environment. What we observe may have been optimal at some time in the past, but no longer be so. For another, the phenomenon of *pleiotropy* tells us that natural selection may favor features that are suboptimal taken in isolation, yet part of an optimal package solution. This can occur because a gene can have more than one effect on the phenotype. If the positive effects outweigh the negative ones, it will be favored by natural selection. As an example, consider the existence of male traits in insects that cause physical harm to their mates during copulation. Such harm has been suggested to arise either as a negative pleiotropic side effect of adaptations that give males a reproductive advantage in another context or as a male adaptation in itself. Experiments suggest that the first explanation is more plausible.

The Units of Selection

Natural selection is not only opportunistic and myopic, but also, with two exceptions I shall discuss shortly, fiercely *individualistic*. It does not favor the species or the population, but the individual organism. If a property arising from a mutation increases the relative fitness of the organism, it will be fixed in the population even if it also causes a decrease in absolute fitness. Imagine a population of fish, exposed to predators, initially swimming in scattered schools. If a mutation causes the fish in which it occurs to move to the center of the school, it will be less vulnerable to predation and as a result will tend to leave more offspring. As this behavior spreads in the population, the school will become more compact and thus an easier target for predators. At each step in the process it is better to seek the middle than to be at the outskirts of the school. Yet in terms of absolute fitness the outcome is worse for all than the initial situation, and in terms of relative fitness it is unchanged. Similarly, runaway sexual selection is a plausible explanation of the large and dysfunctional antlers found in some species of deer.

One exception to individualism is *kin selection* (a form of "subindividualism"), in which the gene rather than the individual organism is the unit of selection. The choice of unit does not matter when the effect of a gene simultaneously and in the same proportion increases the presence of the gene in the population and the number of offspring of the organism displaying that behavior. This is the case, for instance, in the evolution of more efficient foraging. But in some cases the gene can benefit even if the organism in which it triggers the behavior does not, namely, when an organism "sacrifices" itself for the sake of close relatives who are likely to have the same gene. When an animal observes a predator and emits an alarm signal, its chances of survival often go down while those of close relatives in the vicinity go up. Since these relatives or some of them will also have the "warning gene," their higher survival chances may cause the gene to spread in the population if they more than offset the lower chances of the animal that emitted the signal. This is not the only possible explanation of this widespread form of behavior, although in some cases it is the most plausible one. In other cases, alarm signals serve to distract predators or to alert all conspecifics (whether kin or nonkin). In still further cases, they may serve to *deceive* conspecifics, for example, to make them move away from some scarce resource. Hence there is nothing intrinsically altruistic or self-sacrificial about alarm signals, although they can, in some circumstances, "mimic" genuine altruism.

Another exception is *group selection* (a form of "supraindividualism"). Consider two populations of fish, one in which the center-seeking mutation has occurred and one in which it has not. Over time, the former will leave fewer offspring than the latter and might ultimately be crowded out. Selection would seem to operate at the level of the group, not of the individual. Yet if the two populations coexist, the second is vulnerable to invaders from the first. Whether the center-seeking behavior is caused by mutation or by in-migration, the outcome is the same, namely, the crowding out of those who do not behave in that way. Similarly, if organisms in a population have a gene that prevents them from overgrazing, thus avoiding "the tragedy of the commons," they might be out-reproduced by less inhibited organisms that lack the gene.

For this reason, group selection has not been seen as a plausible mechanism for generating cooperation or self-restraint. In the light of the theory of altruistic punishment set out in Chapter 15, however, this objection can be met. If the organisms in a population have a gene that make them punish noncooperators, the latter will not gain any reproductive advantage from their free riding. This mechanism can only, however, ensure cooperation where noncooperators can be reliably identified. It seems unlikely to apply to fish with the center-seeking behavior but might well apply to animals that refuse to share food with others.

Kin and group selection provide two mechanisms for the emergence of cooperative behavior, the former based on shared genes and the latter on altruistic punishment. A third mechanism is that of *reciprocal altruism* or "tit-for-tat" in repeated interactions, such as "I scratch your back; you scratch mine" (among some animals quite literally) or "I offer you food when I have a surplus; you offer it to me when you have." The other side of the coin is punishment, or at least abstention from cooperation, when the other party fails to reciprocate. For this mechanism to operate the individuals must interact often enough to make self-restraint worthwhile, remember what others did on earlier occasions, and recognize them when they meet again.

This mechanism seems to account for cooperation in many cases of dyadic interaction; some examples and a counterexample follow. When two capuchin monkeys are offered the opportunity to share food on successive occasions, the second gives more to the first the more it has received from it. Chimpanzees are more likely to share food with those who have groomed them earlier in the day. When two starlings are placed in a situation in which each receives foods when and only when the other presses a lever, they take turns doing so. Females in a nest of vampire bats regurgitate blood meals to others that have failed to obtain food in the recent past. The vampires are able to recognize one another and are more likely to give blood to those that have donated in the past, but also more likely to donate to relatives. In another experiment, each of two bluejays was on a schedule that rewarded it more when it pressed the "selfish lever" A than when it pressed the "cooperative lever" B, regardless of what the other did, and both got more when both pressed B than when neither did. Here tit-for-tat did not emerge: after some initial cooperation the jays ended up consistently pressing lever A.

Reciprocal altruism is not, however, a plausible mechanism for generating cooperation in larger groups. The only punishment strategy that could work is the "grim trigger" response by which defection (non-cooperative behavior) by one member of the group immediately causes all others to cease cooperating, both with the defector and with each other. Intuitively, this extreme reaction does not seem plausible, and empirically it does not seem to occur.

〈〈〈

BIBLIOGRAPHICAL NOTE

In "Selection by consequences," *Science* 213 (1981), 501–4, B. F. Skinner argued for the importance of *three* ways in which behavior can be explained by its consequences: by natural selection operating on individuals, by reinforcement, and (although he does not use that term) by group selection. A useful introduction to reinforcement theory is J. E. R. Staddon, *Adaptive Behavior and Learning* (Cambridge University Press, 1983). A study of how reinforcement theory can be used to shape (rather than explain) behavior is D. Lee and P. Belfiore, "Enhancing classroom performance: A review of reinforcement schedules," *Journal of Behavioral Education* 7 (1997), 205–17. A classic exposition of the theory of natural selection, notable for the insistence on the individualistic nature of selection, is G. Williams, *Adaptation and Natural Selection* (Princeton, NJ: Princeton University Press, 1966). For a discussion of gradient climbing and "the metaphor of fitness landscapes," see Chapter 2.4 of S. Gavrilets, *Fitness Landscapes and the Origin of Species* (Princeton, NJ: Princeton University Press, 2004). An exposition emphasizing the gene as the unit of selection is R. Dawkins, *The Selfish Gene*, 2nd ed. (Oxford University Press, 1990). An excellent introduction to animal signaling is S. A. Searchy and S. Nowicki, *The Evolution of Animal Communication* (Princeton, NJ: Princeton University Press, 2005). For a discussion of how group selection might be made possible by altruistic punishment, see E. Fehr and U. Fischbacher, "Social norms and human cooperation," *Trends in Cognitive Sciences* 8 (2004), 185–90. A seminal study of "tit-for-tat" cooperation between unrelated animals is R. Axelrod and W. Hamilton, "The evolution of cooperation," *Science* 211 (1981), 1390–6.

Chapter 17
SELECTION AND HUMAN BEHAVIOR

❀ ❀ ❀

Variation and Selection

How much of human behavior is chosen or "selected" by some other mechanism than intentional choice? To answer this question, let us first note that any selection mechanism needs a raw material, inputs, to work on. Like the selection process itself, the source of variation can be either intentional or nonintentional (see Figure 17.1).

	Intentional source of variation	Nonintentional source of variation
Intentional selection	Artificial selection in plant and animal husbandry	Gradual improvement of boats Eugenics Selective abortion and infanticide
Nonintentional selection	Selection of firms by market competition	Natural selection (Ch.16)

FIGURE 17.1

287

Nonintentional Variation, Nonintentional Selection

Natural selection has obviously shaped the physical structure of human beings, which offers them opportunities for action as well as constraints on action. Those who try to explain human behavior in terms of natural selection sometimes make stronger claims. They want to explain the behavioral patterns themselves, not merely the structures that make them possible.

The most plausible mechanism is that evolution has produced *emotions* with their characteristic action tendencies. Since a male can never be sure whether he is the father of his offspring whereas the female is not in doubt that she is the mother, we would expect natural selection to produce a stronger tendency to feel sexual jealousy in men than in women. This is confirmed by many homicide statistics. Thus among 1,060 spousal homicides in Canada between 1974 and 1983, 812 were committed by men and 248 by women, but among those motivated by jealousy 195 were by men and only 19 by women. The theory of natural selection also predicts that parents would be more emotionally committed to their biological children, who are carriers of their genes, than to stepchildren. This prediction, too, is confirmed by data. Thus an American child living with one or more substitute parents in 1976 was about 100 times as likely to be abused as a child living with two natural parents. Natural selection may also favor *lack* of emotion. The dangers of inbreeding are kept in check, in humans and in other primate species, by lack of sexual attraction among young who grow up together, whether or not they are related to each other.[1]

Natural selection, operating on groups rather than on individuals, may also have favored emotions of anger and indignation toward those who violate norms of cooperation, motivating punishment even at some cost to the punisher (Chapter 16). A more puzzling question is whether and why selection might have favored the emotion of *contempt*, which is directed toward those who violate social rather than moral norms. Since

---

[1] The incest taboo may, therefore, address a temptation that exists more rarely than has been thought. Freud, by contrast, thought the incest taboo had arisen to counteract an unconscious desire to have sex with close relatives.

many social norms are arbitrary and even dysfunctional (Chapter 22), it is difficult to see how they could be sustained by group selection. Given a tendency for others to ostracize those who violate social norms, reproductive fitness would be better served by respecting the norms if the cost of ostracism exceeds the benefit derived from the norm violation. The puzzle is why this tendency would arise in the first place. Why, for instance, would people disapprove of adultery? Social norms against adultery involve third-party reactions that differ from the second-party reaction of sexual jealousy. Although A might benefit from C's disapproval of B's advances to A's spouse, that benefit does not create a selection pressure on C to behave in this way. Whereas group selection might favor genes that induce "third-party punishment" of free riders, the benefit to the group of third-party punishment of adultery is less obvious. Although the tendency for norms against female adultery to be stronger than those against male adultery suggests an evolutionary explanation, it is hard to see what the mechanism would be.[2]

Other claims are more speculative, such as the idea that *self-deception* in humans evolved because of its evolutionary benefits. The argument goes as follows. It is often useful to deceive others. However, deliberate or hypocritical deception is hard to carry off. Therefore, self-deception evolved to enable people to deceive others successfully. The weakness of the argument is that if self-deception causes one to hold false beliefs, these might have disastrous consequences if used as a premise for behavior. Nobody has made a convincing argument that the *net* effect of these opposing effects tends to be positive, as it would have to be for self-deception to enhance evolutionary fitness.

Even more speculative is the claim that unipolar *depression* may have evolved as a bargaining tool, somewhat similar to a labor strike. For instance, an alleged function of postpartum depression is to induce others to share in raising the child, just as workers go on strike to make employers share the profits. Suicides induced by depression are, on this view, the cost of making a credible threat of suicide. They are, as it were, suicide attempts

---

[2] But any sociobiologist worth his or her salt would probably be able to come up with an "explanation" on half an hour's notice.

that failed to fail. Insomnia is explained as an allocation of cognitive resources to solve the crisis to which the depression is a response, whereas hypersomnia (sleeping more than normal) is explained as a way of reducing productivity and thus enhancing the bargaining efficacy of the depression. The argument, while consistent with some known facts about depression, ignores a host of others, such as that depression as well as suicide run in families, that divorced individuals (with no bargaining partner) are more depression prone than the married or never married, and that stressful life events are neither necessary nor sufficient for depression.

Explaining depression as a bargaining tool is another example of a pervasive search for a *meaning* or *function* of all apparently pointless or dysfunctional behaviors. Up to a point, the search for meaning is a good research strategy; beyond this point, it becomes contrived and, as in some of the examples cited, ultimately absurd. There are so many ways in which harmful traits may be preserved in a population that one cannot take for granted that frequently occurring behavior confers reproductive fitness on the agent.[3] Natural selection has certainly favored the propensity to feel physical pain, and there is no a priori reason why it could not favor the tendency to experience mental pain. But to establish the function of depression it is not enough to offer a just-so story that accounts for some of the known features of the illness. Crucially, the hypothesis must also explain facts over and above those it was constructed to explain (Chapter 1), and preferably "novel facts" that were unknown until predicted by the hypothesis.

Intentional Variation, Intentional Selection

Although this doubly intentional mechanism has been and will remain (we can only hope) unimportant in explaining *human* behavior patterns, considering its structure is nevertheless worthwhile.

In *The Origin of Species*, Darwin wrote that "nature gives successive variations; man adds them up in certain directions useful to him." But it

---

[3] In addition to suboptimal behavior caused by lags and pleiotropy (Chapter 16), they may be maintained by a variety of other genetic mechanisms related to the fact that sexually reproducing organisms have two different variants (alleles) of each gene.

is not merely a case of "Nature proposes; man disposes," since, as he also observed, the input can be modified by human behavior:

> A high degree of variability is obviously favourable, as freely giving the materials for selection to work on; not that mere individual differences are not amply sufficient, with extreme care, to allow of the accumulation of a large amount of modification in almost any desired direction. But as variations manifestly useful or pleasing to man appear only occasionally, the chance of their appearance will be much increased by a large number of individuals being kept; and hence this comes to be of the highest importance to success. On this principle Marshall has remarked, with respect to the sheep of parts of Yorkshire, that "as they generally belong to poor people, and are mostly in small lots, they never can be improved." On the other hand, nurserymen, from raising large stocks of the same plants, are generally far more successful than amateurs in getting new and valuable varieties.

Today, we can add that artificial selection can also be enhanced by inducing mutations. In addition, the maintenance of "genetic libraries" can prevent the reduction of genetic variation that is otherwise the inevitable result of selection for particular traits.

With regard to the selection process itself, Darwin distinguished between two *levels of intentionality*:

> At the present time, eminent breeders try by methodical selection, with a distinct object in view, to make a new strain or sub-breed, superior to anything existing in the country. But, for our purpose, a kind of Selection, which may be called Unconscious, and which results from every one trying to possess and breed from the best individual animals, is more important. Thus, a man who intends keeping pointers naturally tries to get as good dogs as he can, and afterwards breeds from his own best dogs, but he has no wish or expectation of permanently altering the breed.

Nonintentional Variation, Intentional Selection

There are many cases in which a new organism or a new form arises by accident and is then either accepted of rejected on the basis of intentional choice. Whereas natural selection tends to produce an equal number of male and female organisms, gender-biased infanticide and more recently gender-based abortion can create a serious sex imbalance in the population. In India and China alone, around 80 million women are "missing" for this reason. Eugenic policies have been widely used to prevent the mentally ill and mentally retarded from reproducing. In Nazi Germany, around three hundred thousand to four hundred thousand individuals were forcibly sterilized on these grounds. As prenatal screening techniques improve, selective abortion may become an important determinant of the makeup of human populations. If further advances make it possible to determine the sex of the child at conception, selection will have been replaced by intentional choice.

Random variation combined with intentional selection may also shape the development of artifacts. When the Norwegian minister and sociologist Eilert Sundt visited England in 1862, he learned about Darwin's theory of natural selection (published in 1859) and set about to apply a variant of it to boat construction:

> A boat constructor may be very skilled, and yet he will never get two boats exactly alike, even if he exerts himself to this end. The variations arising in this way may be called *accidental*. But even a very small variation usually is noticeable during the navigation, and it is then *not accidental* that the seamen come to *notice* that boat that has become improved or more convenient for their purpose, and that they should recommend this to be *chosen* as the one to *imitate*. . . . One may believe that each of these boats is perfect in its way, since it has reached perfection by one-sided development in one particular direction. Each kind of improvement has progressed to the point where further developments would entail defects that would more than offset the advantage. . . . And I conceive of the process in the following way: when the idea of new and improved forms had first been aroused, then *a long series of prudent experiments*, each involving extremely small changes, could lead to the happy result that from the boat constructor's shed there emerged a boat whose like all would desire.

In this text, Sundt improved on Darwin in a crucial respect.[4] Whereas Darwin confessed to ignorance about the origin of variation, Sundt hit

---

[4] The improvement was possible, of course, only because he addressed a different problem, since in 1862 nobody had the conceptual wherewithal to imagine that the source of variation in *organisms* could be random replication mistakes. This leap became possible only after Mendel had shown the

on the idea of locating its source in *errors of replication*, similar to typographical errors and to (what we know now to be) mutations in the DNA. The imperfection of the boat builder – his inability to make perfect copies – is a condition for the ultimate perfection of the end result. Sundt carefully notes that the outcome of the process is a local maximum, from which no further improvements can occur by incremental changes. In the very last sentence, he also suggests that the process may turn into artificial selection, when people engage in deliberate experiments rather than letting variations arise by chance. As did Darwin, he suggested that intelligence or intentionality may occur at two levels: first when people *notice* than one model is more seaworthy than a previous one, and then when they *understand* that improvements could be accelerated if chance variation were replaced by systematic experiments.[5]

Intentional Variation, Nonintentional Selection

The working of economic markets has some features in common with natural selection. The analogy has two versions, one relatively close to natural selection and one more remote. They share the premise that given the multiple limitations of human rationality, firms or managers are *inefficient* in the sense that they are unable to calculate the production and marketing decisions that will maximize their profit. Nevertheless the market mechanism will weed out inefficient firms, so that at any given time mainly efficient firms will be observed. Everything happens "as if" managers were efficient.

In the first and simplest version, all firms are constantly *trying* to increase their profits by processes of imitation and innovation. Although imitation by itself does not generate new inputs for selection to operate on, *imperfect* imitation may, as noted, have this result. Innovation is also, by definition, a source of new inputs. When – through sheer luck – innovation

---

discrete nature of the units of inheritance (genes) and Watson and Crick demonstrated that replication was involved in the process of inheritance. I wonder what Darwin would have answered had Sundt asked him whether the source of biological variation might not be imperfection in the reproductive machinery.

[5] In this way, one could also prevent the unfortunate situation that would arise if boat builders became so good that they never made mistakes.

or imperfect imitation enables a firm to produce at lower cost, it can undersell its rivals and drive them out of business unless they, too, adopt the more efficient ways. By either mechanism, bankruptcy or imitation, these efficient techniques will spread in the population of firms. If we assume that both imitation and innovation occur predominantly in small steps and that competition takes place in an otherwise constant environment, it will bring about a local maximum of equilibrium profits.

The second version denies that firms are always trying to maximize profits. Instead, they use *routines* or rules of thumb that are maintained as long as profits are at a "satisfactory" level. In a neologism, they "satisfice" rather than maximize. What this means may depend on many factors, but we may assume for simplicity that a firm whose profits are consistently below the satisfactory level will either go bankrupt or face the threat of a hostile takeover. The simplest routine is to do everything as before as long as profits are at a "satisfactory" level. More complicated routines could include setting prices by a constant markup on costs or investing of a certain percentage of profits in new production. The idea of satisficing is reflected in such sayings as "Never change a winning team" or "If it ain't broke, don't fix it." In one perspective, satisficing could even be optimal. In a phrase I quoted earlier, "The greatest of all monopoly profits is a quiet life."

Suppose now that profits fall below the satisfactory level. A firm that has been doing the same thing year in year out may be the victim of an organizational analogue of rust or sclerosis. External shocks such as a rise in oil prices or a change in an important exchange rate may increase costs or reduce revenue. Consumer demand may change; rivals may come up with better methods or new products; or workers might impose a costly strike on the firm. Whatever the cause (which may even be unknown to the firm), unsatisfactory profits will induce a search for new routines by some combination of innovation and imitation. Either procedure is likely to be predominantly local, in the sense of being limited to alternatives close to the existing routines. Large changes of any kind may be too costly for a firm that is in financial trouble (Chapter 9), and nonincremental innovations are also conceptually more demanding.

The process of imitation is obviously biased toward the behavior of successful rivals. Whether innovation is random or directed depends on the perceived causes of the crisis that triggered it. If the fall in profits below the acceptable level resulted from a rise in oil prices, the firm may bias its search in the direction of methods that will economize on oil.[6] If it resulted from a change in the exchange rate between the dollar and the euro, the firm is more likely to search randomly. In all cases, however, there is a strong intentional component in the firm's behavior. The decision to change the current routines is intentional, as is the decision about how much to invest in innovation or in imitation. The choice of models to imitate is deliberate, and as just noted, the firm may intentionally bias the search for new routines in a particular direction.

The new routines that result from this process are then exposed to the blind forces of market competition. If they enable the firm to attain a satisfactory level of profit, it will switch off the search until a new crisis arises. If they do not, the firm may try again or have to declare bankruptcy. Sooner or later, nonsatisficing firms are eliminated. In itself, this process does not tend to produce profit-maximizing firms. To see how that could happen, we need to bring *competition* more explicitly into the picture. If we assume that as one of their routines firms invest a fixed percentage of profits in new production, those that by sheer luck have hit upon a better routine than their competitors will expand so that over time their routines become more heavily represented in the population of firms.[7]

Selection Models in the Social Sciences

The usefulness of these models depends on a simple empirical question: what is the rate at which inefficient firms are eliminated compared to the

---

[6] Unless further increases are to be expected, rationality does not require the firm to look for *oil-saving* innovations, since no one can know what the set of feasible innovations looks like (see also Chapter 14). Yet the increase in the price of oil will tend to make these innovations more salient.

[7] In this version they will not deliberately try to drive their rivals out of the market, for instance, by using the high profits to sell below cost until the others give up, since they have no concern for more-than-satisfactory profits.

rate of change of the environment? In the previous chapter I raised the same question with regard to natural selection and made the indirect argument that the highly fine-tuned adaptation of organisms to their environment suggests that the latter must have changed relatively slowly. In the case of the economic environment, we can make a more direct assessment. In the modern world, firms are exposed to unprecedented rates of change. If they were reduced to incremental tracking of the environment, firms would be chronically unfit. Successful firms are more likely to be those that are capable of *anticipating* change, by aiming ahead of the target. This strategy, too, will fail much of the time, but at least not all the time. Moreover, because of their political clout large corporations may also be able to *shape* the environment in which they operate. In an earlier age of cutthroat capitalism among small firms, selection mechanisms of the kind I have described may or may not have been important – we do not know. Today, they are unlikely to explain much of what we observe.

There is also a more general issue at stake. When attacked for the lack of realism of their assumptions, rational-choice theorists routinely assert that they only claim to explain behavior on the assumption that people act "as if" they maximize utility (or profit, or any other aim). Often, they add that this assumption can be justified by some kind of selection mechanism. In the economic sphere, market competition is supposed to do the job. I have argued that it cannot.[8] The most general way of stating my objection is perhaps that even if it could be shown that market competition does improve efficiency through elimination of inefficient firms, there is a vast step from "improving efficiency" to the ultrasophisticated as-if maximization imputed to firms in economic models.

In the political sphere, electoral competition is supposed to ensure that the only politicians we observe are those who are elected or

---

[8] In addition to the general arguments I have cited, the economics of team sports offers a possible objection to the idea that profit maximization is brought about by selection. If profit-maximizing baseball or football teams used their profits to buy up all the best players in their league, their superiority would become so overwhelming that the games would lose much of their uncertainty, and hence of their fun, and hence of their profit-generating ability.

reelected; hence one can assume that all politicians act "as if" they are concerned only with their election prospects. The leap from a concern with election to an *exclusive* concern is not justified, however. A methodologically unprejudiced look at politics suggests that there are three kinds of political actors: opportunists (who only care about getting elected), reformers (who care about their policies' being implemented), and activists or militants (who care more about "making a statement").[9] The view of politics as based on the interaction among these three groups in each party – and among different parties – is clearly more realistic than the "ice cream stall" model of politics (Chapter 19) according to which vote-maximizing parties would all converge to the center. For a striking refutation of the claim that politicians are motivated only by reelection concerns, consider the line of French politicians originating in Jean Jaurès and passing through Léon Blum, Pierre Mendès-France, and Michel Rocard, all of whom were transparently motivated by a desire to promote the impartial values of social justice and economic efficiency. It has to be said, though, that in Rocard's case his distaste for electoral politics did detract from his political efficacy.

Outside the arenas of competition, "as-if" rationality has even less justification. Consumer choices, voting behavior, church attendance, choice of career, and most other behaviors one could name are not subject to selection mechanisms that mimic rationality. They are, to be sure, subject to *constraints* that can reduce the importance of choice in general and of rational choice in particular (Chapter 9). Constraints operate before the fact, to make certain choices unfeasible. Selection operates after the fact, to eliminate those who have made certain choices. Although both mechanisms contribute to the explanation of behavior,

---

[9] The three groups can be more formally distinguished as follows. Opportunists prefer to propose policy A to policy B when the probability of winning at A is greater than the probability of winning at B, given that the opposition party is proposing some fixed C. Militants prefer to propose A to B when the average party member would derive higher utility at A than at B (independently of what C is). Reformists prefer to propose A to B, given that the opposition is proposing C, when the expected utility of the average party member is higher at A than at B. Thus opportunists are concerned only with probabilities, activists only with utilities, and reformers with both.

they cannot, jointly or singly, account for all of it. Choice remains the core concept in the social sciences.

⟨⟨⟨

Bibliographical Note

The data on homicide statistics and child abuse are from M. Daly and M. Wilson, *Homicide* (New York: Aldine de Gruyer, 1988). For objections to their explanation, see Chapter 7 of D. Buller, *Adapting Minds* (Cambridge, MA: MIT Press, 2005). For two sides of the self-deception argument, see R. Trivers, *Social Evolution* (Menlo Park, CA: Benjamin-Cummings, 1985) (favoring an evolutionary explanation), and V. S. Ramachandran and S. Blakeslee, *Phantoms in the Brain* (New York: Quill, 1998) (opposing it). For two sides of the adaptive nature of depression, see E. H. Haggen, "The bargaining model of depression," in P. Hammerstein (ed.), *Genetic and Cultural Evolution of Cooperation* (Cambridge, MA: MIT Press, 2003) (favoring an evolutionary explanation), and P. Kramer, *Against Depression* (New York: Viking, 2005) (opposing it). The analysis of markets in terms of natural selection originates in A. Alchian, "Uncertainty, evolution, and economic theory," *Journal of Political Economy* 58 (1950), 211–21. Its most sophisticated version (which does *not* support "as-if" maximization) is R. Nelson and S. Winter, *An Evolutionary Theory of Economic Change* (Cambridge, MA: Harvard University Press, 1982). The theory of "satisficing" derives from H. Simon, "A behavioral theory of rational choice," *Quarterly Journal of Economics* 69 (1954), 99–118. The economics of team sports is the subject of D. Berri, M. Schmidt, and S. Brook, *The Wages of Wins* (Standard, CA: Stanford University Press, 2006). The distinction among opportunists, reformers, and activists is taken from J. Roemer, *Political Competition* (Cambridge, MA: Harvard University Press, 2001). On "as-if" arguments see also the Bibliographical Note to Chapter 1.

V

INTERACTION

Social interaction can take many forms. (1) The outcome, for each agent, depends on the outcomes for others. This interdependence of outcomes can arise if the material or psychic welfare of others affects my own psychic welfare (Chapter 5). (2) The outcome of each can depend on the actions of all. This interdependence reflects general social causality (Chapter 18), illustrated in such phenomena as (human-made) global warming. (3) The action of each depends on the (anticipated) actions of all. This interdependence is the specific topic of *game theory* (Chapters 19 and 20), which also integrates (1) and (2) within its framework. (4) The beliefs of each depend on the actions of all. This interdependence can arise by a variety of mechanisms, such as "pluralistic ignorance" or "informational cascades" (Chapter 23). (5) The preferences of each depend on the actions of all. This interdependence is perhaps the least well-understood aspect of social interaction. Although I touch on some aspects of the question at various places, notably in Chapter 22, I offer no comprehensive account.

These interdependencies can arise through decentralized action by individuals who stand in no organized relation to each other (Chapter 24). Much of social life has more structure, however. Many outcomes occur through procedures of collective decision making – arguing, voting, and bargaining – through which groups of individuals reach decisions that are binding on them all (Chapter 25). Finally, organizations operate by rules that are designed to put the incentives of individuals and goals of the system in line with each other (Chapter 26).

《《《

Chapter 18
UNINTENDED CONSEQUENCES
❊ ❊ ❊

Unintended Consequences of Individual Behavior

Things do not always turn out the way we intend. Many events occur unintentionally. Sometimes, the causes are trivial, as when we press the accelerator instead of the brake or hit the "delete" button by mistake. Some mechanisms are more systematic, however. While there can hardly be a "general theory of unintended consequences," one can at least begin to compile a catalogue. I consider cases in which the consequences are not only unintended, but also unforeseen. Foreseeable "side effects of action" are not intended for their own sake, especially if they are negative, but I shall not count them as "unintended consequences of action."

Unintended consequences can arise from individual behavior as well as from social interaction. Beginning with the former, we can use a simple extension of the desire-opportunity framework that was set out in Chapter 9 (see Figure 18.1).

While actions are shaped by desires (or preferences), they can also shape desires. Thus in addition to the intended outcome of an action, there is sometimes an unintended one: a change of desire. Addiction is a good example. Under the influence of addictive drugs, people begin to discount the future more heavily, thus weakening the deterrence effect of the long-term harm from addiction. Had this effect been anticipated, it might have prevented the agent from embarking on the path to addiction, but typically it is not. Similar phenomena are observed in more

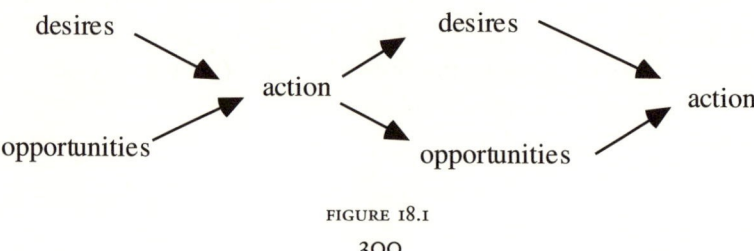

FIGURE 18.1

ordinary situations. I go to the party intending to have only two drinks so that I can drive home, but after the second drink my resolve dissolves in alcohol and I take a third one. Had I known, I might have taken one drink only.

Desires can also be affected by an unconscious preference for novelty or change ("The grass is greener on the other side of the fence"). In H. C. Andersen's tale "What Father Does Is Always Right," the farmer goes to the market in the morning to sell or exchange his horse. First, he meets a man with a cow, which he likes so much that he exchanges the horse for it. In successive transactions, the cow is then exchanged for a sheep, the sheep for a goose, the goose for a hen, and, finally, the hen for a sack of rotten apples. The farmer's road to ruin is paved with stepwise improvements. Each time the farmer believes himself to be better off by the exchange, but the net result of all the exchanges is disastrous.[1]

The "endowment effect," an implication of loss aversion (Chapter 12), also illustrates choice-induced but unintended preference change.[2] Many goods acquire greater subjective value for the owner than they had before she bought them, as shown by the fact that her minimal selling price typically exceeds her maximal buying price by a factor ranging from 2 to 4. Since most goods are evaluated as a loss when given up and as a gain when acquired and since losses count more heavily than same-sized gains, this is what loss aversion predicts. In addition, experiments show that prospective buyers underestimate the minimal resale price they would accept, showing that the preference change is indeed unforeseen.[3]

---

[1] More formally, imagine a person who regularly (although not consciously) adjusts his desires so that he prefers more strongly the commodity of which he currently has less. Suppose he is exposed to the following sequence of two-commodity bundles: $(1/2, 3/2), (3/4, 1/2), (1/4, 3/4), (3/8, 1/4). \ldots$ Then if at a given time he is consuming bundle n in the sequence and for the next period is offered the choice between bundle n and bundle $n + 1$, he will always choose the latter since it offers more of the commodity of which he currently has less. But since the sequence converges to zero, these local improvements bring about overall ruin. The effect is similar to that in which an agent can be bled to death by cycling preferences (Chapter 11), but the mechanism is different.

[2] By accident, the term "endowment effect" has come to be used both for the tendency to overvalue items in one's possession and for the utility a person may derive in the present from utility in the past (Chapter 2). The two meanings are entirely unrelated.

[3] Indeed, it is hard to see how it could be foreseen. The person would have to use two baselines simultaneously, the pre-purchase state relative to which the good is a gain and the post-purchase state relative to which it is a loss.

Another mechanism that could produce this "bolstering effect," the tendency, that is, to cast one's choices in a positive light once they have been made, is offered by the theory of cognitive dissonance (Chapter 1).

As an example of how action may shape *opportunities* in unintended and unforeseen ways, consider the bully who is able to get his way in transactions with others because they usually prefer to yield rather than stand up to him. An unintended consequence of his behavior may be that others shun him, so that he has fewer opportunities for transactions with them. He does well in each encounter, but he has fewer of them. The latter consequence may be not only unintended and unforeseen, but unperceived. As far as he can see, bullying works.[4] If he does notice the negative effects of his behavior, he might still persist in it if the positive effects outweigh them. In that case, the negative consequences will be foreseen but not intended for their own sake.

Often the choice of one option today will remove certain options from the feasible set in the future. This effect may be foreseen: my budget constraint may allow me to buy one car, but not two. Sometimes, however, the agent may not know that the choice has irreversible consequences. A peasant may have a piece of land on which there are some trees and some fields. To get more land for cultivation, and wood to burn, she cuts down the trees. The deforestation causes erosion, leaving her with less land for cultivation than she began with. In a set of cases that I shall discuss shortly, erosion may be the outcome of *collective* behavior, if for instance erosion occurs on the farmer's plot if and only if both she and her two neighbors carry out deforestation. But it is also possible and quite common for an individual single-handedly and unknowingly to undermine her future opportunities for action. The culprit is a *cognitive deficit*: the agent cannot predict future consequences of present behavior. In other cases, it may occur through a *motivational deficit*: the agent attaches low weight to the (known and certain) future consequences compared to immediate gains (Chapter 6).

---

[4] This limited perspective is shared by some social scientists, who argue that emotions such as anger can be "rational," or at least adaptive, because they enable agents to get their way in encounters with others.

Externalities

Let me now turn to unintended consequences of *interaction*, a theme that was one of the key ideas of the emerging social sciences. In Adam Ferguson's memorable phrase, history is "the result of human action, but not the execution of any human design." His contemporary, Adam Smith, referred to an "invisible hand" that shapes human affairs. Half a century later, Hegel invoked the "cunning of reason" to explain the progress of freedom in history. About the same time, Tocqueville made a similar claim that in the progress of democracy, "everyone played a part: those who strove to ensure democracy's success as well as those who never dreamt of serving it; those who fought for it as well as those who declared themselves as its enemies." A few years later, Marx referred to people's "alienation" from their own action, claiming that "this fixation of social activity, this consolidation of what we ourselves produce as a material power above us, growing out of our control, thwarting our expectations, bringing to naught our calculations, is one of the chief factors in historical development up till now."

Among these writers only Adam Smith and Marx provided specific mechanisms for the production of unintended consequences. In modern language, they emphasized how *externalities* of behavior may aggregate to produce outcomes neither intended nor foreseen by the agents. In stylized form, imagine that each of many identical agents takes a certain action to promote his interest. As a by-product of that action, he also imposes a small cost or confers a small benefit (a negative or positive externality) on each of the other agents (and on himself). Each agent, then, is the target of many such actions. Adding up the effects, and then adding the sum to the private benefit of the agent caused by his action, we get the final outcome that the agents generate through their actions. Since we assume that they are identical, their initial states, the states they individually intend to bring about, and the states they collectively do bring about may each be represented by a single number, x, y, and z, respectively.[5]

---

[5] Many economists would not count all the phenomena I list here as externalities. They would include pollution, but not market-generated effects such as Keynesian unemployment. For my purposes, however, what matters is what they have in common: in pursuit of a benefit for himself,

Suppose first that z > y > x, a positive externality. This was Adam Smith's main interest: when an agent directs his "industry in such a manner as its produce may be of the greatest value, he intends only his own gain, and he is in this, as in many other cases, led by an invisible hand to promote an end which was no part of his intention. Nor is it always the worse for society that it was no part of it. By pursuing his own interest he frequently promotes that of the society more effectually than when he really intends to promote it." In market competition the aim of each firm is to make a profit by producing more cheaply than the rivals, but in doing so they also benefit the customers. The customers, too, might in their capacity as workers or managers be in a similar position to benefit others through their competitive efforts. The result has been spectacular secular growth. The effect may or may or may not have been foreseen but was certainly "no part of" their intention.

Suppose next that y > z > x, a weak negative externality. The agents are made better off as a result of their effort, but, because of the costs they impose on each other, not as much as they expected to be. People commuting to work by car may be better off than they would be by using public transportation if the latter is poorly developed, but congestion or pollution prevents them from benefiting as much as they expected. If the externality is produced by congestion, they can hardly fail to notice it. If, however, it is produced by pollution, it might take a while before they understand that they are mutually harming themselves rather than being victims of (say) factory pollution.

Suppose finally that y > x > z, a strong negative externality. The agents are all made worse off as a result of everybody's trying to become better off. This was one of Marx's main charges against the decentralized capitalist economy. His main account of capitalist crises, the "theory of the falling rate of profit," had this general structure. To maintain or increase profits, he argued, each capitalist has an incentive to replace labor by machinery. When all capitalists do so simultaneously, however, they are collectively sawing off the branch they are sitting on, since the

---

each individual imposes a small cost or benefit on everybody else *and on himself.* A firm laying off workers or cutting wages will cause a small reduction in the demand for its own products.

ultimate source of profit is the surplus value generated by labor. The argument is seductive but on closer analysis turns out to be wrong in all sorts of ways. More interesting is another observation that Marx made in passing and that later become a cornerstone of the theory of unemployment produced by John Maynard Keynes. Each capitalist, Marx noted, has an ambiguous relation to the workers. On the one hand, she wants the workers *she* employs to have low wages, since that makes for high profits. On the other hand, she wants all *other* workers to have high wages, since that makes for high demand for her products. Although it is possible for any one capitalist to have both of these desires satisfied, it is logically impossible for this to be the case for all capitalists simultaneously. This is a "contradiction of capitalism" that Keynes spelled out as follows. In a situation of falling profit, each capitalist responds by laying off workers, thus saving on the wage bill. Yet since the demand of workers directly or indirectly is what sustains the firms, the effect of all capitalists' simultaneously laying off workers will be a further reduction in profit, causing more layoffs or bankruptcies.

There are many cases of this general kind. Overfishing, deforestation, and overgrazing ("the tragedy of the commons") may be individually rational, but collectively suboptimal or even disastrous. If each family in a developing country produces many children as insurance against poverty in old age, overpopulation will generate more poverty. In a water crisis, each individual who uses water for nonessential purposes causes a slight increase in the probability that the authorities may cut the water supply for a few hours each day, affecting essential purposes as well. These consequences may or may not be foreseen. A crucial feature of this category of unintended consequences is that even when they are foreseen, the behavior will be the same. As I explain in the next chapter, it is a *dominant strategy*: it is rational to choose it regardless of what others are doing.

Internalities

A partially similar argument applies to "internalities," defined as the benefit or harm a person's choice at one time may confer on the welfare he derives from later choices. Metaphorically speaking, internalities are externalities

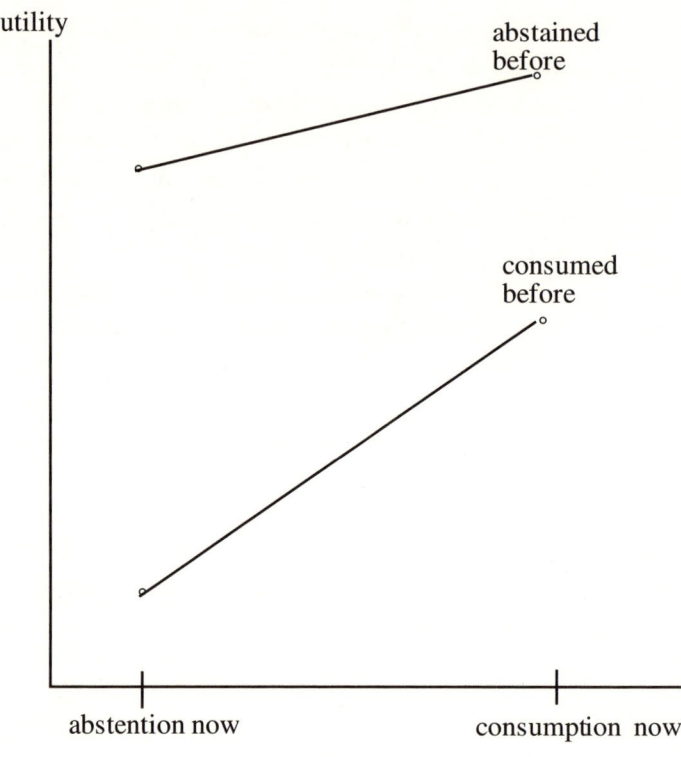

FIGURE 18.2

that a person imposes on his "later selves." In the discussion of child custody summarized in Figure 11.3, I argued that time spent with the child creates a positive internality for the parent. Addiction provides an important example of negative internalities. The more a person has consumed in the past of an addictive substance, the less pleasure she derives from current consumption. This "tolerance" effect may also occur with nonaddictive goods. Even if you love butter pecan ice cream, you are likely to be satiated if you have it five times a day. In addiction, however, past consumption has a further effect. While it makes current consumption less pleasurable than it would have been had the agent not consumed in the past, it also increases the welfare difference between consuming and not consuming in the present ("withdrawal"). Schematically, see Figure 18.2.

Thus regardless of whether she has abstained or consumed in the past, the agent is better off in the present by consuming than by not consuming. Consumption is a dominant strategy. At the same time, repeated consumption makes her worse off at all times (except for a few times in the beginning) than repeated abstention, just as the dominant strategy of having many children can make everybody worse off. There are of course obvious differences between externalities and internalities. One is the temporal asymmetry: whereas all individuals can harm one another, later selves cannot hurt earlier selves. Another is that the successive selves are really just time slices of *one* decision maker, whereas different individuals are not spatially distinct parts of one superorganism. Once *the* person (the one and only) understands that his present choices have a negative effect on the welfare he can derive from later choices, he has an incentive to change his behavior. Whether the incentive is strong enough depends on the severity of the withdrawal symptoms and on the extent to which the agent discounts future welfare. Some agents who would never have taken the first step had they known the consequences may choose not to quit once they are hooked.

The Younger Sibling Syndrome

Unintended consequences of social action can also be produced by what I shall call the *younger sibling mechanism*. Before I explain this phrase, let me illustrate it with a famous example from economic theory, the "cobweb," also called the "hog cycle" because it was first put forward as an explanation of cyclical fluctuations in hog production. It has a much wider application, however. Fluctuations in the shipbuilding industry have often had the same pattern, with a seller's market followed by overinvestment and glut. When students make career choices on the basis of current demand for graduates, they may collectively undo the basis for their decisions.

Hog farmers must decide one year ahead of time how much they want to put on the market in the next year, a decision that is determined by the price they expect hogs to fetch and the cost of producing them. An increase in expected price will induce farmers to produce more, as reflected in the upward-sloping supply curve in Figure 18.3.

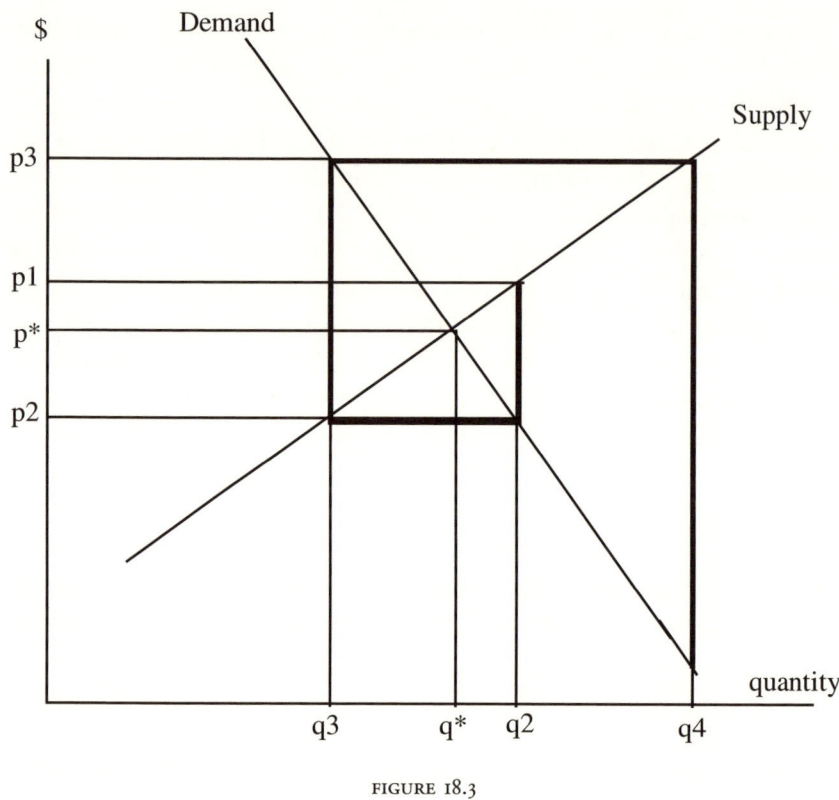

FIGURE 18.3

Assume that in year 1 the price for hogs is p1. Expecting that prices will remain the same in year 2, farmers put q2 on the market next year. At this volume, however, the market-clearing price is p2 rather than p1. Expecting that prices will remain at that level in year 3, farmers produce volume q3 for that year. The market-clearing price will be p3, inducing farmers to produce q4 in year 4, and so on. In this case, prices and volumes form an outward spiral or "cobweb" pattern indicated by the bold lines in the diagram. Pleasant surprises alternate with unpleasant ones, but the expected outcome never occurs. If the relative slopes of the supply and demand curves are modified, the result could be an inward spiral converging to the equilibrium price p* and equilibrium volume q*.

There is something irrational about the behavior of the farmers. Each of them believes that *he* is free to vary his output to maximize his profits, while tacitly assuming that others are just mechanically doing what they did last year. While perhaps irrational, the behavior is certainly intelligible. A French philosopher, Maurice Merleau-Ponty, said that our spontaneous tendency is to view other people as "younger siblings."[6] We do not easily impute to others the same capacity for deliberation and reflection that introspection tells us that we possess ourselves, nor for that matter our inner turmoil, doubts, and anguishes (see Chapter 23). The idea of viewing others as being just as strategic and calculating as we are ourselves does not seem to come naturally.

Three examples from voting behavior can also illustrate the idea. Suppose I am a member of the left wing of the Socialist party in my country. I would much prefer to have the Socialists rather than the Communists in power, but since the polls predict a solid Socialist majority I vote Communist to make my party move to the left. I do not, however, pause to ask myself whether other left-wingers might think along the same lines. If many of them do, the Communists might win. The intention to produce the top-ranked outcome (a Socialist victory with a strong Communist showing) may generate the third-ranked outcome (a Communist victory). In what is probably a more common scenario, if many voters stay home because they are confident that their party will win, it may lose. Finally, recall the Chirac example from Chapter 12. A possible explanation for his disastrous calling of early elections may have been his failure to anticipate that the voters would infer his beliefs from his decision rather than simply behave, mechanically, as they said in the polls that they would.

The failure to see others as intentional and maximizing agents is observed when legislators or administrators propose policies that are undermined when agents adjust to them. According to Roman law, the stealing of a single horse or ox made a man a cattle thief, whereas it would not be a crime if he stole fewer than four pigs or ten sheep. A commentator on the law wrote that "in such a state of the law one would

---

[6] He actually wrote "younger brother."

expect thefts of three pigs or eight sheep to become abnormally common." To promote security of employment, many countries have adopted legislation making it illegal to lay off workers who have been employed, say, two years or more. Employers rationally respond by outsourcing or by offering workers temporary contracts, thus reducing security of employment. Cities may build highways to reduce congestion, only to find that because more people take their cars to work the roads are just as jammed as before and more pollution is generated. The government may try to limit immigration to those who are married to a person who is already legally in the country, with the effect of inducing people to marry just for this purpose. Draft exemptions for students create an incentive to go to college. Even the creation of explicit incentive systems may backfire. Thus when the Chicago Public School System in 1996 created a system in which badly performing schools would be punished in various ways, it did not occur to the designers that in addition to creating an inventive for teachers to work harder, the system encouraged them to inflate the grades, as did in fact happen.

The younger-sibling syndrome can have important social consequences, as two examples will bring out. Tocqueville notes that in the decades preceding the French Revolution, the upper classes publicly denounced the vices of the regime and its devastating impact on the people, as if the latter were deaf to what they were saying, "This reminds me of the sentiment of Mme Duchâtelet, who according to Voltaire's secretary did not mind undressing in front of her menservants, unpersuaded as she was that valets were men." The secretary, in his memoirs, wrote in fact that "great ladies regarded their lackeys only as automata." This simultaneous show of contempt toward the lower classes and denunciation of their misery prepared minds for the Revolution. More recently, the argument behind the "Phillips curve," according to which the government can choose, if it so desires, to realize low unemployment at the cost of high inflation, presupposes that the social actors are unaware of this policy. When governments tried to achieve this end, however, strategic behavior by rational trade unions and other actors undermined their efforts and produced instead "stagflation" – high inflation *and* high unemployment.

Unlike the unintended consequences produced by externalities, those generated by the younger sibling mechanism may end when the agents understand it. There are no dominant strategies in the cases I have described, only strategies that are optimal on the (usually implicit) assumption that others are less rational than one is. Once all agents view each other as rational, their behavior may converge to a fully predictable outcome. All hog farmers will expect the equilibrium price to prevail. Acting on that expectation, they will produce the equilibrium volume. Their shared belief is self-fulfilling. This idea is the topic of the next chapter.

❰❰❰

Bibliographical Note

The impact of addiction on time discounting is documented in L. Gordano et al., "Mild opioid deprivation increases the degree that opioid-dependent outpatients discount delayed heroin and money," *Psychopharmacology* 63 (2002), 174–82. The note offering a model of Andersen's tale is inspired by C. C. von Weiszäcker, "Notes on endogenous change of tastes," *Journal of Economic Theory* 3 (1971), 345–72. For a discussion of Marx on unintended consequences, see my *Making Sense of Marx* (Cambridge University Press, 1985), Chapter 1.3.2 and passim. The addiction model derives from G. Becker and K. Murphy, "A theory of rational addiction," *Journal of Political Economy* 96 (1988), 675–700. A superb conceptual study of unintended consequences is T. Schelling, *Micromotives and Macrobehavior* (New York: Norton, 1978). For the idea of internalities, see R. Herrnstein et al., "Utility maximization and melioration: Internalities in individual choice," *Journal of Behavioral Decision Making* 6 (1993), 149–85. The example from the Chicago Public School System is taken from B. Jacob and S. Leavitt, "Rotten apples: An investigation of the prevalence and predictors of teacher cheating," *Quarterly Journal of Economics* 118 (2003), 843–77.

Chapter 19

STRATEGIC INTERACTION

❀ ❀ ❀

Strategic Interaction with Simultaneous Choices

The invention of *game theory* may come to be seen as the most important single advance of the social sciences in the twentieth century. The value of the theory is partly explanatory, but mainly conceptual. In some cases it allows us to explain behavior that previously appeared as puzzling. More important, it illuminates the structure of social interaction. Once you see the world through the lenses of game theory – or "the theory of interdependent decisions," as it might better be called – nothing looks quite the same again.

I first consider games in which agents make simultaneous decisions. The goal is to understand whether and how n agents or *players* may achieve an unenforced coordination of their *strategies*. Often, we shall look at the special case of n = 2. The players may be able to communicate with each other, but not to enter into binding agreements. To any n-tuple of strategies, one chosen by each agent, there corresponds an *outcome*. Each agent ranks the possible outcomes according to his or her *preference order*. When needed, we shall assume that the conditions for representing preferences as cardinal utilities are satisfied (Chapter 11). The *reward structure* is the function that to any n-tuple of strategies assigns an n-tuple of utilities. Although the word "reward" may suggest a monetary outcome, the word will be used to refer to psychological outcomes (utilities and ultimately preferences). When, as is often the case, the monetary or material reward structure and the psychological reward structure diverge, only the latter is relevant.

As briefly mentioned in the last chapter, an agent may have a strategy that is *dominant* in the sense that regardless of what others do, it yields a better outcome for her than what she would get if she chose any other strategy. Her *outcome* may depend on what others do, but her *choice* does not. In other cases, there is genuine interdependence of choices. If others drive on the left side of the road, my best response is to drive left too; if they drive on the right, my best response is to drive right.

An *equilibrium* is an n-tuple of strategies with the property that no player can, by deviating from his equilibrium strategy, unilaterally bring about an outcome that he strictly prefers to the equilibrium outcome. Equivalently, in equilibrium the strategy chosen by each player is a best response to the strategies chosen by the others, in the weak sense that he can do *no better* than choosing his equilibrium strategy if others choose theirs. The strategy need not, however, be optimal in the strong sense that he would do *worse* by deviating unilaterally. In the general case, a game may have several equilibria. We shall see some examples shortly. Assume, however, that there is only one equilibrium. Assume moreover that the reward structure and the rationality of all players are common knowledge.[1] Under these assumptions, we can predict that all agents will choose their equilibrium strategy, since it is the only one that is based on rational beliefs about what others will do.

Some games with a unique equilibrium turn upon the existence of dominant strategies. The phrase "turn upon the existence of dominant strategies" can mean one of two things, illustrated in panels A and B of Figure 19.1.[2] In an accident involving two cars, both are harmed. In an accident involving a pedestrian and a car, only the former is harmed. Car-car accidents occur if at least one driver is careless. If both are careless, the outcome is worse. Car-pedestrian accidents occur only if both are careless. Taking due care is costly. From these premises, it follows that in the car-car case, taking care is the dominant strategy for each driver. In the car-pedestrian case, no-care is dominant for the driver.

---

[1] A fact is common knowledge if all know it, all know that all others know it, all know that all others know that all others know it, and so on. To avoid reliance on the phrase "and so on," which suggests an infinite sequence of beliefs, the idea may also be stated as follows: there is no n such that the fact is common knowledge up to level n in the sequence but not at level n + 1. For a simple illustration, common knowledge may be realized in a classroom. When the teacher tells a fact to the students, they all know it, know that others know it, and so on.

[2] By convention, the first number in each cell represents the payoff for the "row player" who chooses between the top and bottom strategies, and the second the payoff for the "column player" who chooses between the left and right strategies. Depending on the context, the payoffs may be cardinal utilities, ordinal utilities, money, or anything else that the players may be assumed to maximize. In Figure 19.1, payoffs may be seen as standing for ordinal utilities, reflecting preferences over outcomes. Here and later, equilibria are circled.

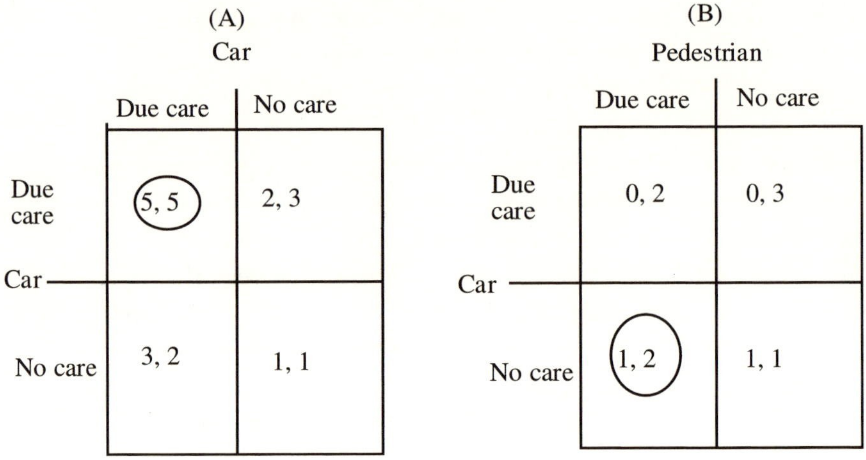

FIGURE 19.1

The pedestrian has no dominant strategy, since due care is the best response to no care and no care the best response to due care. Since he knows that the driver has no-care as a dominant strategy and, being rational, will choose it, the pedestrian will nevertheless choose due care.[3]

Games in which all players have dominant strategies are quite common and empirically important, as we shall see. Theoretically, they are somewhat trivial, except when they are repeated over time. Games in which some players have dominant strategies that can induce clear-cut choices in others are less common but also important. They have stronger informational requirements, however, since in our example the pedestrian needs to know the possible outcomes for the driver as well as for himself, whereas the two drivers only need to know their own outcomes. Often, we can impute dominant strategies to others without much trouble. We do not usually, for instance, look both ways before crossing a one-way street because we assume that the fear of drivers of being liable for an accident will make them obey the one-way rule.

---

[3] According to some legal analyses, an important function of tort law is to use the system of fines and damages to change the reward matrix so that the emerging equilibrium has some desirable property (efficiency or fairness).

A special class of games has *coordination equilibria,* often called "conventions," in which each player not only has no incentive to deviate unilaterally, but also would prefer that nobody else does so. In an equilibrium in which everybody drives on the right side of the road, an accident might occur if I deviate *or* if anyone else does. In this case, the equilibrium is not unique, since driving on the left side has the same properties.[4] Often it does not matter what we do as long as we all do the same thing. The meanings of words are arbitrary, but once they are fixed, they become conventions. In other cases, it does matter what we do, but it is more important that we all do the same thing. I return to some examples shortly.

Two Duopoly Examples

Some games have unique equilibria that do not turn upon the existence of dominant strategies. Duopoly behavior is an example (see Figure 19.2).

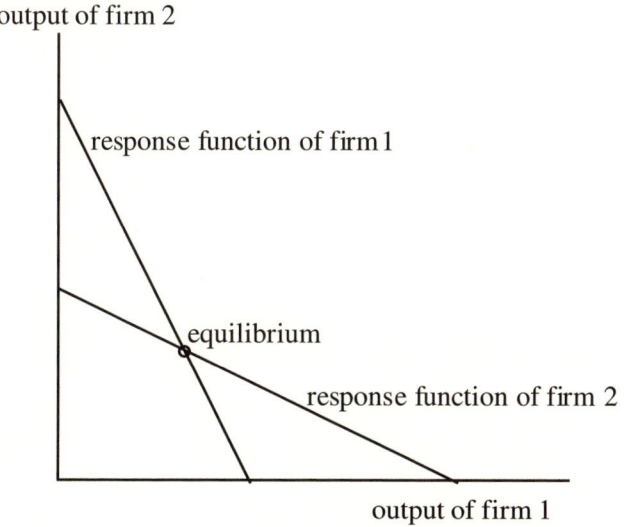

FIGURE 19.2

---

[4] Although the nonuniqueness does not follow from the formal definition, this seems to be a general feature of real-life coordination games.

When two firms dominate a market, lower production by one firm will induce higher prices and an expansion of production by the other firm. In other words, each firm has a "best response" schedule that tells it how much to produce as a function of the output of the other firm. In equilibrium, the output of each firm is a best response to the output of the other. This statement does not imply that they could not do better. If they formed a cartel and restricted their production to below-equilibrium levels, both would earn greater profits. Yet these collectively optimal levels of production are not best responses to each other. The firms are, in fact, facing a Prisoner's Dilemma (defined in Figure 19.3).

For another case of duopoly, consider two ice cream vendors on a beach, trying to find the best location for their stalls on the assumption that customers (assumed to be evenly distributed across the shoreline) will go to the closer stall. There is no dominant strategy. If one of them puts up a stall some distance left of the middle of the beach, the best response of the other is to position himself immediately to the right, to which the best response of the first is to move right again, and so on, until their stalls are beside each other at the middle of the beach. This unique equilibrium is obviously not the best for the customers in the aggregate. For them, the best outcome is one in which each stall is positioned halfway between the middle and one end of the beach. Although this outcome is just as good for the sellers as the equilibrium outcome, these positions are not best responses to each other. This model has also been applied to explain the tendency for political parties (in a two-party system) to move toward the middle of the political spectrum.

Suppose, however, that when both stalls are at the middle customers close to the ends abstain from buying ice cream because it would melt by the time they walked back. If no customer is willing to walk more than half the length of the beach, one-quarter to get to the stall and one-quarter to get back, the optimal consumer outcome is also the unique equilibrium since neither has an inventive to relocate. Suppose the beach is 1,000 meters long. If the seller at 750 meters moves his stall to 700, he will lose the 50 customers between 950 and 1,000 who are not willing to walk more than 500 yards and gain the 25 customers between 475 and

500 to whom his stall is now closer than the other – a net loss. A similar argument might also explain why political parties never converge fully to the middle, since extremists at either end might prefer to abstain rather than vote for a centrist party. In addition, as I noted at the end of Chapter 17, it is simply not plausible to view vote maximization as the only aim of political parties.

Some Frequently Occurring Games

A few simple interaction structures, with payoffs as in Figure 19.3, occur very often in a great variety of contexts.[5] C and D stand for "coopera- tion" and "defection." In the Telephone Game the column player is the one who first called. In the Focal Point Game, A and B can be any pair of actions such that both players would prefer to coordinate on either than not to coordinate but are indifferent between the two ways of coordi- nating.

The games illuminate the structure of the two central issues of social interaction – *cooperation* and *coordination*. In a society with no coop- eration for mutual benefit, life would be "solitary, poor, nasty, brutish, and short" (Hobbes). That it would be *predictably* bad is a meager consolation. In a society where people were unable to coordinate their behavior, unintended consequences would abound and life would be like "a tale told by an idiot, full of sound and fury, signifying nothing" (*Macbeth*). Both cooperation and coordination sometimes succeed, but often fail abysmally. Game theory can illuminate the successes as well as the failures.

The Prisoner's Dilemma (PD), the Stag Hunt, and Chicken involve in one way or another the choice between cooperation and defection (noncooperation). The Prisoner's Dilemma is so called because the fol- lowing story was used to illustrate it in an early discussion. Each of two prisoners, who have been involved in the same crime but are now in separate cells, is told that if he informs on the other but she does not

---

[5] Although stated here as two-person games, they easily generalize to the case of many agents. An n + 1-person version of the Prisoner's Dilemma, for instance, is illustrated in Figure 24.2.

	C	D
C	3, 3	0, 4
D	4, 0	(1.5, 1.5)

Prisoner's Dilemma

	C	D
C	(4, 4)	1, 3
D	3, 1	(2, 2)

Stag Hunt/ Assurance Game

	C	D
C	2, 2	(1, 3)
D	(3, 1)	0, 0

Chicken

	Ballet	Boxing
Ballet	(1, 2)	0, 0
Boxing	0, 0	(2, 1)

Battle of the Sexes

	Redial	Do not redial
Do not redial	(2, 2)	0, 0
Redial	0, 0	(1, 1)

Telephone Game

	A	B
A	(1, 1)	0, 0
B	0, 0	(1, 1)

Focal Point Game

FIGURE 19.3

inform on him, he will go free and she will go to prison for ten years; if neither informs on the other, both will go to prison for one year; and if both inform on each other, both will go to prison for five years.[6] Under these circumstances, informing is a dominant strategy, although both would be better off if neither informed. The outcome is generated by a combination of the "free-rider temptation" (going free) and the "fear of being suckered" (getting ten years).

The negative externalities discussed in the last chapter can also be viewed as many-person PDs. Some other examples follow. For each worker (assuming selfish motivations) it is better to be nonunionized than to join a union, even when it is better for all if all join and gain higher pay. For each firm in a cartel it is better to break out and produce a high volume to exploit the high prices caused by the output restrictions of the other firms, but when all do that, prices fall to the competitive level; profit maximization by each firm undermines the maximization of joint profits. The Organization of Petroleum Exporting Countries (OPEC) cartel is vulnerable in the same way. Other examples are situations in which everybody has to run as fast as he can to stay in the same place, such as the arms race between the United States and the former Soviet Union, political advertising, or students writing papers for a teacher who "grades on the curve."

The idea of the Stag Hunt is often imputed to Jean-Jacques Rousseau, although his language was somewhat opaque.[7] In more stylized form, it involves two hunters who can choose between hunting stag (C) and a hare (D). Each can catch a hare by himself, but the joint effort of both is necessary (and sufficient) to catch a stag. Half a stag is worth more than a hare. It takes more time and effort to catch hares when both are trying because the noises the hunters make scare them away. As in the Prisoner's

---

[6] The payoffs for the Prisoner's Dilemma in Figure 19.3 might seem artificial. For the present purposes, all that matters is the (ordinal) ranking of the outcomes. Later, the payoffs will be reinterpreted as monetary rewards.

[7] "If a deer was to be taken, every one saw that, in order to succeed, he must abide faithfully by his post: but if a hare happened to come within the reach of any one of them, it is not to be doubted that he pursued it without scruple, and, having seized his prey, cared very little, if by so doing he caused his companions to miss theirs." This could be read as saying that pursuing hares is a dominant strategy.

Dilemma, there is a risk of being a sucker, hunting for stag while the other goes for a hare. There is no free-rider temptation, however. The game has two equilibria, in the upper left-hand and lower right-hand cells.

Although the first equilibrium is clearly better, it may not be realized. To see why this might happen we can drop the assumption that the payoff structure is common knowledge and allow the agents to have mistaken beliefs about the payoff structure of other agents. Actions taken on these beliefs will form an *equilibrium in a weak sense* if, for each agent, the actions taken by the others confirm his beliefs about them. Assume, for instance, that in a Stag Hunt each agent falsely believes the others to have PD preferences. Given that belief, the rational action is to defect, thus confirming the belief of the others that *he* has PD preferences. This society might end up with high levels of tax evasion and corruption. I return to such cases of "pluralistic ignorance" in Chapter 23. In another society, where people correctly believe others to have Stag Hunt preferences, a good equilibrium will emerge in which people pay their taxes and do not offer or take bribes. "Cultures of corruption" might be a belief-dependent, not a motivation-dependent, phenomenon.

International control of infectious diseases can have the structure of a Stag Hunt. If only one country fails to take the appropriate measures, others will not be able to protect themselves.[8] For another example, consider counterterrorist measures. If only one of two nations invests in such measures, it benefits the other as well as itself. If the costs exceed the benefits to itself, it will not invest unilaterally. Yet if both invest, the ability to pool information may lead to a greater security level for each than it could achieve by exploiting the investment of the other.

In these examples, the payoff structure arises from the causal nature of the situation. In the Stag Hunt and the disease control case, the "threshold technology" implies that individual efforts are pointless. In the counterterrorism case, the underlying cause is something like economies of scale: ten units of effort have more than twice the effect of five units. In other cases, the payoff structure is due to the fact that the

---

[8] This is a huge simplification, made simply for the sake of illustration.

agents care for other things than their own material rewards. In such cases, it is more common to refer to the game as an Assurance Game (AG). Even if the material payoff structure is that of a PD, each individual may be willing to cooperate if he is *assured* that others will. The desire to be fair, or the reluctance to be a free rider, may overcome the temptation to exploit the cooperation of others. Alternatively, altruistic preferences may transform a PD into an AG.

Let us interpret the payoffs in the PD in Figure 19.3 as monetary rewards and assume that each person's utility equals his monetary reward plus half the monetary reward of the other. In that case, the utility payoff will be as in Figure 19.4 – an AG. The PD may also be transformed into an AG by a third mechanism, if an outside party attaches a penalty to the choice of the noncooperative strategy D. If we again interpret the payoffs in the PD in Figure 19.3 as monetary rewards, *and* assume that this is all the agents care about, deducting 1.25 from the reward to defection will turn it into an AG. A labor union might, for instance, impose formal or informal sanctions on nonunionized workers. Finally, one might transform a PD into an AG by rewarding cooperation, for example, by offering a bonus or bribe of 1.25 to cooperators. Promises of reward have to be respected, however, whereas a threat does not have to be carried out if it works. If the free-rider payoff is very high, the benefits from cooperation may not be large enough to fund the bribes.[9] In some cases, though, rewards are used. Workers who join a union may benefit not only from higher wages, which usually accrue equally to nonunionized workers, but also from pension plans and cheap vacations offered only to members.

The game of Chicken is named after a teenage ritual from the 1955 movie *Rebel Without a Cause*. Los Angeles teenagers drive stolen cars to a cliff and play a game in which two boys simultaneously drive their cars off the edge of the cliff, stopping at the last possible moment. The boy who stops first is "chicken" and loses. In another variant, two cars drive toward each other and the one who swerves first is

---

[9] Whether one uses punishments or rewards, the costs of establishing the system and monitoring the agents also have to be funded by the gains from cooperation. In practice, this can easily make such arrangements impossible or wasteful.

	C	D
C	(4.5, 4.5)	2, 4
D	4, 2	(2.25, 2.25)

FIGURE 19.4

"chicken." In each of the two equilibria, each agent does the opposite of the other. Even with common knowledge of the payoff structure and of the rationality of the agent, we cannot predict which of the equilibria (if any) will be chosen. From the point of view of rational choice, the situation is *indeterminate*. In the second ("swerve") version of the game, a player might try to break the indeterminacy by (visibly) blindfolding himself, thus inducing the other to swerve. Yet this creates the same predicament with the two options being "blindfolding" and "not blind-folding" rather than "swerving" and "not swerving."[10] It is a deeply frustrating situation.

On one understanding of the arms race, it has the structure of Chicken. The Cuban missile crisis is often cited as a case in which the two superpowers were locked in a Chicken-like confrontation and the USSR "blinked first." Another example is that of two farmers who use the same irrigation system for their fields. The system can be adequately maintained by one person, but both farmers gain equal benefit from it. If one farmer does not do his share of maintenance, it may still be in the other farmer's interest to do so. The Kitty Genovese case can

---

[10] Similarly, the "solution" to the Prisoner's Dilemma that consists of each person's promising to cooperate merely recreates the PD with the choices being "keeping the promise" and "reneging."

also be seen in this perspective, if we assume that each neighbor would prefer to intervene if and only if nobody else did.

Turning now to questions of *coordination*, consider first the Battle of the Sexes. The stereotype behind the story is the following. A man and his wife want to go out for the evening. They have decided to go either to a ballet or to a boxing match after work and to settle the final choice over the telephone. His phone breaks down, however, so they have to decide by tacit coordination. They have a common interest in being together, but divergent interests about where to go. As does the game of Chicken, this game has two equilibria, coordinating on the ballet or on the boxing match. And as in that game, there is no way common knowledge of the payoff structure and of rationality will tell the couple where to meet. Once again, the situation is indeterminate.

Games of this kind arise when coordination can take many forms, all of which are better for all agents than no coordination at all, but each of which is preferred by some agents to the others.[11] In social and political life, this seems to be the rule rather than the exception. All citizens may prefer any political constitution (within a certain range of possible regimes) to no constitution at all, because long-term stability is important in enabling them to plan ahead. When the law is fixed and hard to change, one can regulate one's behavior according to it. Yet each interest group may prefer a specific constitution in the range over the others: creditors lobby for a ban on paper money in the constitution, each political party favors the electoral system that will favor it, those with a strong candidate for the presidency want that office to be strong, and so on.

Multiple coordination equilibria also arise when different societies initially develop different standards of weight, length, or volume and later discover the potential benefits from a common solution. Continental Europe and the Anglo-Saxon world retain separate standards in these areas. Unlike the case of multiple constitutional solutions, the obstacle to agreement is not permanent divergence of interest, but short-term transition costs. The choice of standard might also, however, be a game of

---

[11] As we shall see later (Chapter 25), this question of dividing the benefits from cooperation can also be studied within *bargaining theory*, a more specialized branch of game theory.

Chicken. Assume, implausibly, that the standard is written into the constitution as an entrenched clause (immune to amendment). Each country will then have an incentive to commit itself before the other does.

The Telephone Game is defined by the need for a rule to tell the parties what to do when a phone conversation is accidentally interrupted. There are two coordination equilibria: the redialing is done by the person who made the call in the first place or by the person who received it. Either rule is better than having both redial or neither. Yet in this case, unlike the Battle of the Sexes, one equilibrium is better for both than the other. It is more efficient to have the caller do the redialing, since he is more likely to know which number to call. Rational, fully informed agents will converge on the superior coordination equilibrium. This statement ignores, however, the cost of redialing. If the cost is large, the game becomes a Battle of the Sexes.

Consider finally the Focal Point Game, which can be illustrated by a variant of the Battle of the Sexes. The spouses have agreed to watch a movie that is playing both in movie theater A and movie theater B but have postponed the choice of venue. We assume that neither is closer or otherwise more convenient than the other. As in the Battle of the Sexes, information, rationality, and common knowledge by themselves will not tell them where to go. There might, however, be a psychological cue in the situation that will serve as a "focal point" for coordination. If the couple had their first date in theater A, this might make them converge to that location. In this case, the cue is a purely private event. In other cases, cues might be shared by a large population. Among New Yorkers, for instance, folklore says that if you get separated from your companion you meet at noon under the main clock at Grand Central Station. And even when there is no folklore, many people would still go to the railway station, since in many cities the railway station is the most important building of which there is only one.[12] Its uniqueness renders it attractive as a focal point. Noontime has the same property.[13]

---

[12] In New York City, those ignorant of the folklore would not go to Grand Central Station, since the presence of Penn Station makes it nonunique. Instead, they might coordinate on the Empire State Building.

[13] Although midnight, too, is a focal point, it is inferior to noontime because of the inconvenience.

This focal point effect is easily demonstrated in experiments. If you ask all members of a group to write down a positive integer (whole number) on a piece of paper and tell them that they will get a reward if all write down the same number, they invariably converge on 1. There is a unique smallest integer, but no unique largest one. In other contexts, 0 may emerge as the unique focal point. In debates during the cold war whether the United States might use tactical nuclear weapons without triggering an escalation into full-blown nuclear war, various ideas were suggested for a "bright line" that would allow limited use. In the end, it was decided that *no use* was the only focal point.

Pascal made a similar observation about the importance of custom: "Why do we follow old laws and old opinions? Because they are better? No, but they are unique, and remove the sources of diversity." Elsewhere he wrote:

> The most unreasonable things in the world become the most reasonable because men are so unbalanced. What could be less reasonable than to choose as ruler of a state the oldest son of a queen? We do not choose as captain of a ship the most highly born of those aboard. Such a law would be ridiculous and unjust, but because men are, and always will be, as they are, it becomes reasonable and just, for who else could be chosen? The most virtuous and able man? That sets us straight away at daggers drawn, with everyone claiming to be most virtuous and able. Let us then attach this qualification to something incontrovertible. He is the king's eldest son: that is quite clear, there is no argument about it. Reason cannot do any better, because civil war is the greatest of evils.

This reasoning can actually influence the choice of a king when there are several pretenders to a throne. In the choice of king in the French Restoration, Talleyrand successfully argued that the legitimate heir of the last king of France was the unique focal point that could prevent divisive conflicts. As he wrote in his memoirs, "An *imposed* King would be the result of force or intrigue; either would be insufficient. To establish a durable system that will be accepted without opposition, one must act on a principle." Later, Marx argued that the Republic of 1848 owed its existence to the fact that it was the second-best option for each of the two branches of the royal family. Tocqueville made a similar observation to explain the stability of the rule of Napoleon III. Democracy, too, can be seen as a focal-point solution. When there are many competing qualitative grounds on which people can claim superiority – wisdom, wealth, virtue, birth – the quantitative solution of majority rule acquires unique salience. Former colonial countries in which tribes speak different languages may choose the language of the colonizer for official purposes. Litigating parties easily converge on a proposal that is everybody's second-best option.

In 1989, the reburial of Imre Nagy provided a focal point for 250,000 people to march in the streets of Budapest to signal their disaffection with the regime. As in the previous examples, the focal point allowed cooperation through coordination. In conflictual situations, focal points can have quite different effects. In the Crimean War the French general Pélissier decided to stage the second attack on Sebastopol on June 18, 1855, because he wanted to please Napoleon III by gaining a victory on the anniversary of the Battle of Waterloo. As this date and its importance to the French were common knowledge, the Russians were able to anticipate and defeat him.

One lesson from this survey is that a given real-world situation can be modeled as several different games, depending on additional assumptions. The arms race has been modeled as a PD, as Chicken, and as an AG. Joining the labor union may be a PD or an AG. Redialing has been seen as a Battle of the Sexes or as a Telephone Game. Coordination of weights and measures could be a game of Chicken or Battle of the Sexes. The fine grain of interaction structures may not be immediately visible. By forcing us to be explicit about the nature of the interaction, game theory can reveal unsuspected subtleties or perversities.

Sequential Games

Let me turn more briefly to games in which agents make *sequential decisions* (I discuss such games at greater length in the next chapter) and begin by a simple example that demonstrates the power of game

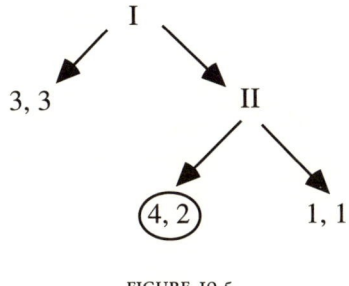

FIGURE 19.5

theory to clarify interaction structures that were only dimly understood earlier.[14]

In Figure 19.5, two armies are confronting each other at the border of their countries. General I can either retreat, leaving the status quo (3, 3) in place, or invade. If he invades, General II can either fight, with outcome (1, 1), or concede a contested piece of territory with outcome (4, 2). Before I makes his decision, II may be able to communicate an intention to fight if attacked, hoping to induce I to choose (3, 3) rather than (1, 1). However, *this threat is not credible*. I knows that once he invades, it will be in II's interest to concede rather than to fight. The unique equilibrium outcome is (4, 2). This equilibrium concept is not the static "best-response" concept we have been discussing so far. Rather, it is a dynamic concept that begins with the later stages of the game and works back to the earlier ones. (The technical term is "backward induction.") First, we ask what it would be rational for II to do if I invaded. The answer, "Concede," leads to the outcome (4, 2). I's choice, therefore, is between a course of action leading to (3,3) and one leading to (4,2). Being rational, he chooses the latter.

As Thucydides observed in *The Peloponnesian War*, promises also have to be credible for the other side to base its behavior on them.

> Oaths made in support of any reconciliation had only momentary validity, as they were made by each side only in the absence of any other source of strength to get out of an impasse; but whoever found the opposition off-guard at a given moment and seized the first opportunity for a bold strike,

[14] I retain the assumption that rationality and information are common knowledge.

enjoyed a revenge sweeter for having exploited good faith than winning in an open fight. . . . For no word was reliable enough, nor any oath formidable enough, to bring about reconciliation, and all who found themselves in a superior position, figuring that security could not even be hoped for, made provisions to avoid injury rather than allow themselves to trust anyone.

The person who received the promise, in other words, should ask himself whether it would be rational for the promiser to keep his word. Allowing for communication in the Trust Game (Chapter 15), for instance, the second player might try to induce the first to make a large transfer by promising to make a large back transfer. If there is nothing to hold him to his word, the promise is not credible. In *Democracy in America*, Tocqueville comments sarcastically on a letter of the secretary of war to the Cherokees, in which he "states that they must abandon hope of retaining the territory they presently occupy, but he offers them the same positive assurance once they have crossed the Mississippi, *as if he will then have the power he now lacks.*" Economic reform in China has been vulnerable to a similar problem. When the government introduced market reforms in agriculture it promised the farmers fifteen-year leases on the land to give them an incentive to improve it. Since there is no way of holding an autocratic government to its promise, many farmers disbelieved it and used the profits for consumption instead. An autocratic government is *unable to make itself unable* to interfere.

The notion of credibility is central in the "second-generation" game theory that began around 1975. (The first generation began around 1945.) Once we take the idea seriously, we are led to ask how agents might *invest in credibility* to lend efficacy to their threats and promises. There are several mechanisms. One is by *reputation-building*, for instance by investing in a reputation for being somewhat or occasionally irrational. Thus it has been reported that President Nixon, encouraged by Henry Kissinger, deliberately cultivated an erratic style to make the Soviets believe he might act against the American interest if they provoked him. Also, people might carry out threats when it is not in their interest to do so in order to build a reputation for toughness that will make others believe their threats on later occasions.

Another mechanism is *precommitment*, discussed in Chapter 13. There, precommitment was viewed as a second-best rational response to the agent's proclivity to behave irrationally. In the strategic context, precommitment can be fully rational. In the game depicted in Figure 19.5, General II might build a "Doomsday machine" that would automatically launch a nuclear attack on the other country in the case of invasion. If both the existence of this machine and the fact that its operation is outside the control of country II are common knowledge, it would deter the invasion. Alternatively, II might use the strategy of "burning his bridges," that is, of cutting off any possibility of retreat. Again, General I would be deterred if he knew that General II has no alternative to fighting if invaded.

In some cases, both parties may try to use precommitment to get an edge over the other. In labor-management bargaining, strike threats and boycott threats may not be credible. The management knows that as the workers have mortgages to pay and families to support they cannot afford to go on strike very long. The labor union knows that as the firm has delivery contracts to fulfill, it cannot afford to have production come to a halt. To enhance the credibility of their threats, the union might invest in a strike fund (perhaps jointly with other unions) and the management might invest in large inventories. Alternatively, the negotiators on each side might state their minimal demands and maximal offers publicly, thus making sure they will incur high reputation costs if they concede. Such a "precommitment game" might be either a PD or a game of Chicken, depending on the structure of the subsequent game.

❰❰❰

Bibliographical Note

The best elementary introduction to game theory is A. Dixit and S. Skeath, *Games of Strategy*, 2nd ed. (New York: Norton, 2004). Among more advanced treatments, I suggest F. Vega-Redondo, *Economics and the*

Theory of Games (Cambridge University Press, 2003). An encyclopedic survey with many applications is R. Aumann and S. Hart, *Handbook of Game Theory with Economic Applications*, vols. 1–3 (Amsterdam: North-Holland, 1992, 1994, 2002). Applications to specific topics are found in J. D. Morrow, *Game Theory for Political Scientists* (Princeton, NJ: Princeton University Press, 1994), and in D. Baird, H. Gertner, and R. Picker, *Game Theory and the Law* (Cambridge, MA: Harvard University Press, 1994). A classic study of conventions is D. Lewis, *Convention* (Cambridge, MA: Harvard University Press, 1969). It is largely inspired by another classic, T. Schelling, *The Strategy of Conflict* (Cambridge, MA: Harvard University Press, 1960), in which the idea of focal points was first expounded. Schelling's work also provided the intuitive foundation for the "second generation" of game theory, formally developed in R. Selten, "Re-examination of the perfectness concept for equilibrium points in extensive games," *International Journal of Game Theory* 4 (1975), 25–55. For various precommitment techniques in political games, see J. Fearon, "Domestic political audiences and the escalation of international disputes," *American Political Science Review* 88 (1994), 577–92. For their use in wage bargaining, see my *The Cement of Society* (Cambridge University Press, 1989).

Chapter 20
GAMES AND BEHAVIOR

❀ ❀ ❀

Intentions and Consequences

The conceptual structure of game theory is illuminating. Does it also help us *explain behavior*? Consider the game-theoretic rationale for burning one's bridges or one's ships. This behavior could be undertaken for the strategic reasons set out in the last chapter, but also for others. The *Oxford English Dictionary* gives the following quotation from E. R. Burroughs, *Tarzan of the Apes*: "Because she had been afraid she might succumb to the pleas of this giant, she had burned her bridges behind her." This is not a piece of strategic reasoning. Rather, the woman in question seems to fear that she might yield to entreaties if she did not make it impossible for herself to do so. Even in the military sphere, such nonstrategic rationales might be as important as the strategic ones. A commander might burn his bridges lest fear of the enemy make his soldiers take flight. He might want to prevent *himself* from deserting, if he is afraid that he might give in to weakness of will. Commander A might burn his bridges or ships to signal to enemy commander B that B cannot count on A's troops' running away. This was apparently the reasoning of Cortes when, telling his sailors (credibly but not truthfully) that his fleet was not seaworthy, he burned all his ships but one. (Also, by burning the ships he could add the sailors to his infantry.) To differentiate among these various explanations, we need to determine the intentions of the agents. Actual benefits of bridge burning are neither necessary nor sufficient to establish an explanation in terms of expected benefits (Chapter 3).

Although game theory explains behavior by appealing to the intentions of the actors to bring about certain consequences, it can also account for situations in which some of the actors do not care about the consequences. Consider for instance the interaction between the European Union and the new entrants from Eastern Europe. The old member states might be tempted to impose conditions for entry that would entail permanently lower agricultural subsidies for the new states, compared to those of same-size old states. In material terms, the new states would benefit so much from entry that they would be better off as second-rank members than as nonmembers, although less well off than they would be as full members. In psychological terms, the insult of being treated as inferior might cause them to reject such conditions.[1] Anticipating this reaction, the old states might be induced to offer entry on terms of full equality. The belief that material terms were not all the new states cared about might get them better material terms.

Since I was not privy to the entry negotiations, these remarks are conjectural. We know, however, that arguments of this kind were made at the Federal Convention in Philadelphia in 1787 in the debate over the terms of accession of future western states. Gouverneur Morris and others proposed that these should be admitted as second-rate states, so that they would never be able to outvote the original thirteen states. Against this view, George Mason argued strongly for admission with the same rights as the original states. First, he argued from principle: by admitting the Western states on equal terms, the framers would do "what we know to be right in itself." To those who might not accept that argument, he added that the new states would in any case be unlikely to accept a degrading proposal.

> If the Western States are to be admitted into the Union, as they arise, they must be treated as equals, and subjected to no degrading discriminations. They will have the same pride & other passions which we have, and will either not unite with or will speedily revolt from the Union, if they are not in all respects placed on an equal footing with their brethren.

Mason refers to the "pride and passions" of the new states, not to their self-interest. Even if it would in fact be in their interest to accede to the union on unequal terms rather than remain outside, they might still, out of resentment, prefer to stay outside. At the same time, he appeals to the self-interest of the old states, not to their sense of justice. In the terminology of

---

[1] In 2003 President Chirac offered an example of this attitude when he responded to expressions of support for U.S. policy in Iraq by East European politicians by saying that they had missed a great opportunity to keep silent, adding that they had obviously not been very well brought up.

Chapter 4, he is telling them that because the new states might be motivated by *passion rather than by interest*, it would be in the interest of the old states to act as if they were motivated by *reason rather than by interest*.

This situation has been studied experimentally by means of the Ultimatum Game and Dictator Game (Figure 20.1). In the Ultimatum Game, one person (the Proposer) can propose a distribution (x, 10−x) of ten dollars between him and another person (the Responder). Offers can be made only in whole dollars. If the Responder accepts, that distribution is implemented. If the Responder rejects the proposal, neither gets anything. Although the game has been studied in many variants, I focus on one-shot interactions under conditions of anonymity. Because subjects interact through computer terminals they do not know the identity of their partner. Often it is also made clear to them that the experimenter will be unable to determine who made which choices, thus eliminating the possibility that their decisions might be influenced by the desire to please her. When subjects play the game many times, they never meet the same partner, thus allowing for learning but not for reputation building.

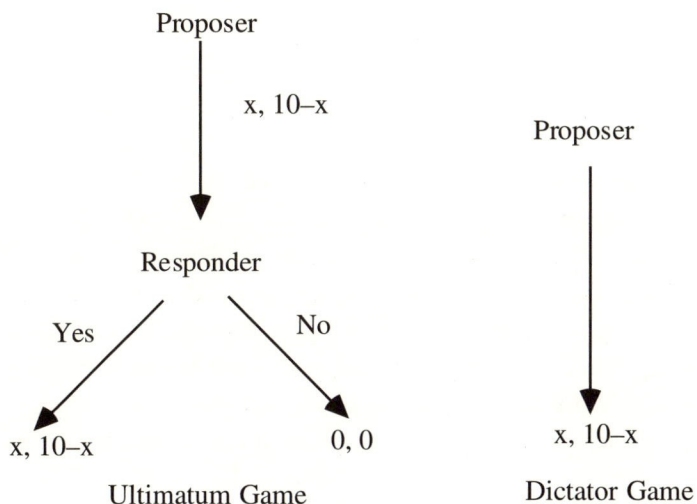

FIGURE 20.1

Under these conditions, there is maximal scope for the decisions to reflect unfettered self-interest.

Assuming that both agents are rational, are self-interested, and have full information about the payoff structure and that these facts are common knowledge, the Proposer will offer (9, 1), which the Responder will accept. If offers could be made in cents, the Proposer would offer (9.99, 0.01), which would still be accepted, since something is better than nothing. In experiments, proposals are typically around (6, 4). Responders usually reject proposals offering them 2 or less.[2] They are willing to cut off their nose to spite their face. Clearly, one of the assumptions is violated. By virtue of the way the experiment is set up, we can exclude lack of information and lack of common knowledge about information. We cannot exclude, however, failure of rationality or non–self-interested motivations.

The Proposer might be an *altruist*, who prefers a somewhat equal allocation to one in which he gets everything. Although altruism toward perfect strangers who are not in any obvious need is a somewhat strange idea, it is at least consistent with rationality. We can reject this hypothesis, however, by comparing behavior in the Ultimatum Game to behavior in the Dictator Game. In the latter, which is not really a "game" at all, the Proposer unilaterally allocates the money between him and the Responder, leaving the latter no opportunity to respond. If proposals in the Ultimatum Game were dictated only by altruism, allocations in the Dictator Game should be no different. In experiments, though, Proposer behavior is much less generous in the Dictator Game. Clearly, the behavior of the Proposer in the Ultimatum Game is driven, at least in part, by the expectation of rejection of ungenerous offers.

To explain this rejection, we might assume that Responders will be motivated by *envy* to reject low offers, and that self-interested Proposers, anticipating this effect, will make offers that are just generous enough to be accepted. If this explanation were correct, we should expect that the frequency of rejection of (8, 2) should be the same when the Proposer is

---

[2] I say "typically" and "usually" because of the considerable variation in the findings. Some of the variation is gender based, some culture based.

free to propose any allocation and when he is constrained – and known to be constrained – to choose between (8, 2) and (2, 8). In experiments, the rejection rate is lower in the latter case. This result suggests that Responder behavior is determined by considerations of *fairness*. For the Proposer to offer (8, 2) when he could have offered (5, 5) is seen as more unfair than when his only alternative was one that was equally disadvantageous to him. What matter are *intentions*, not outcomes.

This interpretation is supported by the importance of strong reciprocity in other games such as the Trust Game (Chapter 15). People are sometimes willing to punish others, at some cost and no benefit to themselves, for behaving unfairly. This practice seems to violate one of the canons of rationality enumerated in Chapter 12: in a choice between acting and doing nothing, a rational agent will not act if the expected costs exceed the expected benefits. Explanations in terms of altruism or envy would not violate this principle. For an altruist, the outcome can be better when he benefits another at some cost to himself, and for the envious person when he harms another at some cost to himself. Such behavior violates the assumption of self-interest, but not the rationality assumption. By contrast, the fairness explanation seems to violate the latter. Strong reciprocity induces behavior similar to what we do when we stumble over a stone and kick it in retaliation: it does not help and just aggravates the pain.[3]

Backward Induction

In the Ultimatum Game, the game shown in Figure 19.5 and other sequential games, the equilibrium is found by backward induction. In the Ultimatum Game, the Proposer anticipates how the Responder might react to a given proposal and then adjusts his behavior accordingly. In these examples, the calculations involved are very simple. In other experiments, subjects might have to carry out longer chains of reasoning. Two subjects may be told, for instance, to go through three rounds of offers and counteroffers to divide a sum of money, which

---

[3] A possible objection to this analysis is that, as we saw in Chapter 15, people may derive pleasure from punishing others and, moreover, that the expectation of pleasure may be what *motivates* the punishment.

shrinks 50 percent for each round of offers.[4] At each point, an agent can either accept the proposal and go "right" or make a counterproposal and go "down." Rationality, self-interest, and common knowledge then induce the following reasoning.

The person making the first proposal (Player I) will have to take into account whether Player II will prefer that division to one in which he would get a larger share of a smaller pie. At the same time, Player I knows that Player II will not make a proposal that would make I worse off by accepting it than he would be by going to the last round. In Figure 20.2, Player I can get at least 1.25 by taking all that is left in the third round. Player II cannot, therefore, offer him less than 1.25 in the

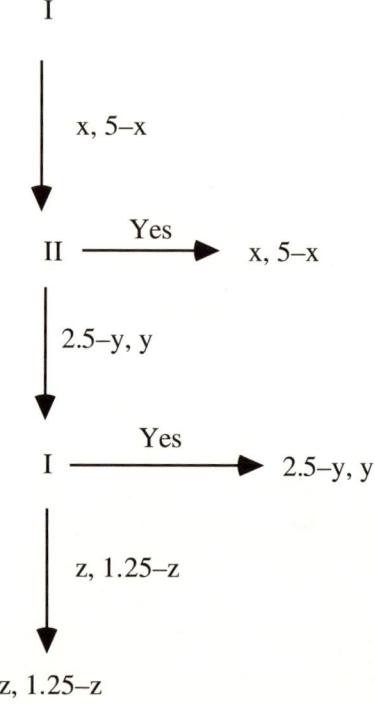

FIGURE 20.2

---

[4] The shrinking may be seen as an effect of time discounting (Chapter 6).

second round, leaving 1.25 as the maximum for himself. Knowing this, Player I will offer (3.75, 1.25) and II will accept.

In experiments, the mean offer made by I is (2.89, 2.11), substantially more generous than the equilibrium offer. Clearly, one or more of the assumptions is violated. (1) The first player might be altruistic. (2) He might fear that the other player might reject the equilibrium offer because he is incapable of following the logic of backward induction. (3) He might himself be unable to follow that logic.[5] The first and second hypotheses can be eliminated by telling the subjects that they are playing against a computer that is programmed to respond optimally. In that case the average first offer is (3.16, 1.84), which remains substantially more generous than the equilibrium. Since the subjects making the high offers could hardly have altruistic feelings toward a computer or believe it to be incompetent, they must be incompetent themselves.

It is not that the task is difficult. Once subjects have the logic of backward induction explained to them, they perform impeccably in further games. Rather, the experiment shows that this kind of reasoning does not come naturally to human beings. Even simple forward-looking reasoning may not occur spontaneously, as shown by the Winner's Curse (Chapter 12). The "younger sibling" syndrome (Chapter 18) has some of the same flavor. It is not that people cannot understand, on reflection, that others are as rational and capable of deliberation as they are themselves, only that their spontaneous tendency is to think about others as set in their habits rather than as adjusting to their environments.

Some Failures of Rational-Choice Game Theory

Among many other findings that reveal the predictive failures of game theory, I shall discuss the "finitely repeated Prisoner's Dilemma," the "Chain Store Paradox," the "Centipede Game," the "Traveler's Dilemma," and the "Beauty Contest."

---

[5] Unlike what is the case in the Ultimatum Game, Player I has no reason to fear that Player II might reject the equilibrium offer as unfairly low, since Player I has both the first and the last word.

When subjects play many successive PDs against one another and know which round will be the last, we observe a substantial proportion of C choices, often exceeding 30 percent. An intuitive explanation is that a player may choose C in one round in the hope that the other will reciprocate ("tit-for-tat"). Yet if the players adopt backward induction, they will understand that in the final game both will choose D since there will not be an opportunity to influence behavior in a later game. In the penultimate game, too, the players will choose D since the behavior in the final game is given by the previous argument. This argument "zips back" all the way to the first round, thus inducing defection in all games.

A chain store has branches in twenty cities, and in each city it faces a potential challenger. The challenger has to decide whether to set up a store to share the market with the chain store or stay out of the city. The chain store has the option of responding aggressively by predatory underpricing, thus bankrupting the rival but also imposing a loss on itself, or agreeing on market sharing. The payoffs are as in Figure 20.3; the first number in each pair is the payoff to the potential entrant.

Backward induction in a single game yields (5, 5) as the equilibrium outcome: the rival enters and the chain store accepts sharing the market. Yet, thinking ahead to later challenges, the chain store might decide to behave more aggressively and ruin the entrant, at some cost to itself, to deter potential entrants in other cities. But if we apply backward-induction reasoning to the sequence of twenty games, this strategy is not viable. In the twentieth game, there are no further benefits to be had from behaving aggressively, so the firm might as well share the market

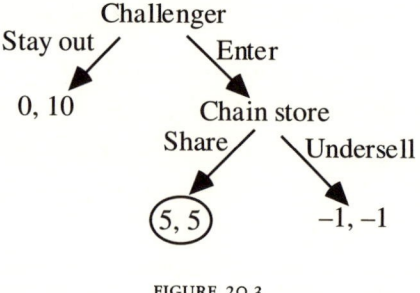

FIGURE 20.3

with the entrant. But that implies that there are no benefits to be gained from predatory pricing in the nineteenth game either, and so on, back to the first game. Although the extent of predatory pricing in actual markets is controversial, it does show up in experimental markets.

The Centipede Game[6] is shown in Figure 20.4 (payoffs in dollars). Backward induction tells Player I to choose Stop at the beginning, leaving each of the two with one-sixteenth of the payoffs they could have obtained by continuing all the way to the end. In one typical experiment, 22 percent chose Stop at the first choice "node," 41 percent of those who remained chose Stop at the second node, 74 percent of those still remaining then chose Stop at the third node, and of the remaining, half chose Stop at the fourth node and half chose Go. The deviation from the (circled) equilibrium predicted by backward induction is large, as is the average increase in gains for the players.

To explain these instances of apparently irrational cooperation and predation, one might stipulate the existence of *uncertainty* about some aspect of the games. Real-life players are rarely faced with a finite and known number of rounds. Often, they might believe that the interaction will continue for an indefinite time, so that there is no final round from which backward induction could begin. In such cases, mutual adoption of tit-for-tat may be an equilibrium in the iterated PD. (It is not unique, since "Always defect, always defect" is also an equilibrium. Structurally,

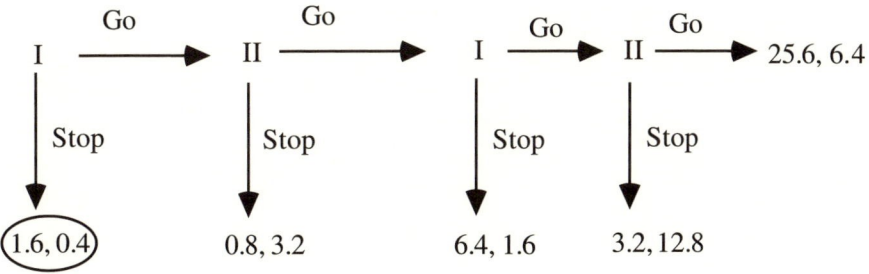

FIGURE 20.4

---

[6] The name refers to a version of the game with 100 nodes.

this is a bit like the Assurance Game, with one good equilibrium and one bad.) If real life induces tit-for-tat behavior, agents may apply it to laboratory situations in which it is not optimal.

Alternatively, an agent might be uncertain about the type of player she is facing. Suppose there is common knowledge that there are some irrational individuals in the population. It is known that some agents will always cooperate, that others use tit-for-tat in finitely iterated PDs, that still others will use predatory pricing to deter entrants even in the twentieth city, and so on. It is not known, however, exactly who these individuals are. Any agent might, with some positive probability, be irrational. In the Chain Store Paradox, a potential entrant will be deterred if the probability she assigns to the chain store manager's being irrational is sufficiently large. The manager, knowing this, has an incentive to engage in predatory pricing toward the first entrant to make others believe he is irrational. When potential entrants in other cities observe this behavior, they use Bayesian reasoning (Chapter 11) to assign a higher probability to his being irrational. It may not be high enough to deter them, but if he does it again and again, it may eventually reach a level at which it is more rational for them to stay out. A similar argument might explain cooperation in the finitely iterated PD and the Centipede Game.

Yet another possibility is that in the iterated Prisoner's Dilemma and the Centipede Game cooperation has something of a focal-point quality. Although *rational* individuals would defect on the first occasion, *reasonable* persons would not. Although this suggestion (about which more later) is pretty vague, it rings truer, to me at least, than the arguments based on uncertainty about the other person's type. For one thing, these arguments require players to carry out enormously complicated calculations, which take up many pages in textbooks. For another, introspection and casual observation suggest that we do not, when making decisions in everyday life, think about others in this way. When I trust somebody with a small amount of money, but not with a large one, it is not because I assign a small probability to his being unconditionally trustworthy, but because I judge that he can be trusted only when the stakes are not very high.

In the Traveler's Dilemma, two players simultaneously state claims, between eighty dollars and two hundred dollars, for lost luggage. To discourage excessive claims, the airline pays each traveler the minimum of the two claims, adds a sum R to the person who made the lower claim, and deducts the same amount from the person who made the higher claim. Consider a pair of claims such as (100, 150), yielding payoffs of (100 + R, 100 − R). This pair cannot be an equilibrium, since the first player would have an incentive to claim 149, yielding a payoff of 149 + R, to which the second player would respond by claiming 148, and so on. As this example suggests, the unique equilibrium occurs when both claim 80. In experiments, this outcome is in fact observed when R is large. When R is small, however, subjects make claims closer to the upper limit of 200. Again, my intuition is that something like focal-point reasoning is operating. Each traveler knows that given the gains from coordinating on a high claim it would be silly to adopt the equilibrium strategy, and she expects the other to know it too.

John Maynard Keynes compared the stock market to a Beauty Contest. He had in mind contests that were popular in England at the time, in which a newspaper would print 100 photographs, and people would write in to say which 6 faces they liked most. Everyone who picked the most popular face was automatically entered in a raffle, in which they could win a prize. Keynes wrote, "It is not a case of choosing those [faces] which, to the best of one's judgment, are really the prettiest, nor even those which average opinion genuinely thinks the prettiest. We have reached the third degree where we devote our intelligences to anticipating what average opinion expects the average opinion to be. And there are some, I believe, who practise the fourth, fifth and higher degrees."

In a game inspired by Keynes's remarks, subjects are asked to pick a number between 0 and 100. The player whose number is closest to two-thirds of the average of all the numbers chosen wins a fixed prize. The average is constrained to be 100 or less, implying that two-thirds of the average is constrained to be 67 or less. Hence for any average resulting from the choices of the other players, 67 will be closer to two-thirds of that average than will any number larger than 67. But when numbers are constrained to be 67 or less, two-thirds of the average is constrained to be 44 or less, and so on, until one reaches the unique equilibrium of 0. In experiments, very few subjects choose 0; the average number is around 35. For someone to choose this number, he must believe that most others choose larger numbers – the younger sibling syndrome. The fact that this number is about two-thirds of the average of the whole range, 50, suggests that the typical subject might believe that others pick a number at random while he is free to optimize. Alternatively, the typical subject might believe that others go through two rounds of elimination, leaving him free to optimize by adding a third round.

I have been suggesting that when people fail to conform to the predictions of game theory, it may be because they are *less than rational* or *more than rational*. The younger sibling syndrome is certainly a failure of rationality, as is the inability to carry out simple backward induction. To be reasonable is to transcend the traps of rationality – to concentrate on the fact that both players can gain while ignoring the best-response logic. As I have said, the latter idea is somewhat akin to the focal-point notion, but only somewhat. Focal points are equilibria, whereas cooperation in the finitely repeated Prisoner's Dilemma, a high claim in the Traveler's Dilemma, or the choice of Go in the Centipede Game is not. What these choices have in common with focal-point choices is a hard-to-define and highly context-dependent property of obviousness and reasonableness.

This argument might seem more similar to magical thinking (Chapter 7) than to focal-point reasoning. To ignore the Sirens of rationality is to follow John Donne's injunction in "The Anniversary":

Who is so safe as we? where none can do
Treason to us, except one of us two.
True and false fears let us refrain.

To ignore *true* fears seems irrational, or magical. (The same holds for ignoring true prospects of gain.) Alternatively, and this is how I prefer to view it, such behavior reflects a higher standard than mere rationality.[7] These are difficult issues, and readers are invited to make

---

[7] I am not referring to the idea of *reason* (Chapter 4), in the sense of impartial motivations, but to a somewhat more everyday notion. The (inchoate) idea I have in mind is related to the fact that people cooperate more frequently in a Prisoner's Dilemma when it is described as a "Community Game" than when it is described as a "Wall Street Game."

up their own minds. Some of the questions are pursued in the next chapter.

❪❪❪

Bibliographical Note

C. Camerer, *Behavioral Game Theory* (New York: Russell Sage, 2004), is the source for most of the examples in this chapter. A useful analysis of the conditions under which the predictions of standard game theory break down is J. K. Goeree and C. A. Holt, "Ten little treasures of game theory and ten intuitive contradictions," *American Economic Review* 91 (2001), 1402–22. The apparently simple idea of backward induction turns out to harbor deep paradoxes, some of which are set out in the Introduction to my *The Cement of Society* (Cambridge University Press, 1989). The game illustrated in Figure 20.2 is taken from E. Johnson et al., "Detecting failures of backward induction," *Journal of Economic Theory* 104 (2002), 16–47. The Traveler's Dilemma is taken from K. Basu, "The traveler's dilemma: Paradoxes of rationality in game theory," *American Economic Review: Papers and Proceedings* 84 (1994), 391–5.

Chapter 21
TRUST

❀ ❀ ❀

Lowering One's Guard

Egoism, said Tocqueville, is "the rust of society." Similarly, it is often said that trust is "the lubricant of society."[1] Everyday life would be impossibly difficult if we could not trust others to do what they say they will do, at least to some extent. Although scholars have defined trust in various ways, I shall use a simple behavioral definition: to trust someone is to lower one's guard, to *refrain from taking precautions against an interaction partner*, even when the other, because of opportunism or incompetence, could act in a way that might seem to justify precautions.[2] By "opportunism" I mean shortsighted or "raw" self-interest, unconstrained by either ethical or prudential considerations. Typical opportunistic acts that may justify others' taking precautions include telling a lie, cheating on an exam, breaking a promise, embezzling money, being unfaithful to one's spouse, or choosing the noncooperative strategy in a Prisoner's Dilemma.

One may or may not trust *oneself* to keep a bargain, stay away from alcohol, or keep the ship on a steady course when the Sirens are calling. Distrust of oneself is revealed by precommitment or by the construction of private rules (Chapter 13). These strategies can be costly, however, because of signaling effects. If others observe one instance of such precautionary behavior toward my future selves, they may infer, incorrectly as we saw in Chapter 10, that I lack self-control in general. Hence they may be reluctant to trust me on occasions when (1) my lack of self-control could be costly for them, (2) no precommitment devices are available, and (3) private rules are irrelevant, as they would be in a one-shot encounter. In many societies, there are norms against total abstention from alcohol as well as norms against drunkenness (Chapter 22).

---

[1] In an older literature on economic development, *corruption* was sometimes assigned the role of lubricant.

[2] Trust thus understood involves a *double abstention*, one party's refraining from precautions in the hope that the other will refrain from opportunistic behavior.

Distrust can take one of two forms. On the one hand, one may simply abstain from interacting with a potential partner when the interaction would make one vulnerable to incompetence or opportunism. On the other hand, one may engage in the interaction but take precautions against these risks. Trust, therefore, is the result of two successive decisions: to engage in the interaction and to abstain from monitoring the interaction partner. Because the decision to abstain from interaction is hard to observe, one may easily underestimate the amount of distrust in society. One might easily think there is more distrust in a society where people are constantly keeping tabs on each other than in one where they largely keep to themselves. Yet on closer inspection one would find that the latter is very inefficient because of the many mutually beneficial bargains that are never struck.

Montaigne described one trusting response: "When I am on my travels, whoever has my purse has full charge of it without supervision." Other instances of showing trust may involve refraining from acts such as the following:

- Reading one's spouse's diary
- Using proctors to monitor students during exams
- Checking the credentials of a prospective employee
- Asking for a deposit from a tenant
- Insisting on written and legally enforceable contracts
- Asking a less wealthy partner to sign a prenuptial agreement
- Hiding money from one's children
- Locking one's front door when leaving the house
- Precommitting oneself to punish defectors in a PD
- Asking for a second medical opinion or a quote from a second car mechanic

As noted, the object of trust can be other people's *ability* or their *motivation*. The distinction is vividly illustrated in the history of resistance movements. In the German-occupied countries during World War II, it happened from time to time that resistance members were killed because they were thought to be German agents. It also happened, although more rarely, that they were killed because they could not be trusted to hold their tongue. A person might turn out to be a drunkard and be executed by the resistance so that he would not reveal dangerous information when drunk. To take a more mundane example, I might question a car mechanic's skill or I might question his honesty. When I ask for a second medical opinion it is often because of worries about the first doctor's competence, although I might also be concerned that she is recommending needless surgery to line her own pocket. In the I following shall mainly discuss the issue of honesty.

Reasons for Trust

There are a number of reasons why people may refrain from taking precautions.[3] (1) The cost of taking precautions might exceed the expected benefits, either on a given occasion or over life as a whole. If there is a car mechanic in my village and I would have to travel fifty miles by taxi to get a second quote, it might not be worth it. More generally, life is too short always to fear one might be taken advantage of. The occasional loss that results from trusting the untrustworthy is small compared to the peace of mind that goes with lack of worry. (2) The very act of taking precautions can provide information that can be exploited by opportunists. Montaigne cites the Latin saying *Furem signata sollicitant. Aperta effractarius praeterit* (Locked houses invite the thief: the burglar passes them by when they are wide open). (3) The idea of taking precautions might be incompatible with the agent's emotional attitude toward the other person. When people are in love, they may refuse to engage in the cool calculation involved in a prenuptial agreement. The verse from Donne cited in Chapter 20 is appropriate in this context too: "True and false fears let us refrain." (4) I might have prior beliefs about the trustworthiness of the other person. (5) I might try to *induce* trustworthiness by trusting him or her.

---

[3] I use "refrain" to indicate a *deliberate* abstention. In some of the cases I discuss, the idea of taking precautions, for example, by reading the diary of a spouse, may never have crossed the person's mind. Yet this is not "blind trust" as I shall define it later, if the agent had the *opportunity* of taking precautions. For the other person in the relationship, the fact that the agent had the opportunity but did not use it is a telling sign, whether or not the abstention is perceived as deliberate.

In the following I shall focus on (4) and more briefly on (5). While many scholars define trust exclusively in terms of (4), I believe the focus on deliberate restraint has the advantage of highlighting the *interaction* between the truster and the trustee. If the trustee *perceives* the lack of precautions, the perception might cause him to act differently than he would have otherwise. In case (2) this happens because he infers that there will be no *occasion* for opportunistic behavior. In other cases, to be discussed later, the perception may change his *motivation* to behave opportunistically, reflecting a pre-analytical intuition that trust has a certain self-fulfilling quality. The same is true of distrust. As Proust noted, "As soon as jealousy is discovered, it is considered by its object as a lack of trust which gives her a right to deceive us."

Reasons for Trustworthiness

People may be perceived as *trustworthy* on a number of different grounds. I shall discuss four: past behavior, incentives, signs, and signals. Often, we know – or believe we know (see Chapter 10) – from observation of other people that they consistently keep their promises, abstain from lying, treat property that is not their own carefully, and so on. Moreover, a person who knows himself or herself to be (un)trustworthy will tend to think others are (un)trustworthy too (the so-called false consensus effect) and therefore tend to (dis)trust them. As La Bruyère said, "Knaves easily believe others as bad as themselves; there is no deceiving them, neither do they long deceive."[4] There is experimental evidence that this mechanism does in fact operate. Conversely, A may trust C because he knows that B, whom he trusts, trusts C. The inference may not be valid, however, because B's trust in C might simply be due to the false consensus effect. As these examples show, we often trust or distrust people for bad reasons, believing others to be either more like us or "more like themselves" (more consistent in their behavior) than they in fact are.

---

[4] La Rochefoucauld thought differently: "People are never deceived so easily as when they are out to deceive others."

In the small international community of diamond merchants, where the temptation for opportunistic behavior is enormous, a verbal agreement without witnesses is as binding as a written contract. A merchant who violated an agreement might pocket a temporary gain, but would be shunned *ever* afterward by *all* other merchants.[5] He would also be unable to pass on the business to his children, as is often the custom in the diamond community. In the case of New York diamond merchants, most of whom live in ultra-Orthodox Jewish communities, a cheater would also suffer social ostracism. The latter mechanism cements the trustworthiness but is not necessary for it. The incentive to maintain a reputation for honesty and trustworthiness is often sufficient.

Signs are *features* of individuals that are thought, rightly or wrongly, to indicate trustworthiness. In a study of what makes taxi drivers willing to trust their passengers not to rob or assault them, women were perceived as more trustworthy than men, older people more than younger, whites more than blacks, the wealthier more than the poorer, the self-absorbed more than the inquisitive, the candid more than the shifty. A Spanish taxi driver in New York would find Spanish passengers more trustworthy than those belonging to other ethnic groups. Catholic drivers in Belfast would find Catholic passengers more trustworthy than Protestants, and vice versa for Protestant drivers. More generic features are having eyes that are not too closely set to each other and looking one's interlocutor in the eyes.

Signals are *behavior* that provides evidence of trustworthiness. These may include the deliberate production or mimicking of signs. For instance, it appears that a good way to generate a frank look is to focus on the root of the nose of one's interlocutor. In this case, the signal will work only if the other person believes that a frank look is a reliable indicator of behavior and ignores how easy it is to fake it. Other behavior works as signals if it is too costly for untrustworthy individuals to afford it. To forge a signature successfully, long practice may be required,

---

[5] This is not the simple tit-for-tat mechanism, in which a player who defects in one round and is punished in the next round may be forgiven if he resumes his cooperative behavior. Rather, it is a "grim trigger" mechanism by which a single defection precludes redemption by good behavior later on.

whereas writing one's own signature is essentially costless. A poor man might dress up as a Wall Street banker to appear trustworthy to the taxi driver but is unlikely to do so since the costs would be greater than what he could expect to get from the robbery. By contrast, waving the *Wall Street Journal* to hail a taxi is something anyone can afford and hence does not discriminate between the trustworthy and untrustworthy. To the extent that trust relies on the belief that the interaction partner has a long time horizon (a low rate of time discounting), costly displays of physical fitness and slimness can serve as a signal, given the (false) belief that farsightedness as a character trait obtains either across the board or not at all.

Often, we trust people because we perceive them to be motivated not only by their self-interest. Sometimes, however, we trust people only if we see them as self-interested. In *The Maltese Falcon*, Mr. Gutman tells Humphrey Bogart, "I don't trust a man who doesn't look after himself." Napoleon said that Talleyrand was not be trusted because he never asked any favors for his family. As president of France, François Mitterrand was said to be similarly distrustful of those who never asked him for favors. More generally, a major problem for confidence tricksters and swindlers is to make their victim believe that they are acting out of self-interest. Suppose I walk up to someone and tell him that there is a fortune to be made by investing a small amount of money up-front. His first question will be "Isn't this to be good to be true?" His second question will be "If it really is true, why do you want to share the opportunity with me rather than taking all for yourself?" The successful con artist is able to elicit the trust of his victim by telling a plausible story to explain why he is induced by self-interest to give up part of the gains. In the absence of a prior history of interaction, claims of benevolent motivation are not credible.

Just as people can be (perceived as) more or less trustworthy, they may be more or less *trusting*. That is, if both A and B have the same beliefs about C (or no beliefs at all), A may trust C and B may not. The propensity to trust others is especially important in getting cooperative ventures off the ground. In repeated interactions, cooperation can be sustained by reciprocity *except in the first round*, where there is no prior history of interaction. To get it started, the parties must cooperate unconditionally in the first round. A trusting individual would follow "tit for tat": cooperate in the first round and reciprocate in later rounds. As the proverb has it, "Fool me once, shame on you; fool me twice, shame on me." A distrustful person would follow "tat for tit": defect in the first round and reciprocate in later rounds. In two-person interactions, two trusting individuals are needed to get cooperation off the ground.

How Trust May Induce Trustworthiness

Being trusted may induce trustworthiness, when the other party *knows* that one has refrained from taking precautions that one might have taken. Referring to the servant who had charge of his purse, Montaigne wrote, "He could cheat me just as well if I kept accounts, and, unless he is a devil, by such reckless trust I oblige him to be honest." This form of reciprocity differs from that which is embodied in the tit-for-tat strategy in the PD. Tit-for-tat can be an equilibrium strategy when the game is played an indefinite number of times and the two choices in any given game are made simultaneously. Montaigne's observation, by contrast, applies to one-shot games in which one party makes her choice, and makes it known, before the other party makes his choice. Experiments about the propensity to cooperate in a one-shot PD confirm this intuition. In one study, subjects were told the choice of the other player before making their own. When a player knew that the other player had defected, only 3 percent chose to cooperate. When he knew that the other had chosen to cooperate, 16 percent cooperated.

Another experiment may be cited to bring out the fine grain of trust. This Trust Game is played in two conditions. In both, the "investor" has the option of transferring anywhere between 0 and 10 of his endowment of 10 monetary units (MU) to a "trustee." The experimenter then triples any amount sent, so that if the investor sends 10, the trustee receives 30. The trustee can decide to transfer any amount from 0 to the whole augmented sum (30 in the same example) back to the investor. Finally, if the investor decides to make a transfer he also has to state the amount he wishes the trustee to transfer back to him.

These features define the inappropriately labeled (or so I shall argue) "trust condition." In the "incentive condition," the investor is also given the option of stating, at the time he makes the transfer and announces the desired back transfer, that he will impose a fine of 4 MU on the trustee if he transfers back less than the desired amount. Some investors use this option, others do not. If they do not, the trustees know that the investor had the option but refrained from using it. The findings from the experiment are that the largest back transfers are made in the incentive condition when no fine is imposed and the smallest in the same condition when a fine is imposed, back transfers in the trust condition being at an intermediate level. This effect was anticipated by investors, who invested about 30 percent more in the "incentive, no fine" condition than in either of the others.

The "incentive, no fine" condition corresponds to my definition of trust. What the experimenters call the "trust condition" I would rather call *blind trust*. It is manifested when precautions are *excluded*, as distinct from the case in which they are *not chosen*. The striking finding is that (nonblind) trust induces more cooperation than blind trust. Lowering your guard makes a difference.

People can also trust, or distrust, *institutions*. They may trust a bank to remain solvent or prefer to keep their savings under a mattress. They may trust a court to be impartial in a dispute between neighbors or prefer to take justice in their own hands. Strictly speaking, these cases do not conform to the definition I gave at the outset, since there are no (or few) precautions citizens can take when dealing with an institution except refusing to deal with it. When I trust my bank, it is a form of blind trust. To a marginal extent, my trust affects the likelihood that it will in fact remain solvent, but only because my contributing to the reserves of the bank makes it somewhat less vulnerable to a run. By contrast, Montaigne's trust in his servant induced trustworthiness by the shame or guilt the latter would feel if he betrayed the trust.

Yet as Montaigne also argued, these beneficial consequences of trusting others are essentially by-products (Chapter 4). If you refrain from taking precaution for the sole purpose of making the other behave well, you are unlikely to succeed. "It is an excellent way to win the heart and mind of another man to go and trust him, putting yourself in his power – provided it be done freely, quite unconstrained by necessity, and on condition that the trust we bring is clear and pure, and that at least our brow is not weighed down by hesitations."

❮❮❮

Bibliographical Note

Evidence that the trustworthy are those who trust others is offered in D. Glaeser et al., "Measuring trust," *Quarterly Journal of Economics* 115 (2000), 811–46. The diamond merchant community in New York is analyzed by B. Richman, "Community enforcement of informal contracts: Jewish diamond merchants in New York" (working paper, Harvard University, Olin Center for Law and Economics, 2002). The use of signs and signals by taxi drivers to determine the trustworthiness of their passengers is the topic of D. Gambetta and H. Hamill, *Streetwise* (New York: Russell Sage, 2005). The ways to make a scam appear credible are analyzed in a neglected book by N. Leff, *Swindling and Selling* (New York: Free Press, 1976). The experiment about cooperation in a one-shot Prisoner's Dilemma is reported in E. Shafir and A. Tversky, "Thinking through uncertainty: Nonconsequentialist reasoning and choice," *Cognitive Psychology* 24 (1992), 449–74. The results from the Trust Game described in the text are reported in E. Fehr and B. Rockenbach, "Detrimental effects of sanctions on human altruism," *Nature* 422 (2003), 137–40.

Chapter 22
SOCIAL NORMS
❀ ❀ ❀

The Collective Consciousness

Sociologists sometimes refer to the "collective consciousness" of a community, the set of values and beliefs shared (and known or believed to be shared) by its members. On the value side, the collective consciousness includes moral and social norms, religion, and political ideologies. On the belief side, it includes opinions about factual matters as well as about causal relations, ranging from rumors about the white slave trade to beliefs about the perverse effects of unemployment benefits. In this chapter I consider social norms and their operation. In the next chapter, I consider modes of collective or, better, interactive belief formation. There is a double asymmetry in my treatment of values and beliefs. On the one hand, I have little to say about the emergence of social norms, not because the question is uninteresting but because I find it too hard. On the other hand, I have little to say about the substance of popular or collective beliefs. Their content varies greatly in time and space, whereas the mechanisms of emergence, propagation, change, and collapse of beliefs are more invariant.

The Operation of Social Norms

Consider two statements:

Always wear black clothes in strong sunshine.
Always wear black clothes at a funeral.

The first injunction is a matter of instrumental rationality, since the air between the body and the clothes circulates more rapidly when the garments are black. The second expresses a social norm, which has no obvious instrumental significance. The existence and importance of social norms cannot be doubted. The proximate causes involved in their operation are reasonably well understood. Yet their ultimate origin and function (if any) remain controversial.

A social norm is an injunction to act or to abstain from acting. Some norms are unconditional: "Do X; do not do Y."[1] They include the norms not to eat human flesh, not to have sexual intercourse with a sibling, not to break into the queue, never to wear red clothes (as some mothers tell their daughters), to wear black clothes at a funeral, to begin with the outermost knife and fork and work inward toward the plate, to treat the sickest patient first. Other norms are conditional: "If you do X, then do Y," or "If others do X, then do X." In many groups, there is a norm that the person who first suggests that some action be taken is then charged with carrying it out;[2] as a result, many good suggestions are never made. A childless couple may feel subject to a norm that whoever first suggests they have a child will have a larger share in raising it; as a result some couples who would like to have a child may remain childless.[3] There may not be a norm telling me to send Christmas cards to my cousins, but once I begin there is a norm to continue and another norm telling my cousins to reciprocate. Yet although conditional, these norms are not conditional on any *outcome* to be realized by the action, as is the injunction to wear black in strong sunshine.

More examples will be offered later. First, however, I need to say something about what lends causal efficacy to social norms and how they differ from other norms. A simple response to the first question is that social norms operate through informal *sanctions* directed at norm violators. Typically, sanctions affect the material situation of the offender, either by the mechanism of direct punishment or by the loss of opportunities caused by social ostracism. A farmer who violates community norms may see his barn burned down and his sheep disemboweled. Alternatively, he may find his neighbor denying his request for help with the harvest. The mechanism of *gossip* can act as a multiplier on

---

[1] In the following, "conditional" and "unconditional" refer to the content of the social norm. As noted in Chapter 5, all social norms are conditional in the sense that their operation is contingent on the presence of an observer.

[2] This norm may be linked to focal-point reasoning.

[3] Hence the norm induces a game of Chicken.

these sanctions, by adding third-party sanctions to the original second-party punishment.

Consider what a cattle farmer might do when a neighbor's cattle repeatedly trespass on her land. She may seize the cattle, at a benefit to herself and at some cost to the neighbor. She may destroy the cattle or reduce their value (e.g., by castrating a bull), at no benefit to herself and some cost to the neighbor. She may herd the offending livestock to some distant place, at some cost to herself and to the neighbor. Or she might cut off all relations with the neighbor (ostracism). The last response could be inefficient, however, in that it might not deter future trespasses. The first response might be seen as an aggressive taking rather than as a punishment. The second and especially the third responses are more adequate, in that they clearly indicate an intention to punish, if need be at some cost to the punisher.

In general, however, I believe that ostracism or avoidance is the most important reaction to norm violations. If instead of repeated trespass the neighbor had engaged in a one-shot break of promise, cutting off relations would have been the more natural reaction. This claim is supported by the general idea that social norms operate through the *emotions* of shame in the norm violator and of contempt in the observer of the violation (Chapter 8). Because the action tendency of contempt is avoidance, which often causes material losses for the ostracized person, there is a link between the emotional response and the imposition of sanctions. Yet the sanctions are often more important as a vehicle for the communication of emotion than they are in their own right. Moreover, the cost of sanctioning *to the sanctioner* may be especially important in communicating the strength of his emotion.

The sanction theory of social norms runs into an obvious problem: what motivates the sanctioners to punish? What is in it for them? Typically, sanctioning is costly or risky for the sanctioner. Even if he does not give up an opportunity for mutually profitable interaction, the expression of disapproval might trigger an angry and even violent reaction in the target. There is an important distinction here between spontaneous disapproval and deliberate shaming. The latter can easily backfire, causing the target to be angry rather than ashamed. Even when the disapproval is in fact spontaneous, the target may, perhaps self-servingly, interpret it as intentional shaming and react accordingly. For this reason, sanctioning is a risky business. Why, then, do people engage in it?

One answer might be that nonpunishers themselves risk punishment. This no doubt happens. In a society with strong norms of revenge one might expect that a person who fails to shun someone who fails to take revenge would herself be shunned. Among schoolchildren, a child might be more willing to interact with a "nerd" when not observed by classmates. Yet a child who abstains from joining the mob in harassing a child who is friendly to the nerd is unlikely himself to be harassed. Hence the third-party harassers are not likely to be motivated by the fear of punishment. Experimentally, the question might be examined by seeing whether third parties would punish Responders who, by accepting very low offers in the Ultimatum Game, fail to punish ungenerous Proposers. I would be surprised if they did, and even more surprised if fourth-party observers punished nonpunishing third parties. At a few removes from the original violation, this mechanism ceases to be plausible.

A more parsimonious and adequate explanation of sanctioning relies on the spontaneous triggering of contempt and the associated action tendency. Anger, too, may be involved, because of the fluid distinction between social and moral norms. Also, *flaunting* one's violation of social norms is likely to trigger anger rather than contempt because it tells other people that one does not care about their reactions. Although these spontaneous action tendencies may be kept in check by the costs and risks of sanctioning, they may be capable of overriding the latter. Ostracizing the nerd who could help his classmates with homework is costly, as was the refusal of aristocrats under the *ancien régime* to let their daughters marry wealthy commoners. When a "taste" for discrimination takes the form of refusing to employ or buy from members of despised minority groups or women, economic efficiency may suffer. Often, such behavior reflects the operation of social norms rather than of idiosyncratic individual preferences, as shown by phrases such as "Jew-lover" or "nigger-lover" used to condemn those who go against the norm.

What Social Norms Are Not

Social norms need to be distinguished from a number of related phenomena: moral norms, quasi-moral norms, legal norms, and conventions. Although the dividing lines may be fluid, there are clear-cut cases in each category. Both moral and quasi-moral norms (Chapter 5) are capable of shaping behavior even when the agent believes herself to be unobserved by others. By contrast, the shame that sustains social norms is triggered by the perceived contempt of others. The corresponding action tendency is to escape from their accusing stares: to hide, run, and even kill oneself.

Legal norms differ from social norms in that they are enforced by specialized agents who typically impose direct punishment rather than ostracism, experiments with legal "shaming" notwithstanding. Legal and social norms interact in numerous ways. In 1990, for instance, some state legislators in Louisiana pushed for reduction of criminal sanctions applicable to informal punishers of flag burners. Even after an edict of 1701 allowed the French nobility to engage in commerce (only wholesale, not retail), it was more than fifty years before they overcame the social norms prohibiting the practice. In some communities, there are social norms against appealing to legal norms, whereas in others people litigate at the drop of a hat.

Conventions, or convention equilibria, can in principle be enforced through the sheer self-interest of the agent, without any action by others. As noted in Chapter 19, they are often quite arbitrary. At the first day of a conference, each participant may find his or her seat more or less randomly. On the second day, a convention has been created: people converge to their chosen seats because doing so is the obvious (focal-point) allocative mechanism. On the third day, the convention has hardened into an entitlement: I get angry if another participant has taken "my" seat. Yet although the social norm cements the arbitrary convention and makes it more likely to be respected, it is not indispensable. Among New Yorkers, there is a convention to celebrate New Year's Eve in Times Square, but since few people would know whether a given person showed up or not, there is little opportunity for sanctioning. Even if the norm of driving on the right side of the road were not reinforced by social norms and legal norms, the dangers to the driver of switching into the left lane would be a strong deterrent.

A complex category is that of unwritten legal and political norms such as constitutional conventions.[4] These are usually not legally enforceable, although courts may take account of them in decisions. Instead, they are enforced by political sanctions, or the fear of such sanctions. Until 1940, for instance, the American constitutional convention that nobody could serve as president more than twice was enforced by the belief that anyone who tried to do so would be defeated. Such norms, of which there are many, have some of the flavor of social norms, since they are enforced by the diffuse force of public opinion rather than by specialized agencies. Other political conventions are better seen as equilibria in repeated games. In many parliamentary systems there is, for instance, a convention that when an administration leaves office its internal documents are sealed and become available (to historians) only after several decades. Although any given administration might be tempted to open the archives of its predecessors and use them as political ammunition, the knowledge that this would set a precedent for its successor to do the same is sufficient to deter it from doing so. This is not a convention in the sense of Chapter 19, since each administration would prefer to deviate from it as long as others do not.

Norms and Externalities

There are norms against those who impose small negative externalities on many others (Chapter 17). When people litter in the park, spit in the street, urinate in the lake, or drink from the office coffee pot without dropping a quarter into the cup, they usually try to do so unseen. Even when they do not actually fear sanctions, the mere thought that others might think badly of them may deter them from performing these actions when observed. Norms of this kind are socially useful in the

---

[4] The phrase "constitutional convention" is used about two entirely different aspect of constitutions: the unwritten norms that supplement the written constitution and the constituent assemblies that are often used to adopt a written constitution.

strong sense that they make *everybody* better off. The norm against spitting in public places is an especially good example. Before one knew how contagious diseases were spread, spitting was a perfectly acceptable practice and widely catered to by spittoons. Once the mechanism of contagion was understood, "No spitting" signs appeared in many public places. Today, the norm is so entrenched (in some countries at least) that the signs have been taken down.

In this example, we can observe the norm emerging and claim with some confidence that it came about *because* it was in the public interest. The danger was perceived, a legal norm was created, and the social norm followed. Whether the perception of negative externalities can create social norms *without* the intermediary step of public intervention is more questionable. The mere fact that a norm is needed, and perceived to be needed, does not automatically bring it about. In developing countries, there is no social norm to limit family size. Social norms against overgrazing and overfishing have not emerged spontaneously to prevent the tragedy of the commons. There is no norm regulating the use of antibiotics, although their excessive use imposes externalities on others through the development of more resistant microorganisms. Norms against playing music on the public beach and against using cell phones in the concert hall also owe (I conjecture) their origin to action by the relevant authorities. Over and over again, we find that outside intervention is necessary to stop people from imposing these negative externalities on each other. In some cases, as in the norm against spitting, people may refrain even when the legal norm disappears or ceases to be enforced. In others, such as China's "one-child" policy, it seems unlikely that the behavior would persist if the regulation were to be lifted.

Smaller groups may be able to impose these norms without external intervention. In the workplace, there is often a strong norm against rate busters, because it is believed that their efforts might cause the management to lower the piece rate. (In this case the externality takes the form of an increase in the probability of a rate cut.) Although the management might want to commit itself to a policy of fixed piece rates, to induce workers to make a stronger effort, it may not be able to make a credible promise to this effect. Strikebreakers, too, are often heavily sanctioned by their fellow workers. It is perhaps significant that these two cases involve common opposition to an adversary. In a "game against nature" such as overgrazing, solidarity does not seem to emerge as easily, because free riding is not seen as *betrayal*. In this perspective, one would not expect the spontaneous emergence of a norm against shirking in firms that offer team bonuses, since violations of that norm only hurt other workers without benefiting the "enemy" (but see Chapter 26).

Other social norms target negative externalities that one group of people imposes on another. The norm against smoking, even in places where it is still legally allowed, is an example.[5] In many Western societies today, guests who smoke often abstain without even asking the host whether they would be allowed to. What one might call "noise externalities" underlie the norm "Children should be seen but not heard." There are two ways in which this injunction could be a social norm and not merely a form of parental punishment. First, children might ostracize other children who violate the norm. Second, parents might ostracize other parents whose children violate it. In train compartments, those who want to impose a "fresh air externality" on others usually lose the contest with those who impose a "stuffy air externality." The reason may be that closed windows are perceived as the default option and hence as a normative baseline.

Norms and Conformism

Some social norms are little but injunctions *not to stick one's neck out.* Inhabitants of small towns everywhere will recognize the "Law of Jante" written down (in 1933) by one who got away:

Thou shalt not believe thou *art* something.
Thou shalt not believe thou art as good as *we.*
Thou shalt not believe thou art more wise than *we.*
Thou shalt not fancy thyself better than *we.*

---

[5] The most important externality is caused by smoke inhalation (passive smoking). It is sometimes also claimed that smokers impose a negative externality on other smokers who want to quit but cannot resist the desire to smoke triggered by the visual cue of others smoking.

Thou shalt not believe thou knowest more than *we*.
Thou shalt not believe thou art greater than *we*.
Thou shalt not believe *thou* amountest to anything.
Thou shalt not laugh at *us*.
Thou shalt not believe that anyone is concerned with *thee*.
Thou shalt not believe thou canst teach *us* anything.

These norms can have very bad social consequences. They can discourage the gifted from using their talents and may lead to their being branded as witches if nevertheless they use them. Luck, too, is frowned upon. Among the Bemba of Northern Rhodesia, it is said that to find a beehive with honey in the woods is good luck; to find two beehives is very good luck; to find three is witchcraft.

Codes of Honor

Strong and often subtle norms can regulate behavior in feuds, vendettas, duels, and revenge more generally. The norms define the actions that call for a retaliation or a challenge, the conditions under which and the means by which it can or must be carried out, and the fate of someone who fails to live up to the primary norm. Beginning with the last, the failure to take revenge often causes a kind of civic death, in which the agent is completely cut off from normal social relations. Within his family, his opinion counts for nothing; if he ventures outside his home, he is met with ridicule or worse. It is a paradigmatic situation of contempt, inducing intolerable shame.

Anything that can be seen, however remotely, as an insult to the agent's honor can trigger retaliation. In prerevolutionary Paris, the vicomte de Ségur, a prominent rake about town, amused himself by writing small epigrams in verse. A rival who was jealous of his reputation wrote a little verse himself subtly mocking Ségur's verses. As revenge, Ségur seduced the rival's mistress and then, when she announced that she was pregnant, told her that he had just been using her to get back at his rival and that now that he had attained his aim he was no longer interested in her. (She subsequently died in childbirth.) He went back to

Paris and told the story to anyone who would listen, never encountering disapproval. *Les liaisons dangereuses*, it seems, was but a feeble imitation of reality.

In nineteenth-century Corsica, there were four circumstances that justified or required vengeance: when a woman had been dishonored, when an engagement had been broken, when a close relative had been killed, and when false testimony in court led to the conviction of a member of one's family. In one case, a notary was convicted of homicide on false testimony and subsequently died in prison. His brother became a bandit and over a period of years killed all fourteen prosecution witnesses. These are all cases of vengeance for the sake of *maintaining* one's honor. The system of honor also included, however, actions undertaken for the purpose of *gaining* honor. Montaigne refers to "what is said by the Italians when they wish to reprove that rash bravery found in younger men by calling them *bisognosi d'honore*, 'needy of honour.'"

In the American South people react more strongly to perceived insults than do northerners. Homicide rates are higher in the South, and people express stronger approval of violent reactions to affronts. In an ingenious study, a confederate of the experimenter bumped into the subject, "accidentally on purpose," and called him an "asshole." Afterward cortisol levels (reflecting reactions to the incident) and testosterone levels (reflecting preparation for future aggression) rose dramatically more in southern than in northern subjects. In another experiment, subjects continued walking down the hallway where they had been "bumped" and saw a large football player type (a confederate) walking toward them in a determined manner. The hallway had been cluttered with tables so that there was room only for one person to pass at a time, essentially creating a game of Chicken. Southerners went much closer to the other person (three feet) before they "chickened out" than did northerners (nine feet).

Do codes of honor serve any social function? If they do, can the function explain why they exist? The idea that the practice of revenge is a useful form of population control is too arbitrary to be taken seriously. An alternative view, that norms of revenge provide a functional equivalent of organized law enforcement in societies with a weak state, is also implausible. The

Mediterranean and Middle Eastern societies that have subscribed to these norms have had levels of violence and mortality rates among young men far above what are found elsewhere.[6] As suggested by the observation by Montaigne just quoted, norms of revenge and the larger code of honor in which they are embedded may *light as many fires as they put out*. Often, feuds create more disruption than they control.

Others have argued that norms of honor evolve in sparsely settled herding societies, in which a reputation for willingly using violence serves as a useful, even indispensable, deterrent to theft. The culture of honor in the American South has been explained in this perspective. Over and above the general problems of functional explanation, this analysis runs into the difficulty that codes of honor were equally strong in the court of the French kings in the seventeenth and eighteenth centuries, to name only one nonrural example. Some of those who focus on codes of honor in the urban aristocracy rather than among rural herders then come up with another functional explanation: in the absence of war the nobility "needed" duels to keep up their warlike spirit. If one does not provide a mechanism by which the need would generate its own satisfaction, this argument is worthless. These polemical comments do not imply that I have a better explanation to offer.

Norms of Etiquette

A further set of social norms are those involved in rules of manners or *etiquette*. Codes of dress, language, table behavior, and the like are often relentless in their detail, condemning to ostracism those who miss the smallest nuance.[7] In all societies there is a norm regulating the appropriate distance from other people to maintain on social occasions. If one moves inside the private space of a person (in the United States perhaps

---

[6] One might object that the relevant comparison is with the level of violence that would obtain in the "state of nature." If that state is defined by an exclusive concern with self-interest and the absence of any statelike agencies, it would not produce violence motivated by envy, spite, or anger. The anticipation of forceful appropriation by the strong of the goods produced by the weak might have a chilling effect on production, thus preventing actual violence from occurring.

[7] In aristocratic societies, *gross* deviations are sometimes accepted, when seen as deliberate rather than as evidence of rule ignorance. Proust's Charlus is an example.

fifteen inches) one risks being shunned as uncouth. The norm is unusual, however, in that the individuals concerned are often unaware of its existence and operation. Most norms of etiquette are highly codified, often literally so. They are not only (for the most part) pointless but also sometimes even cruel in their consequences, as when a five-year-old girl goes home in tears because her friends ridiculed her new stroller for her baby doll on the grounds that it *had no brakes*. In prerevolutionary Paris, a young officer, wealthy but not noble, tried to gate-crash a ball at Versailles. "He was treated so severely that in his despair over the ridicule with which he was covered, at a time when ridicule was the worst of all evils, he killed himself when he came back to Paris."

The puzzle is why these intrinsically trivial matters take on such importance. The disproportionate disapproval triggered by a breach of etiquette may be due to the unfounded belief that people are all of a piece (Chapter 10), so that someone who violates an unimportant norm is likely also to violate more consequential ones. Also, the violation of trivial norms of etiquette may be seen as a nontrivial show of disregard for what other people think. This leaves unexplained, however, why the unimportant norms exist at all. The puzzle is not why this or that norm exists, but why people would ever attach any significance to intrinsically inconsequential matters. Once they are *seen* as important, however, the norms *become* important regulators of behavior. If somebody turns up for a job interview in a bank wearing a pink leather jacket, it can only mean that he or she either is deliberately flaunting the social norm or is tone-deaf to the expectations of others. In either case, the behavior offers a good reason for giving the job to someone else.

Again, functional explanations are very common. The subtle rules of etiquette among the elite exist, allegedly, in order to make it more difficult for outsiders to "crash the party" by imitating the rule-governed behavior. There is no doubt that these rules often have the *effect* of keeping upstarts down, but that does not offer an explanation of why they exist. As many self-proletarianized students have discovered, it is very difficult to break into the working class for someone was not born in it. In Norway in the 1970s, for instance, young Maoists found that making fun of the royal family was a sure way of alienating themselves from the class they were trying to join. Yet nobody has suggested that the norms of the working class exist *in order to* make it more difficult for outsiders to pass themselves off as workers. The argument makes no more sense for the norms of the elite.

Norms Regulating the Use of Money

In addition to legal bans on using money to buy babies, votes, school grades, organs for transplantation, and (sometimes) sex, there are many social norms that regulate appropriate and inappropriate uses of money. Some of these operate among friends and neighbors, such as the norm against asking another adult in a suburban community to mow one's lawn for money (Chapter 12). When neighbors have to cooperate on raising a fence, they often make contributions in kind, perhaps by one's providing the labor and the other the raw materials. Even when it might have been more efficient for one of them to do all the work and be reimbursed by the other, the norm against financial transactions between neighbors excludes this solution. In the United States, professors in private universities would not, unless they are close friends, dream of asking each other how much they are paid.

Other norms, perhaps surprisingly, regulate the use of money in relations among strangers. There is a norm, for instance, against walking up to the person at the head of a bus line and offering him or her money in exchange for the place.[8] This norm is obviously inefficient: if the person who is asked agrees to move to the back of the line in exchange for the money, both agents benefit and nobody is hurt. According to Tocqueville, such norms against open display of wealth in public are specific to democratic societies: "Do you see this opulent citizen? . . . His dress is simple, his demeanor modest. Within the four walls of his home, luxury is adored." There are even norms regulating talk about money or awareness of the monetary aspect of a transaction. The double

---

[8] If the person said that he needed to get home quickly because he had a sick child at home, he might well be allowed to move to the head of the line, but the person whose place he took would typically remain second. Since this act imposes costs on all the other persons who are waiting for the bus, their approval must somehow also be obtained.

menus still offered to couples in some restaurants, one without prices for the woman and one with prices for the man, reflect a norm that gallantry should be untainted by monetary concerns. When carrying a bottle of wine to a party, you are supposed to remove the price label.

Norms of Drinking

If social norms were invariably geared to enhance the welfare of the individual or of society we might expect them to be directed against heavy drinking that is perceived to have harmful short-term or long-term consequences. There are indeed many norms of this kind. Some norms, usually linked to religion, demand total abstinence. Islam and some Protestant sects have absolute bans on alcohol. Secular norms, by contrast, often enjoin drinking in moderation. The Italian norm "Never drink between meals" has the dual effect of limiting total consumption and of reducing the rate of absorption of alcohol, thus buffering the short-term effect on the body. In Iceland, there are norms against drinking in the presence of the children and against drinking on fishing trips.

Alcohol-related norms do not, however, always enhance welfare. There are norms that condemn abstinence, as well as norms that enjoin people to drink heavily. Among the Mapuche Indians of Chile, drinking alone is criticized, and so is abstinence; such behavior is seen as showing lack of trust. The traditional French culture condemns both the teetotaler and the drunkard. In Italy, distrust of abstainers is expressed in a proverb, "May God protect me from those who do not drink." In youth subcultures of many countries, abstainers are subject to heavy pressure and ridicule. Conversely, there are many societies in which heavy drinking is socially prescribed. In Mexico and Nigeria, the macho qualities shown in the ability to drink heavily are much admired. In pre-revolutionary Russia, excessive drinking was obligatory in the subculture of young officers.

When abstinence is condemned or when heavy drinking is socially mandatory, would-be abstainers may have to resort to subterfuge. In Sweden, a common question is "Do you want sherry, or are you driving?" It is so accepted that abstaining alcoholics often say they are driving because this relieves them of the social pressure that otherwise would certainly be exerted by the host to convince the guest to have a drink. The norm of drinking can only be offset by another norm (against drunk driving). Similarly, it has been argued that conversions to Protestantism provide an alternative for some Latin Americans who want to opt out of the system of community governance in which even the rituals often involve heavy drinking and drunkenness. Again, the norm of drinking can only be overridden by another norm, which in this case has the backing of religion.

These are cases of the strategic use of norms. Conversely, people can behave strategically to get around the norms. Some ancient Chinese considered alcohol itself to be sacred and drank it only in sacrificial ceremonies; eventually, they would sacrifice whenever they wanted to drink. In Spain, at certain hours, not to drink on an empty stomach is a tacit cultural proscription, so food will be included with the drinking. In both cases, we observe a reverse of the original causal link: rather than obeying the conditional norm of drinking only when they are doing X, people do X whenever they want to have a drink.

The Norm of Tipping

Tipping for service is not a negligible phenomenon. Estimates of tips in U.S. restaurants range from $5 billion to $27 billion a year; adding tips to taxi drivers, hairdressers, and others would yield a larger figure. Estimates of the fraction of income that waiters derive from tips range from 8 percent (the Internal Revenue Service assumption) to 58 percent for waiters serving full-course meals. In some contexts tipping may seem puzzling, in others less so. If you go to the same hairdresser each time you need a haircut, you tip to ensure good service; the same applies for meals in your favorite restaurant. Tipping in one-shot encounters, such as a taxi ride or a meal in a restaurant you do not expect to visit again, is more puzzling. Such behavior is in fact doubly puzzling: it cannot be sustained by two-party interaction over time, nor by third-party sanctions at the time of the encounter. If you are the only passenger in the taxi, other people are rarely in a position to know whether you tip the taxi driver adequately; nor are other customers in the restaurant likely to notice how much you tip your waiter.

Tipping, it has been argued, is an efficient way of remunerating waiters. It is obviously easier for the client to monitor the quality of service than it is for the restaurant owner. Hence decentralizing the monitoring function and linking reward to observed performance are a way of overcoming the "principal-agent problem" (how to prevent workers from shirking) that besets many contractual relationships (Chapter 26). Tipping, therefore, might be part of an "implicit contract" for the purpose of enhancing efficiency. But as Sam Goldwyn said, an unwritten contract isn't worth the paper it's written on. The argument, like many other attempts to explain social norms, is merely a piece of unsupported functionalism. The idea that restaurant owners who forbid tipping are eliminated in the competition with those who allow it is entirely conjectural, and in any case would not explain why customers do tip in the latter. Also, when assessed empirically, tipping does not seem to pass the appropriate efficiency tests. It does not, for instance, appear to be more prevalent in occupations where monitoring is easier. The fact that waiters often pool their tips also undermines the efficiency argument.

I do not know why there is a norm to tip in certain occupations and not in others. Once a norm exists, however, we can understand why people tip: they simply do not like the idea that others, such as a disappointed taxi driver, might disapprove of them, even if they do not expect to meet them again. Being the object of the contemptuous stare of the other is not necessary. It may be enough simply to know or have to reason to believe that the other feels contempt. To take another example, the belief that others might disapprove explains why I abstain from picking my nose on the subway platform when a train is passing by without stopping, even if there are no other people on either platform.

Why Norms?

The importance of social norms for the regulation of behavior and the proximate mechanism by which they operate are, as I said, fairly well understood. I do not believe, however, that we have a good understanding of their origin. There are two separate questions. First, what is the evolutionary origin of the correlative emotions of shame and contempt that sustain social norms? In other words, why are there social norms at all? Second, why do specific norms exist in specific societies? How and when do they arise; how and when do they disappear?

A simple answer to the first question is that we care intensely about what other people think about us. We seek their approval and fear their disapproval. This answer, however, only raises the same question at one remove: why should we care about what other people think about us? In some cases, to be sure, a reputation can be useful and worth cultivating. Yet the thought that the taxi driver might think badly about us if we do not leave a tip is entirely divorced from reputational concerns. Also, since the reason others think badly about us is that we have violated a social norm, explaining norms by the desire that others not think badly about us is to some extent circular.

Concerning the second question, the most common answer is that norms emerge to regulate externalities. There is something to this idea if we add, as I argued we should, that social norms against imposing negative externalities on others are usually ushered in by an outside authority. There is a general social norm to obey the law. If fines were seen as prices, and prison as no more stigmatizing than a stay in a hospital, there would be no such norm, but in general these reactions to lawbreaking are not seen as equivalent to other, objectively equal burdens. People feel ashamed of going to jail and try to hide the fact if they can.[9] When the law bans behavior that imposes negative externalities on others, the social norm of obeying the law may spill over into a norm against that behavior. The norm may persist even if the law that gave rise to it falls into disuse. This outcome may be hard to distinguish, however, from the emergence of the "good equilibrium" in an Assurance Game (Chapter 19). If the state induces cooperation by punishing defectors and then dismantles the punishment apparatus, people may continue to

---

[9] In Norway, there used to be a mandatory three-weeks' prison sentence for drunk driving. Some people took a sunlamp with them into the prison cell, to acquire a tan they could use to buttress their story of having taken a holiday.

cooperate because each person's top-ranked situation is the one in which she and everybody else cooperate (there is no free-rider temptation).

With regard to many of the other norms I have discussed, such as the norm against offering money to buy someone's place in the bus queue, norms of etiquette, or norms of tipping, it is harder to come up with an explanation of their emergence and persistence. One line of argument, often offered by economists, is that the persistence of norms can be explained as equilibrium behavior and that their emergence is a matter of accident and history about which social science has little to say. Since an implicit premise of this book is that the dividing line between social science and history is artificial and pointless, I cannot agree with the latter claim. As to the former, I have argued that social norms typically do not exhibit the best-response logic that characterizes strategic games. When, unobserved, I observe another violating a norm, sanctioning the violator is typically not a best response.

❮❮❮

Bibliographical Note

This chapter builds on, and (I hope) improves on, the account of norms I proposed in *The Cement of Society* (Cambridge University Press, 1989) and, more succinctly, in "Social norms and economic theory," *Journal of Economic Perspectives* 3 (1989), 99–117. Influential discussions of social norms are J. Coleman, *Foundations of Social Theory* (Cambridge, MA: Harvard University Press, 1990), R. Ellickson, *Order Without Law* (Cambridge MA: Harvard University Press, 199), and E. Posner, *Law and Social Norms* (Cambridge, MA: Harvard University Press, 2000). I learned from all of them but was not persuaded by any. For an instructive criticism of Posner see the review by R. McAdams, *Yale Law Journal* 110 (2001), 625–90. Useful discussions of unwritten constitutional norms or conventions are found in two articles by J. Jaconelli, "The nature of constitutional convention," *Legal Studies* 24 (1999), 24–46, and

"Do constitutional conventions bind?" *Cambridge Law Journal* 64 (2005), 149–76. The Law of Jante is taken from A. Sandemose, *A Fugitive Crosses His Trail* (New York: Knopf, 1936). The role of witchcraft in sustaining norms against sticking one's neck out is discussed in K. Thomas, *Religion and the Decline of Magic* (Harmondsworth, England: Penguin, 1973). I discuss codes of honor and revenge in Chapter 3 of *Alchemies of the Mind* (Cambridge University Press, 1999). The story about the vicomte de Ségur is taken from *Les mémoires de la Comtesse de Boigne* (Paris: Mercure de France, 1999), vol. 1, pp. 73–4. These memoirs (ibid., p. 38) are also the source of the story about the young officer who killed himself out of shame for being ridiculed. Norms of etiquette are the topic of P. Bourdieu, *Distinction* (Cambridge MA: Harvard University Press, 1987), with a distinctly functionalist slant. The experimental studies on "the culture of honor" are reported in R. Nisbett and D. Cohen, *The Culture of Honor* (Boulder, CO: Westview Press, 1996). The examples of norms of drinking are taken from my *Strong Feelings* (Cambridge, MA: MIT Press, 1999). The misadventures of self-proletarianized students in Norway are charted in a wonderfully amusing novel, unfortunately not translated into English, by D. Solstad, *Gymnaslærer Pedersens beretning om den store politiske vekkelsen som har hjemsøkt vårt land* (Oslo: Gyldendal, 1982). For norms against asking another person how much he earns, see M. Edwards, "The law and social norms of pay secrecy," *Berkeley Journal of Employment and Labor Law* 26 (2005), 41–63. The efficiency-based explanation of the norm of tipping is offered by N. Jacob and A. Page, "Production, information costs and economic organization: The buyer monitoring case," *American Economic Review* 70 (1980), 476–8. It is criticized in M. Conlin, M. Lynn, and T. O'Donoghue, "The norm of restaurant tipping," *Journal of Economic Behavior & Organization* 5 (2003), 297–321, which proposes an account closer to the one sketched here.

Chapter 23
COLLECTIVE BELIEF FORMATION

❀ ❀ ❀

Tocqueville on Conformism

The mechanisms of belief formation I considered in Chapter 7 operate for the main part at the level of the individual, in the sense that the beliefs held by one person owe little to those held or expressed by others. In this chapter I discuss some mechanisms of collective or interactive belief formation. To illustrate the distinction, consider Tocqueville's analyses of American conformism. One explanation why Americans tend to have the same ideas is simply that they live under similar conditions: Since "men equal in condition. . .see things from the same angle, their minds are naturally inclined towards analogous ideas, and while each of them may diverge from his contemporaries and form beliefs of his own, all end up unwittingly and unintentionally sharing a certain number of opinions in common." Another explanation relies on the pressure to conform: "In America the majority erects a formidable barrier around thought. Within the limits thus laid down, the writer is free, but woe unto him who dares to venture beyond those limits. Not that he need fear an *auto-da-fé*, but he must face all sorts of unpleasantness and daily persecution."

This last passage suggests that people conform outwardly, because of social pressure, but not necessarily inwardly. As he also writes, if you hold a deviant view, "your fellow creatures will shun you as one who is impure. And even those who believe in your innocence will abandon you, lest they, too, be shunned in return." Other passages suggest that conformism reaches all the way to the soul, so that people eventually develop a sincere belief in the majority view. Two mechanisms are suggested, one "cold" or cognitive and another "hot" or motivational. On the one hand, "it seems unlikely. . .that everyone being equally enlightened, truth should not lie with the greater number." On the other hand, the fact that "American political laws are such that the majority is sovereign . . . greatly increases its inherent influence over the intellect, for there is no more inveterate habit of man than to recognize superior wisdom in his oppressor."

Experimental Findings

I have cited Tocqueville at some length (and shall cite him again in this chapter), because of his acute insights into these matters. The questions he identified – outward versus inward conformism, and cognitive versus motivational mechanisms – are very much with us today. To address them I shall first cite some classic experiments on conformity.

In the most famous experiment, subjects were asked to indicate which of three lines A, B, and C was closer in length to a given line D. There were three conditions: private, doubly public, and singly public. In the private condition, subjects stated their answer when no one else was present, besides the experimenter. In this case 99 percent indicated that D was closest to B, suggesting the unambiguous correctness of this answer. Yet in the two public conditions a substantial minority of subjects gave different replies. In both conditions, the subject answered after several others (confederates of the experimenter) had unanimously said that A was closer in length. In the doubly public condition, in which the subject gave his answer in the presence of the confederates, about one-third agreed that A was closer.[1] In the singly public condition, in which subjects stated their opinion privately after they had heard what the others said, conformism was reduced but not eliminated.

The excess conformism in the doubly public condition was arguably due to *fear of disapproval*. The residual conformism in the singly public condition could be due to *learning* ("so many others are not likely to be wrong") or to *dissonance reduction*. The latter explanation seems the more plausible. Those who conformed privately with the majority are unlikely to have done so on the basis of rational learning only, given the poor

[1] In Chapter 5 I discussed how observing others can trigger behavior similar to theirs by the quasi-moral norm of fairness, whereas being observed *by* others may trigger similar behavior through the fear of disapproval. In belief formation, observation by others can also produce conformity through fear of disapproval, whereas conformity produced by the observation of others occurs either by learning or by dissonance reduction.

cognitive status of the majority view. Some motivational factor must have been at work.

Another experiment strengthens that interpretation. Here the subjects had a more ambiguous task, detecting the distance a light source in a dark room had traveled. Although the source was in fact immobile, isolated subjects judged it to have traveled about four inches (the "autokinetic effect"). Having heard one confederate say that the light had moved between fifteen and sixteen inches, the subjects estimated the distance to be about eight inches. With two confederates making estimates in the sixteen-inch range, the estimate of the subjects was about fourteen inches. The presence of one confederate, that is, led to a four-inch increase in the estimate, and that of a second to a further six-inch increase.

In a process of Bayesian learning (Chapter 11) I can rely on other observers to correct my perception or memory. Their estimates of some fact, such as the distance traveled by the light, can serve to modify my initial assessment. How *much* they will affect it depends on my beliefs about the reliability of their perception and on the number of these other observers. In this experiment, the subject would presumably attach the same reliability to each confederate. Whatever that reliability might be, the change in his estimate caused by one confederate's stating the distance as sixteen inches should be greater than the additional change caused by the second confederate.[2] This contradicts the findings, however, since the second confederate caused a *greater* adjustment than did the first. There seems to be a dissonance-reduction effect, caused by the discomfort of finding oneself disagreeing with the majority, which cannot be reduced to rational learning.

The second experiment had a further, interesting feature. It ran for several "generations," over which the confederates were gradually replaced by naïve subjects. Thus in the second generation of a two-confederate experiment, one confederate was replaced by a naïve subject from a first-generation experiment, while in the third generation the

---

[2] In the numerical example used to illustrate Bayesian learning in Chapter 11, each new piece of confirming evidence brings about a smaller increase in probability than did the previous one. This "decreasing marginal value of new information" is a quite general phenomenon.

other confederate was also replaced by a naïve subject from an earlier generation. In subsequent generations all participants were naïve subjects who had been previously exposed either to confederates or to other subjects who had been exposed to confederates, and so on. The experiment was designed so that the newly inducted subject in each generation spoke after the two others. The designers of the experiment had anticipated that the artificially high estimates would be maintained indefinitely, but were proved wrong. After about six generations in three-person groups and eight generations in four-person groups the estimates converged to four inches, that is, the distance estimate given by isolated subjects. The belief in the emperor's new clothes did not perpetuate itself indefinitely. If some cultural beliefs with poor support in reality do maintain themselves over time, it could be because the discrepancy is hard to observe or because they are supported on other grounds. The use of lotteries to identify good hunting or fishing sites, as is the practice in some societies, may have survived because of their religious significance.

Pluralistic Ignorance

At the outset of this chapter I distinguished between two reasons why people at a given time might hold or profess similar beliefs: because they are influenced by similar conditions (correlation) or because they influence each other (causation). A special case of the first is provided by the many examples of simultaneous discoveries, such as the invention of the calculus by Newton and Leibniz more or less at the same time. Although no one knows exactly what the "similar conditions" were in that case, the idea may have been "in the air." For another case of the simultaneous appearance of similar ideas consider the idea of the emperor's new clothes. Hans Christian Andersen's tale was published in 1835. In the second volume of *Democracy in America*, published in 1840, Tocqueville came up with a similar idea to explain the apparent stability of majority opinion:

> Time, events, or individual efforts by solitary minds can in some cases ultimately undermine or gradually destroy a belief without giving any

external sign that this is happening. No one combats the doomed belief openly. No forces gather to make war on it. Its proponents quietly abandon it one by one, until only a minority still clings to it. In this situation, its reign persists. Since its enemies continue to hold their peace or to communicate their thoughts only in secret, it is a long time before they can be sure that a great revolution has taken place, and, being in doubt, they make no move. They watch and keep silent. The majority no longer believes, but it still appears to believe, and this hollow ghost of public opinion is enough to chill the blood of would-be innovators and reduce them to respectful silence.

A passage from Tocqueville's *Old Regime* (1856) makes a similar point about religion. In the course of the French Revolution "those who retained their old faith became afraid of being alone in their allegiance, and, dreading isolation more than heresy, joined the crowd without sharing its beliefs. So what was still only the opinion of a part of the nation came to be regarded as the opinion of all, and from then on seemed irresistible even to those who had given it this false appearance."

In these passages, Tocqueville refers to beliefs that people *profess* to hold (or abstain from disavowing), not to beliefs they actually and sincerely hold. In this respect his analysis differs from behavior in the moving-light experiment and in the singly public condition of the line-matching experiment.[3] This is not, however, a hard and fast distinction. As I have argued in several places, it is not always clear what it means to "believe" that something is the case. Even in the singly public condition, the "belief" of the subjects who said that A was the matching line may have been somewhat faint. They might not, for instance, have been willing to bet money on the proposition. Also, stating a belief may, under some circumstances, induce a tendency to endorse it (Chapter 7).

Modern psychology rediscovered Tocqueville's insight under the heading of "pluralistic ignorance." In extreme cases, nobody believes in

---

[3] Actually the moving-light experiment was doubly public, leaving scope for insincerity. Yet the ambiguous nature of the task presumably facilitated sincere, or quasi-sincere, adoption of the exaggerated belief. I assume that the reason for the procedure was that the study of successive generations would have been hard to do in a singly public condition.

the truth of a certain proposition but everybody believes that everybody else believes it. In more realistic cases, most people do not believe it but believe that most people do. Both situations differ from the pathological cases in which everybody publicly professes a certain belief while knowing that nobody actually holds it in private. Communism displayed this *culture of hypocrisy* to an extreme degree, at least in its final gerontocratic stage. Pluralistic ignorance and cultures of hypocrisy can be sustained by the same mechanism, namely, fear of disapproval or punishment for stating deviant views. The difference is that in pluralistic ignorance, the disapproval is horizontal – meted out by fellow citizens who falsely believe they have to ostracize deviants lest they themselves be ostracized. As Tocqueville notes, nonshunners of deviants may be shunned. By contrast, the culture of hypocrisy works by vertically imposed punishment: those who do not express enthusiasm for fulfilling the plan or hatred of the class enemy are likely to lose their jobs or worse. The vertical punishment may then induce horizontal measures, if people avoid or punish deviants lest they be punished as deviants themselves.

Pluralistic ignorance also differs from the mechanism underlying the passive-bystander syndrome observed in the Kitty Genovese killing. In (a stylized version of) the latter case, each individual believed that the passivity of others justified his or her own. The cause cannot have been social pressure or a desire to conform to group norms, since the thirty-eight bystanders were too isolated from each other to form a community. Rather, the passivity seemed justified by an *inference:* since nobody else seemed to be doing anything, the situation could not be very serious. The "raw data" (her cries) were overwhelmed by this inference. We shall look more closely at this mechanism shortly. Here I only want to note that the situation did not involve pluralistic ignorance, since there was no discrepancy between what each person privately believed and the beliefs he or she imputed to others.

The culture of drinking has been shown to illustrate pluralistic ignorance. On many American campuses, there is a culture of heavy drinking among undergraduates, especially male. Most students do not feel comfortable with the heavy levels of drinking but go along because they believe, wrongly, that most others do.[4] Their drinking behavior conforms to what they wrongly believe to be the typical attitude on campus rather than to their private attitudes. Another example can be taken from an experiment in which students were told to read an article written in a deliberately obtuse style that made it virtually incomprehensible, and then asked how well they had understood it and how well they thought others had understood it. In one condition, the students had the option of seeking out the experimenter and asking for assistance; in another they were expressly told they could not do so. Even in the former condition, no students went to see the experimenter because the procedure for doing so required that they risk embarrassing themselves. Each student seems to have believed, however, that whereas he or she stayed put out of fear of embarrassment, others did so because they understood the article and needed no help. Hence students in that condition tended to believe that others had understood the article better than they had themselves. The difference disappeared in the other condition. Conjecturally, this effect might be due to an "older sibling syndrome." As noted in Chapter 18, we are all aware of our own inner anguishes and fears, but since we do not have direct access to the inner life of others, we tend to see them as more mature and self-possessed.

In the study of drinking on campus, it was also found that over time private attitudes, beliefs about the attitudes of others, and behavior moved into line with one another, raising the question of the *stability* of pluralistic ignorance. There are in fact two ways in which it might disappear: by the false beliefs about others becoming true or by people ceasing to hold them. If each person adopts the belief he or she (falsely) imputed to others, that imputation would in fact become true. This would most likely happen by dissonance reduction, caused either by the discomfort of disagreeing with the majority or the discomfort of saying one thing and believing another. This seems to be what happened with drinking on campus.

---

[4] It may be true, however, both that most students do not drink and that most friends of most students drink, if those who drink have more friends than those who do not.

On the other hand, the situation might unravel.[5] Suppose that 20 percent of group members show in their behavior that they do not hold the belief in question, and that the remaining 80 percent pay lip service to it because they require more than 20 percent of nonconformists in the group to become nonconformists themselves. Specifically, suppose that in a group of 100, there are 20 nonconformists, 10 who would be willing to "come out" if at least 25 have already done so, 15 who would do so if at least 35 have, and 55 who would join if at least 50 have shown their true colors. As stated, the majority culture is stable. Imagine, however, that 5 of the most conformist individuals leave or die and are replaced by 5 nonconformists. In that case, the majority would unravel. The 25 nonconformists would create the conditions for 10 more to join them; the resulting 35 would attract 15 more, thus generating the requisite threshold for the remaining 50 to join. Instead of referring to the process as the *unraveling of conformism*, we may also see it as the *snowballing of nonconformism*. We shall observe a similar dynamic in collective action (Chapter 24).

Conformism may unravel in many other ways. The little child in Andersen's tale is reflected in the line-matching experiments: when a *single* confederate stated the veridical opinion that D was the closest in length to B, the conformism all but disappeared. For another example, consider the widespread belief in both England and France prior to the Reformation that the king could heal scrofula by touching the sick person. The Reformation undermined this belief, since Catholics in France and Anglicans in England now were compelled to explain why the evidence in the other country was spurious. But recognizing the possibility of large-scale collective error turned out to be dangerous, since the allegedly invalid proofs used to support the belief in the other country were not very different from the ones invoked in one's own.

Another mechanism for unraveling is the publication of an opinion survey. Prior to the 1972 referendum over Norwegian entry into the Common Market (as it was called then), the government, the main political parties outside government, and the major newspapers were all

---

[5] The extinction of false beliefs in the moving-light experiment is also a form of unraveling, due to the fact that in each generation subjects use their own "raw data" to adjust the estimated distance somewhat downward compared to what they hear from others.

massively in favor of entry. Although, as the referendum showed, there was a popular majority against entry, each individual opponent would have been led to believe himself or herself a member of a small minority had not the opinion polls indicated otherwise. Without the polls, the outcome of the referendum would in all likelihood been different. Some of those opposed to entry would have abstained from voting, since the outcome would have been seen as a foregone conclusion. Also, the movement that was formed to persuade the undecided would have remained small and uninfluential. In the period between the introduction of universal suffrage and the rise of opinion surveys, the scope for pluralistic ignorance about political matters must have been considerable.

Rumors, Fears, and Hopes

Another tale by Hans Christian Andersen, "There Is No Doubt About It," illustrates how "one little feather may easily grow into five hens" through successive exaggerations. The study of rumor formation and propagation is not, to my knowledge, very far advanced. The main contributions are by French (and some Anglo-American) historians, taking their lead from the pathbreaking study of the "Great Fear" of 1789 by Georges Lefebvre. In addition to the Great Fear, they have studied rumors, virtually all of them false, related to:

- the return of Napoleon after his two defeats in 1814 and 1815
- the complete restoration of the *ancien régime*
- a socialist leveling in the wake of the 1848 Revolution
- a massive invasion of Germany in March 1848 of French impoverished workers, plundering, burning, and killing
- a conspiracy among the doctors to "poison the people"
- a conspiracy among the clergy and the nobility to "starve the people"
- impending tax reductions
- impending tax increases
- *francs-tireurs* shooting at German soldiers from the rooftops when Germany invaded Belgium in 1914
- tens of thousands of Russian soldiers joining the allied troops in August 1914

Drawing on these studies it is possible, I think, to identify some general issues and perhaps to draw some conclusions. Let me begin, however, with some empirical observations. First, the idea of one feather's turning into five hens does not exaggerate the magnifying effect of rumor. After the insurrection of the workers in Paris in June 1848, two men who were observed on the side of a country road became ten, three hundred, six hundred in the telling and retelling, until finally one could hear that three thousand "levelers" (*partageux*) were looting, burning, and massacring. Thirty thousand soldiers were sent out to counter the threat. An investigation revealed that one of the two was insane and that the other was his father, who was in charge of him. In the same period, a peasant invented a fantasy to scare a child; soon thereafter more than a thousand men were in arms to defeat the nonexistent "brigands."

Second, it is sometimes possible to identify with some precision the origin, speed of propagation, and mechanisms of propagation of the rumors. The Great Fear of 1789 originated near-simultaneously but independently (coordinated by harvest time) in seven different places and then traveled (at an average speed estimated to four kilometers per hour) to embrace most of the country. The rumor of an invasion of Germany by French unemployed workers in 1848 traveled at a comparable speed. In both cases, it has been estimated how much the rumor slowed when crossing a mountain and at night. In many cases, the actions elicited by rumor were themselves, as we shall see shortly, the inspiration of rumor. Often, rumor was also propagated by individuals purporting, whether sincerely or not, to be in the possession of information: public officials, vagabonds, traveling hawkers, shepherds, soldiers returning from the front. Rumor also spread by the ringing of church bells that could be heard in nearby villages. In the later period, newspapers and letters were an important source of rumors. Official denials of the substance of a rumor often served to feed it.

Lefebvre summarized part of his explanation of the Great Fear by saying that "the people scared itself" (*le peuple se faisait peur à lui-meme*). The belief that brigands were approaching caused the mobilization of troops, which other peasants from a distance mistook for brigands.

When a village rang the church bells, the detachments sent out by neighboring villages were mistaken for enemies. In 1848, a warning shot of a cannon in one French village was interpreted in neighboring villages as the din of battle. When rumors of an impending invasion of French paupers reached Germany in March 1848, road workers on the French side of the Rhine crossed the river in a hurry to return to their homes and families. Others, watching from a distance, may have thought they were the French approaching.

In many cases, the substance of the rumor was the existence of a conspiracy against the people, orchestrated by the government or the elite. A natural event – a bad harvest, a series of fires, an outbreak of cholera – was imputed to intentional agency. (As noted earlier, the people often saw the elites as moved by malevolence rather than by interest.) The same mental habit often caused the authorities to impute a common intentional source to what were in effect independently arising rumors. From the fact that similar rumors arose simultaneously in different parts of the country the authorities inferred, correctly, that they must have a common cause. Instead of identifying that cause as a shared objective situation, such as a bad harvest, the authorities inferred, incorrectly, that an intentional agent was at work. Rumors about conspiracies were inseparable from the belief that rumors were created by conspiracies.

In a comment on the tendency for rumors to grow, Montaigne offered what may have been the first analysis of the micromechanisms of rumor transmission:

> The distance is greater from nothing to the minutest thing than it is from the minutest thing to the biggest. Now when the first people who drank their fill from the original oddity come to spread their tale abroad, they can tell by the opposition which they arouse what it is that others find it difficult to accept; they; they then stop up the chinks with some false piece of oakum. . . . At first the individual error creates the public one: then, in its turn, the public error creates the individual one. And so it passes from hand to hand, the whole fabric is padded out and reshaped, so that the most far-off witness is better informed about it than the closest one, and the last to be told more convinced than the first. It is a natural progression. For whoever believes anything reckons that it is a work of charity to

convince someone else of it; and to do this he is not afraid to add, out of his own invention, whatever his story needs to overcome the resistance.

This is a somewhat charitable account, as Montaigne imputes to the spreader of rumors nothing but the desire to persuade others of what he believes to be true. In his analysis of the Great Fear, Lefebvre cites other and more murky motives. Some individuals may have been motivated to exaggerate the danger lest they be accused of cowardice. To display incredulity was both to invite accusations of serving the counter-revolution by putting the people to sleep in the midst of danger and to risk offending the amour propre of those who called the alarm. In analyses of nineteenth-century rumors it has been argued that vagabonds naturally tended to spread the rumors that their listeners would like to hear (a form of induced self-deception) – the return of Napoleon I to please his followers or the illness of Napoleon III to please his opponents. Similarly, hawkers offered the most sensationalist rumors that would attract a wide audience. Concerning the rumors of Belgian *francs-tireurs*, their accuracy appeared incontrovertible once they had been used as a premise for bloody reprisals. How else, the Germans may have thought, could their atrocities be justified? And when the rumors were passed on by injured soldiers sent home from the front, who would have dared to contradict them?

Writers on rumors emphasize how they arise out of the "collective consciousness," in the form of preexisting schemata that can be activated even by insignificant events. Popular beliefs about the malevolence of the elites and their tendency to form conspiracies against the people are among the general conditions that make rumors credible, in addition to the specific factors listed. Beliefs about the insatiable need of government for higher taxes and more soldiers also made it easy for apparently neutral actions such as statistical surveys to trigger rumors that tax increases and conscriptions were impending. In 1914, German beliefs about the nature of Belgian resistance were formed by the activation of schemata of the *francs-tireurs* created in the Franco-Prussian War in 1870–1. These schemata usually had some basis in reality, even when the specific beliefs they inspired had none.

I have cited several times the proverb "We believe easily what we hope and what we fear." The rumors I have discussed illustrate both possibilities. The return of Napoleon, a tax abatement on the occasion of a regime change, and the Russian soldiers' joining up with the allied forces, all bear witness to the power of hope. (In the case of Napoleon, though, there were also those who feared his return.) Yet one historian of rumors in nineteenth-century France claims that "in general rumors are systematically much more pessimistic than euphoric" – fear is more prevalent than hope. To verify this claim one might try to count episodes of wishful and counterwishful thinking, to see whether the latter do in fact dominate the former. This would probably be a hopeless endeavor, however, both because one could not possibly establish a representative sample and because it would be hard to know how much importance to give to each episode.

A more promising approach is to draw on the distinction between beliefs and quasi-beliefs that I proposed in the introduction to Part II; the main difference is that only the former are used as a premise for action. If we consider episodes of rumor formation, it appears to be a fact almost without exception that *only fear-based rumors cause people to modify their behavior.* In the episodes of rumor formation from eighteenth- and nineteenth-century France, peasants harvested the grain before it was ripe to prevent its destruction by "brigands," sold their harvest without even retaining seed grains because they feared all would be confiscated, hid their valuables when it was rumored that they would be taxed, married to avoid conscription, and hoarded salt when a new salt tax was rumored. Rumors that the brigands were approaching had a decisive influence on the course of the French Revolution. Among other things it caused peasants to attack the castles of their seigneurs, actions that in turn triggered the decrees of August 4, 1789, abolishing feudalism. Ethnic riots, similarly, are often triggered by rumors about an impending attack by the other group.[6] Counterwishful thinking generated by fear seems to have great power to influence behavior. By contrast, wishful thinking generated by hope seems to have been embraced more for its

---

[6] The role of emotion in riots is confirmed by their documented tendency to occur more frequently in hot weather.

consolation value. This asymmetry seems quite robust. While it does not prove that fear-based rumors are more numerous, it does show them to be more important for the explanation of behavior.

The main exception to the asymmetry I have come across occurs in financial markets, where hope-fueled rumors are often based on speculative bubbles. The "irrational exuberance" of the 1990s was certainly used as a basis for – ultimately self-defeating – action. At the same time, financial markets also show the influence of irrational pessimism. Little seems to be known, however, about the mechanics and dynamics of *interactive* belief formation in these markets. There seems to be a complex interaction among those who act on the basis of rumors, those who act on the basis of price changes caused by rumors, and those who act on the basis of rumors when they are supported by price changes. Although some agents act on beliefs that are rational, given their evidence, some of that evidence is the outcome of irrational actions taken on the basis of unfounded rumors.

The asymmetry seems to be limited to interactive belief formation. At the level of the individual, wishful thinking is certainly no less capable of generating behavior than is counterwishful thinking. Moreover, casual observation suggests that at the individual level the latter mechanism is less common than its opposite. The interactive nature of rumors seems, in ways we do not well understand, to generate patterns that deviate from those we observe when individuals form their beliefs in isolation from one another.

Informational Cascades

Rumors can also arise by entirely rational belief formation, through a mechanism known as "informational cascades." Suppose that each individual in a group has access to some private information about some matter. All form their beliefs sequentially, each one relying on his or her private information *and* on the beliefs expressed by their predecessors (if any) in the sequence. Each villager, for instance, might have some private evidence about the presence of brigands in the vicinity and use it, together with what he has heard from others, to form the opinion he then passes on. Voting by roll call can have the same dynamic, if the matter at hand turns only on beliefs about factual issues and not on preferences. Each member of an assembly will rely not only on her own information but also on what is revealed by the vote of those who precede her in the roll call. For a third example, consider a journal referee for a paper who learns that (but not why) a referee for another journal had favored rejection.

In these situations people use the conclusions of the belief formation process of others as indirect inputs to their own belief formation, without knowing the direct inputs (the private information) others used to form their conclusions. It may then happen that rational individuals end up with false beliefs, although they would have reached the correct conclusion had each of them had access to the "raw data" of their predecessors and not only to their conclusions. In the referee example, the second reader might, if he had read the first report, have spotted bias or faulty reasoning. Yet if he only knows the conclusion of the first report and the fact that the first journal is highly respectable, he should rationally take into account the negative opinion of the first referee together with his own assessment. If the latter is favorable but only slightly so, he may end up recommending rejection. A third reviewer with a strongly favorable personal opinion might also (rationally) favor rejection if she learns that two previous referees did so. Yet the outcome may be suboptimal (relative to the aims of the scholarly community), since the second and third referees favored publication and the first may have been only mildly against it.[7] If the reviewers had read the article in the inverse order, the conclusion would have been different ("path-dependence").

❮❮❮

Bibliographical Note

The line-matching experiments, first carried out by Solomon Asch, are described in any textbook on social psychology, for example, E. Aronson,

---

[7] Various conformity-reducing practices may be understood in this perspective. When (as used to be the case in Norway) the internal grader at university exams sends the student's answer to an external grader, he does not pass his own grade along. For the same reason, when seeking a second medical opinion, one should not tell the second doctor what the first said.

The Social Animal, 9th ed. (New York: Freeman, 2003). The moving-light experiment is described in R. C. Jacobs and D. T. Campbell, "The perpetuation of an arbitrary tradition through several generations of laboratory microculture," *Journal of Abnormal and Social Psychology* 62 (1961), 649–58. For drinking on campus, see D. A. Prentice and D. T. Miller, "Pluralistic ignorance and alcohol use on campus: Some consequences of misperceiving the social norm," *Journal of Personality and Social Psychology* 64 (1993), 243–56. For the students exposed to the incomprehensible article, see D. T. Miller and C. McFarland, "Pluralistic ignorance: When similarity is interpreted as dissimilarity,"*Journal of Personality and Social Psychology* 53 (1987), 298–305. The unraveling scenario relies on T. Kuran, *Private Truths, Public Lies* (Cambridge, MA: Harvard University Press, 1995). The observation about the effect of the Reformation on the belief in the king's power to heal is due to M. Bloch, *Les rois thaumaturges* (Paris: Armand Colin, 1961). The studies of rumor formation on which I have drawn are G. Lefebvre, *La grande peur de 1789* (Paris: Armand Colin, 1988); F. Ploux, *De bouche à oreille: Naissance et propagation des rumeurs dans la France du XIXᵉ siècle* (Paris: Aubier, 2003); R. Cenevali, "The 'false French alarm': Revolutionary panic in Beden, 1848," *Central European History* 18 (1985), 119–42; M. Bloch, "Réflexions d'un historien sur les fausses nouvelles de guerre," *Revue de synthèse historique* 33 (1921), 13–35; and C. Prochasson and A. Rasmussen (eds.), *Vrai et faux dans la Grande Guerre* (Paris: Editions La Découverte, 2004). A detailed catalogue and analysis of rumors in ethnic riots are found in D. Horowitz, *The Deadly Ethnic Riot* (Berkeley: University of California Press, 2001). For rumors in the stock market, see A. M. Rose, "Rumor in the stock market," *Public Opinion Quarterly* 15 (1951), 61–86. An introduction to the mechanism of informational cascades is S. Bikchandani, D. Hirshleifer, and I. Welch, "Learning from the behavior of others: Conformity, fads, and informational cascades," *Journal of Economic Perspectives* 12 (1998), 151–70.

Chapter 24
COLLECTIVE ACTION
❀ ❀ ❀

The Living Flag

In *Lake Wobegon Days* Garrison Keillor describes Flag Day in his mythical town. Herman, the organizer of the parade, bought a quantity of blue, red, and white caps and distributed them to the townspeople so that they could march through the streets as a Living Flag, while he stood on the roof of the Central Building to take a photograph. Right after the war, people were happy to comply, but later they had second thoughts:

> One cause of resentment was the fact that none of them got to see the Flag they were in; the picture in the paper was black and white. Only Herman and Mr. Hanson got to see the real Flag, and some boys too short to be needed down below. People wanted a chance to go up to the roof and witness the spectacle for themselves.
>
> "How can you go up there if you're supposed to be down here?" Herman said. "You go up there to look, you got nothing to look at. Isn't it enough to know that you're doing your part?"
>
> On Flag Day, 1949, just as Herman said, "That's it! Hold it now!", one of the reds made a break for it – dashed up four flights of stairs to the roof and leaned over and had a long look. Even with the hole he left behind, it was a magnificent sight. The Living Flag filled three streets below. A perfect Flag! The reds so brilliant! He couldn't take his eyes off it. "Get down here! We need a picture!" Herman yelled up to him. "How does it look?" people yelled up to him. "Unbelievable! I can't describe it," he said.
>
> So then everyone had to have a look. "No!" Herman said, but they took a vote and it was unanimous. One by one, members of the Living Flag went up to the roof and admired it. It *was* marvelous. It brought tears to the eyes, it made one reflect on this great country, and in Lake Wobegon's place in it all. One wanted to stand up there all afternoon and just drink it in. So, as the first hour passed, and only forty of the five hundred had been to the top, the others got more and more restless. "Hurry up! Quit dawdling! *You've* seen it! Get down here and give someone else a chance!" Herman sent people up in groups of four, and then ten, but after two

hours, the Living Flag became the Sitting Flag and then began to erode, as the members who had a look thought about heading home to supper, which infuriated the ones who hadn't.

"Ten more minutes!" Herman cried, but ten minutes became twenty and thirty, and people snuck off and the Flag that remained for the last viewer was a Flag shot through by cannon fire.

In 1959, the Sons of Knute took over Flag Day. Herman gave them the boxes of caps. Since then, the Knutes have achieved several good Flags, though most years the attendance was poor. You need at least four hundred to make a good one. Some years the Knutes made a "no-look" rule, other years they held a lottery. One year they experimented with a large mirror held by two men over the edge of the roof, but when people leaned back and looked up, the Flag disappeared, of course.[1]

The Wobegonians face a collective action problem, albeit an unusual one. Each is tempted to go up on the roof or, in the later experiment, to look into the mirror. But if they all do that, the Flag *unravels* or disappears, and there is nothing to look at. To solve the problem, they resort to classical coordination techniques: to impose a "no-look rule" to prevent free riding, to take turns, to have a lottery. The first is not very satisfactory, since there is little point in forming a Flag nobody can see.[2] The others ensure that some people can watch but not so many that there is nothing to watch. They demand, however, centralized coordination, backed by organizations and sanctions. The challenge is to understand how people sometimes solve their collective action problems by decentralized action.

Unraveling and Snowballing

If people were left to their own devices, the Flag would *literally* unravel. Unraveling in a metaphorical sense has also been shown in

---

[1] New York: Viking, 1985.

[2] God could see it, of course. In some medieval churches many wonderful capitals are so high up that nobody can see the details without binoculars, which were not invented when they were built. But since God could see them, it did not matter. The Wobegonians do not seem to have had the same religious fervor.

public goods experiments. Subjects are endowed with a certain sum of money and told that if they contribute some of it to a common pool it will be multiplied and the multiplied amount then distributed equally to all subjects, whether or not they have made a contribution themselves. (This is a many-person PD, played a number of times among the same subjects.) If all subjects were rational and self-interested, nobody would contribute anything. In fact, even in anonymous interactions subjects start out by contributing on average 40–60 percent of their endowments. In subsequent rounds contributions decline steadily until they stabilize around 10 percent. One possible explanation is that most people are willing to contribute if and only if others contribute at a certain level. The level may vary across individuals, so that some require a high average contribution to trigger their own donations, whereas others will make a contribution as long as a few others do or even if no one else does. The unraveling may then occur as shown in Figure 24.1.

At the outset, people believe that others will contribute OD on average. Some individuals are utterly selfish and contribute nothing, but others are moved by norms of fairness to make a contribution. The sum total of their contributions adds up to OH. This smaller amount (OH = OC) is then used as a basis for the expected amount in the next game. Some of those who were willing to give when expected contributions were OD now drop out, so that the resulting contributions fall to OG. In subsequent rounds, more and more contributors drop out when the level of contribution falls below that at which they are willing to contribute, until the process stabilizes at OA = OE. At this point, actual and expected contributions coincide.

One may also observe the opposite phenomenon, "snowballing," rather than "unraveling." An example was the buildup of crowds on successive Sundays in Leipzig prior to the demolition of the Berlin Wall in 1989. In revolutions and rebellions, too, a small number of initial participants may grow into a movement that brings the government down. Before we can try to understand such phenomena, however, the structure of collective action problems has to be spelled out more carefully. For the time being we can abstract from the sequential aspect of the

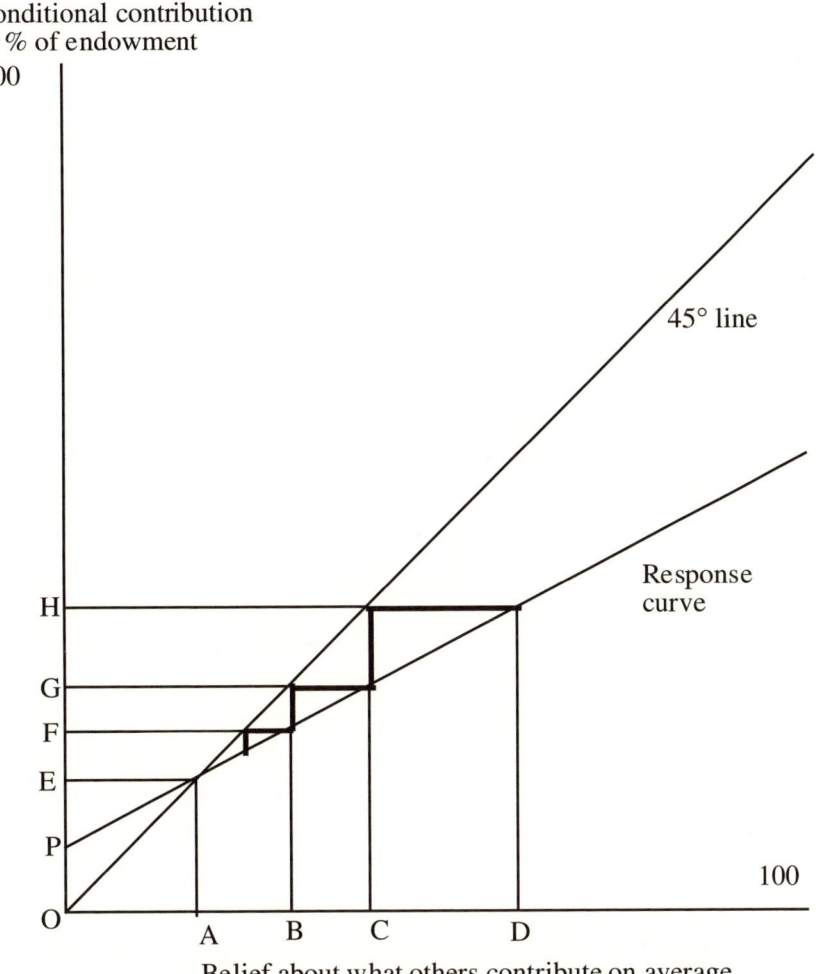

Conditional contribution
as % of endowment

FIGURE 24.1

examples just given and define a collective action problem simply in terms of the relation between individual choices and collective outcomes.[3]

---

[3] I shall write as if individual choices are binary (individuals either cooperate or do not) and as if outcomes are continuously variable (a public good, such as clean air, may be provided to a smaller

The problem is closely related to issues I have discussed in earlier chapters. Collective action problems arise in the presence of negative or positive externalities that generate a many-person PD or a related situation. To *define* a collective action problem, I shall limit myself to a subset of the motivations that may animate the agents in such situations. Specifically, agents are supposed to be motivated only by the costs to them of participating and by the personal benefits they derive from the outcome of the collective action. A worker on strike, for instance, is supposed to look only at the risk of losing his job or his wage for the duration of the strike, and at the prospect of a higher wage (for him) if the strike is successful. By contrast, we may have to appeal to a broader set of motivations to *explain* the choice of the cooperative strategy in these situations.

Providing a positive externality has direct costs or risks for the agent. In the public goods experiment, the cost is that of giving up part of one's endowment. In the march in Leipzig, it was that of being beaten up by the police. At the same time, the agent provides a small material benefit for those with whom she interacts. In the experiment, each of the other subjects received some fraction of her contribution. The subject, too, derived a material benefit (she got the same fraction), but obviously less than her cost. In Leipzig, each marcher provided an extra focus for the attention of the police force (assumed to be constant) and thus made it marginally less probable that any given comarcher would be beaten up. Thus if we limit ourselves to the direct costs and benefits of cooperation, individual defection beats individual cooperation. At the same time, in both cases universal cooperation beats universal defection. If all contribute their whole endowment to the common pool, they all get the same multiple back. If all denizens of Leipzig go into the streets, the risk for any one of them of being beaten up is close to 0, while the chances of the hated regime's falling move close to 1.

or larger extent). In reality, individuals may differ in *how much* they contribute, not merely in *whether* they do. I shall not take this complication into account. Also, some public goods are "lumpy" or discrete. If individuals in a community lobby to keep the local school open, it will either close or remain open. This complication can be finessed by interpreting the outcome as the continuously variable *probability* of the public good's being provided.

The Technology of Collective Action

We can show this situation diagrammatically. In a group of n + 1 individuals, Figure 24.2 indicates how the payoff to a given individual varies as a function of his own behavior and of that of the others. The behavior of others is indicated along the horizontal axis, which measures the number of cooperators (among the others). If the individual is also a cooperator, his utility, measured along the vertical axis, is indicated along the R line AB in the diagrams. If he is a noncooperator, his utility is measured along the L line OC. The L and R lines intersect the vertical axes in the order that defines the ordinary (two-person) PD: the most preferred outcome is unilateral noncooperation (free riding), the next best is universal cooperation, the third best universal noncooperation, and the worst outcome unilateral cooperation (being exploited). As in the two-person case, noncooperation is a dominant strategy, since the L line is everywhere above the R line. In contrast to the two-person case, however, we can define a number of cooperators M that can make themselves better off by cooperating, even in the presence of free riders whom they make even better off. The line OB shows the *average* benefit to everybody, cooperators and noncooperators,

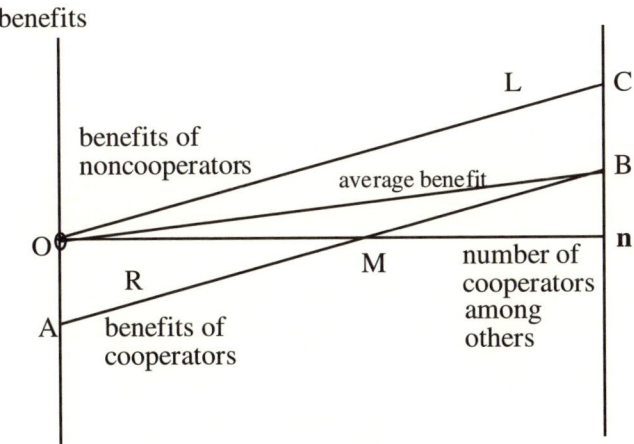

FIGURE 24.2. Redrawn from T. Schelling, *Micromotives and Macrobehavior* (New York: Norton, 1978)

as a function of the number of cooperators. As the number of agents is constant, OB will also reflect the *total* benefit produced by cooperation.

The situation in Figure 24.2 reflects a special case. It assumes that the cost of cooperation, measured by the distance between the L and R curves, is constant. In other cases, the cost of cooperation increases as more people cooperate. As people join call-in campaigns for public radio, the lines become congested and it takes more time to get through. It may then happen that the last to join[4] actually reduce the average benefit, because the cost to them of participating exceeds the sum of the benefits they generate for everybody else (and for themselves). The cost may also be high initially and then decrease. As more people joined up in Leipzig, the government forces had to spread themselves more thinly. In that case, too, for a similar reason, the first cooperators may actually have made the situation worse (in the sense of reducing the average benefit).

Figure 24.2 also assumes that the benefits of cooperation, given by the L line, are a linear function of the number of cooperators. Each new cooperator adds the same amount to everybody's welfare. Increasing marginal benefits can be illustrated by cleaning a beach of litter: the last bottle that is removed makes more of an aesthetic difference than the penultimate one. Decreasing marginal benefits are also frequent. A simple example is calling city hall about a pothole in a middle-class urban area: the first person who takes the time to call could make the probability 0.4 that the hole will be fixed, the second raise it to 0.7, the third to 0.8, the fourth to 0.85, the fifth to 0.88, and so on. Sometimes, both the first and last contributors add little, whereas those in the middle are more efficacious. A few revolutionaries or strikers do not make much of a difference, and when almost everyone has joined it matters little whether the few uncommitted do so too. In social movements, this pattern is probably typical.

The marginal benefits of cooperation may even be negative over some range of cooperators. Unilateral disarmament can make all nations worse

---

[4] Here and elsewhere, words such as "first," "middle," and "last" can refer to the times at which successive cooperators join, as in building a revolutionary movement. But they can also refer to simultaneous acts of cooperation, as in voting. To say that the last voters add little is to say that the benefit created in a situation in which everyone votes is nearly the same as the benefit created when almost everyone votes.

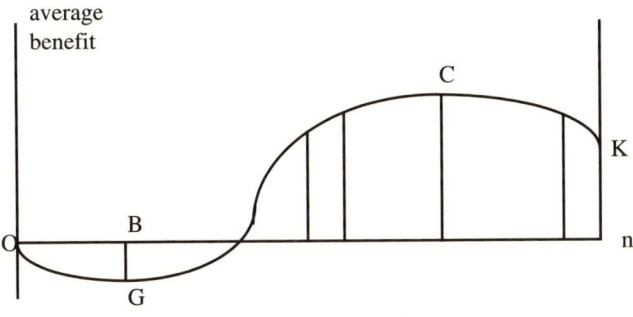

FIGURE 24.3

off if it creates a power vacuum to be invaded, thus unleashing a general war. Isolated acts of rebellion may give the authorities a pretext for cracking down on potential rebels as well as on the actual ones. Conversely, there may be too many cooperators. Suppose that in wartime everybody insists on joining the army, so that industries vital to the war effort are understaffed and the war is lost. If everyone insists on helping out with the dinner at the outing, the many cooks may spoil the broth.

As these remarks show, the technology of collective action differs from case to case. In the following, I focus on the case shown in Figure 24.3, which I believe to be fairly typical of social movements trying to bring about a change of policy. The first contributors incur high costs or risks and produce few benefits for others. They may, in fact, harm others rather than benefit them. Their net contribution is negative. The last contributors also produce few benefits. In some cases, their cost may be decreasing, as I suggested. In other cases, all who fight for a cause may incur considerable costs or risks until the adversary capitulates. Those who joined the French resistance in 1944 often did little damage to the Germans, but all ran a considerable risk to their lives.

Overcoming the Free-Rider Problem

I have defined the collective action problem in terms of *rational outcome-oriented self-interested motivations*. These are, typically, insufficient to elicit cooperation since, regardless of what others do, the individual is better off not cooperating. Let me mention two exceptions to this statement.

The first arises if the *same* agents are faced *repeatedly* by the same collective action problem. In an ongoing interaction of this kind, cooperation may be sustained by a *grim trigger strategy*: cooperate as long as everybody else does, and defect forever if a single other agent defects once.[5] There is some evidence that cartels, for instance, maintain themselves in this way. The decisions to abstain from gas warfare in World War II may also have been due to fear of retaliation, but more probably to operational drawbacks of the method. These cases are not typical, however. Workers, for instance, do not decide every year whether to renew their union membership. Rebellions and revolutions are one-shot movements to which the argument from repeated interaction does not apply. Other campaigns, crusades, and drives usually have too little structure for cooperators to identify noncooperators. To explain how cooperation arises in such cases we must look elsewhere.

The second exception arises if there is an outside agent, typically an organization that can impose selective punishment on noncooperators and/or selective rewards for cooperators. The state may punish individuals who impose negative externalities on others, by smoking in public or spitting in the street. Unions may offer cheap vacations to their members. Revolutionary movements may promise activists central positions in the postrevolutionary government. These "solutions" to the collective action problem rely on centralized enforcement, not on decentralized action by the individuals directly concerned. Note, however, that the existence of an organization capable of changing the incentives of social agents may itself be the result of successful collective action. Also, promises to reward activists after the victory may not be credible. In many cases, ranging from Henri IV in 1594 to Charles de Gaulle in 1945, charismatic leaders have disappointed their followers by appointing or retaining officials from the

---

[5] Unlike the finitely iterated PD, this statement refers to a situation of indefinite duration. Whether in a given case trigger strategies form an equilibrium depends on the cardinal payoff structure and on the rate of time discounting of the agents. In principle, other strategies might also generate a cooperative equilibrium, but only the trigger strategy has the requisite focal-point quality.

defeated regime in leading positions. Militants do not always make good administrators.

In decentralized one-shot collective action situations cooperation will not arise if all agents are fully rational, all have outcome-oriented self-interested motivations only, and these two facts are common knowledge. (This statement is a logical truth, not an empirical claim.) Referring to Figure 24.3, we may distinguish a number of motivations that can trigger and sustain cooperative behavior. In the stylized scenario I shall sketch, these kick in successively, each of them (except the first) relying on the presence of agents motivated by the preceding ones. Although the particular scenario does not apply to all cases, I believe that one of its features has universal validity. Successful collective action, when we observe it, is not the work of identically motivated individuals. Rather, it is the outcome of *mixed motivations* – both at the individual level and across individuals.[6] In the following I shall identify half a dozen such motivations that I believe to be present, in various proportions, in many collective action situations.

Cooperation needs some individuals who are not motivated merely by the costs and benefits to them. Two categories of such individuals are what I shall call *full utilitarians* and *selfless utilitarians*. The first will cooperate if and only if their contribution increases the average benefit. In Figure 24.3, they require that the number of cooperators has already reached a point OB where their action has useful consequences. The second category will cooperate if and only if their contribution increases the average benefit, *not counting the costs to them*.[7] In some of the examples I gave earlier, cooperation had negative effects only because the costs to the cooperator exceeded the sum total of benefits. The selfless utilitarian will not be deterred if her action has negative effects in this sense. She will, however, abstain from cooperating if her action imposes direct harm on others. Many would-be initiators of social movements have found themselves in this predicament. They may, as noted, be

---

[6] To prevent complicating the discussion, I consider only variations across individuals.

[7] This asymmetry is captured in several proverbs: "Friendship is to forget what you give and to remember what you receive" and "Never forget a service rendered you, forget immediately one you have rendered."

afraid of causing employers or authorities to take repressive measures that will hurt other group members and not merely themselves.

If they do not experience this problem, the selfless utilitarians may be numerous enough to raise the number of cooperators to OB, where the full utilitarians enter. If the selfless utilitarians are too few, or if the predicament I described deters them from acting, *unconditional cooperators* are needed to create the critical number OB that will trigger the full utilitarians. These actors take a number of shapes – they may be Kantians, saints, heroes, fanatics, or they may be slightly mad. What they have in common is that they act neither as a function of the expected consequences of their action, nor as a function of the number of other cooperators. Fanatical Nazis, for instance, joined the NSDAP at a time when its prospects were little more than a pipedream. Utilitarians, by contrast, act as a function of the expected consequences of their action. Although their expectation may itself be a function of the number of other cooperators, their action is not directly triggered by that number (Chapter 5). If the curve OGCK in Figure 24.3 did not dip below 0, both types of utilitarians would act as first movers themselves.

A further category of actors would never act as first movers, however. These are the individuals whose motivation is triggered by the observation of others' cooperating or by the knowledge that cooperators can observe them (Chapter 5). A first subset of this group are motivated by the quasi-moral norm of fairness: it is not fair for us to remain on the sidelines while others are taking risks for our common cause. This motivation may vary in strength, in the sense that the cooperation of different individuals may be triggered by different numbers of cooperators. Those whose cooperation is triggered by a low threshold may hence contribute to trigger that of those with a higher one. A second subset are motivated by social norms. If noncooperators can be identified and subjected to social ostracism, as is usually the case at the workplace, for example, cooperators may shame them into joining. Shamefulness, too, has degrees. Some may be shamed into joining by a single remark or act of avoidance, whereas others will join only if exposed to the pressure of many group members, including (perhaps especially) those who were themselves shamed into joining.

A final category are those who join the movement for its "process benefits" – because it is fun or otherwise personally appealing. For some people, marching and singing in the streets, or sampling whatever entertainment is offered, can be desirable in itself, independently of the cause. For others, joining the movement may be seen as an occasion for "consciousness raising" or "character building." Although the desired states are essentially by-products (Chapter 4), implying that those who seek them directly are likely to be disappointed, they may nevertheless join for that reason. Because these individuals are outwardly indistinguishable from the other categories, they, too, may serve to trigger the adhesion of those with high thresholds for joining.

This typology of motives does not offer an explanation for successful collective action, only a framework for explanation. There are many different motivational mixes that can create the requisite snowball effect. In some cases, the movement may not be able to recruit enough cooperators, if the first movers are too few to attract the utilitarians or the first movers and the utilitarians together are too few to attract those whose cooperation is conditional on that of others. In other cases, the process may never take off at all, because there are no first movers. The outcome depends on the distribution of the motivations in the population, and on the technology of collective action. It also depends on organization and leadership, in ways that I have ignored here in order to focus on the pure case of decentralized choices.

⟪⟪⟪

Bibliographical Note

The public good experiment with unraveling is described in E. Fehr and U. Fischbacher, "The nature of human altruism," *Nature* 425 (2003), 785–91. For snowballing in Eastern Europe, see R. Petersen, *Resistance and Rebellion: Lessons from Eastern Europe* (Cambridge University Press, 2001). This work also shows how several motivations may exist together within one individual, not only (as in my text) in different individuals. I discuss some variations of the technology in *The Cement of Society* (Cambridge University Press, 1989). Other variations are discussed in G. Marwell and P. Oliver, *The Critical Mass in Collective Action* (Cambridge University Press, 1993). An elegant overview is T. Sandler, *Collective Action* (Ann Arbor: University of Michigan Press, 1992). An application that takes account of the fact that individual agents may differ in their resources as well as in their motivations is J. Bowman, *Capitalist Collective Action* (Cambridge University Press, 1993). Grim trigger cooperation in cartels is discussed in C. Lipson, "Bankers' dilemmas: Private cooperation in rescheduling sovereign debts," in K. A. Oye (ed.), *Cooperation Under Anarchy* (Princeton, NJ: Princeton University Press, 1986). The case of the New York diamond merchants discussed in Chapter 23 is also relevant here. An account of collective action that emphasizes vertical relations between leaders and followers is S. Kalyvas, *The Logic of Violence in Civil War* (Cambridge University Press, 2006).

Chapter 25
COLLECTIVE DECISION MAKING

❀ ❀ ❀

Often, members of a group – from the family to society as a whole – need to regulate matters of common concern by making decisions that are binding on them all. Consider again the question of regulating water consumption during periods of scarcity (Chapter 5). Sometimes, this collective action problem may be resolved by decentralized decisions, through a combination of moral, quasi-moral, and social norms. Often, however, the city council has to limit the water supply or reduce consumption by banning certain uses, such as watering the lawn or filling up swimming pools. When collective action fails, collective decision making may be required.

For another example, take the practice of voting in national elections. The choice whether to vote or stay home is a classic collective action problem. Knowing that his or her voice makes no difference to the outcome, each citizen has a personal interest that dictates abstention. Yet if everybody abstained, or if voting dropped to very low levels, democracy itself might be in danger of being replaced by a dictatorship or an oligarchy, against (almost) everybody's interest. In many democracies voting does in fact reach respectable levels, from 50 percent to 80 percent, as a result of decentralized decisions by the citizens. Some may ask themselves, "But what if everybody abstained?" Others may say to themselves, "Since most others bother to vote, it is only fair that I should do so too." Still others may calculate that "although the impact of my vote on the viability of democracy is tiny, it is important if multiplied by the large number of other citizens it affects." In a small village, some may fear that "if I stay home, my neighbors will notice and express their disapproval."

If these motivations, singly and combined, prove too weak, voting may fall to disastrously low levels, in a process that is in part self-reinforcing ("Since few others bother to vote, why should I?"). To reverse this process, parliament may legislate to make voting obligatory and to impose a fine on nonvoters and submit the law to the approval of the voters in a referendum. When voting on whether voting ought to be made obligatory, the citizens face a choice that is very different from the one they confront when contemplating whether to vote in ordinary elections with nonmandatory voting. The options are not "I vote" versus "I stay home" but "Everybody votes" versus "Everybody is free to stay home."[1] If many of those who prefer the second option in the first choice prefer the first option in the second choice, they will *decide collectively* to make voting obligatory.

Collective decision making is about making a *policy choice*. Before entering into the process of collective decision making, each member has certain policy preferences, which derive from his or her fundamental preferences together with a set of causal beliefs about ends-means relations. The basic goal of collective decision making is to *aggregate* individual policy preferences by one of three mechanisms to be discussed shortly.[2] The aggregation may also induce a *transformation* of individual policy preferences, and it may create an incentive for individuals to *misrepresent* their policy preferences. The interaction among aggregation, transformation, and misrepresentation of preferences can make for considerable complexity.

In many of the cases I shall discuss, a smaller group of individuals make decisions that are binding on a larger group. Sometimes, they are delegated to do so, as representatives of or negotiators for the larger body. In that case, they may be constrained by the knowledge that their decisions will have to be ratified by their constituency, or that they will not be reelected if they fail to achieve satisfactory results. In other cases, the larger society has no power, short of a revolution, to influence those who make the decisions that shape their lives. Yet even here we may talk of collective decision making within the elite. After the fall of Stalin, there followed collective leadership by the Politburo. The Chilean junta

---

[1] To put it differently, the option "I stay home but everybody else has to vote" will not be among the options in the referendum.

[2] Although the phrase "aggregation mechanism" is usually reserved for voting procedures, I use it here to denote any process in which actors who may have initially different preferences interact to bring about a decision that all of them accept as binding.

that exercised power from 1973 to 1980 had a highly structured internal mode of collective decision making.

The three aggregation mechanisms I shall consider are *arguing, bargaining,* and *voting*. I believe that this is an exhaustive list. Although some collective decisions are made by a randomizing device, as when an assembly flips a coin to break a tie or leaders are chosen by lot from the population at large, the decision to adopt this procedure must itself have been made through arguing, bargaining, or voting. I shall not discuss the intriguing question whether one of these three procedures is in the same sense more basic than the others, for example, whether the decision to resolve a certain question by voting must itself be made by arguing. Instead I shall investigate the properties of each procedure, including their important pathologies.

Let me first give some examples of the three procedures. Pure argument is observed (or at least is supposed to be the rule) in juries for which unanimity is required. Even here, some jurors may resort to tacit bargaining by virtue of their greater ability to hold out, that is, their lesser impatience to get out of jury work and back to their ordinary life.[3] Because time always matters when a decision has to be made, and because the participants in the process often discount the future at different rates, this case may in fact be typical.

Pure bargaining is illustrated by sequential "divide-a-dollar" games in which the parties make successive offers and counteroffers. The outcome is determined by the bargaining mechanism and the bargaining power of the parties, that is, the resources that enable them to make credible threats and promises. The process is illustrated in Figure 20.2.

Pure voting was Rousseau's conception of collective decision making. The citizens were to form their preferences in isolation from one another so as not to be contaminated by eloquence and demagogy. Because they would also cast their votes in isolation from one another, vote trading would be excluded. In actual political systems this ideal is never realized. It may be illustrated, perhaps, by certain low-stake decisions such as the

---

[3] In early English jury trials the practice of starving the jurors (or having them pay for their own food) until they reached a unanimous decision may also have conferred greater bargaining power on some than on others.

election of members to a scientific academy whose main function is to elect new members.

Mixed arguing and voting, without bargaining, may be illustrated by hiring and tenure decisions in a university department. These are supposed to be governed only by deliberation about the merits of the candidate followed by a vote. Although this ideal does not always correspond to the reality, it sometimes does. In good departments there is a norm against logrolling, reinforced by a norm against voting without explaining one's vote.

Mixed arguing and bargaining, without voting, is illustrated by collective wage bargaining. When a union and management are deciding how to divide the income of the firm, it might appear as if only bargaining is taking place. On closer inspection, however, there is always a substantial amount of arguing about factual matters, such as the financial well-being of the firm and the productivity of the labor force.

Mixed bargaining and voting occurs when members of a labor union have to ratify, by voting, a wage agreement negotiated by their representatives. In such situations, the expected outcome of voting serves as the threat point of bargaining.

Political decision making, whether by a committee, an assembly, or the population at large, often involves all three procedures.[4] Again, this fact follows from the need to reach a decision sooner rather than later. Voting tends to arise when an issue has to be decided urgently, so that the participants do not have the time to deliberate until they reach unanimity. More prosaically, they may not be motivated to search for unanimity. If the decision is more urgent for some participants than for others, the possibility of bargaining also arises, since those who can better afford to wait may demand concessions in exchange for an early decision. In standing committees and assemblies, bargaining also arises through logrolling, which is due to unequal intensity of preferences over the issues to be traded off against each other. Other bargaining mechanisms in legislatures include filibustering and "the politics of the empty chair"

---

[4] Even general elections may offer scope for bargaining. If voting is public, voters and candidate may haggle over the price of votes.

by which a group may exploit the rules of quorum to obtain what it could not achieve by other means.

In such cases, the sources of bargaining power are created within the assembly itself. In other cases, the decision makers can draw on resources that exist independently of the assembly – money and personnel. In 1789, the debates in the French constituent assembly were suspended between the king's troops and the crowds in Paris, the latter being initially a weapon that the deputies could wield against the former and later a threat that some deputies deployed against others. In 1989, the quasi-constitutional or preconstitutional Round Table Talks in Poland were suspended between the threat of Soviet intervention and the prospect of economic paralysis. If a vote cannot be bought with the promise of another vote, as in logrolling, it can be bought with money, for instance, with the allocation of party funds for purposes of reelection campaigning.

As will be clear from this discussion, the three modes of collective decision making may be seen as three steps in an idealized sequence, in the sense that each of them arises naturally from the preceding one. Although arguing intrinsically aims at unanimity, in the sense that it is based on reasons that are supposed to be valid for all, this end is rarely achieved. To settle the issue, voting is needed. Because voting often takes place among individuals who have many issues to decide on, it naturally gives rise to bargaining in the form of logrolling.

Arguing

Arguing is the effort to persuade by reason giving. Ever since Pericles' eulogy of Athens, this mode of decision making has been closely linked to democratic politics:

> Our public men have, besides politics, their private affairs to attend to, and our ordinary citizens, though occupied with the pursuits of industry, are still fair judges of public matters; for, unlike any other nation, we regard the citizen who takes no part in these duties not as unambitious but as useless, and we are able to judge proposals even if we cannot originate them; instead of looking on discussion as a stumbling-block in

the way of action, we think it an indispensable preliminary to any wise action at all.

The link between the institution of public debate and "wise action" can be somewhat indirect. Often, the main effect of the public setting is to exclude overt appeals to interest. In a public debate, a speaker who said, "We should do this because it is good for me" would not persuade anyone, and would, moreover, be subject to informal sanctions and ostracism that would make her less effective in the future. Even those who are motivated solely by interest are constrained by the public setting to present their policy proposals as motivated by more impartial values. This process of *misrepresentation* of preferences differs from that of *transmutation* (Chapter 4) in the same way as deception differs from self-deception. It is the interest of the speaker, not her need for self-esteem, that causes her to misrepresent her interest as reason. Her interest may also cause her to make the misrepresentation hard to perceive, by arguing in impartial terms for a policy that deviates somewhat (but not too much) from the one that would coincide perfectly with her interest. The misrepresentation might, in fact, backfire, if it were too obvious. Hence *the need to disguise one's fundamental preference may induce a shift in one's policy preference*, by what we may think of as "the civilizing force of hypocrisy."

In many societies, property has been used as a criterion for suffrage. One may, to be sure, offer impartial arguments for this principle. At the Federal Convention, Madison argued that the stringent property quali-fications for the Senate, rather than protecting the privileged against the people, were a device for protecting the people against itself. But as noted, there is something inherently suspicious about such arguments, which coincide too well with the self-interest of the rich. It may then be useful to turn to literacy, as an impartial criterion that is *highly but imperfectly* correlated with property. At various stages in American his-tory literacy has also served as a legitimizing proxy for other unavowable goals, such as the desire to keep blacks or Catholics out of politics. American immigration policy has also used literacy as a proxy for criteria that could not be stated publicly. Proposals to screen immigrants by testing them for literacy in their native language were usually justified as a way of selecting on the basis of individual merit, a widely accepted impartial procedure. The real motivation of the advocates of literacy was, however, prejudice or group interest. Patrician nativists wanted to exclude the usually illiterate immigrants from central and southeastern Europe. Labor feared that an influx of unskilled workers might drive wages down.

It would obviously be wrong to think that arguing can *always* be reduced to more or less subtle ways of promoting one's interest. If that were the case, there would be no point in misrepresentation since nobody would ever be taken in.[5] If speakers are motivated by a sincere desire to promote the public good, argument and debate may change their beliefs in ways that induce a change in policy preferences. This is especially likely to occur if the various members of a group have access to different information, so that they can improve the quality of their decisions by pooling their knowledge.[6] If the body is a representative one, it is then important to select delegates with widely different back-grounds. In electing representatives to a national assembly, for instance, this consideration speaks in favor of proportional voting with a low threshold or no threshold at all.[7] One might also require representatives from an electoral district to be residents of that community.

People also, although perhaps more rarely, argue about fundamental preferences and change them as a result of debate. Often, change occurs through the discovery of hidden similarities between cases or the expo-sure of superficial similarities. Many people are opposed, for instance, to the mandatory use of "cadaver organs" for transplantation purposes. They believe that if the family has religious objections to this procedure, their feelings ought to be respected. Against this view one might point to

---

[5] Similarly, the argument has been made that if *all* animal signals were deceptive, the deception would have no point.

[6] Recall, however, that this improvement is more likely if they pool their raw data than if they simply pool the conclusions reached on the basis of raw data (Chapter 23).

[7] Other considerations, notably the need for effective governance, may speak in favor of majority voting or proportional voting with a high threshold. In elections to constituent assemblies, in which governance is a secondary consideration, there is a tendency to choose delegates by proportional voting.

the mandatory use of autopsies in the case of suspicious deaths, even when the procedure is contrary to the religious beliefs of the family. If invasive measures are in order to determine the cause of death, one might argue that they should also be acceptable for the purpose of saving lives. Change can also occur when a general principle is seen to contradict intuitions about particular cases. A person might accept mandatory use of cadaver organs on utilitarian grounds but balk at the implication that one would be justified in killing one randomly chosen person and using heart, kidneys, lung, and liver to save the lives of five others.[8] As a result, an initial unqualified utilitarianism might be revised to take account of nonconsequentialist values (Chapter 4).

The benefits of arguing may be undermined, however, by the effects of *speaking before an audience*. Public-minded individuals may, no less than others, be subject to amour propre that makes them reluctant to admit in public that they have changed their mind. In Chapter 3 I noted that this was the main reason Madison gave, long afterward, why the Federal Convention was held behind closed doors with silence imposed on the delegates. His argument might, however, seem to conflict with a traditional argument for opening assembly debates to the public. Many legislative decisions have a strong short-term impact on legislator interests. If the decision-making process is shielded from the public eye, arguing about the common interest will easily degenerate into naked interest bargaining. Allowing the public to follow the proceedings and observe the votes tends to limit such self-serving scheming and, as a by-product, promote the public good. As Bentham wrote, "The greater the number of temptations to which the exercise of political power is exposed, the more necessary is it to give to those who possess it, the most powerful reasons to resist it. But there is no reason more constant and more universal than the superintendence of the public." Or as the American judge Louis Brandeis said, "Sunlight is the best disinfectant."

---

[8] Utilitarians tend to deny that this implication follows. They argue, typically, that the negative effects of the fear and uncertainty that would be generated by the knowledge that one might be chosen as a "random donor" would more than offset the benefits of the practice. *But how do they know this?* I suspect that they reason backward, from the obvious unacceptability of the practice to the existence of costs that would exclude it on utilitarian grounds, rather than forward, from the demonstration of costs to the rejection of the procedure.

These remarks point to a tension in the process of arguing. If debates are held in public, the quality of argument will suffer. If they take place behind closed doors, arguing may degenerate into bargaining. The tension may be attenuated, however, if the matters to be decided leave little room for the play of private interest. Constituent assemblies may be less prone to self-serving decisions than ordinary legislatures, not because the delegates are more impartially motivated but because (or to the extent that) their interests have less purchase on the issues at hand. Also, as I have noted several times, because of the long-term perspective of constitutional design self-interest may to some extent mimic the desire to promote the public good.

Voting

Voting may be needed when arguing fails to generate a consensus on policy. Voting systems vary greatly. In popular voting, dimensions of variation include the franchise, the mode of voting (secret versus open), the majority needed for a decision, and, in some referendum systems, the quorum. In assembly votes, the main dimensions are the quorum, the size of the majority, and the choice between roll-call voting and show of hands (and similar procedures, such as "shouting" or "sitting and standing"). Secret voting in assemblies is rare, but not unheard of. In the French Assemblée Constituante of 1789–91, the president of the assembly was chosen by secret ballot. In recent times, Italy and Colombia have practiced secret voting in parliament. Note that secret voting is to be distinguished from closed proceedings in which no auditors are allowed. The latter may be combined with public voting that enables the assembly members to make credible promises of logrolling, which would be impossible with secret voting. By contrast, if the proceedings are open to the public some auditors may have a negative reaction if they see their representatives voting against their preference on one issue, since they cannot observe the gains thus made possible on another.

In the following I restrict myself to majority voting. Even though this is not a universal practice, the decision to adopt proposals by a larger majority such as three-fifths or two-thirds would itself, it seems, have to be made by simple majority. Constituent assemblies, which often impose qualified majorities for future constitutional amendments, almost invariably use simple majority voting in their own proceedings.[9] The idealized model in which constituent assemblies behind the veil of ignorance decide by unanimity that they will decide by majority voting once the veil is lifted has little relevance for actual constitution making. I shall ignore the issue of quorum, except to note that abstention or the "politics of the empty chair" can be used by a minority to block a decision that would have passed had it shown up and voted against it.

The lack of consensus that makes it necessary to decide by voting may derive from diverging fundamental preferences, diverging beliefs, or both. As an example, consider the debates over unicameralism versus bicameralism in the French Assemblée Constituante of 1789. Very broadly speaking, the assembly contained three roughly equal-sized groups. The reactionary right wanted to set the clock back to absolute monarchy, the moderate center wanted a constitutional monarchy with strong checks on parliament, and the left wanted a constitutional monarchy with weak checks on parliament. On the issue of bicameralism, the constellations were, highly simplified, as shown in Table 25.1.

In the end, bicameralism was defeated by the alliance of reactionaries and radicals. This general phenomenon – policy agreement based on preference differences and belief differences that cancel each other – is quite common. One might even achieve unanimity on that

TABLE 25.1

	Fundamental Preferences	Beliefs	Policy Preferences
Reactionaries	Destabilize the regime	Bicameralism will stabilize the regime	Unicameralism
Moderates	Stabilize the regime	Bicameralism will stabilize the regime	Bicameralism
Radicals	Stabilize the regime	Bicameralism will destabilize the regime	Unicameralism

[9] The South African constitution of 1996 is a partial exception. The requirement that it be adopted by a qualified majority was laid down in the interim constitution of 1993, which was itself adopted by bargaining rather than voting.

basis,[10] although obviously of a different kind from the one that might emerge in the "ideal speech situation" in which speakers are motivated only by the common good and are willing to listen to argument.

In my stylized rendering of the debate, a majority believed that bicameralism would stabilize the regime and a (different) majority wanted to stabilize the regime (see Table 25.1). If collective decisions had been made by first aggregating beliefs by (sincere) majority voting, next aggregating fundamental preferences by (sincere) majority voting, and finally taking the action that according to the aggregate belief would best realize the aggregate preference, *bicameralism* would have been the choice. (To prevent this outcome, the reactionaries could have falsely stated a belief that bicameralism would destabilize the regime, thus creating a majority for that belief and hence a majority for the choice of unicameralism.) To my knowledge, this "double aggregation" procedure is never used in practice. Given the complexities of aggregating policy preferences directly, any such system would probably be unmanageable.

In the debate over bicameralism, voters differed in their beliefs as well as in their ultimate goals. In other cases, they may be similar in one of these two respects and differ in the other. Since what is actually observed and aggregated are policy preferences, it may be hard to disentangle the two factors that go into their making. In the abstract, we may nevertheless try to determine the effects of majority voting on the aggregation of beliefs (assuming identical goals) and on the aggregation of fundamental preferences (assuming identical beliefs). According to Tocqueville, democracy (i.e., majority voting with a large franchise) was superior to other systems in both respects. "The moral ascendancy of the majority rests in part on the idea that there is more enlightenment and wisdom in an assembly of many than in the mind of one, or that the number of legislators matters more than the manner of their selection, [and] on the principle that the interests of the many ought to be preferred to those of

---

[10] In the French assembly, this outcome occurred in May 1791 when radicals, moderates, and reactionaries joined forces in voting for a law that made the members of the constituent assembly ineligible for the first ordinary legislature. The aim of the radicals was to weaken the legislature in favor of the club of the Jacobins; that of the reactionaries to weaken it in favor of the king. The vote was unanimous, since the moderate center, "drunk with disinterestedness" (Chapter 5), enthusiastically voted to deny themselves a role in the future legislature.

the few." Democratic officials may "commit grave errors" but "will never systematically adopt a line hostile to the majority."[11]

Consider first aggregation of beliefs. There is a long-standing debate whether an extended or a narrow franchise is the better procedure for arriving at correct beliefs – whether the many are wiser than the few. According to Aristotle, this was a matter of weighing quantity (the number of participants in the political process) against quality (the competence of the participants):

> Quality may exist in one of the classes which make up the state and quantity in the other. For example the low-born may be more numerous than the noble or the poor more than the rich, yet the more numerous class may not exceed in quantity as much as they fall behind in quality. Hence these two factors have to be judged in comparison with one another. Where therefore the multitude of the poor exceeds in the proportion stated [so as to offset their inferior quality], it is natural for there to be a democracy.

In modern language, the issue can be stated in terms of Condorcet's "jury theorem." Suppose that members of a jury state their (independent) beliefs about whether the accused has in fact done what the prosecutor claims he did, and that each of them has a greater than 50 percent chance of being right. Condorcet showed that if the jury decides by majority voting, its chance of getting it right increases with the size of the jury,[12] and converges to certainty when the jury becomes indefinitely large. Also, for a given size of the jury, the chance of the majority's getting it right increases when the chance of each jury member's getting it right goes up.[13] Hence, as Aristotle suggested, one may improve the outcome either by increasing the number of jurors or by increasing their qualifications.[14]

---

[11] He does not ask, though, whether the occasional liability to *grave* mistakes might not be more serious than the *systematic* bias of a nondemocratic regime. Although Tocqueville claimed that because of its favorable geographical situation the United States could afford to make mistakes, that might not be true of other countries.

[12] Assuming, contrary to what is argued in the next paragraph, that the likelihood of each voter's being right is unaffected by an increase in the number of voters.

[13] The chance of the majority's getting it right also increases if one requires a qualified majority, such as 60 percent. In that case, however, one might get a "hung jury" in which neither the guilt nor the innocence of the accused gathers the required majority.

[14] One might also try to ensure that the conditions of Condorcet's theorem obtain by making it more likely that the beliefs of the voters are in fact independent of each other. In this perspective,

Going beyond Aristotle, we can observe that qualifications may be a direct function of number rather than of socioeconomic position. In social-science language, the competence of voters may be "endogenous" to the system rather than given "exogenously." Suppose one has to choose between two political systems, oligarchy and democracy, both deciding by majority vote but with different size of the franchise. In a democracy voters will rationally decide to remain ignorant, since the impact of each on the outcome is very small.[15] In an oligarchy, voters will invest more in gathering information since each of them has a larger impact.

Bentham noted that this argument also applies to voting in an assembly: "The greater the number of voters the less the weight and the value of each vote, the less its price in the eyes of the voter, and the less of an incentive he has in assuring that it conforms to the true end and even in casting it at all." In responding to the argument that an assembly (he had in mind the French Assemblée Constituante of 1789) ought to be numerous, since "the probability of wisdom increases with the number of members," he wrote that "the reduction that this same cause brings in the strength of the motivation to exercise one's enlightenment offsets this advantage." In this quality-quantity trade-off there will be an optimal size of the electorate of maximizes the probability that majority voting will yield the correct belief.[16]

Consider next aggregation of preferences by voting. The two main and closely related problems that arise are *misrepresentation* of preferences and *indeterminacy* of the outcome. Beginning with the first, people may have

---

Rousseau's proposal to ban discussion prior to deliberation might make sense. At the same time, if deliberation improves the quality of beliefs, it cannot be an objection that it also makes them less independent of each other. The conditions of the theorem are sufficient for majority voting to produce a good outcome, but not necessary.

[15] Since the decision to vote is itself irrational (Chapter 12), one might ask whether citizens might not also irrationally invest in information about the issues at stake. In the present context, however, the relevant issue is whether citizens invest more when the franchise is narrow than when it is wide, just as more voters may turn out when the election is seen as close.

[16] In the abstract the optimum could be at one of the extreme ends – either a single individual or all adult persons. Under reasonable assumptions, there is more likely to be an "interior maximum." If the optimal size is small, one might choose the voters at random among the citizens at large to ensure that they do not represent sectarian interests. In this perspective, voting would be a *function* rather than a *right*.

an incentive to vote for other proposals or candidates than those they most would prefer to see adopted or elected. The choice of the open rather than the secret ballot can induce this phenomenon. In classical Athens, most decisions by the assembly were by a show of hands, with the result that some citizens may have been afraid to vote their minds. Thus Thucydides states that "with the enthusiasm of the majority [for the Sicilian expedition], the few that liked it not, feared to appear unpatriotic by holding up their hands against it." (By contrast, the decisions in the large Athenian jury courts were by secret ballot.) The choice of roll-call vote rather than other methods, such as "standing versus sitting," can also intimidate voters. In the constituent assemblies in Paris (1789–91) and in Frankfurt (1848), radicals routinely demanded roll-call votes in important matters, with the implicit and sometimes explicit threat that they would expose those who voted against radical proposals to popular violence by circulating lists with their names. Even if there was a clear majority under the "standing versus sitting" system, which made it difficult to identify how individuals cast their vote, the outcome might be reversed upon roll-call vote.[17]

Misrepresentation can also arise with the secret ballot. In essentially all voting systems situations can arise in which a voter, by voting for an alternative other than her first-ranked one, can bring about an outcome that she prefers to the one that would have occurred had she voted sincerely.[18] (An exception could arise if candidates or proposals were chosen by a randomizing device, with the probability of an alternative's being chosen equal to the proportion of voters favoring it. In this case,

[17] For a more recent example, when the 1964 Civil Rights Act was being debated in the U.S. House, the chair of the Rules Committee (Howard Smith) introduced what he thought of as a killer amendment: he proposed that the bill prohibit discrimination on grounds of sex as well as race and national origin. The House leadership, sharing Smith's belief that the amendment might kill the bill, attempted to get liberal Democrats to vote against the proposal, and, according to some accounts, many of these members would have been personally willing to do it if only such a vote could have been held in private. But the galleries were filled with women's interest groups who were there to observe behavior on nonrecorded (teller) votes, and, in this circumstance, liberal members were unwilling to go along with the leadership and vote down Smith's amendment. As it turns out, the Smith amendment did not lead to the defeat of the bill but rather to the inclusion of gender as one of a group of statutorily protected classes.

[18] More technically: in nondictatorial and nonprobabilistic voting systems, expressing one's true preferences is not in general a dominant strategy. Systems can be devised, however, in which sincerity is an *equilibrium* in the sense of being the best response to the sincerity of others. The details are complicated and do not reflect features of real-world voting systems.

the problem of the "wasted vote" would not arise. The disadvantages of the system are obvious and explain why it has never been chosen.) The desire to see one's first-ranked option win by a margin that is not too wide may induce one to vote against it. In Chapter 18 I mentioned, for instance, how Socialists might vote for Communists in order to move the platform of their party to the left. If it is certain that one's first-ranked option will not be chosen, one may vote for the best alternative of those that have some chance of winning. Some voting systems also create an incentive to rank a candidate or proposal preferred by other voters less favorably than one's real preferences would dictate (see the example later), or to introduce new alternatives for the sole purpose of making the choice of one's preferred alternative more likely.

In some cases, the outcome of majority voting is indeterminate. Suppose there are three blocs of roughly equal size in a municipal assembly, representing, respectively, the business community, industrial workers, and social service professionals. The assembly is to choose among building an indoor swimming pool, subsidizing the local symphony orchestra, or building a golf course. Conforming to the stereotype of these groups, suppose that (after long debates) they rank the options as shown in Table 25.2.

If the alternatives are held up against each other in pairwise votes, there is a majority of businesspeople and workers who prefer the golf course to the orchestra, a majority of businesspeople and professionals who prefer the orchestra to the pool, and a majority of professionals and workers who prefer the pool to the golf course. Hence the "social preferences" are *intransitive* or *cycling*. In the case of individual choice, transitivity was a requirement of rationality (Chapter 11). In the present context, the question is not so much one of rationality as of determinacy.

TABLE 25.2

	Businesspeople	*Workers*	*Professionals*
Golf course	1	2	3
Orchestra	2	3	1
Pool	3	1	2

If all the municipal council has to go by is the rankings in Table 25.2, it is hard to see how they could make any decision at all. Since the vote was taken because the council was unable to reach consensus, more debate is unlikely to help. If one could measure the *intensity* with which the various groups prefer one of the options to another, or the extent to which the options satisfy objective needs, one might be able to say that one option was unambiguously superior to the others. There is no general procedure, however, that allows us to compare degrees of preference intensity or of need satisfaction across individuals.[19] Asking them how much they value the options, for instance, by making them rank them on a scale from 0 to 10, is pointless. For one thing, we cannot know whether a given score (e.g., 7) means the same thing for members of the three groups. For another, asking them to rank the options would give them an incentive to misrepresent the intensity of their preferences, for example by assigning 10 to their top-ranked option and 0 to the others.

It is not clear how important this problem of "cycling social preferences" is in practice. It cannot arise if individual preferences are "single peaked," meaning that the options can be ranked from "highest" to "lowest" in such a way that the preferences of each individual are steadily increasing toward his or her most preferred policy and steadily decreasing as one moves away from it. In many cases, this is a reasonable property of preferences. If an individual's preferred tax schedule is 20 percent, he or she will prefer 19 percent to 18 percent and 21 percent to 22 percent. Moreover, there are no instances of an assembly's simply throwing up its hands and declaring that because there is no "popular will" no decision will be made. In fact, if the status quo is one of the options, this idea is incoherent. Some decision is always made, whether by default (retaining the status quo), by adoption of a traditional voting procedure, or by manipulation of the agenda.

---

[19] That is why classical utilitarianism, which tells us to maximize the sum total of individual utilities, is difficult to apply in practice. This problem should not lead one to think that it is always meaningless to compare degrees of welfare across persons. Institutions as well as individuals carry out such comparisons routinely, with great confidence. Yet since the comparisons are based on intuitions rather than on measurements, there will be many cases in which they fail to yield unambiguous results.

Yet the fact that a decision is reached does not imply that it embodies the popular or "general" will in some nonarbitrary sense. For a constellation of (sincere) preferences such as the one given in Table 25.2, the very idea of a general will is meaningless. How often do such constellations occur? Political scientists have offered a number of examples. Others have argued that the alleged examples have been misdescribed, and that a closer examination refutes these specific claims about cycling majorities. I shall describe two cases that appear to be genuine instances of cycling preferences.

On October 8, 1992, the Norwegian parliament decided that the future airport for the Oslo area should be located at Gardermoen (I shall refer to this option as alternative G). Other options were Hobøl (alternative H) and a solution that involved a combination of Gardermoen and the existing Fornebu airport (alternative D). The options were not to be held up against each other but considered successively against the status quo. Once an option received a majority of the votes, it was adopted.[20] Although this serial voting was the traditional voting system in the parliament, other systems are possible, for example, holding the options up against each other in pairwise votes until one winner remains. With successive voting, the order in which the options are voted on can be decisive, as we shall see shortly.

The *expressed* party preferences, which with unimportant exceptions coincided with the votes of the deputies, were as follows:

The Labor Party (63 deputies) : G > D > H
A coalition of the Socialist Left Party, the Christian Democrats, and the Agrarian Party (42 deputies): D > H > G
The Conservative Party (37 deputies): H > G > D
The Progress Party (22 deputies): H > D > G
One independent deputy: G > H > D

Assuming these to be the *sincere* preferences, social preferences were cycling: D beats H 105 to 60, H beats G 101 to 64, and G beats D 101 to 64.

---

[20] As all were preferred to the status quo, one was sure to be adopted.

Before voting, parliament voted on the order in which the alternatives should be considered. Labor proposed G-D-H, whereas the president of the parliament proposed D-H-G. When the proposals were held up against each other, Labor's won. If the president's proposal had won, Labor would probably had voted for D, since otherwise its failure to garner a majority for D would have led to the adoption of its bottom-ranked proposal, H. Under the order that was adopted, the Conservative Party was in a similar predicament. In the end, the Conservatives voted for G, since if they had voted against it, their bottom-ranked proposal, D, would have won. Although it is abstractly possible that Labor was insincere in stating D as its second-ranked option, and that it did so only to make the Conservative Party believe that voting against G would lead to the adoption of D, there is no evidence to that effect. If this was in fact the case, social preferences would not be cycling, since H would beat both D and G.

In the second example it is pretty much excluded that the cycling preferences could be a mere artifact of misrepresentation. It arose in the context of deciding the order of demobilization from the American army after World War II. Getting out early was a scarce good, which had to be allocated fairly. To determine the criteria, the army conducted large-scale surveys among the enlisted men. In a survey in which the criteria were held up against each other in pairwise comparisons, the rankings showed some collective inconsistency. Thus 55 percent thought that a married man with two children who had not seen combat should be released before a single man with two campaigns of combat; 52 percent rated eighteen months overseas as more important than two children; and 60 percent rated two campaigns as worth more than eighteen months overseas. It is most unlikely that the respondents were misrepresenting their preferences.[21]

---

[21] The authors of the study from which I take these findings wrote that "a high degree of internal consistency on such intricate hypothetical choices was hardly to be expected," suggesting that the problem was one of individually inconsistent rankings. If the majorities had added up to more than 200 percent, this suggestion would have been justified. As they add up only to 167 percent, it is quite possible that the rankings were individually consistent and yet gave rise to a collective intransitivity. The study was published in 1949, two years before Kenneth Arrow's pathbreaking work on preference aggregation and the inconsistencies to which it is vulnerable.

Bargaining

Bargaining is the process of reaching agreement through credible threats and promises. A spouse may threaten to litigate for sole custody of a child unless the other spouse agrees to joint custody. In wage bargaining, workers can threaten to strike, to work to rule, or to refuse overtime work, while employers can threaten with lockouts or plant closings. The management of a firm may threaten to fire an employee unless he works harder at his job. One country may threaten to invade another unless it makes territorial concessions. In a constituent assembly, a delegate from one territorial unit may threaten to walk out unless the assembly adopts a mode of representation that is to the advantage of that unit. American senators may threaten with filibustering to make the president withdraw a nomination. Congress may threaten to refuse to vote the budget if the president uses a veto to override legislation.

Turning to promises, a member of a group that decides by voting may promise to vote for a proposal that is important for one of her colleagues, on the condition that the latter votes for one that matters to her (logrolling). The seller of a house may promise not to begin renegotiating if a buyer meets his asking price. Similarly, a kidnapper may promise to release the victim once the ransom has been paid, rather than retaining the victim and making a new demand. Conversely, a government may promise to let a terrorist out of jail once his co-terrorists have released the victim they have kidnapped. A victim of kidnapping may promise not to describe the appearance of the kidnappers to the police if they release him. A person in a Prisoner's Dilemma situation may promise to cooperate if the other does so as well.

The outcome of bargaining depends on the *credibility* of threats and promises. A threat is credible if the agent making it can be expected (for whatever reason) to carry it out if the other person refuses to comply. "Your money or your life" is more credible than "Your money or my life." A promise is credible if the agent can be expected (for whatever reason) to keep it once the other person has complied. "I shall draw the illustrations once you have written the text" is a credible promise, since the person making it will have an incentive to keep it. In the Trust Game that I discussed in Chapter 5 and Chapter 15, the trustee has no material incentive to keep a promise to return half the gains created by the transfer of the investor.

The credibility of *threats* depends on objective as well as subjective factors. Objective factors can be divided into outside options and inside options. An outside option is what a party to the bargaining would obtain if the negotiations broke down irrevocably. In wage negotiations, the outside option for the workers would be the wage they could get in another firm or the level of unemployment benefits. In bargaining over child custody, the outside options are defined by the expected outcome of litigation. At the Federal Convention in Philadelphia, the outside option was what a state might obtain by withdrawing from the union (and possibly allying itself with another nation). A threat to withdraw from bargaining is credible only if the party can show that it will do better outside the relationship than it would fare by accepting the offer of the other party.

An inside option is what the parties have at their disposal during the bargaining process itself, determining how long they can hold out. For the workers, the inside option may be given by the size of the strike fund. For the parents, it might be given by the allocation of temporary custody to one of them. In Philadelphia, the inside option was determined by the eagerness of the delegates to get back to urgent business in their home states. Inside options affect the credibility of threats because they determine whether a party has an incentive to carry them out. A strike threat by the workers may not be credible if (the firm knows that) they have no strike fund and most of them are married and have high mortgage payments to be serviced.

More generally, the threat to impose a harm on another party is not credible if doing so will also harm oneself substantially. Members of Congress cannot credibly threaten to refuse voting the budget if the president knows that this measure would seriously damage both their reputation and their own ability to get things done. A member (Lanjuinais) of the French constituent assembly argued in 1789 that the future legislature would not be able to use its control over revenue to prevent the king from using his veto. Since "stopping the payment of taxes" for this purpose would be "like cutting your throat to heal a wound in the leg," the threat to do so would not be credible.

On the subjective side, threats are more credible if the agent has (and is believed by the other party to have) a long time horizon. The more patient bargainers have an edge since their opponents may be willing to trade off the *size* of a concession against the *time* at which it is made.[22] In the Paris-based negotiations between the United States and North Vietnam, the latter country made a good opening move when their delegation took out a *two-year lease* on a house, thus signaling that they were not in any hurry. Risk neutrality or a low degree of risk aversion may also give a party an edge in bargaining. A risk-averse parent who has good chance of being awarded custody by the court may nevertheless agree to joint custody (Chapter 11). A further subjective factor that can lend credibility to threats is placing a relatively low value on what the other party has to offer compared to what one is being asked to give up. In divorce bargaining, one parent may be able to force a favorable financial deal because the other parent cares strongly about getting custody of the children.

Having a long time horizon also affects credibility in another manner. If I fail to carry out a threat in a current interaction because it would be costly to do so, my ability to make credible threats in future interactions will suffer. The idea is perhaps more easily understood if stated in a converse way: I may carry out a threat in a current interaction even when I have no incentive to do so, in order to build up a reputation for being someone whose threats have to be taken seriously. If the other person understands the logic of this argument, I may not have to carry out any threat at all. There is no reputation building in a literal sense, only in a "virtual" sense. More commonly, I might have to carry out a few "counterinterested" threats to signal to the world that I am that kind of

---

[22] This formulation is somewhat misleading. In a bargaining game like the one shown in Figure 20.2 the agreement will be struck immediately on the basis of backward induction, in which the rate of time discounting of the parties plays a role. The bargaining is "virtual," not actual. Yet it remains true that the more impatient party will get less because it matters more to it to get it right away.

person. In the comments on the Chain Store Game in Chapter 20 I referred to both possibilities.

The credibility of *promises* also depends on both objective and subjective factors, although in somewhat different ways. The credibility of a promise depends crucially on the agent's being able to deliver. Consider for instance a failed attempt at logrolling in the French constituent assembly in the fall of 1789. In three meetings between the leader of the moderates, Mounier, and the radicals Barnave, Duport, and Alexandre Lameth, the latter three made the following proposal. They would offer Mounier both an absolute veto for the king and bicameralism, if he in return would accept that the king gave up his right to dissolve the assembly, that the upper chamber would have a suspensive veto only, and that there would be periodic conventions for the revision of the constitution. Mounier refused outright, arguably because he did not believe in the ability of the three to deliver on their promise, since the assembly did not have parties in the modern sense of disciplined groupings that can be made to vote as a single bloc.

For another instance, consider promises of immunity to prosecution for outgoing leaders in transitions to democracy. Promises to this effect were made, accepted, and broken in Argentina in 1983, in Uruguay in 1984, and in Poland and Hungary in 1989. (In the Latin American countries threats of a military coup then forced compliance.) In retrospect, the generals and party leaders should have understood that these promises were not credible, since the negotiating incoming leaders could not guarantee that courts and legislatures would respect them. In Poland, the negotiators for the opposition in the Round Table Talks, who belonged to the left wing of Solidarity, argued that *pacta sunt servanda* – promises are to be kept. When the right wing of the movement gained power, they ignored the pledge.

The subjective conditions of credibility include, once again, a long time horizon. If the agent has a low rate of time discounting and knows that she will interact again with the person to whom she has made a promise (or with other persons who can observe her behavior), she has an incentive to keep it. Logrolling in legislatures, for instance, can be maintained by such anticipations. (In constituent assemblies, which only meet once, the incentive for keeping one's promise of reciprocating should be weaker, and hence fewer such promises should be made.) An agent may also be able to create a disincentive for himself to renege on his promise. Although kidnappers normally have no reason to believe a promise by their victim that he will not reveal their identity to the police, he can make it credible by giving them a piece of damaging and verifiable information about himself that *they* could reveal if arrested.

As the subjective conditions or mental states that shape the outcome of bargaining cannot be directly observed, bargainers have an interest in misrepresenting them, by verbal or nonverbal behavior. For all we know, the North Vietnamese negotiators took out a long lease merely to convey the *impression* that they were patient. In logrolling, each side will exaggerate the importance of what she is being asked to give up in order to force a large concession by the other. When workers claim to attach great importance to costly safety measures at the workplace, it may be a stratagem to justify a big wage increase as the price of forgoing them. In many cases, attempts to deceive may be too transparent to work. If a divorcing parent claims great concern for getting custody of the children to get a favorable financial settlement, the other parent may be able to document a consistent lack of interest in the children before the marriage began to break down or the recent acceptance of a job that involves a great deal of traveling. A farsighted parent might, however, anticipate this problem and lay the groundwork for a claim to care about the children before the other parent understands that the marriage is breaking down.

Like parties engaged in arguing, bargainers can have an incentive to misrepresent their interest as based on principle. The reasoning behind the misrepresentation is different, though. In arguing, the parties want to prevent the opprobrium of basing their proposals on naked interest. In bargaining, no opprobrium attaches to expression of interest. Firms and workers are supposed to be concerned with profits and wages, not with the common good. Bargainers may nevertheless gain a strategic advantage from framing their demands in terms of principle. They may claim that in backing down from a principle-based claim they are making a greater concession, and hence expect greater concessions from the other side, than if mere interest is at stake. If each side employs this tactic, however, the bargaining may break down.

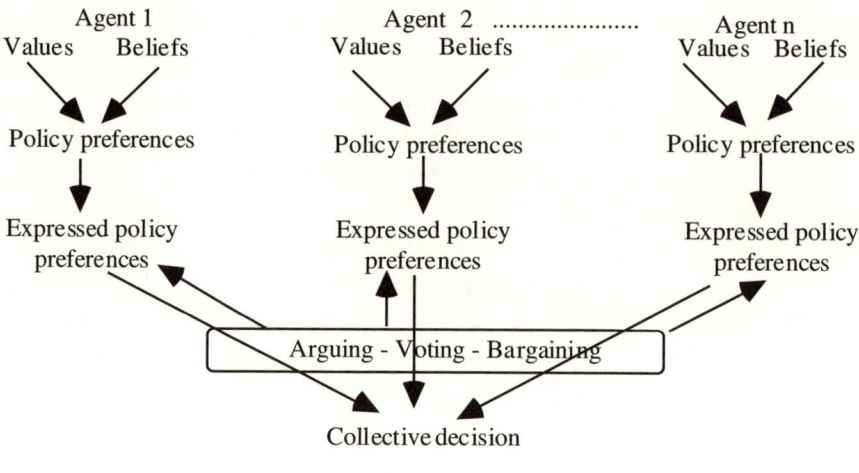

FIGURE 25.1

Summary

Pulling together the various strands of this chapter, the process of collective decision making can be represented as shown in Figure 25.1. The central point is perhaps that each of the mechanisms of collective decision making – arguing, voting, and bargaining – creates an incentive to misrepresent some aspect of one's preferences. In other words, an *aggregation mechanism contributes to shaping the inputs to the mechanism itself*. The expressed policy preferences are a function both of the real policy preferences and of the mechanism that aggregates expressed policy preferences. The welfare impact of misrepresentation is ambiguous. By virtue of the civilizing force of hypocrisy, the effects may be socially beneficial. In other cases, generalized use of this tactic may create a Prisoner's Dilemma type of situation, in which everybody loses.

⟪⟪⟪

BIBLIOGRAPHICAL NOTE

For mechanisms that are in some respects intermediate between collective action and collective decision making, see E. Ostrom, *Governing the Commons: The Evolution of Institutions for Collective Action* (Cambridge University Press, 1990). For a survey of countries with compulsory voting and the sanctions they adopt on nonvoters, see http://www.idea.int/vt/compulsory_voting.cfm. A luminous if occasionally eccentric discussion of arguing and voting is J. Bentham, *Political Tactics* (Oxford University Press, 1999). The passages quoted from Bentham (translated from French) are in the equally interesting *Rights, Representation, and Reform* (Oxford University Press, 2002), pp. 35 and 122. For misrepresentation induced by deliberation, see Chapter 5 of my *Alchemies of the Mind* (Cambridge University Press, 1999). For the difference between ordinary legislatures and constituent assemblies, see my "Constituent legislatures," in R. Bauman and T. Kahana (eds), *Constitution and the Legislature* (Cambridge University Press, 2006). For the vote on bicameralism in 1789, see J. Egret, *La révolution des notables* (Paris: Armand Colin, 1950). The "double aggregation" procedure is discussed in C. List, "The discursive dilemma and public reason," *Ethics* 116 (2006) 362–402. The discussion of Condorcet's jury theorem draws on D. Karotkin and J. Paroush, "Optimum committee size: Quality-versus-quantity dilemma," *Social Choice and Welfare* 20 (2003), 429–41. A full treatment of the history of the secret ballot is H. Buchstein, *Öffentliche und geheime Stimmangabe* (Baden-Baden: Nomos, 2000). The note on the Civil Rights Act of 1964 is taken more or less verbatim from H. Brady and J. Ferejohn, "Congress and civil rights policy: An examination of endogenous preferences," in I. Katznelson and B. Weingast (eds.), *Preferences and Situations* (New York: Russell Sage, 2005). For a discussion of strategic voting, see Chapter 2 in D. Austen-Smith and J. Banks, *Positive Political Theory II* (Ann Arbor: University of Michigan Press, 2005). G. Mackie, *Democracy Defended* (Cambridge University Press, 2003), contains extensive analyses of cycling social preferences, and a claim that almost all alleged examples of cycling in legislatures are based on flawed readings of the evidence. The example of Oslo airport is taken from A. Hylland, "The Condorcet paradox in theory and practice," in J. Elster et al. (eds.), *Understanding Choice, Explaining Behavior: Essays in Honour of Ole-Jørgen Skog* (Oslo Academic Press, 2006). The example of the demobilization of American soldiers is taken from S. Stouffer (ed.), *The American Soldier* (Princeton, NJ: Princeton University Press, 1949). The seminal work on bargaining is T. Schelling, *The Strategy of Conflict* (Cambridge, MA: Harvard University Press, 1960). A classic work on bargaining in action is H. Raiffa, *The Art and Science of Negotiation* (Cambridge, MA: Harvard University Press, 1982). An informal introduction to bargaining theory is my *The Cement of Society* (Cambridge University Press, 1989).

Chapter 26
ORGANIZATIONS AND INSTITUTIONS

❀ ❀ ❀

Organizations and Institutions

Examples of organizations include the local supermarket, General Electric, the American Congress, the Catholic Church, the German Constitutional Court, France, and the United Nations. Examples of institutions include the family, constitutions, paper money, the market economy, and transitional justice. Organizations and institutions may be related as "token" and "type," that is, as an instance of a concept and the concept itself. The stock exchange is an institution (a type), the New York Stock Exchange an organization (a token of that type). The nation-state is an institution, France is an organization. Some organizations, such as the United Nations, are not tokens of any institution, however. Conversely, some institutions, such as the market economy, have no organizational tokens. Special markets, though, such as the market for pollution permits, can be organizations. Although I shall mostly discuss organizations, they are best understood against the background of institutions.

Organizations are *collective actors*, defined by their capacity for centralized decision making. In some cases, their creation can be traced back to a specific moment in time, such as July 4, 1776, for the United States or October 24, 1945, for the United Nations. In other cases, such as France or the Catholic Church, it is more appropriate to say that the organizations *evolved* or *emerged* than that they were created. Although it may be hard to pin down the exact moment at which a loosely structured aggregation of individuals crystallizes into a collective actor with an enduring identity over time, there will be a moment when we can tell that it has happened.

Institutions are *ways of doings things* that emerge or evolve gradually, although once they have taken on a definite shape they can be consciously adopted and implemented by organizations. Consider for instance the 1989–90 transitions in Eastern Europe. The new democracies adopted the institution of the market economy and created stock exchanges and other organizations to implement it. In their constitutions, they organized the institution of constitutional courts with the power to strike down unconstitutional laws. When dealing with their autocratic predecessors, they adopted institutions of transitional justice.

These three institutions, the market economy, constitutional courts, and transitional justice, have not always existed. Although Adam Smith was not necessarily wrong when he asserted, as a universal fact, "a certain propensity in human nature ... to truck, barter, and exchange one thing for another," that propensity can be kept in check by others. In particular, it may be blocked by the distrust that characterizes the "warre of everyone against everyone" in Hobbes's state of nature. To overcome that distrust, institutions may be necessary. Under primitive conditions, "truck and barter" may be too risky, if the strong can simply grab the possessions of the weak without offering anything in return. It is better, then, to keep one's possessions to oneself, out of sight. Even when that basic problem is overcome by policing, free riding and distrust may still be impediments to the efficient functioning of markets. If I have a good idea about how to manufacture a certain product more cheaply, I may be reluctant to develop it if I know others can take it over without incurring the costs of development. The institution of the patent system is a response to this problem. If borrowers want to use their house or land as collateral, lenders will not be forthcoming unless they can be sure that the property is not mortgaged several times over. To assure them, the state has to create a cadastre they can consult before offering the loan. These institutions, which can now be taken over directly in highly elaborate forms by new states, took centuries to emerge.

It may seem obvious today that if a country has a constitution, it also needs a political mechanism to strike down unconstitutional laws. Typically, this task ("judicial review") will devolve on a court, whether it is a mixed court that also has other tasks, as in the United States, or a specialized constitutional court, as on the European continent. Historically, however, constitutions existed well before judicial review.[1] Although the constitution of the United States created a Supreme Court that was authorized to strike down state legislations, it was not expressly authorized to declare federal laws to be unconstitutional. When the court in 1803 arrogated that power to itself in *Marbury v. Madison*, it was essentially an act of bootstrapping. In 1854, the Norwegian Supreme Court also took it upon itself to exercise judicial review, which is not mentioned in the constitution of the country. In 1971, the French Constitutional Council authorized itself, against the express intentions of the writers of the constitution in force, to strike down legislation that violated the Declaration of the Rights of Man and of the Citizen from 1789. The Israeli Supreme Court has also given itself the right to strike down legislation that violates one of the country's Basic Laws, thus turning its partial constitution into a full-blown one. Although each of these decisions was controversial at the time, all but the last-mentioned have hardened into uncontested features of the institutional landscape.

Today, there is an expectation that leaders of repressive regimes will be held to account legally when they fall or step down. If the new domestic leaders do not take an initiative on their own, the international community may take on the task itself (Rwanda and the former Yugoslavia), exercise pressure on the successor regime (Indonesia), or create hybrid courts with both national and international judges (Sierra Leone and Cambodia). There is, today, something like an institution of transitional justice. If we go back in time, however, extrajudicial killing, for purposes of revenge or incapacitation, has always been the typical mode of dealing with leaders of repressive regimes. The decision by the allies in 1814 and 1815 to exile Napoleon rather than execute him was an important step in the process of "staying the hand of vengeance." At the end of World War II many allied leaders wanted the main Nazi criminals to be shot on sight as outlaws rather than being subject to trials. In the end, however, the Nuremberg trials offered a near-exemplary respect for the need to convict on evidence and to satisfy the requirements of due process. Some of the

---

[1] The Netherlands still does not have judicial review. Swedish judicial review is constrained by the constitutional proviso that a law has to be "obviously" unconstitutional for the court to strike it down. Presumably such laws would rarely be passed in the first place.

accused were in fact acquitted. In some German-occupied countries there were elements of "wild" popular justice in 1944–5, but they were quickly replaced by the rule of law. When the Communist regimes fell forty-four years later there was general agreement that in addressing their wrongdoings one should not emulate their unlawful practices.

The Problem of Monitoring

An organization may have *members* or *employees*. Members can also be employees, as in workers' cooperatives. Members interact horizontally, through the processes of arguing, bargaining, and voting that I discussed in the previous chapter. The vertical relations between employees and their superiors have a different character. To simplify, assume that the organization has a single executive ("the principal") and many employees ("the agents"). A *principal-agent problem* arises when, as is often the case, the principal and the agents have different interests. Workers may have an interest in a moderate work pace, whereas the manager may wish them to make a stronger effort. If he tries to make the two interests coincide by paying workers according to effort, he may find it difficult or costly to monitor how hard they are working. Traditionally, that was the task of the foreman, but how can the manager be sure that the foreman is not demanding bribes from the workers or using his authority to promote his own financial or sexual ends? The nineteenth-century workplace was often characterized as "the tyranny of the foreman." In such cases, who shall guard the guardians? As we shall see shortly, these problems may also arise when principal and agents coincide, as in workers' cooperatives.

Similarly, the head of a state agency has an interest in employees' being honest, in the sense of not taking or demanding bribes from the public. She also has an interest in efficiency, so that the size of the public sector can be kept to a minimum. Employees can have opposite interests in both respects. If they are motivated only by their economic self-interest, they will take bribes when they can get away with it. As a consequence of their interest in power, agents also have an incentive to swell the size of their departments and to multiply the number of subordinates. Again, monitoring may be difficult. The principal may sometimes catch an agent taking a bribe, but in general this is not a method she can rely on. She may try to reduce opportunities for corruption, for instance, by having competitive bids for public contracts, but this precaution does not help if agents tailor the contracts so as to favor particular suppliers. Because agents often have a near-monopoly on information, principals may be unable to tell which requests for more hirings are justified and which are not.

Subordinates are not the only ones that may have incentives out of line with the organization. American university presidents have had to step down when it turned out that they were awarding themselves huge salaries or had their homes redecorated at the organization's expense. One American vice president (Spiro Agnew) had to resign when he was exposed for corruption. Kleptocracy – the rule of thieves – has become an exceedingly familiar phenomenon across the world. Although they are principals in one sense, such leaders may also be subject to monitoring. Yet overseers (voters, boards of trustees, shareholders, the World Bank, or the International Monetary Fund) have often been conspicuously unsuccessful in regulating the behavior of chief executive officers or heads of state. As in other cases, they may lack either the *information* needed to correct excesses or the *incentive* to do so.

In workers' cooperatives, a conflict may arise between workers as principals and workers as agents. Speaking to the Social Science Congress in 1863 Sir James Kay Shuttleworth said, with respect to the cooperative Lancashire cotton mills:

> [Then] arose the formidable question – What benefits should the shareholders have in this mill beyond the ordinary profits? The first claim that was practically put forward in such societies was, that a preference should be given to the families of the shareholders in selecting the workers in the mill. . . . . He had witnessed on his own property the failure of one of these concerns. There was a desire to introduce into the concern the principle of cooperation to this extent, that the shareholders should have the advantage of the employment of their families in the mills. The immediate effect of that was this, that instead of producing a stricter discipline and that close attention to the working of machinery, which was

so necessary in cotton mills (and he might mention that the discipline of a regiment was inferior in strictness to that of a cotton mill), at their quarterly or half-yearly meetings most vexatious complaints were made by the workers against the overlookers, and an overlooker who had dared to discharge a worker who was a shareholder, was in extreme danger of being dismissed at the next meeting.[2]

Another frequently occurring problem in cooperatives arises from their reluctance to lay off their members in times of low demand. Commenting on the downfall of the Wolverhampton Plate-Locksmiths in 1878, a contemporary wrote that

> if the business had been carried on by a private manufacturer, he would probably have discharged the workmen for whom, from the falling off of the demand for plate-locks, he could not find profitable employment, and applied himself to develop the trade that remained. But this would have involved on the body of workers who formed the society an amount of self-sacrifice for which they were not prepared. Instead, they worked for stock, in the hope that the demand would revive. As it did not revive before their resources were exhausted, they inevitably came to grief. Debts multiplied upon them; the best workers fell away.

Solutions to the Principal-Agent Problem

Shirking, proliferation of hirings, corruption, and similar problems may be countered by acting either on the incentives of the agents or on their opportunities (Chapter 9). The latter solution is hard to implement. To be effective, an agent needs some independence and freedom of action. Slaves have rarely been used in occupations that demand application and care. It may prove impossible to structure the situation so that the agent

---

[2] In 1875 the managing director of the Ouseborn Co-Operative Engine Works Company made similar complaints to explain the failure of the company: "The time rules of the Ouseborn, including the rule that each day counts its own overtime, the excessive restrictions upon labour from a section of our men, the small proportion of our apprentices, the frequent discussions and deputations, the excessive amount of overtime required to enable us to finish our contracts, and generally, the want of discipline resulting from the impression that every man was his own master – all contributed to increase the cost of production."

is free to pursue the aims of the principal while literally unable to pursue his own. One may try to approximate this goal by having decision makers serve for such a short period that it is hard to bribe them. The jury system and the American electoral college (in its original conception) have been justified on these grounds (among others). Short tenure of elected officials (often combined with nonreeligibility) and frequent rotation of appointed officials are also supposed to reduce the opportunity for corruption. The latter practices have severe efficiency costs, however. By the time officials have finally become familiar enough with the job to do it well, they may have to leave it.

Acting on incentives may seem more promising. By rewarding hard work or imposing fines on shirkers, for instance, one may align the incentives of agents with those of the principal. In occupations in which individual effort can be measured by individual output, piece wages may solve the problem. Sometimes, however, the technology only allows the firm to measure the output of a group of workers. Also, the use of individual piece wages can be counterproductive. If you pay each member of a soccer team (or the attackers on the team) as a function of the number of goals he scores, the team as a whole will perform less efficiently. A good team player is one who will pass the ball to someone else in a better position to score. The firm might then try to solve the problem by establishing a team bonus system so that workers might have an incentive to monitor each other.

Yet if, as is often the case, the costs of monitoring exceed the benefits that accrue to the person who is responsible for it, he or she has no *material* incentive for monitoring. A soccer player may not find it worth the trouble (which might be considerable) to berate prima donna behavior by a team member. While a social norm against shirking may develop, the empirical evidence on this point is ambiguous. The norms are more likely to develop in small groups, both because members can more easily observe each other and because each member is more severely hurt by the free riding of any other member. Yet even here they may not emerge in a completely spontaneous manner (Chapter 22). The norm against prima donna behavior or selfish play in soccer may owe much to the strategies of the coach, who can punish players who think too much about themselves and too little about the team. There is anecdotal evidence, though, that players punish those who do not pass the ball to those are in a better position by not passing the ball to them.

The question of who shall guard the guardian, or monitor the monitors, might in theory be solved by something like a *circular system*, in which each person in a chain has a direct material incentive to punish the person on her left, since if she does not, she will be punished by the person on her right. In practice, no such arrangements seem to exist. Soccer players do pass the ball to those who pass it to those who do not. Free-riding temptations may, however, be mitigated by *trust*. If firms offer wages above the going rate, workers (or some of them) may respond by making an extra effort. The snag is that the firm may not have an incentive to set up this scheme. Although total output (and hence total income) will go up, so will the total wage bill. If the net result is lower profits, the firm is better off offering the competitive wage.

The Organization of Distrust

Political constitutions often aspire to be a circular system of checks and balances, in which the performance of each institution is monitored by another. This aspiration is not realized in all actual constitutions, perhaps not in any. The constitutional machinery usually rests on an "unmoved mover" or "unchecked checker," a part that is monitoring the performance of other parts while not being subject itself to monitoring. In the United States, the Supreme Court occupies this position. In other countries, it is occupied by parliament. In Romania, for instance, parliament can overrule decisions by the constitutional court if it strikes down its legislation (a legacy from the Communist era, when parliament was formally omnipotent and de facto impotent). In France, too, parliament was the unmoved mover until 1971. Yet within the Anglo-American tradition at least, constitutional design rests on the principle, formulated by David Hume, "It is ... a just political maxim, that every man must be supposed to be a knave." Constitutions, in this perspective, are a form of organized distrust.

The American constitution is perhaps the most elaborate expression of this attitude. Striking features of the debates at the 1787 Federal

Convention and the document they produced are the constant concern with the potential for corruption, bribes, and threats and the need to close any loopholes through which they might enter. To cite one example, the Special Committee on representation that reported on July 9 recommended that "as the present situation of the States may probably alter as well in point of wealth as in the number of their inhabitants, that the Legislature be authorized from time to time to augment ye. number of Representatives." In response, Edmund Randolph was "apprehensive that as the number was not to be changed till the Natl. Legislature should please, a pretext would never be wanting to postpone alterations, and keep the power in the hands of those possessed of it." Along similar lines, George Mason argued, "From the nature of man we may be sure, that those who have power in their hands will not give it up while they can retain it." More weakly, we should say with Hume that those in power are to be *assumed* to try to retain it. Although some politicians may (and all will claim to) be working for the common good, we should economize on trust. More strongly, we should assume that those who have power will use it to retain *and expand it* if they can. Constitutions, in this perspective, are devices for preventing them from doing that. It is not the only thing that constitutions do, but it is often one of the things they aim at doing.

The power of this normative framework to *explain* the adoption of actual constitutions depends on the extent to which framers pursue the common good rather than their particular interests or passions. As I noted toward the end of Chapter 13, one can certainly not take it for granted that they are exempt from the latter motivations. Yet the normative pressure to act *as if* they are motivated by reason – the civilizing force of hypocrisy – may be stronger in a constituent assembly than in an ordinary legislature. Also, as I argued in the previous chapter, the purchase of self-interest on the issues to be decided tends to be less in the constituent setting. For this reason, constituent assemblies operating behind closed doors may be able to reduce the distorting effect of passion without paying the cost of excessive interest-based bargaining.[3]

---

[3] I am not entirely comfortable with this negative view of passion. Hegel claimed that "nothing great in the world has been accomplished without passion." Tocqueville wrote that in times of crisis people either fall below or rise above their normal level. Moreover, impartiality does not exclude

Given this caveat, let me sketch a stylized example of how organized distrust could be embodied in a series of interlocking provisions. Many of the features are found in actual systems. Others are included mainly to illustrate the lengths to which one might have to go to close all possible loopholes.

1 To prevent the government from *engaging in political justice*, the constitution should either require juries for criminal trials or stipulate that judges be assigned randomly to cases (or selected by some other mechanical procedure). In the absence of clauses of this kind, the government could put its political opponents on trial and ensure their conviction by hand-picking the judge.

2 To prevent the government from *manipulating the electoral system*, the electoral law, down to quite specific details, should be written into the constitution and not be left to statutory determination. Redrawing electoral districts to take account of population changes could either be done by a mechanical formula or be entrusted to an independent commission. Recent American and French history shows many instances in which the government of the day has modified the electoral rules to stay in power.

3 To prevent the government from *manipulating the flow of information*, state-owned radio and television should be governed by independent commissions ("the British model"), not appointed by the government ("the French model"). Privately owned media should also be protected. Airwaves should be allocated by independent commissions. The government should be barred from rationing resources that are vital for the media such as paper and printer's ink, or one might entrust such decisions to an "independent rationing board." The combination of unmanipulated elections and unmanipulated media has been shown to be highly effective in preventing famines and other disasters. If those who are tempted to act contrary to the public interest know that their activities will be exposed to the electorate, which can then turn them out of office, they are less likely to engage in such behavior.

---

passion, as demonstrated by the French framers in 1789 who were "drunk with disinterestedness." One of the most impressive of them, the comte de Clermont-Tonnerre, said that "anarchy is a frightening yet necessary passage, and the only moment one can establish a new order of things. It is not in calm times that one can take uniform measures." Yet even though enthusiasm may produce admirable ends, it may undermine the clearheaded thinking needed to realize them.

4 To prevent the government from *manipulating monetary policy* as an instrument for reelection, that policy should be entrusted to an independent central bank. An alternative but less attractive solution would be to let monetary policy be decided by a computer program constructed by three monetary economists drawn randomly from the five top-ranked economics departments in the country and revised every five years.

5 To prevent dogmatic or ideological central bankers from *enacting disastrous monetary policies*, it should be possible to dismiss them if there is a supermajority (two-thirds or three-quarters) for doing so in parliament. They should have a limited tenure (unlike the former governors of the Italian Central Bank) and only be able to serve once (unlike the current Italian governor).

6 To prevent the government from *manipulating statistical information* as an instrument for reelection, data gathering should be entrusted to an independent Bureau of Statistics. In Britain, the Chancellor of the Exchequer has taken steps to boost trust in official figures by making the Office of National Statistics independent of government (*Financial Times*, December 2, 2005). A headline in the *New York Times* (September 22, 2002) said, "Some experts fear political influence on crime data agencies." Political pressures on the labor statistics have also been reported ("Bureau of Labor Statistics Should Be Investigated," *New York Post*, September 29, 2000). In subtler cases, the choice of an econometric forecasting model may also be at stake. Clearly, the less crime and the less unemployment people believe there is, and the better the prospects for growth, the better the chances of reelection for incumbents. In addition to barring the government from using monetary policy to manipulate the reality, one should prevent it from using statistics to manipulate beliefs about reality.

7 To prevent the government from *starving the opposition*, the main political parties should receive subsidies as a fixed function of their proportion of the votes and their proportion of the seats in parliament. The amount of subsidies should be fixed in the constitution and might be linked to the price of gold.[4]

---

[4] A corresponding desire to make the constitution as explicit and nonmanipulable as possible was behind Madison's desire to fix the salaries of federal judges "by taking for a standard wheat or some other thing of permanent value."

8   To prevent the government from *enacting self-serving legislation*, the constitution could stipulate that certain categories of laws should only take effect a certain time (one year or more) after being adopted. By this mechanism there would be created an artificial veil of ignorance, behind which even self-interested parties might be induced to take impartial measures.

9   To prevent the government from *bypassing these restrictions* by using its majority in parliament to amend the constitution, amendments should require supermajorities, delays, or both. The amendment clause itself should be entrenched, that is, be immune to amendment.

10 To prevent the government from *ignoring these restrictions*, as was formerly the case in France, the constitution should provide for judicial review by an independent Constitutional Court or Supreme Court.

11 To prevent the government from *manipulating judicial review* by increasing the number of judges on the Constitutional Court or the Supreme Court, that number should not be left to statute, as it is in the United States and several other countries, but be fixed in the constitution.

12 To prevent dogmatic or ideological judges on the Constitutional Court or the Supreme Court from *ignoring large popular majorities*, it should be possible to dismiss them if there is a supermajority (two-thirds or three-quarters) for doing so in parliament. Unlike what is the case for the justices on the American Supreme Court, their length of tenure should be limited. Also, they should not be reeligible.

As this example indicates, a constitution can be an intricate machinery. If one of the interlocking pieces is missing, others may be rendered inefficacious or harmful (see later discussion). At the same time, there is a real danger that the constitution could be so rigid that it prevents the political system from responding to emergencies. Constitutional constraints on monetary policy or on electoral laws might, in a given case, be disastrous. At the Federal Convention in Philadelphia George Mason observed that "though he had a mortal hatred to paper money, yet as he could not foresee all emergences, he was unwilling to tie the hands of the Legislature. He observed that the late war could not have been carried on, had such a prohibition existed." Similarly, when in 1946 the Italian parliament decided against constitutionalizing monetary stability, one of the objections referred to the need for the government to be free to act in times of war. In 1945, de Gaulle manipulated the French electoral system to keep the Communists out of power. Commenting many years later on a proposal to write the electoral law into the constitution, he said that "one never knows what might happen. There might be, one day, once again, reasons to revert to proportional voting for the sake of the national interest, as in 1945. We should not tie our hands." In retrospect, France ought to be grateful that the constitution did not include the electoral law.

The problem can be summarized in two famous observations on the American Constitution. Commenting on the Ku Klux Klan Act of 1871, John Potter Stockton said that "constitutions are chains with which men bind themselves in their sane moments that they may not die by a suicidal hand in the day of their frenzy." In 1949, Robert Jackson stated that "the bill of rights is not a suicide pact." There is no easy way to ensure that a constitution intended as a suicide prevention device does not one day turn into a suicide pact.

The Problem of the Second Best

Disregarding this issue, let us now assume that if the twelve conditions I have enumerated (or others of the same general kind) are satisfied, the political system will in some sense, which for present purposes we need not make very precise, be *optimal*. In the real world, this outcome is unlikely to be achieved. It is hard to get everything right. One might, however, want to *approximate* the optimum as closely as possible, on the apparently reasonable assumption that the more of the conditions for optimality that are satisfied, the closer one will get to the optimum. This assumption is false. Under very general conditions, it is not true that a situation in which many, but not all, of the conditions for an optimum are fulfilled is necessarily, or is even likely to be, superior to a situation in which fewer are fulfilled. Referring to the twelve devices cited earlier, it is not clear a priori that judicial review without a check on the judges is better than no judicial review at all, or independent central banks with no check on the bankers better than a system that leaves monetary policy in the hands of the government.

Tocqueville's discussion of the *ancien régime* in France may be read in this perspective. That system was characterized by a number of features that would be absent in a well-ordered society. The royal administration had wide, ill-defined, and arbitrary powers. The venality of office made a rational bureaucracy impossible. The obstruction of the *parlements*, highly politicized courts mostly acting for self-serving reasons, made it difficult to pursue consistent policies. Yet, Tocqueville argued, given the first of these features, the presence of the other two was in fact beneficial:

> The government, in its desire to turn everything into money, had first put most public offices up for sale and thus deprived itself of the faculty to grant and revoke them at will. One of its passions had thus greatly interfered with the success of the other: its greed had worked counter to its ambition. In order to act it was therefore continually reduced to using instruments it had not fashioned itself and could not break. Hence it often saw its most absolute wishes enfeebled in execution. This bizarre and faulty constitution of public functions took the place of any kind of political guarantee against the omnipotence of the central government. It was a strange and ill-constructed sort of dike that divided the government's power and blunted its impact. . . . The irregular intervention of the courts in government, which often disrupted the proper administration of affairs, thus served at times to safeguard liberty: it was a great ill that limited a still greater one.

In his analysis of English law in the eighteenth century, James Fitzjames Stephen noted that excessive emphasis on technical details of the law "did mitigate, though in an irrational, capricious manner, the excessive severity of the old criminal laws." Commenting on Islamic criminal law, he similarly wrote that it "mitigated the extravagant harshness of its provisions by rules of evidence which practically excluded the possibility of carrying them into effect." Similarly, the Ottoman empire, tsarist rule in Russia, Mussolini's Italy, and Franco's Spain have all been characterized as "despotism tempered by incompetence." Compared to the relentlessly efficient Nazi Germany these regimes were, in fact, benign.

Tocqueville also noted when *ancien régime* officials tried to replace the hated *corvée* (forced labor on the highways) with a tax to be used to maintain the roads, they gave it up out of fear that "once this fund had been established, there was nothing to prevent the Treasury from diverting it to its own use, with the result that soon taxpayers would be saddled with a new tax and the duty of forced labor as well." This phenomenon is quite common. When politicians propose that publicly funded hospitals must give priority in health queues to individuals who could be helped to get back into the work force, they usually promise to channel the social gains thus generated back to the hospital, so that other patients will benefit rather than suffer. Hospital administrators tend to be skeptical of such proposals, suspecting that the gains will simply go to fill government coffers. In California, proposals to allocate water to the farms that can make best use of it, to generate a surplus that could be used to improve the water supply to other farmers, have met with similar skepticism. A situation with two suboptimal elements – an inefficient priority system for allocating scarce goods and a government that does not respect its promises (or those of its predecessor) – may be better than one in which the first is removed.

These cases are a bit like what happens when policymakers eliminate animals that create a nuisance for human populations, only to find that an even greater nuisance is created by the organisms they kept in check. Thus when Mao Tse-tung decided to eliminate sparrows because they ate grain, he had to reimport them later from the Soviet Union when the pests they kept down flourished, with catastrophic ecological results. Societies, no less than ecological systems, may have apparently absurd or noxious features whose removal might produce even greater ills. It is probably for this reason, among others, that Edmund Burke and his followers have been so adamant in their criticism of rationalist institutional design.

This line of reasoning can be taken too far. When workers gained the right to vote, opponents argued that the elimination of an injustice toward the workers would destabilize society in all sorts of ways and create an even greater injustice toward the rich, whose wealth the poor could be expected to confiscate. This argument puts on the same foot two sets of considerations that do not have the same weight. But as this is a book about explaining social phenomena, not about assessing them from a normative point of view, I shall not pursue the matter.

❨❨❨

BIBLIOGRAPHICAL NOTE

I take the distinction between organizations and institutions from C. Offe, "Institutions' role in the distribution and control of social power," in I. Shapiro, S. Skowronek, and D. Gavlin (eds), *The Art of the State* (New York University Press, 2006). The "rise of the market" is a central theme in D. North, *Structure and Change in Economic History* (New York: Norton, 1981). The emergence of judicial review is the topic of E. Smith (ed.), *Constitutional Justice Under Old Constitutions* (The Hague: Kluwer, 1995). For the emergence of transitional justice, see G. J. Bass, *Stay the Hand of Vengeance* (Cambridge, MA: Harvard University Press, 2001). A useful reader on (what I somewhat idiosyncratically call) organizations is C. Ménard (ed.), *The Political Economy of Institutions* (Cheltenham: Edward Elgar, 2004). The problem of aligning individual and organizational incentives is the topic of J.-J. Laffont and J. Tirole, *A Theory of Incentives in Procurement and Regulation* (Cambridge, MA: MIT Press, 1994). A comprehensive handbook on corruption is A. Heidenheimer, M. Johnston, and V. LeVine (eds.), *Political Corruption* (New Brunswick, NJ: Transaction Publishers, 1989). The references to nineteenth-century English cooperatives are taken from B. Jones, *Co-operative Production* (Oxford University Press, 1894; New York: Kelley, 1968). The idea of a "circular system" of mutual monitoring is discussed in E. Kandel and E. Lazear, "Peer pressure and partnership," *Journal of Political Economy* 100 (1992), 801–17, and in R. Calvert, "Rational actors, equilibrium, and social institutions," in J. Knight and I. Sened (eds.), *Explaining Social Institutions* (Ann Arbor: University of Michigan Press, 1995) (reprinted in Ménard, *The Political Economy of Institutions*). The relative importance of trust and incentives in firms is discussed in E. Fehr and A. Falk, "Psychological foundation of incentives," *European Economic Review* 46 (2002), 687–724. The Humean origins of the American constitution are traced in M. White, *Philosophy*, The Federalist, *and the Constitution* (Oxford University Press, 1987). The quote from de Gaulle is taken from A. Peyrefitte, *C'était de Gaulle*, vol. 1 (Paris: Fayard, 1994), p. 452. The idea of the second best was introduced in R. G. Lipsey and K. Lancaster, "The general theory of the second best," *Review of Economic Studies* 24 (1956), 11–32. I discuss Tocqueville's analyses of the *ancien régime* in "Tocqueville on 1789: Preconditions, precipitants, and triggers," in C. Welch (ed.), *The Cambridge Companion to Tocqueville* (Cambridge University Press, 2006). The passages quoted from Stephen are in his *History of the Criminal Law of England* (London: Macmillan, 1883; Buffalo, NY: Hein, 1964), vol. 1, p. 284, and vol. 3, p. 293. The reference to Mao Tse-tung is in J. Chang and J. Halliday, *Mao: The Unknown Story* (New York: Knopf, 2005), pp. 430–1. I state my views on the normative basis for institutional change in Chapter 4 of *Solomonic Judgments* (Cambridge University Press, 1989).

CONCLUSION: IS SOCIAL SCIENCE POSSIBLE?

❀ ❀ ❀

What Counts as Science?

The answer to the question whether a social science is possible, or perhaps already exists, depends on the criteria for what is to count as science. An external criterion could be the following: a discipline has become a science when (1) there is general agreement among its practitioners at any point on what is true, what is false, what is conjectural, and what is unknown within its domain; (2) there is a process of cumulative progress by which theories and explanations, when discarded, are discarded forever; (3) the main concepts and theories can be expressed in terms clear and explicit enough to be understood by anyone who is willing to expend time and effort; and (4) the "classics" of the discipline are read mainly by historians of sciences. As Alfred Whitehead said, "A science that hesitates to forget its founders is lost."

This description is intended to capture roughly the status of the contemporary natural sciences. Criterion (1) is not literally and fully satisfied by any of these disciplines. Controversies exist, for instance, over string theory, punctuated equilibrium, or the relative importance of nature versus nurture in human development. Yet the depth of disagreement is easily exaggerated by those outside the relevant scientific community, who may not appreciate the huge amount of shared agreed-upon knowledge that is the background of controversy and sometimes mistake tentative explorations for definite claims. Criterion (2) is usually satisfied. There are very few if any reversals in the history of natural science, no neo-Newtonians rebelling against Einstein or neo-Lamarckians rebelling against Darwin. The transformation of what may have been semi-obscure or awkward theories when first formulated into easily assimilated textbook material testifies to the general satisfaction of (3). With rare exceptions, mainly in biology (Darwin, d'Arcy Wentworth Thompson, Claude Bernard), criterion (4) is also satisfied.

Using these criteria I shall now propose an assessment of the soft, the qualitative, and the quantitative social sciences. After some brief dismissive remarks on soft social science, I shall make a case for qualitative social science. More controversially, I shall also make a case against quantitative social science, at least in some of its more prominent forms. The proponent of qualitative social science, therefore, is in the uncomfortable position of fighting a two-front war, with the constant risk of one opponent accusing him of being in league with the other.

Soft Social Science

The "soft" social sciences have more in common with certain forms of literary criticism (or with literature) than with empirical qualitative investigations. Postmodernism, postcolonial theory, subaltern theories, deconstructionism, Kleinian or Lacanian psychoanalysis, and similar theories have been exposed for the obscurantisms they are by many writers, perhaps most effectively by Alan Sokal. As he remarked in an interview, the lack of a shared language for rational discussion makes it impossible to criticize these pseudotheorists head-on. Instead, you have to make them shoot themselves in the foot, as he did most effectively by getting one of their journals to publish an article he submitted on the hermeneutics of quantum gravity, chock-full of meaningless but impressive-sounding jargon.

Although members of these coteries may develop a style of discussion among themselves that suggests a degree of satisfaction of criterion (1), it merely amounts to a form of pseudointersubjectivity in which shared verbal reflexes masquerade for rational agreement. Criteria (2)–(4) are rarely if ever satisfied. No ideas seem to be discarded forever. Most striking, perhaps, is the nonsatisfaction of (3). Derrida may dazzle by his language, but his "teachings" are not *teachable*. There are no "how-to-do-it" textbooks of deconstructionism (although there are many surveys or "mappings" and "negotiations"), largely because its practitioners tend to proceed by insinuation and rhetorical questions rather than stick their necks out to make definite assertions. Maybe the closest to a textbook is Frederick Crew's set of parodies *Postmodern Pooh*. With regard to (4), the cult of ancestors, with obligatory references and exegeses, seems to be mandatory. (In this paragraph, I have obviously been preaching to the converted.)

Qualitative Social Science

Within qualitative social science I include the bulk of historical writings as well as works that take the form of "case studies" rather than "large n" studies. I believe the best training for any social scientist is to read widely and deeply in history, choosing works for the intrinsic quality of the argument rather than the importance or relevance of the subject matter. Here are some models: James Fitzgerald Stephen, *A History of the Criminal law of England*; E. P. Thompson, *The Making of the English Working Class*; G. E. M. de Ste Croix, *The Class Struggles in the Ancient Greek World*; Joseph Levenson *Confucian China and Its Modern Fate*; Paul Veyne, *Le pain et le cirque*; G. Lefebvre, *La grande peur*; Keith Thomas, *Religion and the Decline of Magic*; Tocqueville, *L'ancien régime et la Révolution*; Max Weber, *Agrarverhältnisse im Altertum*; Gordon Wood, *The Radicalism of the American Revolution*; Jean Egret, *La pré-révolution française*; Denis Crouzet, *Les guerriers de Dieu*; or Martin Ostwald, *From Popular Sovereignty to the Sovereignty of Law* (I have stuck my neck out a bit by including some not-yet-acknowledged classics). What these writers and others of their stature have in common is that they combine utter authority in factual matters with an eye both for potential generalizations and for potential counterexamples to generalizations. By virtue of their knowledge they can pick out the "telling detail" as well as the "robust anomaly," thus providing both stimulus and reality check for would-be generalists.

The same is true for authors of "case studies," among which one of the greatest remains Tocqueville's *Democracy in America*. Although it does not fit neatly into the category, I would also include Joseph Schumpeter, *Capitalism, Socialism, and Democracy*. A seemingly eccentric but, I believe, compelling candidate is Arthur Young's *Travels in France*, covering the years 1787, 1788, and 1789. These are "character portraits" of whole societies or regimes, all of them with a comparative perspective. Marc Bloch, *La société féodale*, also belongs here. Alexander Zinoviev's *The Yawning Heights* is not exactly a character portrait of Soviet Communism, but a caricature in the good sense of the word – eliminating inessentials and isolating core features by exaggerating them. A fully documented version is S. Courtois et al., *Le livre noir du communisme*. The unfolding trilogy by Richard Evans on the Third Reich promises to do for the specific regime of Nazism what Robert Paxton did in *What Is Fascism?* for this more generic regime. Richard Bosworth's *Mussolini* and *Mussolini's Italy*, if read in conjunction with Evans's books, provide striking insights into the difference between a regime whose evil, while real, was largely low grade and one that was evil to the core.

Historical analysis and case studies do not merely provide raw materials for generalization, but often themselves contain implicit generalizations that the author has left for the reader to sort out. Tocqueville, for instance, was a master of the latent generalization. Because of a combination of the historian's and the aristocrat's arrogance he did not deign to spell out his theoretical scaffolding but pretended he was merely putting one foot in front of another. Although *Democracy in America* constantly relies on the desire-opportunity scheme for explaining behavior, it is never stated in so many words. Although *L'ancien régime et la Révolution* relies heavily on the distinction between envy and hatred in the analysis of class relations, readers must figure out for themselves the systematically different causes and effects of these two emotions.

Under the heading of qualitative social science I also include writings that make these generalizations *explicit*. In discussing them I shall proceed not by listing authors or works, but by returning to the puzzles I listed in the Introduction. Very importantly, all the "answers" are subject to the second caveat I mentioned in the Introduction: they satisfy only the minimal condition of implying the explanandum. In some cases I would stick my neck out and say that the explanation I offer is probably the correct one, but in others I would not.

I↬The Mind

- Why do some gamblers believe than when red has come up five times in a row, red is more likely than black to come up next? *Answer*: because they are subject to the availability heuristic.
- Why do other gamblers believe than when red has come up five times in a row, black is more likely than red to come up next? *Answer*: because they are subject to the representativeness heuristic.
- Why do preferences sometimes change through the sheer passage of time? *Answer*: either because of hyperbolic discounting or because of the short half-life of the emotions that generated them.
- Why do many people who seem to believe in the afterlife want it to arrive as late as possible? *Answer*: because their belief is not the kind of belief that serves as a premise for action but merely provides them with some peace of mind whenever they think about death.
- Why are people reluctant to acknowledge, to themselves and others, that they are envious? *Answer*: because they care about their self-image and because envy, in most societies, is near the bottom of the normative hierarchy of motivations.
- Why are people reluctant to acknowledge, to themselves and others, that they are ignorant? *Answer*: because human beings are pattern-seeking animals and because confessing ignorance on important issues produces psychic discomfort.
- Why, among sixteenth-century converts to Calvinism, did the belief that people were predestined either to heaven or to hell induce greater peace of mind than the belief that one could achieve salvation through good works? *Answer*: because magical thinking made them believe that by joining the church they could cause God to have chosen them to be among the elect.
- Why is it (sometimes) true that "who has offended, cannot forgive"? *Answer*: because prideful individuals are so reluctant to admit they have done wrong that they invent reasons why the offended person deserved and continues to deserve his fate.
- Why is shame more important than guilt in some cultures? *Answer*: because a society that has not conceptualized guilt will also display less guilt behavior.

- Why did the French victory in the 1998 soccer World Cup generate so much joy in the country, and why did the fact that the French team did not qualify beyond the opening rounds in 2002 cause so much despondency? *Answer*: because surprise is a magnifier of both positive and negative emotions.
- Why do women often feel shame after being raped? *Answer*: because victims often share the "blame the victim" attitude that follows from the belief that the world is fundamentally a just place.
- Why do humiliating rituals of initiation produce greater rather than lesser loyalty to the group into which one is initiated? *Answer*: because the belief that one has endured great pain for nothing would create cognitive dissonance.

II↪Action

- Why do more Broadway shows receive standing ovations today than twenty years ago? *Answer*: because audiences need to feel that they are getting value for their money.
- Why may punishments increase rather than decrease the frequency of the behavior they target? *Answer*: because the use of harsh punishments causes hate that may offset the fear.
- Why are people unwilling to break self-imposed rules even when it makes little sense to follow them? *Answer*: because they are afraid that a single exception might cause the rule to unravel.
- Why is the pattern of revenge "Two eyes for an eye" instead of "An eye for an eye"? *Answer*: because of loss aversion.
- Why is the long-term yield on stocks much larger than that on bonds (i.e., why does not the value of stocks rise to equalize the yields)? *Answer*: because of a combination of loss aversion and "decision myopia."
- Why do suicide rates go down when dangerous medications are sold in blister packs rather than bottles? *Answer*: because many desires are so short-lived that by the time one has opened the blister pack the suicidal impulse has ended.
- Why did none of thirty-eight bystanders call the police when Kitty Genovese was beaten to death? *Answer*: because each of them

thought that since nobody else intervened the situation was probably not very serious.

- Why did some individuals hide or rescue Jews under the Nazi regimes? *Answer*: because they were asked and were ashamed to refuse.
- Why did President Chirac call early elections in 1997, only to lose his majority in parliament? *Answer*: because he did not anticipate that the voters would derive information from the announcement of early elections that would cause them to vote against him.
- Why are some divorcing parents willing to share child custody even when their preferred solution is sole custody, which they are likely to get were they to litigate? *Answer*: because they are risk averse.
- Why are poor people less likely to emigrate? *Answer*: because they cannot afford the travel costs and cannot use themselves as collateral for a loan.
- Why do some people save in Christmas accounts that pay no interest and do not allow for withdrawal before Christmas? *Answer*: because they know that if they put their savings in a regular account, hyperbolic discounting might induce early withdrawal.
- Why do people pursue projects, such as building the Concorde airplane, that have negative expected value? *Answer*: because of pridefulness or because of loss aversion.
- Why in "transitional justice" (when agents of an autocratic regime are put on trial after the transition to democracy) are those tried immediately after the transition sentenced more severely than those who are tried later? *Answer*: because of the short half-life of the retributive emotions.
- Why, in Shakespeare's play, does Hamlet delay taking revenge until the last act? *Answer*: because Hamlet is subject to weakness of will and because the tension could not be resolved before the end of the play.

III⁀Lessons from the Natural Sciences

- Why are parents much more likely to kill adopted children and stepchildren than to kill their biological children? *Answer*: because only the latter carry their genes.

- Why is sibling incest so rare, given the temptations and opportunities? *Answer*: because natural selection has favored a mechanism inhibiting sexual desire for same-age members of the opposite sex in the same household.
- Why do people invest their money in projects undertaken by other agents even when the latter are free to keep all the profits for themselves? *Answer*: because group selection has favored a tendency to cooperate.
- Why do people take revenge at some material cost to them and with no material benefits? *Answer*: because group selection has favored a tendency to punish noncooperators.
- Why do people jump to conclusions beyond what is warranted by the evidence? *Answer*: because natural selection has favored pattern seeking.

IV ⌒ Interaction

- Why do supporters of a Socialist Party sometimes vote Communist and thereby prevent their party from winning? *Answer*: because each of them is the victim of a "younger sibling syndrome" that prevents him or her from realizing that others might do the same.
- Why do some newly independent countries adopt as their official language that of their former imperialist oppressor? *Answer*: because in a country with many local languages the language of the colonial power is everybody's second-ranked option.
- Why are ice creams stalls often located beside each other in the middle of the beach, when customers would be better off and the sellers no worse off with a more spread-out location? *Answer*: because it is individually rational for each seller to move to the middle regardless of what the other does.
- Why does an individual vote in elections when his or her vote is virtually certain to have no effect on the outcome? *Answer*: because the voter is subject to magical thinking or acts on the categorical imperative.
- Why are economically successful individuals in modern Western societies usually slimmer than the average person? *Answer*: because

they believe (correctly) that other people entertain the (false) belief that people who lack self-control in one domain are likely to lack self-control across the board.

- Why do people refrain from transactions that could make everybody better off, as when they abstain from asking a person in the front of a bus queue whether he is willing to sell his place? *Answer*: because people are more averse to open displays of economic inequality than to hidden ones.
- Why did President Nixon try to present himself to the Soviets as being prone to irrational behavior? *Answer*: because this behavior would lend credibility to threats of mutual destruction that the Soviets otherwise might not have believed.
- Why do military commanders sometimes burn their bridges (or their ships)? *Answer*: because they expect that their opponent, knowing that they will be unable to retreat, will abstain from a costly fight.
- Why do people often attach great importance to intrinsically insignificant matters of etiquette? *Answer*: because they think that someone who deviates from the norms does not care what they think about him.
- Why do passengers tip taxi drivers and customers tip waiters even when visiting a foreign city to which they do not expect to return? *Answer*: because the thought that others think badly about them is painful.
- Why do firms invest in large inventories even when they do not anticipate any interruption of production? *Answer*: because they expect that the investment will deter the workers from striking and thereby ensure that there is no interruption.
- Why, in a group of students, would each think that others have understood an obscure text better than she has? *Answer*: because each of them is the victim of an "older sibling syndrome" that makes her think that if other students do not seek assistance it is not because they are shy.
- Why are votes in many political assemblies taken by roll call? *Answer*: because advocates of popular measures use the procedure to deter those who might otherwise vote against them.

- Why is logrolling more common in ordinary legislatures than in constituent assemblies? *Answer*: because logrolling is sustained by tit-for-tat behavior that requires ongoing interaction over longer periods.

How does qualitative social science fare on the criteria (1)–(4) that I set out earlier? Taking them in inverse order, the classics are not obsolete. I would find it hard to take seriously someone who claimed that classical works are not worth taking seriously today because their findings, when accurate, are fully incorporated into current thinking. They have much more than antiquarian interest. I do not claim, though, that a dialogue with past masters is the only or the best way of generating new insights. Thomas Schelling, for instance, does not seem, in any obvious way at least, to have been standing on anyone's shoulders. Kenneth Arrow may have rediscovered and generalized Condorcet's insight, but he was not influenced by him. The work of Daniel Kahneman and Amos Tversky was as far as I know not generated by knowledge of any precursors. When I once had the occasion to point out to Tversky that one of his distinctions (between "the endowment effect" and "the contrast effect") had been anticipated by Montaigne and by Hume, he replied only that he was happy to be in such good company. Since the scholars I have just named are responsible for what were arguably the most decisive advances in social science over the last fifty years, one obviously cannot argue that the dialogue with the past is the only road to new insight. For another example, when Tocqueville set out to write the *Ancien régime*, he deliberately abstained, he said, from reading any of the previous writings on the subject, limiting himself to archives and to readings that were contemporaneous with the events he studied. He would rather, he said, have to rediscover some truths found by others than be unduly influenced by them. Although there is evidence that he did in fact peek at what had been written earlier, his masterpiece for the most part owed little to others.

This being said, the dialogue with the past can be immensely fruitful, if only to identify the positions one has to refute. It is hard to imagine that non-Marxists such as Weber or Schumpeter could have written what they did if they had not read Marx closely. Direct or positive influence is also common, of course. It seems likely that some recent theories of the evolution of property systems were directly influenced by David Hume, rather than simply claiming him as a precursor. Paul Veyne's work on the psychology of tyranny in antiquity owes much to Hegel's analysis of the master-slave relation. George Ainslie, who has done much to render one of Freud's basic insights analytically persuasive, might not have arrived at his ideas but for Freud's earlier, inchoate version. I suspect that Bentham's *Political Tactics* is still insufficiently mined. In these cases, as in all the others I have in mind, the ideas inspired by the classics have to stand on their own once arrived at. The good use of the classics does not include arguments from authority.

Qualitative social science, in most of the instances I have cited, passes criterion (3) with flying colors. What one might call "the analytical turn" in social science does not in my view rest on the use of quantitative methodology but on a near-obsessive concern with clarity and explicitness. (The concern can take a fully obsessive form among some analytical philosophers.) The importance of distinguishing between conceptual links and causal links among the objects of study is becoming increasingly recognized. "Context" is increasingly read as "fog" rather than as "a rich environment." Compared to earlier scholarship, there is much less essentialism; scholars less frequently ask what democracy or socialism "really" is. There is an acknowledgment that while definitions are to some extent constrained by usage, they do not attempt to capture underlying essences. They are arbitrary stipulations to be judged only by how well they enable us to come up with good explanations for interesting phenomena.

There is also, I believe (or hope), a trend away from what one might call "nondeductive abstract" thinking. In order to be honest, abstract reasoning has to subject itself to the discipline either of deductive logic or of a constant reference to facts that show that the abstract propositions have an application and *make a difference*. In the past, abstractions often took on a life of their own. The meaning of terms could change in the course of an argument, allowing for invalid inferences. Marx, for instance, "deduced" private property from alienated labor as follows: since under capitalism the product does not "belong to" the worker, in the sense that work is not meaningful, it has to "belong to" – be the property of – someone else, the capitalist. A beneficial effect of the relentless professionalization of social science in most educational institutions of the West is to make it much harder to get away with this kind of thing. Appeals to analogy have also become less prevalent, although not absent. While the idea of "human capital" is a valuable extension of the idea of physical capital, the same cannot be said about "consumption capital" (Gary Becker), "cultural capital" (Pierre Bourdieu), and "social capital" (Robert Putnam). At best, these are useless and harmless metaphors; at worst, they open fruitless avenues of research and suggest false causal hypotheses.

It is harder to assess the extent to which qualitative social science satisfies criterion (2). Among historians (including those who write character portraits of a regime), opinions wax and wane. Consider for instance the idea that the Terror was incipient in the French Revolution from the beginning versus the claim that it was the result of the preventable ascent of Robespierre and the equally preventable flight of the king that delegitimized the monarchy and brought about the revolutionary wars. Maybe, according to the latter view, if Mirabeau had lived, none of this would have happened. At any given time, there are some French historians holding either view, but the majoritarian view cycles. Today's discarded view may be tomorrow's dominant one. It is hard to think of any major historical question that has not generated, and does not continue to generate, similar fluctuations. This will presumably always be the case. Even when the data are given and can be fully surveyed, as is approximately the case for ancient history, new generalizations generated by the nonhistorical social sciences may confirm some interpretations at the expense of others.

In the nonhistorical sciences, there is clearly progress, but not of knowledge in a literal sense, Consider again our understanding of why rational agents may want to discard some of their options, for example, by burning their bridges. The insight that such apparently self-limiting behavior can be *fully* rational behavior against an adversary, and not merely a rational protection against one's own irrational propensities, is an irreversible gain in understanding. How many actual episodes of bridge burning or ship burning the idea allows us to explain is another matter. A commander might, as Cortes did, burn his ships simply to prevent the troops from taking flight. The insight into the possibility of cycling majorities is an irreversible one, but the number of actual cases to which it applies is arguably small. The "discovery" – it is more like naming a common preanalytical intuition – that emotions have a short half-life will not be undone, but in any given case there may be mechanisms working in other directions that offset the spontaneous decay. Even if a dominant explanation of a given event or episode is discarded and then resurrected, the building blocks or mechanisms at work in the discarding and resurrection remain. The repertory, or the size of the toolbox, does not shrink.

The qualitative social sciences do not do well with respect to criterion (1). As noted, there can be – in fact there almost always is – disagreement within a given generation of historians. Even disregarding political views that might cause Marxists and liberals to view the Terror differently, there is plenty of room for scholarly controversy. Imputing motivations and beliefs to historical actors, for instance, is a very tricky business. Behavior that one historian takes as a naïve expression of mental states will by another be taken to be strategic. A French aristocrat in exile during the Terror might say that he believes the monarchy will be reinstated soon, yet take out a long lease on an apartment. His contemporaries and the historian are less likely to think him sincere than they are with respect to one who takes out a succession of short leases, yet even the latter may in fact have acted in this way to create an impression of unshakable optimism. His enemies are, in any case, certain to claim he did. Unless the historian is lucky enough to find a document that is unlikely to have a strategic purpose, such as a memento written by the historical actor to herself, the issue can only be resolved by *judgment*. And although good historians are good partly because they have good judgment, they can err.

Within the nonhistorical qualitative social sciences, there can also be substantial disagreements. Mainstream economists sometimes claim that many of the findings of behavioral economics that seem to constitute evidence of irrationality are due to the fact that they are mostly obtained in experimental settings. For a variety of reasons, what people do in artificial laboratory settings may not correspond to their spontaneous behavior in everyday life. Behavioral economists have tried to organize the experiments to meet this objection, by raising the stakes, insulating the subjects from social pressure from other subjects and from the experimenter, and allowing for learning over time. The objection has also been made that subjects mechanically transfer responses that are adaptive outside the laboratory into the experimental setting, where they are maladaptive, for instance by using tit-for-tat strategies in one-shot experiments in which they make no sense. Behavioral economists have responded that there is nothing mechanical about the behavior of the subjects in the laboratory, who can be shown to be capable of a great deal of incentive-based fine-tuning. These are ongoing debates, about which it is hard for a nonspecialist to have an opinion. If I tend to side with the behavioral economists, it may be, to some extent, on the nonintellectual grounds that the opponent of my opponent is my friend.

Quantitative Social Science

I turn now to the quantitative social sciences. These are of three varieties: measurement, data analysis, and modeling. The three are linked, as data analysis often requires measurement (to establish the data) and frequently requires modeling (to tell us which data to look for). I shall focus on modeling, since I know too little about measurement and data analysis, but first a few words about the latter two.

Measuring entities such as consumption per capita, unemployment, the prevalence of corruption, or what the public thinks about the death penalty is an intrinsically difficult operation. For measurements of consumption to allow for comparisons over time and across countries, one has to consider that consumers in different times and places may purchase different items with the same income, that their incomes differ, and that the goods available for purchase may differ. Measuring unemployment is difficult if there is a large underground economy, a large student population, a large incarcerated population, or many people who have given up looking for a job. Measurements of corruption are usually based on perceived levels of corruption, as determined by expert assessments and opinion surveys. For obvious reasons, it is hard to get independent evidence to assess the reliability of these sources. Even when they converge, they might do so because they are subject to a common bias. The measurement of public opinion presupposes that there is stable opinion to be measured. It is well known, however, that irrelevant changes in the questions can make big differences for the response. "Do you favor A?" elicits very different answers from "Do you favor A if the alternative is B?" even when it is clear that B is the only alternative to A. For an example let A be a country's entry into the European Union and B be nonentry. These problems may very considerably affect the robustness of data analysis.

Data analysis (by which I mean statistical analysis) is in a sense the core of modern social science. If our interest is in studying large-scale social phenomena, we know that we shall always be dealing with populations that are heterogeneous in a number of respects, such as health, income, family status, preferences, and place of residence. Any deterministic prediction to the effect that when exposed to external shock X (e.g., an increase in the marginal tax rate) *all* individuals respond by behavior B (e.g., by reducing their labor supply) is doomed to defeat. Instead, one tries to determine how *likely* it is that an individual in a given category will respond in a certain way, by establishing the correlation between membership in that category and the response. These are often highly technical exercises.

They can also be dangerous exercises, in the sense of presenting a number of traps that even skilled scholars may fall into. In Chapters 1 and 2, I briefly mentioned five: data mining, curve fitting, arbitrariness in the measurement of dependent or independent variables, the problem of distinguishing correlation from causation, and the difficulty of identifying the direction of causation. The common practice of using "lagged" values of the variables, correlating the value of one variable at time t with the value of another at time $t + n$, creates further opportunities for tinkering. In addition, the heterogeneity of units of analysis may be a problem. In a statistical analysis of the causes of war, it is not obvious that World War I and World War II ought to be counted on a par with a "soccer war" between two Latin American countries. One might also, however, want to question the practice of eliminating anomalous cases as "outliers" in order to improve the fit. A further problem is that of selection bias, which can arise for instance if opinion polls are based on telephone interviews, which exclude individuals who have no telephone or for some reason do not answer calls.

It is impossible for a nonspecialist such as I to say how often social scientists fall into these and other traps of data analysis. The gold standard has to be prediction or "postdiction," which predicts one part of the observations from analysis performed on another part. Merely finding a pattern in the data is less persuasive, given the endless possibilities for tinkering and fiddling. These, too, could in principle be reduced by scholars' precommitting themselves publicly both to hypotheses and to procedures ahead of the actual analysis. To my knowledge, this device is rarely used.

Modeling is a deductive exercise, which begins with assumptions and concludes with predictions. In the social sciences rational-choice modeling is the most common form, but far from the only one. Increasingly, social scientists propose evolutionary models that do not presuppose rational or even intentional responses to events. Social scientists have also proposed more mechanical models of behavior, that is, models without clear foundations or justifications. The English physicist Lewis Richardson, for instance, proposed a model of the arms race based on two linear differential equations that had no clear psychological rationale. I limit myself to rational-choice modeling of social phenomena.

Rational-choice modeling is pervasive in economics, in which it is now applied well beyond the traditional fields of consumer and producer behavior. There are for instance the economics of suicide, the economics of church attendance, and, more generally, the economic analysis of any activity that in one way or another involves *choice*. The tendency is to remove the conceptual wedge that separates intentional action from rational action: if there is an opportunity for choice, it is assumed that it will be exercised rationally. In political science, rational-choice theory is certainly dominant in the sense of commanding higher prestige and higher salaries and is increasingly becoming a mandatory part of graduate education in elite institutions (in the United States). Applications more often focus on politicians (and sometimes parties or even states) than on voters or citizens. In sociology the minority that applies rational-choice theory to the traditional issues of the discipline has to some extent been preempted by economists with greater command of the tools (the study of trust is an important exception). In social anthropology, which (in the United States) has been moving in the direction of soft social science, rational-choice theory has not gained a foothold.

Is this science? Let me first consider criterion (1). We can take for granted that the modeling is correct, in the sense that the conclusions follow from the premises. Are the conclusions true? Before I address this issue, I want to observe that it is not clear that they are always *intended* to be true, that is, to correspond to the actual world. Rather, they sometimes represent a form of science fiction – an analysis of the action and interaction of ideally rational agents, who have never existed and never will. The analysis of ever-more-refined forms of strategic equilibria, for instance, is hardly motivated by a desire to explain or predict the behavior of actual individuals. Rather, the motivation seems to be an aesthetic one. Two of the most accomplished equilibria theorists, Reinhart Selten and Ariel Rubinstein, have made it quite clear that they do not believe their models have anything to say about the real world. When addressing the workings of the latter, they use some variety of behavioral economics or bounded rationality. To cite another example, social choice theory – the axiomatic study of voting mechanisms – became at one point so mathematically convoluted and so obviously irrelevant to the study of actual politics that one of the most prominent journals in economics, *Econometrica*, imposed a moratorium on articles in this area.

An interesting question in the psychology and sociology of science is how many *secret practitioners* there are of economic science fiction – hiding either from themselves or from others the fact that this is indeed what they are practicing. Inventing ingenious mathematical models is a well-paid activity, but except for the likes of Selten and Rubinstein payment will be forthcoming only if the activity can also be claimed to be relevant; hence the incentive for either self-deception or deception. To raise this question might seem out of bounds for academic discourse, but I do not see why it should be. Beyond a certain point, academic norms of politeness ought to be discarded – a point also made in John Stuart Mill's *On Liberty*, which has been the bible on intellectual freedom since it appeared. I have already dropped any pretense of politeness toward the obscurantists of soft social science and can see no reason to treat *hard obscurantism* any differently.

I have no direct evidence for either deception or self-deception, so I must proceed differently. I shall try to show, that is, that what rational-choice practitioners do is often so removed from reality that it is hard to take seriously their claims that they are engaged with the world. At the risk of repeating what I have said in earlier chapters, let me try to summarize my argument in ten points.

1   Many models impute to agents motivations they demonstrably do not have. The routine assumption of exponential time discounting is one example.

2   Some models impute motivations to the agents for which no evidence is offered, such as a particular form of the utility function. One can of course stipulate a function in order to prove possibility theorems ("a rational consumer with decreasing marginal utility *might* do X"), but not to prove anything about the world. In many situations, the assumption that agents are self-interested is also one that has to be shown to be true, not merely assumed.

3   Most models ignore the advances in the understanding of choice associated with prospect theory. Since the theory is stated in terms of gain or losses from a given baseline, it does not analyze behavior in terms of maximizing an objective function defined over outcomes. The maximization format may be indispensable for mathematical manipulation but irrelevant for much of actual behavior.

4   Some models impute cognitive capacities to agents that they may possess but not exercise. They may, for instance, not spontaneously carry out the backward-induction reasoning that is required in many important applications.

5   Many models impute cognitive capacities to agents that they demonstrably do not possess. The point is so trivial that it is almost embarrassing: how can an economist assume that an agent has the ability to carry out calculations that he or she (the economist) needs many pages of highly technical appendixes to spell out? The temptation is strong to say, "Come on! Get real!"

6 Many models impute intentions on the basis of the objective interest of the agent in a particular situation, without pausing to ask whether other motivations – emotions or social norms – might be in play. If we try to explain behavior in turbulent or conflictual situations such as revolutions, for instance, imputing a motive of rational long-term self-interest (reduced to present value by exponential discounting) seems almost ludicrously inadequate. Other models impute intentions on the basis of actual outcomes, thus neglecting the possibility both of mistaken calculations and of calculated gambles.

7 Many models take no account of the fog of uncertainty that surrounds most important decisions, especially when the relevant consequences are in the distant future. Attempts to overcome this problem by assigning subjective probabilities to the outcomes are often arbitrary, as when scholars appeal to the principle of insufficient reason to stipulate a uniform probability distribution.

8 Some models stipulate collectivities (classes or states) as if they were unitary agents, without addressing (in the case of classes) the free-rider problem or (in the case of states) the structure of collective decision making.

9 Some models assume that deviations from rationality either (1) are temporary or (2) will cancel out in the aggregate. As for (1), temporary deviations can have durable results if the situation has a "lobster-trap" structure. As for (2), behavioral economics has shown that since many deviations are systematic and not random, there is no reason to expect them to disappear in the aggregate. The "equity premium puzzle" is an example.

10 Many models rest content with explaining behavior by arguing that it is an equilibrium in a game, without taking the further step of showing why, in situations with many equilibria, this particular one was realized. Moreover, they rarely pause to ask whether the world is not changing so fast that equilibria do not have enough time to establish themselves.

I have noted some typical responses to these objections. One is to cite the hermeneutic problem of establishing motivations in a noncircular way. I agree that this is a serious difficulty, but it is not insurmountable, and even if it were, that would not justify the gratuitous imputation of motivations. Another is to propose the replacement of actual rationality (of real, live agents) with "as-if rationality." I have argued that this is a stratagem that can work only if either of two conditions is satisfied. On the one hand, one might be able to point to a mechanism that is capable of mimicking rationality, *all the way down* to the mathematical appendixes. The problem is that nobody has come up with such a mechanism. Appeal to selection is little more than hand waving, given the huge discrepancy between the crudeness and imperfection of social selection mechanisms and the ultrasophisticated reasoning processes imputed to the agents. On the other hand, one might be able to point to predictions that are so compellingly accurate that we would be forced to accept the theory even if we did not understand how it works. The problem is that the social sciences yield no predictions that even remotely approximate this status.

In fact, if we look more closely at the satisfaction of criterion (1) we observe the coexistence over time of different theories with very different explanations and predictions. Macroeconomics, in particular, stands out in this respect. I have lost track of the current status of Keynesianism, monetarism, and rational expectations, but if one of them had bested the others and had been delivering a steady stream of highly accurate predictions, I think I would have noticed. Is the need for an independent central bank an established truth – or just a fad? For decades now economists have proposed radically different explanations of the high rates of European unemployment, without being able to reach agreement. Do people really work less when they are taxed more? Expert opinions differ. These are not matters on the frontiers of research, where there will always be disagreement, but long-standing questions at the core of the discipline.

Criterion (2) also fails to be satisfied, as indicated by the use of the prefix "neo," as in neo-Keynesianism or neofunctionalism. Criteria (3) and (4) are easily satisfied; in fact, they are oversatisfied. The professionalization of American social science to which I referred earlier has, as its negative side, a crippling narrowness and a self-defeating obsession with the ranking of one's department on some list or other. I conjecture, in fact, that being highly ranked is a state that is essentially a by-product of the search for knowledge rather than for rank. (Proust, as we saw, made a similar observation about musicians.) Moreover, because the dialogue with the past is relegated to the low-prestige subfield of history of economic thought or the slightly more prestigious history of political thought, the narrowness is further compounded. But although the pathologies of hard obscurantism are to be preferred to those of soft obscurantism, it is not a choice we have to make.

The Future of Social Science

Can one do better? Can the scientific aspirations of the social sciences – the quest for prediction, determinacy, and precision – be satisfied at some time in the future? The history of sciences teaches us to be very cautious in making claims about what a given science can and cannot achieve. "They all laughed" at Descartes when he said that animals were machines, but who's got the last laugh now? Any attempt to address the question has to be both tentative and speculative.

The incorporation of findings from neuroscience will certainly provide a stronger basis for psychology and may resolve some ongoing controversies. It has already been claimed, for instance, that brain scans support quasi-hyperbolic rather than hyperbolic discounting. One might also be able to nail down the distinction between anger and indignation if it could be shown that these emotions activate different centers in the brain. The neurophysiology of addiction will certainly continue to enhance our understanding of this puzzling, self-destructive behavior. Yet note that all of these applications involve *motivation* for action. Applications to *perception* such as filling-in phenomena are also plentiful. By contrast, the neuroscience of propositional *beliefs* (and of belief-motivation interactions) does not exist and will not for the foreseeable future. Consider a trivial case of belief updating. I thought it was going to rain tomorrow, but as the sky cleared up I revised my forecast and, as a result, changed my plans. I do not think it is just my lack of imagination (or of scientific expertise) that makes me doubt that we shall soon be able to identify the neurophysiology of even this simple process, and many processes of belief formation are of course vastly more complex. If I am right, then one-half of the belief-desire model of action will for a long time remain impervious to the neuroscientific approach. The same holds even more obviously if we go beyond that model and ask for the "neurons of inspiration" that generate inventions and works of art.

There are two kinds of reasons why the social sciences fail to predict or explain in a strong sense. One is that even for given beliefs and preferences, the action may to some extent remain indeterminate (that is, unpredictable). In decision making under uncertainty or with a high degree of complexity, behavior may be due to what Keynes called our "animal spirits" rather than to identifiable features of the situation to which we react in identifiable ways. People do, to be sure, act on rules of thumb in these cases: the problem is that there are too many of them. There may, for instance, be competing focal points: *do as it was done before* versus *do as the neighbor does*. To say that people "satisfice" rather than "maximize" is not to say much unless we can identify ex ante what constitutes a satisfactory level.

Another reason is our poor understanding of mechanisms of preference formation. Individuals are subject to competing propensities whose relative strengths, in any given situation, are often indeterminate. If I threaten you, will that make you afraid or angry? If both effects occur, which will dominate? If I take a break from my hectic professional life, will my leisure be equally frantic or, on the contrary, utterly relaxed? If my country turns from a dictatorship into a democracy, will my release from political authority cause me to discard religious authority as well or, on the contrary, to seek it out? I have argued that we are often unable to answer such questions about preference formation ex ante, although after the fact we may be able to identify the dominant mechanism.

Could one reduce the indeterminacy by identifying either *triggering conditions* or *triggering probabilities*? I discussed the first possibility in Chapter 2, with somewhat skeptical conclusions, so let me turn to the second. Could one, for instance, specify a distribution in the population of satisficing levels that would at least enable us to predict aggregate behavior? This is, after all, what the social sciences are largely about. Similarly, whether we suppose that some fraction of the population is going to be afraid rather than angry when threatened, or that each of us might react in either way, might it not be possible to quantify the probabilities?

Assuming we could, I still do not think we would gain much explanatory power, because of the immense importance of *context*. Earlier I said that progress in science often follows from relentless abstraction from context. This holds for the social sciences as well, in the sense that we cannot identify propensities or mechanisms except by disregarding many features of the situation or creating a setting in which they are absent. The intuitive notion of conformism, for instance, is complex. It includes the reliance on others as a source of information, the desire to be like others, the desire not to stick one's neck out, and the desire not to be badly thought of by others. If for a specific research purpose we want to define (say) the second of these as what is going to count as conformism, we have to isolate it from the other three dimensions of conformism by creating an experimental setting (or finding a real-life one) in which they are unlikely to be present. We shall probably find that some people do indeed want to be like others, while others desire most of all to distinguish themselves from others. Maybe we could even specify the proportions or probabilities. Yet in a real-life situation, the other dimensions of conformism are likely to be present as well and might exercise an opposite effect. Knowing how people are distributed along one of four dimensions of conformism may not be of much help in predicting conformist *behavior*. Analysis, teasing apart, is doable. Synthesis, putting together, is much harder, and perhaps impossible.

It is easy to imagine how a scholar bent on proving the possibility of a social *science* might respond to this predicament, but I shall not pursue the matter further. Some of us are impressed and overwhelmed by the complexity and instability of human behavior. Others have a gut belief in an underlying regularity that, when uncovered, will enable us to put the social sciences on a par with the natural sciences – be it with physics, chemistry, geology, or meteorology. The future will tell, but I have tried to make it clear where I would place my bets and why.

⊂⊂⊂

INDEX

❮❮❮